COMPREHENSIVE URBAN EDUCATION

PATRICIA B. KOPETZ

University of Tennessee at Chattanooga

ANTHONY J. LEASE

University of Tennessee at Chattanooga

BONNIE Z. WARREN-KRING

University of Tennessee at Chattanooga

PEARSON

Boston ■ New York ■ San Francisco ■ Mexico City ■ Montreal
Toronto ■ London ■ Madrid ■ Munich ■ Paris ■ Hong Kong
Singapore ■ Tokyo ■ Cape Town ■ Sydney

KH

*To Edmund and Virginia Kopetz, and Betsy and Michael Snowden,
for their unfailing support and encouragement; and George and
Dorothy Bowersox, who never provided less than their best attention;*

Dena and Henry, of whom are held the highest expectations; and

Loving husband, David Kring, for all of his support and encouragement.

Series Editor: *Traci Mueller*
Series Editorial Assistant: *James P. Neal, III*
Marketing Manager: *Krista Clark*
Composition and Prepress Buyer: *Andrew Turso*
Manufacturing Buyer: *Andrew Turso*
Cover Coordinator: *Joel Gendron*
Editorial-Production Coordinator: *Mary Beth Finch*
Editorial-Production Service: *Publishers' Design and Production Services, Inc.*
Electronic Composition: *Publishers' Design and Production Services, Inc.*

For related titles and support materials, visit our online catalog at www.ablongman.com

Between the time Website information is gathered and then published, it is not unusual for some sites to have closed. Also, the transcription of URLs can result in typographical errors. The publisher would appreciate notification where these errors occur so that they may be corrected in subsequent editions.

Cataloging-in-Publication data unavailable at press time.
ISBN: 0-205-42416-3

Photo credits appear on page 356, which constitutes a continuation of the copyright page.

Printed in the United States of America.
10 9 8 7 6 5 4 3 2 1   10 09 08 07 06 05

2/7/08

CONTENTS

CHAPTER TWO

Educational Perspectives   33

CHAPTER THREE

Characteristics of Urban Schools   63

CHAPTER FOUR

The Urban Teacher   105

CHAPTER SEVEN

Instruction for Urban Settings   225

CHAPTER EIGHT

Assessment and Evaluation   258

CHAPTER NINE

Partnerships That Work in Urban Settings   301

PREFACE

Teaching today presents an inherently difficult challenge—it is not for those who desire an easy ride or for the faint of heart. During an earlier time, instruction was considered effective when pitched to students in the middle achievement range, often ignoring the learning needs of upper-level and lower-level students. It was not uncommon for lessons to focus upon the process of instructional delivery rather than upon assuring that children were learning. For the most part, educators concentrated upon instructional inputs rather than outputs. The education world has changed in recent years, accelerated by federal and state legislation stressing accountability for learning, the most recent being the No Child Left Behind Act. The concentration is now upon outputs—that is, whether children meet academic achievement standards. This has already changed the teaching dynamic to one in which teachers, more than ever before, are accountable for student learning. There is today greater pressure upon the classroom teacher to cause children to meet academic standards.

The new era in education strikes particularly hard in urban schools that house children of the poor in disproportionately large numbers. Teachers in urban areas face a daunting task given the high levels of accountability now present.

This book can offer assistance as urban teachers face these new and vigorous challenges. While it is not designed to provide a theoretical and foundational view of education, it is intended, for the most part, to be transformational. We believe that those who are considering teaching as their profession of choice have deliberated upon their decision to teach and their deliberation and decision-making process has already provided a good deal of foundational support. The book is transformational in that it aims to transform how one thinks about teaching in an age of high levels of accountability for learning. The presentation is straightforward and realistic.

The book attempts to paint a realistic picture of the prevalent conditions in urban homes, neighborhoods, and schools. It is at times hard-hitting and shocking. No attempt has been made to gloss over the urban conditions that influence school environments. An awareness of the reality of urban settings and the many problems teachers must face will likely leave readers exhausted. They must fully realize that the ills evident in urban areas find their way into the classroom. We make no apologies for the fact that realism may frustrate some. It is far better for each preservice teacher to make a realistic appraisal about teaching in an urban setting, at an early stage, rather than to enter teaching under false pretenses. We see an imperative for teachers to forge a solution to educating urban children and contribute to efforts to erase mediocrity and failure.

In spite of the realism, the book is about being successful as a teacher. It begins with a history of education in which the readers are led to understand that educational issues, particularly equality of educational opportunity, are not a new phenomenon but have been with us from the onset of our nation. What is new is an awakening that our society requires that all individuals must be educated to high levels and our schools stand as beacons lighting the way for all to share and contribute to a better world.

This text is intended to encourage those who would teach urban children. In spite of the problems, urban teachers who are knowledgeable and skilled in dealing with children amidst sound instructional delivery will face the challenges with confidence. They will enable children to reach learning objectives and to crave even greater learning.

This book presents the characteristics of poverty, stressing the special demands of students of poverty and strategies to deal with these demands. It provides information on best practices for effective curriculum and instructional delivery. Strategies for classroom management will help preservice teachers to plan for safe and orderly classrooms conducive to learning. Assessment and evaluation of student performance and the need to utilize assessment data to plan instructional strategies is also stressed. Our aim is to provide those who plan to teach with an arsenal of strategies to be used as needed in their daily teaching. The information is presented to be utilized according to individual determination resulting from discovery and understanding.

America is a great nation that has, and continues, to accept people from all corners of the globe seeking a better life. Many of these individuals settle in urban areas and charge the schools with educating their children. While we are concerned by conditions in many of our urban schools, we are filled with a renewed confidence as we observe a new breed of preservice teachers ready to take on the challenges. They understand the nature of the challenges and accept the accountability for children's learning. It is our sincere hope that this book will increase their knowledge base and their sensitivity and provide them with the skills to positively impact the lives of children.

ACKNOWLEDGMENTS

The authors wish to especially thank Dr. Mary P. Tanner, Dean of the College of Health, Education, and Applied Professional Studies at UTC, for her support that enabled and facilitated collaborative efforts within the Hamilton County School System. Sincerely appreciated is the assistance and guidance provided by Pamala Carter, Rebecca McCashin, Sara Beth Seay, Dana Wilson, Karen Adsit, Charles Hart, Marcus Myers, Dawn Currier, and Chattanooga's Public Education Foundation personnel. We much appreciate Edmund Kopetz's patience and creativity in his designs of the initial computer graphics, charts, and graphs. We thank Elizabeth K. Snowden for her clerical skills and word-processing assistance. We are appreciative of the guidance and friendship of William Jenkins, whose books and seminars gave welcomed insights into the complexity of multicultural issues. We would also like to thank Allan E. Dittmer of the University of Louisville for his comments on the manuscript. We are most grateful to our editor, Traci Mueller; editorial assistant, James Neal, III; and production professionals, Mary Beth Finch and Denise Botelho, for their exceptional guidance and assistance throughout this endeavor.

CHAPTER 1

THE HISTORY OF URBAN EDUCATION

We ain't asking for anything that belongs to those white folks. I just mean to get for that little black boy of mine everything that any other South Carolina boy gets. I don't care if he's as white as the drippings of snow.
—The Reverend J. W. Seals, Summerton, SC, 1953

URBAN PERSPECTIVES

Robert E. Carter
Retired Business Owner
Native American Indian Origin

We were raised learning that there were distinct differences between the races. As a people, we just accepted that that was the way things were.

Genuine pride, honesty, and self-learned wisdom best describe Robert E. Carter. "Growing up in the American Indian culture during the 1940s and 50s," he smiled, "I made the best of all that was available to us." Of the Lumbee Indian Tribe, which numbers 50,000 strong, and is one of the ten largest American Indian tribes in our nation, Carter, from his home nestled in a quiet, suburban pocket of Lumberton, North Carolina, offered with enthusiasm, yet at times poignantly, reflections of past and current activities that continue to affect his family, friends, and other loved ones.

"Historically, we were raised learning of distinct differences between the races. For example, movie theatres were divided into three groupings: White people viewed shows from the main floor, and on the second level there was a seating section divided by a wall where Blacks sat on one side and Indians on the other. Further, families of color were not welcomed in local restaurants. Our families ate at drive-in places when dining away from home." His expressive blue eyes demonstrated his disappointment and frustration with that growing-up era of his life. "As a people, we just accepted that that was the way things were."

Schools were segregated during his grammar school years. There were three local schools: one for Whites, one for Blacks, and one for Indians. At age 12, a young

Robert entered the fourth grade, excited about another year of learning and his newly acquired textbooks. But soon after enrolling in the class, his father informed him that he'd have to quit school to work and help out the family. He was disappointed that this was where his formal learning would end.

Yet education continued to be a high priority for Carter. Growing up, he learned all he could about farming, mechanics, business, and significant public relations knowledge about trust and getting along with all types of people. Later, after marrying his dear wife, Lucille, and raising four children, his quest for the best education for their children was foremost on his mind.

"During the 1960s, we moved into a home directly across the street from a neighborhood elementary school. But the superintendent informed us that our kids would have to attend a school for Native American Indians across the county, several miles away. My wife and I refused that arrangement. We kept the children home and out of school. Well, it happened to our benefit that, at the time [1960s], the Black-lead desegregation movement was strongly flexing its muscle in our region. That threat of disruption and chaos, I'm certain, influenced the superintendent, who only two weeks later personally welcomed our kids' enrollment in the neighborhood elementary school." Yet the Carter children, having attended so-called Indian schools in previous grades, had lots of catching up to do. "They entered grades at the neighborhood school that were, in academic content, a year ahead of the education they received in their former Indian school," Carter lamented.

In closing, Carter held true to his convictions. "People are people, and what's fair and just should be afforded everybody. We've come a long way in people understanding other people. And memories of the past, depicting the way things used to be, are stories that need to be told."

> Note: Among all Native American groups, the Lumbees have the highest percentage of lawyers, doctors, and teachers. But prejudice dies hard, and enmities smolder. The effects of past injustices and segregation often linger longer than we might expect. (J. Humphreys, personal communication.)

WHAT IS URBAN?

This chapter traces the history of education in the United States, particularly as it relates to an understanding of urban schools. Urban schools did not simply appear on the education landscape. They evolved over a long stretch of our history. Each historical period created an influence in the development of education in the United States, and urban schools, as we know them today, evolved.

When we think *urban*, we picture areas of blight, congestion, and crime, and we often think of schools in crisis. While this may be true in some inner-city areas, or in particular sections of inner cities, the picture is not universally accurate. Most city areas in the United States are pleasant and relatively safe living environments where residents value civic pride.

Urban areas are not exclusively big cities. Cities have spread into outlying areas, creating larger urban areas, often referred to as *urban sprawl*. While the problems of the inner cities remain most troublesome, many are not unique to the cities but are found throughout the wider urban area.

Cities are areas where people assemble for some particular reason. The most distinguishing lure of the city is economic. Thus, people live in or near cities. The need to be near cities has created the *urban area*—the city and surrounding area. Cities are where jobs can be found, places of recreation and action, and lively places to visit. The outer urban areas are typically identified with a nearby city. The city is the place where people go to work and to enjoy the many benefits provided, both cultural and recreational.

Cities and suburbs share much of the same destiny. When people flee from the city, they create minicities, or subcultures, by developing the conveniences of cities. The office buildings, shopping centers, theaters, restaurants, and traffic that marked predominantly city environments are readily found in the suburban landscape. Suburbs are becoming more and more urban. As a result, suburban areas are experiencing overcrowded schools, housing shortages, crime, transportation, traffic problems, sanitation issues, and issues related to educating a diverse population of students.

The urban area, then, reaches beyond the city. It is true that the greater intensity of problems exists in cities, especially large inner cities. A definition of an urban area, however, encompasses the city and its surrounding suburban areas. Urban schools reflect the issues found in urban areas. Educators cannot continue to act as if the schools rise above the urban problems. They must understand the reality of the urban situations and accept the challenge of creating or contributing to solutions to its problems.

The business of education is one of educating our youth so that they will be positioned to find meaningful employment, enjoy life, and make positive contributions to society. This is true for all youth regardless of their station in life. The problems of urban areas can mostly be traced to individuals who lack the level of education to find and hold meaningful employment. This leads to an unfortunate cycle of poverty. Because urban areas offer the best possibility to find employment, the uneducated or undereducated and the poor often reside in the inner cities or nearby urban areas.

Urban schools find themselves in a position of being central in the struggle to educate children and bring them out of poverty. This struggle has persisted and today remains unresolved. If the schools can succeed in this mission, our nation and our world will enjoy greater prosperity and quality of life than is presently imaginable.

The schools unfortunately have not been able to accomplish the goal of equal education for all. This is not a negative commentary regarding our schools. Indeed, education in America has produced high levels of intellect for its citizens and the most dynamic economy in the world. We are, without a doubt, the envy of all nations. For this good fortune, we must give much credit to our system of education.

The urban problem is not only one of quality education. The greater problem is one of providing equal education for all. Those who are affluent (upper and middle class) receive access to the best schools and best programs of education. Those who are poor receive less access to the best schools and educational programs. This defines the issue of many urban schools in the United States. The poor are mostly found in urban areas, particularly inner cities. The schools they attend and their treatment in these schools is not on par with the more affluent areas. Given this reality, the problems of urban areas and thus the problems of the poor continue to plague us.

This is not unique to twenty-first century America. Our history is one in which the best education has been reserved for the more affluent, and there has been little or no concern for those who have been less fortunate. That condition is now coming home to roost. Two modern day conditions have created our present dilemmas. First, we are becoming increasingly diverse and the immigrants working in our country are already stricken by severe poverty. Second, our economy is increasingly technologically oriented, and jobs for these immigrants are difficult and often impossible to obtain. Unless we deal with this deadly combination, our society will be overwhelmed and the problems we face in urban areas will intensify.

As we look to improve education and provide equal access to all children in the future, it would be instructive to review our past. American schools, in spite of constant rhetoric, have not at any time provided equal educational opportunity for their children. The lessons of our country's history can help us to see the future more clearly and perhaps to change the course of history.

THE EARLY YEARS

The Colonial Era

Providing universal public education, available for all children, can be viewed as uniquely American. Early American education was influenced by the European model and can be traced to our early colonial days when education was established exclusively for the elite. When the colonists came to our shores, they were not contemplating universal education. Education was viewed as the province of the privileged class. Education "was for the sons (and less frequently for the daughters) of the upper class that they might become the elite leaders of society" (Van Til, 1971). This notion of education for the elite persisted until well into the 1900s; in some respects, the issue of unequal education exists today in spite of eloquent rhetoric extolling education for all.

The goal of equality in educational opportunity has been an evasive goal throughout the history of American education. From our very beginning, stemming back to the Colonial era, the education one received depended upon the particular situation one was placed into by birth.

So it is that the dilemma that we presently face in educating minorities and poor children is not a new phenomenon. It stretches back to our nation's earliest colonial days when education was highly valued. However, education during the early 1600s was targeted to the specific religious values of the time and for select children, as evidenced by the writings and legislation of the period. According to religious views of the day, there was a need for every Christian to read and interpret the Bible. Therefore, there was a necessity for towns to provide means by which learning could occur. Concern for diversity or equality was nonexistent. The primary driving factor pertained to the religious aspects of the society and the continuance of religious beliefs.

In 1625, Puritans took the first step in forming a formal school, known as the Roxbury Latin School. In 1636, the first American college was established at Harvard in Cambridge. Children in the six-to-eight-year age range attended *Dame schools* set up in homes that concentrated upon reading. Dame schools also taught writing and math, but reading was predominant because of the need to understand and live by the Bible (Eastern Illinois University, 2004; George Mason University, 2004).

The Roxbury Latin School and Harvard were designed for male children of upper-level social classes in preparation to hold positions of leadership in the church or the court. Females were not allowed to attend these schools, since world leaders and influential persons were upper-class males. Women remained basically illiterate and not encouraged to gain an education. They were taught in the home the skills necessary to take on the role of housewife and raise a family (Eastern Illinois University, 2004; George Mason University, 2004).

The practice of sorting children according to their perceived roles in life and the desire to concentrate upon the education of certain individuals, so prevalent throughout the history of American education, has its roots in these earliest education efforts. Essentially, the attitude that held it important to educate the upper classes—a divisive issue in urban schools today—began as early as the Colonial era.

In 1647, Massachusetts passed one of the first actions of educational legislation, which was a forerunner of compulsory education, known as the Old Deluder Satan Act. This law reflected the value the early colonists placed upon religion and had at its roots the struggle against the devil (Old Deluder Satan Act, 1647). It was felt that the devil was at the root of all evil and required constant diligence to remain out of his grasp.

The language of the law depicted the religious theme, "it being one chief project of that old deluder, Satan, to keep men from the knowledge of the scriptures, as in former times by keeping them in an unknown tongue" (Old Deluder Satan Act, 1647).

In spite of its simplicity, this law marked the beginning of free and universal education for all. It stipulated that all towns of fifty or more families would be required to provide a schoolmaster to teach children to read and write. Towns of one hundred or more families were to establish a grammar school to prepare children for college (Old Deluder Satan Act, 1647).

Throughout the seventeenth century, education was valued for the religious purposes that dominated the value systems of the early settlers. The schools and the church in the New England colonies were marked by a oneness in which there was no separation. The church remained dominant under the Puritan views. It is clear that education was not the driving force behind the law. Many of our founding fathers came to America to escape religious oppression in England, and they were bent upon the exercise of religious freedom.

The society in the middle colonies was more varied and the population was more flexible in their beliefs and more cosmopolitan in their attitudes. The schools were also driven by religious beliefs and attitudes, but there was greater religious diversity within the population. While the New England region was settled mostly by English settlers, the middle region initially saw mostly Dutch, Swedes, and Germans. The New York area represented the greatest diversity. In the mid-1600s, the population included Dutch, French, Danes, Norwegians, Swedes, English, Scots, Irish, Germans, Poles, Bohemians, Portuguese, and Italians.

The Puritans held a tight control over education in New England. In the middle region, the Dutch Reformed Church greatly influenced early education in New York; and in Pennsylvania, the Quakers established their educational systems. As Dutch and Quaker control waned, other religious groups representing the various immigrant groups which settled in the region began to establish schools. In these early days of our nation, it was evident that the colonists placed great value on educating their youth, but it continued to be religion-based—that is, based on what they valued most: religious freedom (Cincotta, 1994).

While the early settlers valued education for religious purposes, as their economies expanded over time, they began to understand the need for education to enhance and expand commerce. After 1680, the chief source of immigration was no longer England. Masses of refugees left the European continent to escape war and governmental oppression. By 1690, the American population numbered 250,000. From that point on, the population doubled every 25 years. By 1775, there were 2.5 million people living in America. The numbers and diversity of the population needing work brought with them new and aggressive ideas to expand the American economy. New England, with its timber, became a shipbuilding center. Its excellent harbors encouraged trade and supported the growth of the fishing industry. Boston became one of the seventeenth century's greatest American ports.

The middle colonies, surrounded by acreage with rich farmland, stressed farming and other industries such as weaving, shoemaking, cabinetmaking, and craft-type industries. In the south, settlers learned to combine agriculture and commerce, and supported a prosperous lumber industry. The South exported large quantities of rice, indigo (a blue dye obtained from native plants used to color fabric), tobacco, and cotton. The level of export to other countries, particularly Europe, opened America to the world of commerce, and the natural resources available made America a major center of international commerce (Cincotta, 1994).

The religious theme in education remained throughout the period. However, as the nation expanded, religion became less evident. The Puritan emphasis on education, particularly reading the Bible, was a major influence emphasizing the importance of literacy. Two major factors, however, reduced the influence of religion. One was the diversity of the new settlers and their schools operated by various religious denominations and sects. There was greater acceptance and tolerance of varying religious beliefs. Private educational institutions began to appear which had no religious affiliation. Of greater significance was the growth of government-operated schools.

The second impact on education during this period was the rapid growth and reliance of the population upon commerce. With reliance upon commerce came the realization that an educated populace was important. Education needed to be broadened beyond religion to include classical languages, history, literature, mathematics, and the sciences. In large measure, the needs of the economy more and more influenced education, a force that has remained until the present day.

While the poor at this time were not excluded from education, most did not participate. The wealthy benefited from the best education available. Again, colonial America placed great value upon education, and it was mostly for those who could afford to attend. Equal educational opportunity had no roots in colonial America, but there was some evidence that some progress, although not major, was being made.

The Southern Colonies

The southern colonies meanwhile lagged behind New England and the middle colonies in developing an educational system. They were not influenced by the expanding merchant capitalism, as were their northern counterparts. It was the difference in the economic systems, the South being driven by the production of cotton and tobacco, that set them apart. The plantation system created structured rural environments that determined social class. Plantation owners viewed society on the basis of the English gentleman class, in which a small, select group of gentleman landholders ruled over masses of Negro slaves. In addition, there existed yet another class composed of smaller independent farmers and poor whites, who were separate from the large plantations (Butts & Cremin, 1953).

The South existed within the rural farm community structure until well into the 1800s without the influence of the commercial and industrial expansion that was taking place in the North. The dynamic expansion and the movement of numerous immigrants into the North had no effect upon the culture of the South. New ideas were not accepted; change was nonexistent. Therefore, in spite of some progress being made in the North toward equal educational opportunity for all children, the South maintained unequal and segregated schools until the nineteenth century.

According to Butts and Cremin (1953), the South maintained the plantation mentality until the impact of the Civil War brought the disastrous consequences of economic collapse and the need to build a new society.

The problems of educating today's African American children, whose numbers are so prevalent in urban areas, are in large measure the legacy of the southern region's plantation mentality and its dependency upon slavery. Slaves, who were brought to America in large numbers, were valued to work on the plantations. There was no need for them to be educated. In fact, it was desirable to keep slaves in ignorance. In this way, the slave masters could exploit the Negroes who were kept in ignorance, uneducated and lacking in communication skills. The legacy created during this dark period in southern America is one on which we look back with shame and for which we continue to pay a heavy price. Van Til expressed the situation clearly:

> The system of slavery required an elitist education for the sons of the white gentry who would themselves soon become slave masters; a tutorial system of classical instruction became the dominant practice. The education of the slave was antithetical to Southern society. . . . (Van Til, 1971, p. 138)

In many southern states education for slaves was prohibited. A 1790 South Carolina law prohibited the education of slaves with this language:

> . . . All and every person and persons whatsoever, who shall hereafter teach, or cause any slave or slaves to be taught to write, or shall use or employ any slave to be taught to write, or shall use or employ any slave as a scribe in any manner of writing whatsoever, hereafter taught to write; every such person and persons, shall, for every such offense, forfeit the sum of $100 current money. (State of South Carolina, 1790)

As stated earlier, education is strongly influenced by the social forces that are present. Thus, it is not difficult to recognize that the introduction of Negroes to the American shores against their will, to be bought and sold as slaves, embarked our nation in a long and bitter struggle to achieve equality among all races. Negroes were valued as slaves, and there was, therefore, no need to educate them. Indeed, given the circumstances, there were perceived advantages to keeping them uneducated.

America lived within a social paradox in its dream for a free society. The problem of racial segregation was more prevalent in the South as a result of the southern plantation's economy. The great value which early Americans had placed upon education set the stage for the schools to be central to the unraveling of segregation. Education held a central position in American life. It has and continues to be the great goal for both the individual and the society. It has represented the opportunity for individual success and the key to the functioning of a free society. From the earliest time in our nation's history it has been highly valued.

Reaching an understanding of the educational enterprise today requires one to look beyond the culture of present day education to the values that have shaped society and influenced thinking about the education of the youth. Throughout our history, education has been shaped by our hopes and aspirations that drive from our value systems.

Education connects directly with the societal values and needs of which it is a part. American public education expresses our culture and that of the people who form the culture. It is solidly rooted in values that are basic to the American people, and has been from the onset (Kincheloe et al., 1995).

Religion and economic growth were valued by the early American settlers. These drove the beginning stages of our educational system. Education presented a means to an end, a way to continue religious thought and to produce people who would expand the economy of the nation. Thus, education was highly valued, but not for everyone. The elitist view of education in the northern colonies gave way somewhat in the later part of the Colonial era to a more liberal acceptance of education for all. It was in the southern colonies that the notion of equal educational opportunity never saw daylight. It was slavery and an economy that was dependent upon slavery that together represented the greatest barrier to education for all, regardless of the color of one's skin or the level of one's economic social standing.

While problems of elitism and segregation continued into the late 1750s and 1800s, education became more and more valued for its benefits to America's expanding economy, and it became sophisticated and organized. Additionally, Americans became more enamored with the notion that education provided a solution to various social problems. With increasing frequency, Americans demonstrated confidence in the power of an educated people (Microsoft Encarta Online Encyclopedia, 2004).

THE INDUSTRIAL ERA

Pressure of Economic Growth

American life, as we know it, did not come about with the signing of the Constitution. Our way of life, as we know it today, has been evolving over a long period of time and has been shaped by social, economical and political forces. To a great extent, it was between 1779 and 1865 that American society developed its unique character. These years marked the beginning of an industrialized America that brought about demands for significant changes in educational institutions, and narrowed the separation between the social classes. Alexis de Tocqueville observed in his treatise "Democracy in America" that "Among the novel objects that attracted my attention during my stay in the United States, nothing struck me more forcibly than the general equality of condition among people (Bradley, 1945, p. 114).

In 1849, the Massachusetts Supreme Court ruled that segregated schools were permissible under its state constitution, a case that was later used by the U.S. Supreme Court to substantiate the *separate but equal* doctrine of 1896. With the impending Civil War soon to divide the country, as southern states elected to secede from the Union, the Supreme Court's Dred Scott decision in 1857 upheld denying citizenship to Negroes, and punitively ruled that descendents of slaves had "no rights to which the white man was bound to respect" (Holladay, 2004, p. 1).

This period marked the beginning of the industrial expansion and capitalism. The influx of technology from Europe, the rapid expansion of power, communication advances, and transportation led to the migration of people from rural areas into the cities. The expansion was compounded by a tremendous inflow of immigrants to the United States, particularly into cities. These changes would ultimately create great pressures within the educational system that would evolve into the educational environment of the present time.

In the years prior to the mid-1800s, America's schools were represented by a disjointed collection of public and private institutions and agencies dependent upon a particular city or town for their resources. Thus, the quality of education varied widely. Many schools continued to be sponsored by religious organizations in their attempts to foster their religious aims, and most institutions provided schools only for males from wealthy families.

The Common School and Free Public Education

During the late 1700s, Thomas Jefferson advanced the notion of creating a system of free schools supported by taxation. His proposals were not enacted, but they served as a powerful influence for the development of schools in the nineteenth century (Microsoft Encarta Online Encyclopedia, 2004).

During the period of the middle 1800s to 1900, two prominent educators, Horace Mann of Massachusetts and Henry Barnard of Connecticut, proposed the creation of a common school system that would standardize educational content for all children. They agreed that education could transform all youth into literate citizens resulting in an America that could compete with other countries (Microsoft Encarta Online Encyclopedia, 2004).

Their objective was achieved by the end of the nineteenth century and free public education (elementary schools) became available for all American children. By 1918, all states had compulsory education laws. These laws and the rise of the common school did much to transform the culture of education, but although the laws required students to attend school, they did not bring about change in the ongoing problem of equality of educational opportunity.

The growth of high schools, greatly influenced by students graduating from elementary schools, was spectacular. In 1900 only 10 percent of American students ages 14 to 17 were enrolled in high school. Most of these children were from affluent homes. From 1900 to 2000, high school enrollments increased to about 88 percent. Students regarded additional schooling as important to success in an increasingly urban and institutionalized society (Microsoft Encarta Online Encyclopedia, 2004).

Throughout all of the growth and change during the middle 1800s to 1900, the South remained static, unchanged by the commercial and industrial expansion throughout the country. Southerners clung to the plantation mentality and to their dependence upon slavery to keep their agrarian economy alive. It was to remain this way until unraveled by the Civil War, which created economic collapse and social upheaval in our nation. It was the aftermath of the Civil War that forced new thinking in the South, but not without a great deal of conflict and bloodshed.

THE POST–CIVIL WAR YEARS

The Continued African American Struggle

When the Civil War ended in 1865, President Lincoln and Congress enacted the Thirteenth Amendment to the U.S. Constitution that abolished slavery in the United States and guaranteed all Americans equal protection under the law, as well as citizenship to African Americans (Holladay, 2004). What was yet to play out in congressional legislation and in the court systems, regarding human rights and equality in education, was a test of wills with an unsettled people of diverse backgrounds in a young country attempting to practice the established principles for which it was founded.

Change occurred slowly, and in many areas of the South slaves found their lives to be similar to those before the war. Andrew Johnson, who succeeded Lincoln as president, seemed to have little interest in the freedom of Blacks. He appointed proslavery governors in southern states. Under the laws, Blacks who had no employment on a steady basis were arrested and ordered to pay hefty fines, Black children were forced to serve as apprentices in local industries, and Blacks were prevented from buying land and denied fair wages. Most significantly, they were not allowed to vote. There was concern, at the time, that former slaveholders would regain control of the South (Pressly, 1962).

The Civil War was ended, slavery was abolished, but clearly the African American's struggle was far from over. In 1866, Congress passed the Fourteenth Amendment, which ensured that the rights guaranteed to African Americans were protected by the Constitution. The amendment stated that no individual could be denied his or her rights as an American citizen. It did not, however, guarantee African Americans the right to vote. In 1866, Congress passed the Fifteenth Amendment guaranteeing all American citizens the right to vote, regardless of their race (Foner & Mahoney, 1997).

On the education front, progress was being made, but the situation was chaotic. African Americans in the North and South attended segregated schools where their education left much to be desired. There were those, such as the Ku Klux Klan and other White supremacy groups, who intimidated and often killed African American citizens. These groups burned schools attended by African American children and murdered teachers. This intimidation effectively prevented many children from attending school.

Frederick Douglass—fearing that the supremacy organizations were frightening African Americans from exercising their civil rights, including their right to an education—in his famous speech, "The Work Before Us," painted a picture of the American scene. "Rebellion has been subdued, slavery abolished and peace proclaimed and yet our work is not done. . . . We are face to face with the same old enemy of liberty and progress. . . . The South today is a field of blood" (Douglass, 1868).

It was with this backdrop that education existed in America in the late 1800s. The elitist attitude about education was dissipating when it came to education for Whites, but the situation for African Americans remained desperate while the nation struggled with major societal change.

Separate but Equal Schools

In 1875 Congress passed the first Civil Rights Act, which prohibited racial discrimination in public places. The U.S. Supreme Court, however, determined the Act to be unconstitutional. The Court deemed it acceptable for individuals and private businesses to discriminate based upon race. Thus, discrimination in schools was acceptable, resulting in an affirmation of the segregation of African American children in schools. Further, in the landmark case of *Plessy v. Ferguson* in 1896, based upon the nation's dominant beliefs of White supremacy and Black inferiority, the Supreme Court supported the so-called separate but equal decision that substantiated and legalized the practice of establishing racially segregated schools. In fact, a few years later, the Court backed the levying of taxes on citizens of all races to establish public schools for White children only (Holladay, 2004).

Homer Plessy argued in the Supreme Court of the United States that his rights as granted under the Thirteenth and Fourteenth Amendments were violated when he was forced to sit in the Black car on a railroad train. Plessy lost the case, and the impact of *Plessy v. Ferguson* was immense. The Court ruled that it was constitutional to require African Americans and Whites to be separated in restaurants, theaters, restrooms, public conveyances, and schools as long as the separate facilities were equal (Oracle Education Foundation, 2001).

The separate but equal law brought about by *Plessy v. Ferguson* would dominate societal thought for sixty-four years, until overturned by *Brown v. Board of Education of Topeka, Kansas,* in 1954. Under this ruling, African Americans would no longer be required to attend separate, segregated schools which were inferior to White schools. *Brown* dealt a serious blow to school segregation policies. "It is universally honored as one of the great moments of American justice" (Orfield & Eaton, 1996, p. 23).

The history of education in America is rich with success, but the success has not been shared by all. In that respect, education's past is filled with tragedy. In a country that declares that "all men are created equal," and all are guaranteed their civil rights, the reality of inequality is incomprehensible. As can be seen, African Americans suffered most. As we attempt to understand the urban school situation at present, we must understand the elitist mentality that prevailed, but mostly must recognize the plight of African Americans in a segregated society. Much of the urban school dilemma we face today surfaces from the unfortunate decisions made during an earlier time.

AMERICA AND THE WORLD AWAKEN TO INJUSTICE

Recognition of Human Rights

Despite our founding fathers' intents, reflected in legislative initiatives, equality of educational opportunities was not occurring. Education inequality became a true, national concern that erupted in the early- to mid-1900s. The courts were awakening to morally justified decisions mandating all-White law schools to enroll applicants of color: *University of Maryland v. Murray*, 1936; *Missouri ex rel. Gaines v. Canada*, 1938; *Sipuel v. Board of Regents of the University of Oklahoma*, 1948; and *Sweatt v. Painter*, 1950 (Holladay, 2004).

Our country's minority population of African American students proved to be lagging behind in educational gains. True in theory, yet false in practice, the elements of equality in schools failed to exist among schools educating predominantly Black student populations, particularly found in urban settings throughout our nation (Webb, Metha, & Jordan, 2003).

The world at large was reacting positively toward human rights issues. The United Nations, in Article 26 of their enacted "Universal Declaration of Human Rights," in 1948 stated that:

1. Everyone has the right to education. Education shall be free, at least in the elementary and fundamental stages. Elementary education shall be compulsory. Technical and professional education shall be made generally available and higher education shall be equally accessible to all on the basis of merit.

2. Education shall be directed to the full development of the human personality and to the strengthening of respect for human rights and fundamental freedoms. (United Nations, 1998)

Article 26 emphasized that not only does every child—of any size, shape, talent, or intelligence—deserve rights to a free (e.g., publicly supported) education, but also that there is no one single educational environment suitable and appropriate for all children (Clinchy, 2001).

The *Brown* Decision Mandates Desegregation in Schools

Nearly half of the states in the United States enacted discriminatory laws, known as *de jure* [by law] *segregation*, that either required or permitted racial segregation in schools. School racial populations were, therefore, allowed to be separate but equal—until the Supreme Court, in a unanimous opinion, ruled in the case of *Brown v. Board of Education of Topeka, Kansas* in 1954. The *Brown* decision overturned the *Plessy v. Ferguson* ruling of 1896, and pioneered the beginnings of aggressive, legal actions to ensure racial integration in schools. Consequently, segregation (separate education based upon race) in schools was then officially considered unequal, and in violation of the U.S. Constitution. This court ruling, more than any other, was to have a profound effect upon the American education landscape.

Chief Justice Earl Warren in the *Brown* decision of 1954 stated:

> We conclude that, in the field of public education, the doctrine of "separate but equal" has no place. Separate educational facilities are inherently unequal. Therefore, we hold the plaintiffs and others similarly situated for whom the actions have been brought are, by reason of the segregation complained of, deprived of the equal protection of the laws guaranteed by the Fourteenth Amendment.

Understood was the notion that isolating school children into all-White and all-Black schools proved to deprive minority children of equal educational benefits. Further, in *Brown II*, the Supreme Court pushed schools to desegregate "with all deliberate speed." Thus, it was the landmark *Brown* decision that decreed that states hastily implement desegregation plans, including the busing of children from their neighborhood schools into other schools in order to achieve greater racial balance and exposure of minority children to improved educational opportunities (Holladay, 2000; Morrison, 2004).

As we celebrate the victory of desegregation, numerous schools in America remain segregated by race and poverty. Orfield asserts that segregation continues to be encouraged. His words are disturbing:

> The common wisdom passed down by teachers through the generations is that *Brown v. Board of Education* corrected an ugly flaw in American education and American law. We celebrate *Brown* and Martin Luther King, Jr. in our schools, even

when those very schools are still almost totally segregated by race and poverty. Millions of African American and Latino students learn the lessons of *Brown* while they sit in segregated schools in collapsing cities, while almost no students success-fully prepare for college. We celebrate *Brown* as cities and courts consider return-ing African American children to low achieving students segregated by race and poverty."(Orfield & Eaton, 1996, p. 23)

Orfield suggests that after the resignation of Chief Justice Earl Warren in 1969 the court began to return toward decisions favorable for segregation. The *Milliken v. Bradley* decision in 1974 denied a school desegregation plan that pro-posed combining the Detroit School District, with a large African American population, with the surrounding largely white suburban areas. The result was that poor African American and Hispanic children attended segregated city schools while White families moved to the suburbs (Orfield & Eaton, 1996).

Civil rights efforts turned negative during the presidency of Richard Nixon. President Nixon opposed busing to achieve desegregation and supported congressional action to limit urban desegregation. He appointed William Rehn-quist, a staunch conservative who demonstrated consistent hostility to desegre-gation, to the Supreme Court (Orfield & Eaton, 1996).

Sunstein, citing a memo written by Rehnquist in 1952, which was disclosed at Rehnquist's Senate nomination hearings provides insight into his attitude:

> I realize that it is an unpopular and unhumanitarian position, for which I have been excoriated by liberal colleagues, but I think *Plessy v Ferguson* was right and should be reaffirmed. (Rehnquist memo, as cited in Sunstein, 2004)

During the first twelve years which Rehnquist spent on the court, he did not vote to uphold a desegregation issue. Fifteen years after Rehnquist's ap-pointment to the court, President Ronald Reagan elevated him to Chief Justice.

The administration of President Reagan was also not tolerant of segrega-tion efforts. The administration opposition to mandatory segregation was intense and not only were desegregation efforts blocked but existing programs were dis-mantled. A particular target of the administration, as was the case with the Nixon administration, were plans for compulsory busing to achieve racial balance. Much of the antidesegregation activity was accomplished by the Supreme Court. By 1995, 60 percent of sitting federal judges were appointed by Presidents Nixon, Reagan, and Bush, and their conservative agendas brought vulnerability to segregation efforts (Orfield & Eaton, 1996).

During this period desegregation remained under attack. It was, however, surprisingly resilient—and it endured. Many local plans continued forward in spite of the persistent opposition. To be sure, efforts to desegregate our schools was dealt a serious blow by the nation's leadership and, in large measure, by the courts. Through this period, *Brown v. Board of Education* remained the law of the land. Demographers predict that students of color in our school age population will continue to grow at a faster rate than our White population. We must be prepared for this transition in demographics with schools that are sensitive to multicultural issues and offer equal educational opportunities for all.

Racial Integration and Educational Equity Gain Federal Support

Federal funding became more influential in education, greatly benefitting the schools, in response to a national educational emergency resulting from the Soviet Union's successful launch of Sputnik I in 1957. This event, in which Communist Russia sent into orbit the world's first artificial satellite—the size of a basketball and weighing a mere 183 pounds—prompted President Dwight D. Eisenhower and Congress to enact the National Defense Education Act of 1958. For fear that the United States was falling behind its Communist adversaries in students' learning of mathematics and science, $575 million was invested to bettering education and to providing low-interest loans for college students, which would create and enable a stronger national defense of our country (Garber, 2003; Wikipedia, 2004).

In the years following the *Brown* decision and the space race, the United States, under the leadership of President Lyndon Johnson, formally waged the so-called war on poverty through its enactment of the Equal Opportunities Act

(EOA) of 1964. This federal legislation established basic literacy and employment programs to assist low-income participants between the ages 16 and 21 years (Webb, Metha, & Jordan, 2003). In response to a growing concern over disadvantaged preschoolers who demonstrated little or no preparation for entering school, and who were considered at risk of academic failure, the EOA is most heralded for its creation of Project Head Start (Ornstein & Levine, 2000). The newly-designed Head Start programs assisted preschool children from low-income families by offering them a head start in education and was meant to compensate for the lack of preparation they received in their homes and communities. Head Start sought to ensure that, once enrolled in the public school, students would be on equal footing with, and work alongside, their nondisadvantaged peers (Webb, Metha, & Jordan, 2003). In addition to providing for preschoolers' cognitive and social needs, the program offered free healthcare and dental care, all in the federal government's efforts to launch underprivileged children into successful educational experiences (Morrison, 2000).

The Civil Rights Act of 1964 offered more landmark legislation during the Johnson presidency. Important to racial justice in schools, Title VI of the Act banned discrimination in programs and activities that garnered federal funds (Holladay, 2004).

Enacted the next year, the Elementary and Secondary Education Act (ESEA) of 1965 poured more than a billion dollars into school districts, representing the largest amount of designated federal funding to education in U.S. history. Chief among its many provisions to assist educational endeavors nationwide was its establishment of Title I programs. These specialized programs, designed to remediate math and reading skills, created an added learning assistance for low-income, disadvantaged children in elementary and secondary schools in hopes of maintaining and continuing the educational gains experienced from and begun by Head Start (Morrison, 2000; Webb, Metha, & Jordan, 2003).

Controversial studies began to make headlines in pursuit of gaining knowledge about educational equity. In particular, a 1966 landmark study by James Coleman, entitled *Equality of Educational Opportunity*, set out to research, gain, and report contemporary understandings of our nation's educational racial imbalance. Coleman discovered that although schools demonstrated similar curriculum design, teacher training, and salary levels, minority school students yielded achievement levels years behind those of students attending predominantly White schools (Coleman, et al., 1966).

Coleman concluded from his study that what most strongly influenced students' academic achievement was *not* educational structure, or a teacher's learned and practiced pedagogy, but the students' culture—the learned and environmental values, educational levels, work ethics, and family discipline in their immediate familial community. His findings met with national controversy.

Confirming these results from similar studies, President Johnson's Civil Rights Commission subsequently enacted federal legislation to strengthen efforts of planned, racial integration techniques. For example, by busing children to

schools outside their neighborhoods, the Commission set racial integration benchmarks and goals as part of their earnest attempts to prevent African American enrollment from exceeding 85 percent of a schools' total student population (Unger, 2001).

This legislation, once and for all, forced the desegregation of schools, with penalties attached for failure to comply. There was great unrest at the time, as Whites attempted to block African American children from attending all-White schools. But Congress would not be deterred, and sent federal marshals to accompany African American students at schools where African Americans were denied entrance.

To break up residential segregation's influence on the segregating of children in schools, our nation was introduced to the establishment of magnet schools, compensatory education programs, and busing of students to better equalize racial balance in schools. In support of busing, the Supreme Court in 1971 ruled in favor of involuntary busing to achieve racial integration in public schools. Despite the outcries of those vehemently opposed to busing, describing it as a waste of taxpayer dollars and a disruption to the neighborhood school concept, the practice continued in the nation's endeavor to establish a peaceful, integrated society. Court-ordered desegregation mandates relaxed in years to come, particularly by the mid-1980s (Holladay, 2004; Morrison, 2000).

Overall, the 1970s demonstrated unstable times in our nation's educational system. Public unrest over rising taxes, the lowest public school enrollment figures since World War II, and studies that reported dramatic drops in nationally administered Standardized Achievement Test (SAT) scores, led parents and politicians to support back-to-basics education. Among the poorer schools, parents sought help from the judicial system to halt the decline of achievement gains, and resume focus upon ensuring equal educational opportunity among their schools (Webb, Metha, & Jordan, 2003).

Fortunately, efforts to desegregate schools were eventually proving successful. In 1972, Congress authorized special funding to assist school districts to enact and implement firm desegregation plans through the Emergency School Aid Act (ESAA). This endeavor focused on eliminating racial isolation in public schools by providing federal support to school districts to fund their proposed desegregation-related initiatives. This Act, its impact on minority students rigorously evaluated, proved positive results that were subsequently reported in 1976. The findings revealed that resources invested yielded gains in student achievement, sound educational leadership, aggressive parental involvement in the schools, and school staffs' positive attitudes toward the integration process (Ornstein & Levine, 2000).

In 1985, a continuation of this effort further assured that children of all races would receive equal educational opportunities through the Magnet Schools Assistance Program (MSAP), replacing the ESAA. Grants were awarded to school districts that demonstrated the most promising initiatives for desegregating schools. MSAP grant funds were used for curriculum development, community relations, staff hiring and training, extracurricular activities, and the operation of magnet schools (otherwise known as alternative schools). As one of the most promising of desegregation initiatives, magnet schools were designed to group students of all races and cultures from throughout district-wide areas, and provide curriculum focused on particular subject areas, student interests and skills, or special features related to academic specializations. Since its inception, the MSAP has granted nearly $740 million to create, develop, and expand on the original magnet school concept implemented in 1985 (Morrison, 2000). See Figure 1.1, which shows the ESEA influence on school funding.

The efforts of well-crafted federal legislation, successful litigation, and grant awards continued to demonstrate accomplishments in the movement to desegregate schools. In its publication *Education Watch*, the Education Trust, based in Washington, DC, analyzed trends in academic progress since 1975 and extolled the significant academic achievement gains of minority and low-income students during the 1970s and early 1980s. Their accumulated data demonstrated a 50 percent gain during an eighteen-year period between African American and White students, and a 33 percent gain between Hispanics and Whites in that same time period (The Education Trust, 1998).

A NATION AT RISK

American Education in Jeopardy

Despite the encouraging academic achievement gains of minorities during this time, the federal government sought to allay growing public fears of problems inherent in the comprehensive U.S. education system. The National Commission on Excellence in Education, charged to study, assess, and define the state and health of education, was created in 1981. The Commission identified particular focus on students' adjustment and overall progress from the formative years of education through the teenage years, and it examined vocational and technical programs, as well as higher education practices (Ornstein & Levine, 2000).

Following eighteen months of study, *A Nation at Risk: The Imperative for Education Reform*, reported in 1983 the Commission's dramatic findings. The re-

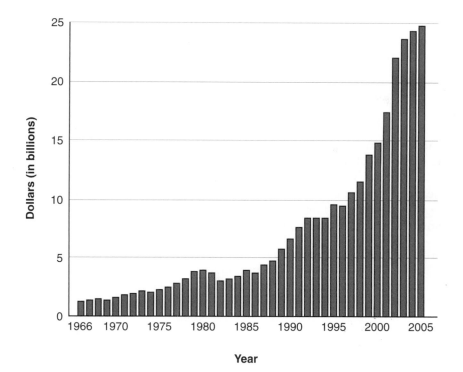

FIGURE 1.1   Federal Investment in the Elementary and Secondary Education Act
Source: 2005 U.S. Budget, Historical Tables, www.ed.gov/about/overview/fed/10facts/edlite-chart
.html#5

port's opening comments acknowledged America's dedication to its educational
intentions:

> All, regardless of race or class or economic status, are entitled to a fair chance and
> to the tools for developing their individual powers of mind and spirit to the utmost.
> This promise means that all children by virtue of their own efforts, competently
> guided, can hope to attain the mature and informed judgment needed to secure
> gainful employment, and to manage their own lives, thereby serving not only their
> own interests, but also the progress of society itself.

The study declared goals that included efforts to "generate reform of our
educational system in fundamental ways and to renew the Nation's commitment
to schools and colleges of high quality throughout the length and breadth of our
land."

The report stated that, historically, Americans had accomplished much in
the nation's continued earnest efforts to educate all among its citizenry. In spite
of these gains, the report stated:

The educational foundations of our society are presently being eroded by a *rising tide of mediocrity* that threatens our very future as a Nation and a people. What was unimaginable a generation ago has begun to occur—others are matching and surpassing our educational attainments. (National Commission on Excellence in Education, 1983)

Schools were encouraged to act as the students' primary resource for improving their social and economic status (Johnson et al., 1996). In summary, the report substantiated public opinion that U.S. schools were ill-prepared to compete in the global economy (Banks, 1999).

Citing new goals to ensure its promise to America, the nation's schools and educational programs launched the quest for academic excellence to defeat the *rising tide of mediocrity* found existent in American public and private education. Among the several recommendations offered in *A Nation at Risk:*

- Raise high school graduation requirements.
- Establish more rigorous and measurable standards and high expectations.
- Devote more effective use of school days by focusing on the Five New Basics (National Commission on Excellence in Education, 1983)

The Five New Basics, applied to the four-year high school curriculum, included studying four years of English, three years of mathematics, three years of science, three years of social studies, and one-half year of computer science. Additionally, college-bound students were strongly recommended to include a study of foreign language for at least two years.

In the years that followed the *A Nation at Risk* report and its recommendations, there occurred a downward trend in U.S. minority students' academic achievement levels. The Education Trust determined that probable causes for the drop were likely threefold:

1. Calling for an end to the *rising tide of mediocrity*, education and business leaders pushed for greater educational goals beyond educational "equity" and raised the bar to reach for academic "excellence";
2. Teachers had begun responding more to the focus on social services, and less on academic learning, to assist students in poverty, which established lower achievement expectations of those economically poor students; and
3. Mastering basic skills was determined to be the highest level of achievement for low-income students, robbing them of exposure to higher-order levels of learning instruction. (The Education Trust, 2003)

America Reacts to Reinvent Its Schools

In 1989, as part of a nationwide push to successfully prepare all students for responsible and productive lives, *America 2000: The President's Education Strategy* challenged educational programs to meet national standards, and held schools accountable for student performance on nationally normed tests. Such initiatives built momentum to further academic improvements as part of a comprehensive movement to "reinvent" America's schools (Clinton, 1991). This initiative fueled subsequent legislation that sustained federal vocational education and training programs, such as the Carl D. Perkins Vocational and Applied Technology Act of 1990. Best known as the Perkins Act, its goals included "developing more fully the academic and occupational skills of all segments of the population" (U.S. Congress, 1990).

To further the reinvention of school's focus, William J. Bennett, a former Secretary of Education, reported on social trends studied from the mid-1960s to the early 1990s. His controversial findings, published in his 1994 book, *The Index of Leading Cultural Indicators*, reported damaging deterioration of the social and moral health of the American society. Startling revelations included the rise in numbers of unwed mothers, a preponderance of minority males in difficulty with the law, and U.S. students' educational achievement lowest among industrialized countries (Bennett, 1999).

To further strengthen schools nationwide and better prepare graduates to compete in the global economy and to reverse the decline of high academic expectations in our nation's schools, the Improving America's Schools Act (IASA) of 1994 significantly enhanced the Elementary and Secondary Education Act that originated in 1965. The legislation continued efforts to ensure educational equity by demanding excellence from all students. Its components included setting high standards for all students, encouraging professional development for teachers, federal funding flexibility to stimulate local initiatives for school improvements, and partnering recommendations that would positively impact all learners. Noted for its creation of the national Even Start program (the Title I component), the IASA was established to encourage adult and child literacy (Morrison, 2000).

The next year Congress introduced the Goals 2000: Educate America Act, passed in 1995, to reinforce and add momentum to setting higher national educational standards. Established goals to be reached by the year 2000 included:

1. With comprehensive federal support of preschool child development programs, that included varied healthcare guidance, all children will start school ready to learn.
2. The high school graduation rate will increase to at least 90 percent.
3. All students exiting grades 4, 8, and 12 will demonstrate competency over the more "challenging" academic areas (math, science, arts, history, etc.) to compete responsibly in the U.S. modern economy.
4. School faculty will have access to continued professional development activities to improve their instructional skills.
5. U.S. students will rank first, globally, in math and science achievement.
6. All U.S. adults will be literate.
7. Schools will be safe, and free of alcohol, weapons, and drugs.

8. Increased parental involvement in the schools will significantly benefit their children. (U.S. Department of Education, 1994)

School integration efforts of the late 1990s demonstrated significant, positive progress, as indicated through extensive research. As shared in the *First Annual School Improvement Report* of 2001, schools in low-income districts exhibited large numbers of their students capable of meeting high educational standards. For schools such as these, and others similarly determined to reach goals of effectiveness, the report recommended that schools adopt sound academic programs, maintain high standards, and offer a focused, strong curriculum (Webb, Metha, & Jordan, 2003).

In spite of the gains in academic achievement, education had not reached the levels of excellence expected. Of particular concern were the many children from minority families and the poor in urban areas, most of whom continued to underachieve. It was acknowledged that progress had occurred, but the urban problems persisted. (See Figure 1.2.)

United States Gets Tough by Enforcing Academic Standards

The most sweeping and structured reform efforts among elementary and secondary education occurred with Congressional reauthorization of the Elementary and Secondary Education Act (ESEA), commonly referred to as the No Child Left Behind (NCLB) legislation of 2002. Referring to NCLB, President Bush stated, "Some say it is unfair to hold disadvantaged children to rigorous standards. I say it is discrimination to require anything less. It is the soft bigotry of low expectations."

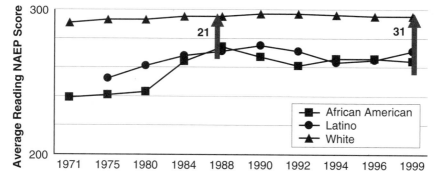

FIGURE 1.2   NAEP Reading Score Trends, 17-Year-Olds

Source: U.S. Department of Education, National Center for Education Statistics. *NAEP 1999 Trends in Academic Progress* (p. 107) Washington, DC: U.S. Department of Education, August 2000 and The Education Trust, Inc. Washington, DC, 2003.

This comprehensive law not only explicitly defines the federal government's role in K–12 education, but endeavors to shrink the achievement gap between disadvantaged and minority students and their peers. As a reauthorization of the Elementary and Secondary Education Act (ESEA) of 1965, the NCLB Act created dramatic new criteria for federal involvement in American education. At its base, the law raises educational standards for all children and promises to assist all children to meet these standards.

The chief intention of NCLB is to (1) raise student achievement, particularly among poor and minority populations, and (2) hold states and local school districts accountable for their allocated federal funds (Bloomfield & Cooper, 2003).

Key among all sections of the legislation is its commitment to unprecedented levels of federal funding that focuses on states meeting academic standards set in reading, math, and science (Learning First Alliance, 2003; Webb, Metha, & Jordan, 2003).

NCLB is based upon four principles:

1. stronger accountability for achievement results;
2. more control and flexibility of education programs at the state and local levels;

3. greater options for parents who choose to send their children to high-performing, safe schools; and
4. an emphasis on successful instruction delivered by high-quality teachers. (Rajala, 2003; U.S. Department of Education, 2003)

Principle One: Accountability for Results.   Accountability begins with keeping parents and their local communities informed of their students' progress, so that positive measures can be undertaken to yield school improvements. Schools will need to determine whether students are meeting the NCLB standards which will require academic performance to be measured. The assessments are designed to determine whether children are learning and to hold schools accountable for learning.

In doing so, the NCLB legislation requires that states measure the progress of their schools and students by annual testing of all students in grades 3 through 8 in reading and mathematics, and at least once in these subjects in grades 10 through 12, by school year 2005–2006. Student achievement in science will be assessed at least once in grades 3 through 8, grades 6 through 9, and grades 10 through 12, by school year 2007–2008. Federal funding is provided for states to design and implement these annual assessments.

Student test results identify which students are making progress and demonstrate to teachers in what academic areas students need improvement. School districts must set annual goals for improvement; those that meet state goals for grade-level work are considered to be making adequate yearly progress (AYP). Test results will be grouped by students who are low-income, of minority status, have disabilities, or have limited English proficiency.

Schools that meet and exceed their AYP are to be rewarded for their success and given a distinguished national rating. In addition, the rating will be accompanied by a 5 percent increase in federal funding (Bloomfield & Cooper, 2003).

Schools that do not demonstrate improvement can expect to receive additional funding assistance to pay for extra support to strengthen achievement amidst a safe learning environment. Over time, schools that continue to fall short of making the AYP face the possibility of restructure, state takeover, or other management options (Learning First Alliance, 2003; U.S. Department of Education, 2003).

The NCLB legislation has led to the development of a national standard in education based upon state-determined academic goals for schools and state-selected, standardized tests that are aligned with curricula to meet the test criteria (Webb, Metha, & Jordan, 2003).

Principle Two: Local Control and Flexibility.   Under the NCLB legislation, schools have the freedom to formulate solutions to local challenges, allowing them to decide their own educational priorities and related initiatives. Federal funding is allocated directly to support the neediest classrooms, where local education agencies support and flex education programs designed to meet their students' specific needs. Allowing school districts the local control of spending federal dollars on school programs best suited for their students is designed to lessen the frustrating red tape of requesting support from the government (U.S. Department of Education, 2003).

Principle Three: Expanded Parental Choices.   NCLB gives parents of disadvantaged children the right to transfer their children from low-performing and/or unsafe schools to better public schools. Parents whose children attend a school that fails to meet its minimal academic growth level for two consecutive years have the right to send their children to a more successful public school, or a charter school, and the school district must pay to transport those children to that school. Charter schools are independent public schools that operate more nontraditionally, and are sponsored and monitored by local or state educational programs.

Following a third consecutive year, parents of disadvantaged students may request that the school district provide additional supplemental education services, including tutoring, after-school assistance, and summer school programs. Expectations of parents include (1) acting as full partners in their child's education, and (2) instilling at home the values and discipline children need that prepare them for success in school (U.S. Department of Education, 2003).

President George W. Bush, upon signing the NCLB into law, gave this advice to parents:

> We know that every child can learn. Now is the time to ensure that every child does learn. As parents, you are your children's first teachers and their strongest advocates. You have a critical role to play—both in how you raise your children and in how you work for meaningful and accurate accountability in their schools. Too many children are segregated in schools without standards, shuffled from grade to grade. . . . This is discrimination, pure and simple. (Bush, 2002)

United States Secretary of Education Rod Paige advised parents as follows:

> No one cares more about your child's future than you do, and no one is better positioned to hold schools accountable for performance than you are. You have a right to know whether your child is really learning at school. . . if your child is not making adequate progress in school, you can and must ask why. A good teacher will be happy to answer your questions. Do your part and ask. (Paige, 2002)

Principle Four: Emphasis on Proven, Instructional Methods.   NCLB holds that teachers demonstrate current best practices in instruction using reliable, evidence-based methods for ensuring that all students read at or above grade level by the third grade. By investing in teacher training and retention efforts among schools, NCLB stresses its desire for quality teaching and retaining the districts' most-qualified, effective teachers (Rajala, 2003).

NCLB purports to provide teachers with tools for quality instruction: scientifically proven methods, materials, and professional development. It is also assumed that teachers are then better protected against frivolous lawsuits (U.S. Department of Education, 2003).

At face value, NCLB would appear to be a sensible law and one that will have a positive effect upon the schools. Logic would indicate that accountability for results, which successfully drives the private sector, can improve academic performance. It is also logical to assume that by quantifying and measuring student performance, greater attention will be given to teaching strategies focused upon assuring that learning is occurring. Whether the positive effects occur, however, is questionable. The law is controversial in a number of aspects and educators remain skeptical and often critical.

The heavy reliance upon student testing is a major area of criticism. Educators continue to feel that tests contain flaws and such heavy reliance should not be placed upon measures that may not be reliable. In addition, educators complain that the law has served to create greater bureaucratic responsibilities upon the schools and the promised financial support has not been forthcoming.

Beyond the controversy and criticisms, there may be a deeper issue. Sarason (1991) asserts that schools are basically intractable with respect to school reform issues. He argues that unless we deal with the complexities of school settings, their structure and dynamics, their power relationships and their underlying value systems, reforms will fail:

> The point they miss is that the classroom and the school and the school system generally are not comprehensible unless you flush out the power relationships that inform and control the behaviors of everyone in the setting. Ignore those relationships, leave unexamined their rationale, and the existing system will defeat efforts at reform. (p. 7)

NCLB is a legislatively imposed reform and, as such, the requirements for change are universal and in the form of mandates. If Sarason is correct, NCLB reform efforts will represent yet another failed attempt to improve our schools since it does not consider the deep intractability of school environments. Sarason does not see this as a "grand conspiracy" to defeat reform but rather that "recognizing and trying to change power relationships, especially in complicated, traditional institutions, is among the most complex tasks humans being can undertake (Sarason, 1991, p. 7).

In spite of the above, teachers will be required to work within the boundaries of NCLB requirements. With the reelection of George W. Bush, his signature education initiative will remain active. Following his reelection, President Bush (2004) stated, "I've earned (political) capital in this election, and I'm going to spend it. You've heard the agenda; Social Security and tax reform, moving this economy forward, education, fighting and winning the war on terror." More specifically regarding NCLB, he stated, "We must continue the work of education reform to bring high standards and accountability not just to our elementary and secondary schools, but to our high schools as well."

While federal reform efforts continue to survive and controversy concerning NCLB remains on the education agenda, teachers in our urban schools must face their students day in and day out and must deliver instruction. That is the reality of teaching. While teachers must remain attuned to the rhetoric, their focus must remain upon the task at hand—delivering instruction that is powerful and effective and that results in high levels of student learning. While this is true for all teachers, it is especially pertinent to those who teach urban children.

SUMMARY

As one reads the history of American education, there is a realization that, while our system of education is sensible, it has *not* provided levels of learning for all students to lead wholesome lives as productive citizens. The right for every child to partake in the best education possible on equal footing with other children is granted to all citizens. Assuring this right has been problematic throughout our history. Over time, however, we have chipped away and at present appear to be increasing our energies toward achieving the elusive goal.

The hard lessons of the era of segregation have been instructive, as our nation has had to deal with the guilt of our actions. The strong message of *A Nation at Risk* has finally awakened our senses. There is today a realization that America must compete with all other nations in a global economy. If we do not prepare our youth to take on that challenge, we run the risk of losing our competitive edge and perhaps our democratic way of life. That risk is simply too great, and our leaders have moved forcefully to remove it from our midst. In spite of our efforts, progress on student academic performance continues to be disappointing.

Since the passage of the ESEA in 1965, through 2003 federal spending to help educate disadvantaged children has exceeded $242 billion (refer back to Figure 1.1). According to the National Assessment of Educational Progress (NAEP) reports on reading, in the year 2000 only 32 percent of fourth graders could read at a proficient level and scores for lowest-performing students have continued to decline (U.S. Department of Education, 2003). That performance is unacceptable.

NCLB endeavors to change the course of education. As such, it presents a challenge for all children to learn at high levels. As educators, we must accept that challenge. Admittedly, the challenge is greatest in urban school districts where the minority and the poor are most concentrated and where the learning gap is greatest. Indeed, the accountability in the law can be frightening, but we must not shrink from our responsibility to cause children to learn and we must accept the challenge with rigor.

Teaching has never been a profession considered easy. It is today inherently more difficult than ever before given the accountability involved. The U.S. Department of Education has published booklets which present and clarify the principle of NCLB. One booklet (2001) aimed at informing teachers suggests that teachers need to understand:

- what high standards mean and do;
- the purpose of assessments;

- how to use test scores to help every student improve;
- how to improve reading instruction; and
- where to turn to for help.

Schools remain very bureaucratic and, as such, they resist change. With accountability, resistance would be a mistake. Teachers cannot concentrate upon socializing children as their primary mission. That must change to one of teaching knowledge and skills. Children can no longer suffer the damage which comes from low expectations. The belief that some children cannot learn, the failure to measure and provide remediation, and the failure to use research-based instructional methods and teaching strategies cannot be tolerated (Wrightslaw News, 2003).

CHAPTER QUESTIONS

1. What factors influenced education during the Colonial era and what evidence is there to substantiate your response?

2. Describe the plight of African Americans as they sought to gain equality of educational opportunity in the years following the Civil War.

3. Discuss the *Plessy v. Ferguson* decision of 1896, which resulted in the separate but equal doctrine, and the *Brown* decision of 1954. What effect did each have upon education?

4. The federal government has increased its involvement in education since the Civil War. Discuss three legislative initiatives that have had an impact upon urban education.

5. How did the National Commission on Excellence in Education's report *A Nation at Risk* change the focus of education from social issues to academic learning, particularly for economically disadvantaged students?

6. Discuss ways in which the No Child Left Behind Act proposes to close the achievement gap between minority and White children.

SUGGESTED WEBSITES

The Civil Rights Project (CRP)
www.civilrightsproject.harvard.edu/research/deseg/deseg_gen.php

Consortium for Policy Research in Education (CPRE)
www.cpre.org/index_js.htm

New Schools, Better Neighborhoods
www.nsbn.org/about/

Northwest Regional Educational Laboratory
www.nwrel.org/index.html

Social Change Online; Racism No Way
www.racismnoway.com.au/classroom/lesson_ideas/20020828_49.html

Urban Network to Improve Teacher Education (UNITE)
www.urbannetworks.net/index.cfm

REFERENCES

Banks, J. A. (1999). *An introduction to multicultural education* (2nd ed). Boston: Allyn & Bacon.
Bennett, W. J. (1999). *The Wilson quarterly: Index of leading cultural indicators* (Summer).
Bloomfield, D. C., & Cooper, B. (2003). NCLB: A new role for the federal government: An overview of the most sweeping federal education law since 1965. *THE Journal (Technological Horizons in Education), 30*(10); *56*(4).
Bradley, P. (ed.). (1945). *Democracy in America by Alexis de Tocqueville.* New York: Vintage Books.
Bush, G. W. (2002). *President Bush signs* No Child Left Behind Act. Wrightslaw. Available: www.wrightslaw.com/news/2002/nclb.sign.htm.
Bush, G. W. (2004). *President George W. Bush post-election press conference. November 4, 2004.* Available: www.gwu.edu/~action/2004/bush/bush110404tr.html.
Butts, R. F., & Cremin, L. H. (1953). *A history of education in American culture.* New York: Rinehart & Winston.
Cincotta, H. (1994). United States Information Agency. Douglass Archives of American Public Address. Available: http://douglassarchives.org/ooah/ooah2.htm (2004, October 20).
Clinchy, E. (2001). Needed: A new educational civil rights movement. *Phi Delta Kappan, 82*(7), 493–498.
Clinton, W. J. (1991). *America 2000: The President's education strategy.* Washington, DC: The White House.
Coleman, J. S., Campbell, E. Q., Holison, C. J., McPartlan, J., Mood, A. M., Weinfeld, F. D., & York, R. L. (1966). *Equality of educational opportunity.* Washington, DC: Government Printing Office.
Douglass, F. (1868). *Life after the 13th Amendment: The work before us.* Available: www.black consciousnetwork.com/frederickdouglas6.htm.
Eastern Illinois University. (2004). *History of American education web project.* Available: www .nd.edu/~rbarger/www7/puritans.html (2004, October 19).
Education Trust, Inc. (1998). *Education watch* (Vol. II). Washington, DC: The Education Trust.
Foner, E., & Mahoney, O. (1997). *America's Reconstruction: People and politics after the Civil War.* Baton Rouge: Louisiana State University Press.
Garber, S. (2003). *Sputnik: The fortieth anniversary.* NASA. Available: www.hq.nasa.gov/office/pao/History/sputnik/.
George Mason University. (2004). *Notes for a History of U.S. Education.* Available: www.mason.gmu .edu/ujosterli/history_US_education.htm (2004, February 2)
Holladay, J. (2004). Brown v. Board timeline, school integration in the United States. *Teaching Tolerance* (25), 42–56.
Humphreys, J. (1999–2004). *Nowhere Else on Earth.* New York: Penguin.
Johnson, J. A., Dupuis, V. L., Musial, D., Hall, G. E., & Gollnick, D. M. (1996). *Introduction to the foundations of American education* (10th ed.) Boston: Allyn & Bacon.

Kincheloe, J. B., Pierce, T. M., Moore, R. E., Drewry, G. N., & Carmichael, B. E. (1995). *White and Negro schools in the South: An analysis of biracial education.* Englewood Cliffs, NJ: Prentice-Hall.

Learning First Alliance. (2003). *The No Child Left Behind Act: Key provisions and timelines.* Available: www.learningfirst.org (2004, October 8).

Microsoft Encarta Online Encyclopedia. (2004). *Public education in the United States.* Available: http://encarta.msn.com/encyclopedia_761571494/Public_Education_in_the_United_States .html (2004, October 21).

Morrison, G. S. (2000). *Teaching in America* (2nd ed.). Boston: Allyn & Bacon.

National Commission on Excellence in Education. (1983). *A Nation at risk: The imperative for education reform.* Washington, DC: U.S. Department of Education.

Old Deluder Satan Act. (1647). Massachusetts State Legislature.

Oracle Education Foundation. (2001). *Plessy v. Ferguson.* Thinkquest. Available: http://library .thinkquest.org/Joll2391/plessy_v_ferguson.htm (2004, October 18).

Orfield, G., & Eaton, S. E. (1996). *Dismantling desegregation.* New York: New Press.

Ornstein, A. C., & Levine, D. U. (2000). *Foundations of education* (7th ed.). Boston: Houghton Mifflin.

Paige, R. (2002). *President Bush signs* No Child Left Behind Act. Wrightslaw. Available: www.wrightslaw.com/news/2002/nclb.sign.htm.

Pressly, T. (1962). *Americans interpret their Civil War.* New York: Collier Books.

Rajala, J. (2003). Education reform (EduHound Extra!). *THE Journal (Technological Horizons in Education), 30*(6); *31*(1).

Sarason, S. B. (1991). *The predictable failure of educational reform.* San Francisco: Jossey-Bass.

Senate Committee on the Judiciary, Hearings on the Nomination of Justice Willliam Hobbs Rehnquist, 99th Congress, 2nd Session, 1986, p. 161–162.

State of South Carolina. (1790). The public laws of South Carolina: An act for the better governing and growing of Negroes and other slaves in This province. *South Carolina, Statutes, The Public Laws of the State of South Carolina.*

Sunstein, C. (2004, May 17) Commentary: From law clerk to chief justice, he has slighted rights: Rehnquist's 1952 memo sheds light on today's court. *Los Angeles Times.* Retrieved July 6, 2005, from www.law.uchicago.edu/news/sunstein_rehnquist.html.

Unger, H. G. (2001). *Encyclopedia of American education.* New York: Facts on File.

United Nations, Department of Public Information. (1998). *Fiftieth anniversary of the universal declaration of human rights.* Available: www.un.org/rights/50/decla.htm (2004, October 23).

U.S. Congress. (1990). *The Carl D. Perkins Vocational and Applied Technology Education Act of 1990 [Public Law 101–392].* Washington, DC: Department of Education.

U.S. Department of Education. (1994). *Goals 2000, Educate America Act [H.R. 1804, Section 101].* Washington, DC: U.S. Government Printing Office.

U.S. Department of Education. (2003). *Introduction: No Child Left Behind [H.R. 1].* Available: www.ed.gov/nclb/overview/index.html (2004, September 20).

Van Til, W. (1971). *Education: A beginning.* Boston: Houghton Mifflin.

Webb, L. D., Metha, A., & Jordan, K. F. (2003) *Foundations of American education* (4th ed.). Upper Saddle River, NJ: Merrill Prentice-Hall.

Wikipedia. (2004). *National Defense Education Act.* Available: www.fact-index.com/n/na/ national_defense_education_act.html (2004, September 1).

Wrightslaw News. (2003). *The No Child Left Behind Act of 2001: What does it mean to you.* Available: www.wrightslaw.com/info/nclb.index.htm (2004, October 21).

CHAPTER 2

EDUCATIONAL PERSPECTIVES

The way in which each of us understands texts
and language is grounded in our cultural,
social, and historical backgrounds.
—Elite Ben-Yosef, 2003

URBAN PERSPECTIVES

Reverend Lurone Jennings
Former Urban Student, Teacher, Coach, and Principal

So I believe that schools should get creative. You have parents going to the basketball and football games, watching the sports, the bands, and the extracurricular activities . . . maybe we need to have PTA meetings or school tables set up at those athletic activities to engage parents in the information and to encourage their (school) involvement.

"As a student, the school aspect was the best part of being raised in the inner-city environment," reminisced Reverend Jennings. "Although my parents cared about what I was up to and what I was doing, they were all wrapped up in their own challenges and struggles. Living in a dysfunctional homelife meant that school was a tremendous outlet for me."

Reverend Jennings, who attended a segregated school of all African American students from the first through the twelfth grade, offered interesting perspectives of the urban schools and their culture. His teachers encouraged him, along with other classmates, to do well in academics in order to progress and succeed in life. "They [teachers] didn't put up with a whole lot of foolishness. They had authority. And they worked together with parents, like a team. There was a combined effort between home and school that would help us realize the importance of education.

"Teachers back then emphasized morality issues, teaching us things that would help us stay away from the folks that were doing the drugs, the drinking, the violence, or the gangs—or those kinds of things that surrounded us in the inner-city community. The teachers were real serious about education and the moral aspects that we needed in order to excel and progress, and they, with our parents, did an excellent job of communicating it.

"Parents also had authority, and would assert that authority in a very serious way to let children know that they meant business when it came to their getting an education. I think parents have to take ultimate responsibility for the success of their children because of what they're able to provide, and offer the energy, drive, support, and importance of education.

"If parents are intimidated by the school environment, then they aren't going to come and participate as we would expect of them. And getting urban parents involved in the schools can be a challenge for teachers. So I believe that schools should get creative. You have parents going to the basketball and football games, watching the sports, the bands, and the extracurricular activities; in a nontraditional sense, but for greater participation, maybe we need to have PTA meetings or school tables set up at those athletic activities to engage parents in the academic information and to encourage their involvement. Perhaps teachers should meet parents right where they are: in their neighborhoods and their communities. As a principal, I encouraged teachers to make a home visit of students who were struggling in school prior to their penalizing students for not turning in homework. I'd say, 'Go visit the child's home and see what you see.' One teacher returned from such an experience in amazement, exclaiming, 'There are fifteen people in a two-bedroom house! And it was so chaotic and noisy—nonconductive to homework completion, for sure.' "

"From my experiences as a student, teacher, coach, principal, and now in service to the Lord, it is clear to me that all the players—parents, teachers, school personnel, community, church ministries, etc.—have great opportunities available for interacting and engaging in and building relationships that perform valuable roles in educating our children."

REALITIES OF URBAN EDUCATION

The Effects of Poverty

The fabric of society in the United States has undergone significant changes following the first two hundred years since its birth as a nation when Western European heritage and English-speaking majority populations were dominant. America is today a nation of increasing populations of people of color and diverse languages, backgrounds, cultures, and heritages. Such dramatic demographic shifts in the United States have created the need for continual, critical evaluation of the state of education in schools, specifically in its classrooms. Critical observations and assessments of the effectiveness of classroom instruction, markedly evidenced by schools' annual, standardized test scores of their students, substantiate serious problems in how well poor students of color are learning. These problems are currently identified in the inequitable achievement gap that exists in test scores between higher functioning White, non-Hispanic students, and lower functioning students of color and most poorer populations.

Simultaneously intensifying this gap is the unacceptable increase in poverty among school-aged children. Poverty, calculated by the Office of Management and Budget, is defined as the income for a family of four of $18,810; for a family of three, $14,680; for a family of two, $12,015; and for unrelated individuals, $9,393 (U.S. Department of Commerce News, 2003, p. 3).

Poverty in America has continued to rise among all ethnic, or non-White, subgroups of the United States population, from 7.2 million in 2002 to 7.6 million poor families in 2003. That indicates an increase of 10 percent of individuals among marginalized subgroups, or diverse populations, subjected to impoverished conditions of existence. As illustrated in Figure 2.1 below, non-Hispanic Whites had the lowest poverty rate of 8.2 percent; Asian Americans revealed the second-lowest rate of 11.8 percent; Hispanics 22.5; American Indians and Alaskan Natives 23.2; and African Americans exhibited the highest poverty rate of 24.4 percent. The numbers of children under the age of 18 living in poverty have likewise increased, rising from 12.1 million in 2002 to 12.9 million in 2003 (U.S. Department of Commerce News, 2003). Teachers need to understand these socioeconomic conditions that are most prevalent in urban schools in order to adjust and design teaching and learning to effectively meet the needs of their diverse population of learners. The implications for the teacher education

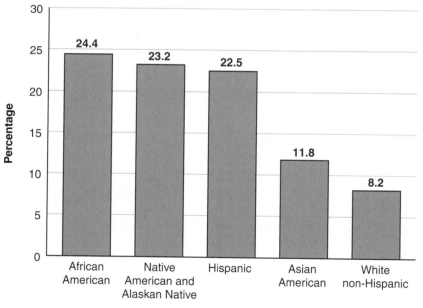

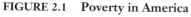

FIGURE 2.1   Poverty in America
Source: U.S. Census Bureau News, 2003.

training necessary for this growing group of impoverished children can be overwhelming and complex. This chapter presents discussions of these and similar issues and ideas to address the needs of this population of learners in urban schools.

Students living in undesirable conditions are challenged to meet academic expectations. For example, when national eighth-grade math student test scores are compared by levels of students' family income, those from families of higher income, or not poor, demonstrate overall higher math skills, with 78 percent achieving at basic to proficient levels. In contrast, students of lower income, or poor, families demonstrate overall lower math skills, with only 47 percent achieving at basic to proficient levels (Education Trust, Inc., 2003a).

Regarding students who continue their education beyond high school, Mortenson's (1997) research reveals that low socioeconomic status (SES) has a negative impact on academic achievement. For example, 60 percent of high-income students graduate from college by age 26, but only 7 percent of low-income students graduate from college by that same age. Further, when comparing specific population subgroups who eventually graduate from college, Figure 2.2 illustrates that certain ethnic groups noticeably lead the way. Nearly 50 percent of Asian Americans have earned at least their bachelor's degree by the

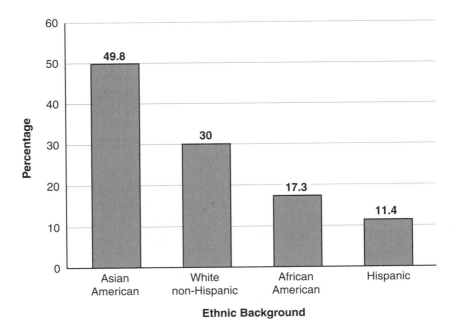

FIGURE 2.2   American Higher Education Attainment by Ethnic Backgrounds

Source: U.S. Census Bureau's Educational Attainment in the United States, 2003.

age of 25, followed by 30 percent of White, non-Hispanic Americans. Falling sharply from there are 17.3 percent of graduates representing the African American population, and 11.4 percent of graduates representing the Hispanic Americans (U.S. Census Bureau, 2003a). Collectively, Figures 2.1 and 2.2 indicate that students of color and of lowest income populations are the least likely to achieve higher levels of education.

Although the United States holds high democratic principles for all students, not all are achieving at the levels they need to succeed in high school, much less to continue on to college. Such realities present a challenge for all teachers, especially those working with significant numbers of low-income students who attend urban schools.

Shifting Educational Paradigms

For most of the twentieth century, public education demographics indicated that majority White students learned in classrooms with students of color, principally African Americans. The educational paradigm for much of the twentieth century was the assimilationist paradigm within which students of color and new immigrants were expected to take on the beliefs, language, and values of the predominant culture in the United States and to become mainstream Americans. Immigrants were expected to forego their native language, learn and use only Standard English and reflect practices of the White, middle-class values. In other words, they were expected to assimilate into the dominant society.

During the 1960s, mainstream American attitudes toward different ethnic groups and cultures were called into question by the Civil Rights movement. From this era the multicultural educational paradigm emerged. This paradigm was the antithesis of everyone assimilating into the existing American mainstream culture. The multicultural paradigm respected the variety of cultures and ethnic groups throughout the U.S. and sought to maintain their respective cultural identities. Equality, equity, and empowerment for marginalized populations are hallmarks of this paradigm (Banks, 1988).

Current concerns in education call for a realistic paradigm that Banks (1988) suggests is broader than any single-faceted paradigm. He calls for a holistic educational paradigm based on a social system that increases the academic achievement of marginalized students as it increases the crosscultural competency of mainstream Americans. He states:

> The school is a micro-culture in which the cultures of students and teachers meet. The school should be a cultural environment in which acculturation takes place: both teachers and students should assimilate some of the views, perceptions, and ethos of each other as they interact. Both teachers and students will be enriched by this process, and the academic achievement of students from diverse cultures will be enhanced because their cosmos and ethos will be reflected and legitimized in the school. (pp. 108–109)

In order for this type of interaction to occur, diverse populations within the school must have equal status and share equal power. Banks concludes that:

> It is essential that schools in Western democracies acculturate students rather than foster tight ethnic boundaries because all students, including ethnic minority students, must develop the knowledge, attitudes, and skills needed to become successful citizens of their cultural communities, their nation-states, and the global world community. (p. 109)

Federal Policies Respond to Growing Needs

Changing demographics during the latter period of the twentieth century has redefined teaching and learning for the twenty-first century. With the 1954 Supreme Court decision *Brown v. Board of Education of Topeka, Kansas*, educational opportunities were expanded for African American students. Subsequently, in 1965, the passage of the Elementary and Secondary Education Act created Title I programs to provide assistance to low-socioeconomic-level schools to meet state-established academic content and performance standards. The Education for All Handicapped Children Act of 1975, passed a decade later, gave children with disabilities the right to a free and appropriate public education (FAPE). Reauthorized and renamed in 1990 as the Individuals with Disabilities Education Act (IDEA), the FAPE expanded the categories of disability to include autism and traumatic brain injury, rehabilitation counseling and social work services, and a commitment to the needs of linguistically and ethnically diverse youth with disabilities. These changes in society that have produced changes in the national laws have led to significant changes in the way in which students' diverse needs must be addressed in the classroom. Today's educational paradigm insists that students with disabilities, students of diverse ethnic origins, students of diverse language backgrounds, and students in poverty all must be served equitably, or fairly, in the public education arena. American education, more than that of any other national educational system in the world, seeks fair and equitable opportunities for all students regardless of race, ethnicity, language, or socioeconomic level.

To further decrease the educational achievement gap between marginalized and mainstream Americans, President George W. Bush in 2001 was instrumental in passing the No Child Left Behind Act (NCLB). This controversial and bold initiative reformed the American education structure to accept a paradigm shift intended to bridge the gap between White students and students of color, between disabled students and nondisabled students, and between low-and middle/upper-socioeconomic groups. Since the states' implementation of this plan, teachers specifically are now required to meet stipulations as "highly qualified" by 2005–2006. Highly qualified is defined as having full state certification, or having passed the state teacher's licensing exam. Teachers test students each year on content aligned with state-designed standards. Student scores should represent those meeting at least adequate yearly progress (AYP). Schools not meeting AYP minimal statistical cutoffs for two consecutive years must develop a two-year plan to turn around the school, making improvements that will raise student scores in schools to meet the AYP score minimum (Webb, Metha, & Jordan, 2003, p. 218). Both school districts and states must announce publicly the yearly report cards on their overall student achievement scores. Chapter 3 presents details of NCLB and other federal initiatives that have influenced education.

Truly the twenty-first century holds new educational challenges for teachers in all environments, but especially for teachers in urban schools. Schools in urban areas across America have a preponderance of poverty, students of color, and students with disabilities. It is in these urban schools where the challenges for teaching and learning are the greatest.

TWENTY-FIRST CENTURY URBAN EDUCATIONAL REALITIES

Preparing Preservice Teachers

We are in a changing and dynamic century, but what does that mean for teaching and learning in an urban setting? How do we meet the challenges to effectively teach *all* children in order for them to make adequate yearly progress? We know that poverty is increasing among school-aged children, that multicultural students whose language is other than English is also increasing, and that students with disabilities, required to be in the least-restrictive environment, are educated in our regular classrooms. These realities create a great challenge for all teachers but affect urban teachers the most.

Since approximately 85 percent of teachers nationally are White, middle-class, and female, it is imperative that we prepare teachers who are culturally sensitive, empathetic, and committed to teaching students of different ethnic backgrounds. What follows are some of the issues and challenges involved in preparing teachers to be successful in the urban environment.

Congruence in Teacher Attitudes, Beliefs, and Expectations

Individuals preparing to teach enter the educational environment with certain beliefs, attitudes, preconceived ideas, and expectations about the students they will be teaching. Females from White, middle-class backgrounds will enter the teaching environment with the beliefs and expectations developed from that culture of White, middle-class America. As they teach those of similar background, there is most likely a congruency in the environment. That is, students for the most part will meet the teacher's underlying assumptions and perform with predetermined expectations. However, when teachers are placed in an environment for which they are *not* prepared, an environment that is quite different from their own personal background and experiences, the expectations and understandings about how students respond and act in the school environment are not likely to be met. This incongruence between teacher and student backgrounds will affect the teachers' ability to successfully meet the needs of the students in the urban setting.

In order to be successful as a teacher of diverse, lower-class, male and female students, teachers must take time to examine the underlying beliefs and attitudes that each brings to this setting. Haberman (1991) reports that an individual's beliefs, attitudes, and expectations originate from parents, early childhood experiences, community, religious practices, and additional significant others. The values that teachers hold based on these initial, intense, in-depth personal experiences guide and influence them for the rest of their lives. Research shows that changing teachers' attitudes and beliefs to properly understand students' of color and poverty attitudes and beliefs is difficult and takes place over time (Bollin & Finkel, 1995; Ladson-Billings, 2000). Sustained discussions, readings, and experiences in real-life situations, extended over time, are crucial to bringing about the changes in teachers' attitudes and beliefs necessary for them to become culturally relevant and effective teachers of multicultural students. The failure to change teachers' attitudes, beliefs, and expectations will result in failure among urban students with whom teachers work, thereby continuing the cycle of failure for these students.

Assimilationist versus Culturally Relevant Pedagogy

Ladson-Billings (2000) argues that specific strategies and methodologies for understanding and teaching African American students are absent from the educational literature. She proposes that this is largely due to the espousal of a pedagogy that one-size-fits-all but in reality supports the academic achievement of mainstream America. In her article "Fighting for Our Lives," she delineates strategies to improve the education of preservice teachers. These include educational students critically examining their own personal and cultural story and writing an autobiography based on their insights, maintaining high expectations and work ethics for their students, and relating their knowledge about the students' home and community to the subject content. Relating home and community knowledge to academic content allows students to make home–school connections and increases their ability to learn. Ladson-Billings promotes teaching that supports cultural competence by respecting the students' home language and using it to scaffold classroom learning (described in Chapter 7). Culturally relevant teachers maintain a sociopolitical critique that creates an awareness of how certain societal and institutional practices lead to and reproduce inequities.

In Ladson-Billings' book *The Dreamkeepers* (1994) she discusses how teachers' beliefs and expectations are shown in their behaviors. She reconceptualizes Winfield's model for culturally relevant teaching and compares this teaching to assimilationist teaching (p. 23). Behaviors toward academically and culturally at-risk students and beliefs about at-risk students are contingent on each other. Those culturally relevant teachers who assume and share responsibility for the achievement of all students in their classes act like conductors and coaches in their approach to students. They seek excellence and hold high expectations for

all students. Culturally responsible teachers strive for excellence and assist students to achieve academic excellence. As conductors they orchestrate the students' learning. They see areas of weakness and make plans to address these by individualizing instruction and using their cultural knowledge to explain concepts to the students. They motivate and inspire students in their learning struggles. As coaches they enlist peers who are experts in an area to assist the students' learning. They encourage and facilitate the learning process by allowing students to take ownership by offering choices. They believe that the students can learn and are capable of achieving academic excellence.

On the other hand, assimilationist teachers seek improvement, maintain the status quo, or shift responsibility to others for the academically and culturally at-risk students in their classrooms. They are termed custodians of the status quo. They either do not believe that these students can do any differently, or they shift responsibility by referring students having difficulty to others, such as tutors or outside sources. They seek improvement for their students through others. The attitude of an assimilationist teacher is extremely detrimental to urban children. A culturally relevant pedagogy is the best means of achieving successful teaching and learning with urban children.

Understanding and Dealing with Urban Children

Jenkins' book *Understanding and Educating African American Children* (2004) contains a chapter entitled, "What Black Children Need in Their Teachers." He reiterates that children of color need teachers who have been trained in their educational programs to meet the demands of a diverse, multicultural classroom. Most of the students of education being trained nationally are White, middle-class, and female. Many of these students are not trained in multicultural settings nor given the skills or understandings that would make them successful and effective in a diverse classroom. Within the United States, numerous universities have been concerned about this issue and are developing educational programs that orient and train students within urban and multicultural settings. Some examples are the University of Memphis, University of Wisconsin–Milwaukee, Johns Hopkins University, Boston College, Michigan State University, and the University of California at Los Angeles. These programs are proving successful in developing students who are ready for the diverse environments in which they will teach.

Jenkins suggests several questions for education majors to ask themselves concerning their suitability to teach in today's multicultural, multilinguistic environment, including, "Do I want to teach children?" "Do I want to teach the best children?" "Do I care enough about kids and this country to give my life to making them both better?" (p. 154). Children of color need teachers who are committed to teaching and to helping them attain high levels of academic success. They do not need teachers who in their sympathy for the difficult circumstances of the children excuse them and accept inferior work or behavior from them. This behavior of teachers only continues the cycle of poverty for the diverse students in their classrooms. They need teachers who will motivate them to do their best and understand how an education opens doors that free them from their difficult circumstances. They need teachers who are strong enough to stand up to them as well as be advocates for them.

Jenkins describes four stages of Black students with White teachers. These stages are helpful to White teachers as they are confronted with negative behaviors in Black students and are seeking positive ways to approach and resolve these behaviors. The four stages are rejection, acceptance, decision and cooperative existence. The last stage is reminiscent of the final outcome of Banks' (1988) holistic educational paradigm where teacher and students learn from each other. In order for a White teacher to be successful in going through these stages with Black students, the teacher must have a secure understanding of who he/she is culturally and be open to growing in their understanding of other cultures (see Table 2.1).

Resistance to Diversity Training

One of the main factors that prevents White preservice teachers from embracing multicultural training is that within the training they are made to feel guilty for being White. Pride in their ethnicity is taken away, and they are not able to healthily accept other cultural groups. Nel (1992) highlights the resistance of preservice teachers to diversity training, suggesting several instructional strategies to minimize teacher resistance: experiential learning in urban schools, understanding the magnitude of the problems facing young people in poverty, extensive readings and documentaries of immigrant and marginalized communities, interviews with diverse students and families, role-plays and simulations that aid understanding the trauma experienced, and finally reflections and discussions of their experiences that allow them to internalize and solidify their changing attitudes and beliefs.

Bollin and Finkel (1995) specifically address the issue of white racial identity as a barrier to understanding diversity. They present the work of Helms (1990), who has developed a six-stage model of White racial identity that gives insight into this issue. These six stages are as follows:

Stage I is naive and presents racial identity as inconsequential;

Stage II is dissonance that occurs as they learn that race does make a difference and are uncomfortable with their sense of privilege;

Stage III is reintegration where they try to explain their differences based on White superiority;

Stage IV is cognitive where they intellectually accept racial differences and work for equity;

Stage V is self-exploration where they begin to define their racial identity and those of other races; and

TABLE 2.1 The Four Stages of Black Students with White Teachers

STAGES	DESCRIPTION	WHAT WHITE TEACHERS CAN DO TO HELP BLACK CHILDREN THROUGH THESE STAGES
1. *Rejection:* Black students reject White teachers. The longer this stage lasts, the greater the educational impairment to the Black child. Anything the White teacher does to shorten this stage does immeasurable good for the student.	Black child denies the White teacher intimate access to her person.	Show understanding of the child's feelings, assure the child that you care, and want to help her get a good education. Be concerned, caring, patient, and sincere. Don't be afraid to discuss present injustices with Black students. Don't take the blame for all past and present injustices of White Americans. White teachers *can* address the racism of Black students. The White teacher should not try to be Black, and one does not have to be Black to understand injustice. Education is not about where you have been, but about where you are going.
2. *Acceptance:* White teacher/Black student relationship reaches its height in academic and social accomplishments.	Black child lets down her guard and allows friendship with White teacher. Highly productive stage. Begins to think critically and make comparisons.	White teachers can help Blacks by reminding them of their own capabilities and their responsibility to live up to those capabilities. The Black child has a chance to prove that she is worthy of the White teacher's effort and interest. Much progress is made. This stage is only temporary. As the student develops her scholarship and confidence, feelings of self-worth are enhanced. At that time, the student begins to see herself as equal to Whites and begins to question and compare.

(continues)

45

TABLE 2.1 (*continued*)

STAGES	DESCRIPTION	WHAT WHITE TEACHERS CAN DO TO HELP BLACK CHILDREN THROUGH THESE STAGES
3. *Decision:* Black students react to the wrong reason for desegregation and retreat back to their community thinking they must give up their Blackness to be accepted as a part of the White community. They choose the comfort of color and all the protection it gives them from the standards of the larger society. They maintain very negative views about their experiences at White schools. Others buy into the White system and become brown versions of White Americans. They receive an education that has no connection to their community and do not give back to it.	Black child rejects White teacher for the second time or enters into the fourth stage.	If Black children are engaged in discussions about cultural diversity and how one can appreciate and learn from another culture while maintaining allegiance to their own, this would significantly lessen their trauma. Not enough of these discussions are held and, therefore, Black children are left to their own conclusions about desegregation. Many Black children believe that the purpose of desegregation is to merge Black culture into White culture, requiring them to lose their Black identity in favor of a White reality. As White teachers understand what is going on inside of their Black students, they can support them and encourage them to talk about their feelings. The great majority of Blacks who have made meaningful contributions to other Blacks and to this country were educated at all-Black schools. White teachers must work to reverse those figures.
4. *Cooperative existence:* Blacks and Whites allow each other to remain different. They see each other as valuable and unique contributors to the richness of the human and American experience.	Black child accepts and builds a trusting relationship with the White teacher.	The ultimate goal of racial understanding should not be just to know other people, but to value them. Races are made up of individuals, not stereotypical groups.

Stage VI is where transculturalization takes place as they internalize a diverse identity and seek to learn more from other racial groups.

West Chester University uses Helms' (1990) framework to evaluate and direct the multicultural awareness of its education students. Texts such as *Black Children: Their Roots, Culture and Learning Styles* by Hale (1986), *There Are No Children Here* by Kotlowitz (1991), and *Among Schoolchildren* by Kidder (1989) are used to encourage new thinking and class discussions.

Bollin and Finkel report that most students initially were angry with the premise of the Hale book that children from the Black culture have differences that need to be accommodated in the classroom in order for the children to be successful in academics. They felt that this was a racist position and that all children should be treated equally. This author as a professor has used Hale's book with preservice students and have found their reactions to the book to be similar. They feel it is a book that pits Blacks against Whites and creates more racism due to describing the differences in the two cultures. Their responses represent the attitudes and beliefs of persons in Helm's Stage I: naive and presents racial identity as inconsequential.

Classroom discussions about race are important to clarifying the students' understanding and acceptance of these ideas. However, reading and discussing racial issues are not enough. For students to extend beyond Stage III (reintegration where they try to explain their differences based on white superiority) they must have sustained time with people of other ethnic groups. Within the context of field experiences such as tutoring and assisting students in a variety of way in the urban classroom, many of the students reported having a critical event that encouraged them to change and move on to Stage IV (cognitive where they intellectually accept racial differences and work for equity).

The authors of this text believe that an understanding of multiculturalism, acceptance, and recognition of diversity in the urban setting is an imperative for teachers. Dealing with different cultures and teaching children from diverse backgrounds requires not only high-level teaching skills, but a willingness to be sensitive to students' learning needs and flexible in instructional delivery.

Star Teachers versus Quitters and Failures

Haberman's *Star Teachers of Children in Poverty* (1995) suggests a list of terms that educators whom he describes as "quitters and failures" often use to describe children in poverty, English language learners, and students of color in terms that they substitute for more offensive terms (p. 21).

> These euphemisms inevitably become recognized for what they are—labels and code words. They might appear to be innocuous when they are initially adopted because they are new terms without a clear history. As these new labels are used, however, it soon becomes clear in the public mind and among educators that the

same groups are being identified: children with low achievement scores; children who are frequently absent; children whose families move frequently; children who are from poverty backgrounds; children who are frequently disciplined and suspended; children from dysfunctional families; children with handicapping conditions; children with language problems; children whose parents are not visible in school; children who are most likely to be victims of crime, physical abuse, and chemical abuse; children who become teenage parents; youth who drop out or are sent to alternative schools; children and youth of color; or of non-English-speaking backgrounds. Added to this common list of attributes are all the other children and youth perceived by educators and the public to be "problems" in the schools. (p. 48)

In contrast to teachers who are "quitters and failures," Haberman describes teachers whom he calls "stars" as having a different attitude toward these students. Where others fail, they succeed in meeting the academic challenges of the students in their classrooms.

Star teachers see their main goal as "turning kids on to learning—i.e., engaging them in becoming independent learners" (p. 15). They are able to convince students that learning is intrinsically useful. Star teachers do not give up on students; they see their potential and believe that they can achieve. They set high standards and hold high expectations for their students and do not accept excuses. Star teachers use real-life situations and problems to engage students in learning. As a result of their belief in their students' abilities to succeed, their students do succeed and this is evident in their academic achievement. Below are examples of successes in high-poverty, high-multicultural schools where teachers and principals believe that change can occur and that the future does not need to repeat the past.

Star Schools, Districts, and States

The Education Trust presents data that demonstrates that schools with low-income and highly diverse populations are able to compete with middle-income, White schools. The Education Trust (2003b) reports in *Dispelling the Myth Online* that Centennial Place Elementary in Atlanta, Georgia, with 79 percent low-income students and 92 percent African American and Hispanic students has outscored 93 percent of Georgia elementary schools in fourth grade reading and 88 percent in fourth grade math in 2002. Englehard Elementary in Louisville, Kentucky, with 82 percent low-income and 53 percent African American students has performed in the top third among Kentucky elementary schools for the last two years. Hambrick Middle School in Aldine, Texas, with 94 percent African American and Hispanic and 85 percent low-income students has performed in the top twentieth percent of all Texas middle schools in both reading and math in seventh and eighth grades over a three-year period.

In addition, certain districts across the nation are reporting gains over time for African American, Hispanic, and poor students. Among these are the Boston, Massachusetts public schools, Long Beach, California Unified School District, and the Aldine, Texas district. States with the largest gains for African American fourth grades as determined by the National Assessment of Educational Progress (NAEP) are North Carolina, California, and Massachusetts, showing gains from 1992 to 2003. States with the largest gains for Hispanic fourth graders as determined by NAEP are North Carolina, South Carolina, and Delaware, showing gains between 1992 and 2003.

The Education Trust's *Achievement in America* (2003a) lists reasons why these schools, districts, and states are outperforming others with poor and diverse students. These include having "clear, high goals for all students and curriculum aligned to those goals" (p. 70), "extra instruction and support provided for students who need it" (p. 86), "good teaching" (p. 88), and "funds" (p. 100). In the schools, districts, and states that seriously utilize these four elements, a difference is made in the lives of African American, Hispanic, and low-income students across America.

In "Dispelling the Myth: High Poverty Schools Exceeding Expectations" six areas are discussed that have been instrumental in helping schools perform at high levels:

1. Use state standards extensively to design curriculum and instruction, assess student work, and evaluate teachers.
2. Increase instructional time in reading and math in order to help students meet standards.
3. Devote a larger portion of funds to support professional development focused on changing instructional practice.
4. Implement comprehensive systems to monitor individual student progress and provide extra support to students as soon as it's needed.
5. Focus their efforts to involve parents on helping students meet standards.
6. Have state or district accountability systems in place that have real consequences for adults in the schools.

In addition to these successes, specific programs have been implemented in various schools nationally that have poor students of color achieving at the same or above the level of their White middle-class counterparts. One such program is the Kamehameha Elementary Education Program (KEEP) (Tharpe & Gallimore, 1988) in Hawaii, a Navajo reservation in Arizona, and schools in Los Angeles. KEEP was begun as a research-and-development program that involved psychologists, anthropologists, linguists, and educators, and was based on inquiry methods over a fifteen-year period. The goal of this research collaborative was to improve the cognitive and educational development of marginalized children. The results of this program revealed that for more than a decade, the poor children of color enrolled in the KEEP system performed at national-norm levels in reading achievement.

The heart of this program was the development of literacy skills through the Center One teacher-child interaction. During this daily activity, small groups of children rotate to Center One where their reading lesson takes place, and they interact with the teacher in discussing a story. The teacher draws upon the background experiences of the students concerning the subject matter and theme of the story to be read. The teacher then gives the students a reason to read by asking a question about the reading section. After a few minutes of reading, the students stop and discuss what they have read.

During this discussion time, the students and teacher engage in a joint instructional conversation. The participation by teacher and student is mutual. The teacher does not monopolize the conversation. The teacher engages the students by using various levels of questioning from recall of details to higher levels of inferential and evaluative thinking. The teacher builds on the responses of the students and remains flexible in guiding the discussion to meet the needs of the learners.

Included in this model is the refining of teacher performance through peer assistance as well as assistance from administrators, consultants, trainers, and specialists. The level of assistance is provided depending on the level needed by the preservice, beginning, or expert teacher. Teachers are observed once a week by a consultant and confer together about the feedback. Consultants and trainers also are assisted in their performances by the program developers and researchers. Each level of this program is closely observed and evaluated on a continual basis so that optimal performance is ensured by all those involved.

Another example of programs that are effective with disadvantaged youth is youth organizations that are located in the inner-city communities. According to Heath and McLaughlin (1993) who studied more than sixty different organizations over a five-year period, the organizations were typically local branches of national organizations such as Boy Scouts, YMCAs, Girls Clubs, and community resource centers that offered a variety of services for neighborhood youth. Young people with the motivation to find a safe place away from the violence and drugs of their neighborhoods sought out these youth programs in their areas. The youth programs described their success in terms of

> helping youth to achieve balance—sure footing and sense of purpose—in their communities as well as an ability to negotiate different roles in different places—to draw on an array of features to give them several identities, all of which are anchored in a secure sense of self. (p. 38)

Youth found positive role models within these organizations that sustained them and gave them a sense of security in the midst of turmoil and insecurity in their lives. In many of the interviews with youth from the inner city, they shared the inevitability of life in prison, death, or early pregnancies. One of the main characteristics of these programs was that they called the young people to participation and commitment. "Inner-city organizations connect youth with larger society, promote a positive sense of purpose and personhood, and provide the resources that youngsters need to reach adulthood" by addressing the multiple needs of youth (p. 55). These needs include tutoring centers, counselors, sports, opportunities to the world of work, and emergency food supplies. These programs act as family for the youth.

These schools and programs, which represent a cross section of America that has high poverty and high multicultural populations, are able to assist students to achieve at high academic levels. Other schools and organizations around the nation with similar demographics can also achieve these results by implementing comparable elements in the organization and curricula within urban settings.

CULTURE, ETHNICITY, AND LEARNING STYLES

The Importance of Teacher Understandings

Ladson-Billings' *The Dreamkeepers*, (1994) discusses the importance of teachers understanding students' cultures in order to make their learning relevant. She proposes that it is not so much what we teach (curriculum), but how we teach African American students that makes the difference in their being motivated to learn. Ladson-Billings indicates that culture does matter. Some examples she gives that are culturally-relevant teaching strategies are using small interactive groups, focusing on reading comprehension instead of pronunciation, and discussing texts based on an overlapping interactional style, for example, many communicating ideas simultaneously.

Failure to understand differences in learning styles, differences in cultural styles of language use and interaction patterns, and differences between classroom culture and the children's out-of-school environment can lead to teachers misreading students' aptitudes and abilities and to misattributions of student deficiency (Delpit, 1992; Perry & Delpit, 1998). According to Perry, Steele, and Hilliard (1997), if teachers bring a limited background knowledge and understanding of ethnic groups to the classroom, their capability to properly assess the students' aptitudes will be limited.

There is not universal agreement that focusing upon culture, ethnicity, and learning styles is helpful for multicultural students. Grant in "Culture and Teaching: What Do Teachers Need to Know?" (1991) describes the contradictions in the literature about culture, ethnicity, and learning styles. Future teachers need to gain knowledge about other cultures; however, some would say that that knowledge could lead to stereotypes and biases. Learning styles could lead teachers to place students into categories and not see each child as an individual who might not fit into that mold.

While various ethnic groups display an inclination toward a particular learning or cognitive style, teachers should be aware that students within these groups are individuals and may not necessarily follow the patterns of the group as a whole. Teachers should also select texts that deal with various ethnic groups in order to foster positive role models for the diverse students in their classrooms, and they should employ a variety of teaching styles to meet the needs of the various learners in their classrooms.

Hale in *Black Children: Their Roots, Culture and Learning Styles* (1986), presents the view that culture influences cognitive styles (Cohen, 1969; Hilliard,

1976, 1992). It is useful for educators to understand the learning and cognitive styles of various cultures. Cohen has identified two major styles of cognitive organization, *analytical* and *relational*. Analytical styles are related to organizational thinking for successful learning in school academics; however, relational thinking styles are related to successful creative arts production: visual, musical, entertainment, athletic, and fashion. American schools are organized mostly around analytical thinking skills and, therefore, students with relational cognitive skills are at a distinct disadvantage. Quite often these children are seen through the lens of a "deficiency orientation" (Sleeter & Grant, 1987) instead of viewing their cognitive style as a strength. A deficiency orientation looks at students and sees their weaknesses and not the strengths they bring to the learning environment. They are spoken of in terms of what they lack instead of what they possess. All students bring abilities and strengths to the academic setting.

Different cultures have different intellectual emphases. Abrahams (1970) has identified the African American approach to music and language as circular rather than the linear approach that is expressive of Western thinking. The two approaches differ in that while the Western culture seeks closure, the African American culture remains open-ended.

Debate continues in the literature concerning whether differences found among ethnic groups based on learning style and personality encourages or discourages ethnic bias and prejudice. Research can be found that agrees with the basic assumption that different cultures support and develop different learning styles and also different personality types. This perspective sees learning style differences related to differences in cultures; that is, certain cultures tend to support certain types of learning styles. For instance, White culture tends to support a field independent/analytical learning style, for example, thinking through situations and deciding upon conclusions to activate; while Black, Native American, and Hispanic cultures tend to support a field dependent/global learning style, for example, seeking input from peers and others, along with their advice and approval, prior to making decisions (Banks, 1988; More, 1990; White, 1992). These basic differences could explain why some ethnic groups' academic achievement is significantly below that of the dominant culture. The conclusion is that if schools and teachers adapt and change the curriculum and instruction to meet the needs of different learners, then certain ethnic groups are more likely to achieve in school. The dominant culture needs to change its educational processes to include more diversity in its approaches to teaching and learning.

Learning Styles and Instruction

In "Building Sociocentric Classrooms: What Ethnic Minorities Can Teach Us," Mikkelson (1991) found that encouraging the more relational style of Black children in story making led to a greater quality and quantity of stories as they piggybacked on each others' stories to create their own. Produced in this way, creating stories becomes a way of sorting out and increasing understanding of real-life situations. Stories are told to share experiences with others and to make sense of life's problems together. By using this style of storytelling, built on the social context rather than the individual context, the lesson becomes a communal process rather than a solitary one.

White (1992) describes the learning styles of African American and Caucasian students that contribute to their academic differences. He describes African Americans as being field-dependent, auditory, and tactile/kinesthetic as their primary processing mode as contrasted to Caucasians as being primarily field-independent and visual. He concludes that Black students need action-oriented curricula and personal involvement in order to be academically successful.

Banks' (1988) research reviewed the effects of ethnicity persistent across social classes in African American and Mexican Americans. These students tend to be more field-sensitive in their learning styles. One instructional implication for this knowledge is that these students relate more effectively to information presented in a story format. Therefore, using stories to present content information to students in social studies, science, and math would be much more interesting, motivational, and thus more understandable to them. The research also suggests that lower socioeconomic students are more externally motivated and need teachers to actively show them the relationship between their hard work and their academic achievement.

Jones (1986) has explored learning styles in relation to gender and ethnic differences. Cross-cultural studies indicate cultural biases in developing learning style differences between genders as well as ethnic groups. Changes in the learning environment may lead to greater success in areas such as math and science for women and Blacks.

Recognizing Learning Styles

The following is an example of how a learning style inventory given to students benefitted both the students and the teachers. Students' learning styles were compared within disciplines, gender, and ethnicity. Using Kolb's Learning-Style Inventory (Kolb, 1985; Serrell, 1983), students rank ordered from one to four (four being how you learn best and one being the least) twelve sets of four learning situations, such as: I am an intuitive person; I look at all sides of issues; I like to analyze things; I like to try things out. From these twelve sets, the four cognitive learning styles evolved as follows:

- accommodator (leader, risk taker, achiever)
- assimilator (planner, theorist, analyst)
- diverger (creator, artist, sensitive to values)
- converger (problem solver, deducer, decision maker)

Profiles of Diverse Groups

According to Table 2.2, Hispanics, Blacks, and Asians identified themselves most often as assimilators and divergers. Divergers are the least-identified learning

style of White students, yet the second highest for Hispanics and Asians. The divergent style is characterized by imaginative ability, sensitivity to people and values, and problem recognition. Divergers identify with right-brain functions of global, holistic, spatial, and intuitive thinking; whereas convergers identify with the left-brain functions of analytical, logical, language, and independent thinking. Both Blacks and Hispanics showed the least inclination toward the converger learning style, with Asians identifying converger as the third lowest. White students, however, chose converger and assimilator as their two main learning styles.

Applications of Learning-Style Differences

Based on the percentages, shown in Table 2.2, students from different cultures show inclinations toward different learning styles. Teachers need to be aware of

TABLE 2.2   Learning-Style Percentages within Ethnicity Spring 1997
Supplemental Instruction Students

	NUMBER	ASSIMILATOR	ACCOMMODATOR	DIVERGER	CONVERGER
White	70	35.7%	17.1%	11.4%	35.7%
Black	9	44.4%	22.2%	22.2%	11.1%
Hispanic	19	42.1%	21.1%	26.3%	10.5%
Asian	11	54.5%	0.0%	27.3%	18.2%

these differences in learning styles among the different groups of students that they teach. Therefore, information should not be presented in one domain; rather, a variety of approaches should be utilized to maximize the learning of the diverse nature of students in classrooms.

Assimilator Teaching Methods and Strategies.   Assimilators learn by thinking through ideas. They take in information logically, process it, and integrate that knowledge with their own observations. They enjoy reflecting on abstract concepts and forming theories and function well in the traditional classroom. These students are content with lectures, text, and research assignments, and are generally able to study successfully on their own.

The following teaching methods and strategies would be effective in the classroom to meet the needs of assimilators:

- Advance Organizers (Ausubel, 1980): Students' cognitive structures are strengthened and they are allowed to organize their knowledge of a particular subject area.
- Concept Attainment Model (Bruner, 1990; Bruner, Goodnow, & Austin, 1967): Data is presented about a certain concept, students view the essential attributes, test the concept, and analyze their thinking about the concept.

Memorization strategies that are appropriate for these learners are:

- Peg System: A number is related to a word that rhymes, producing a mental picture.
- Acrostics: Take the first letter of a word to be learned in processes, dates, lists, etc., and create a word or sentence from each letter or word to aid memory.
- Acronyms: Select a key word from information to be learned and form it into a word or nonsense word that is easy to remember.

Another process that these learners benefit from is called *Socratic Dialogue*. In this strategy, the teacher asks questions that carry students step-by-step through a reasoning process such as an ethnic, religious, or ideological conflict. The teacher asks students to take a position on an issue or to make a value judgment, and then he or she challenges the assumptions underlying the stand by exposing its implications. The teacher probes the students' positions by questioning the relevance, consistency, specificity, and clarity of the students' ideas until they become clearer and more complex. This style uses analogies to contradict students' general statements.

Converger Teaching Methods and Strategies.   Convergers are similar to assimilators in that they take in abstract information; however, convergers take

abstract theories and apply them to real-life problems. They are practically oriented and like to experiment with hands-on technology. These students do well
in lab situations where they can apply what they have learned. A teacher of these
students would need to present factual information and then provide an opportunity to apply that information to a real-life problem.

One teaching method that is appropriate for these learners is using *deductive* reasoning, the process of drawing a conclusion from a principle already
known or assumed. It involves an inference drawn by reasoning from the general
to the particular, as opposed to *induction*, which is reasoning from particular facts
or details to general concepts such as main ideas, concepts, or principles.

Another method is to allow students to explore, manipulate, and experience
for themselves the concepts and principles that have been relayed during a lecture session. The teacher's role is to provide the materials and encouragement
necessary for the students to explore, manipulate, and build on the concepts
given. Lab situations, writing exercises, researching ideas, and building and creating something with the information are some activities from which converger
students gain in their academic knowledge and understanding of concepts.

Accommodator Teaching Methods and Strategies.   Accommodators are dynamic learners. They perceive information concretely and process it actively;
they integrate experience and application. They learn by trial-and-error; they are
risk takers who are at ease with people. Teachers of these students need to enable
their self-discovery with curricula geared to the learners' interests (i.e., an inductive rather than deductive approach). These students prefer variety in instructional methods and especially enjoy experiential learning.

Some preferred teaching methods for these learners involve student-led
class discussions, collaborative/cooperative learning groups, inductive learning
(Joyce & Weil, 2000; Taba et al., 1971), and personal interactions of various
kinds. Also preferred is the Scientific Inquiry Method (Chalmers, 1990; National Research Council, 2000), where an area of investigation is posed to students, students structure the problem, identify the problem in the investigation,
and speculate on ways to resolve the problem. Another method known as the
Group Investigation Model (Dewey, 1916; Thelen, 1981) allows students to
encounter a puzzling situation, explore reactions to the situation, formulate
a study task, and organize for study (problem definition, role, assignments,
etc.). They are then involved in independent and group study, analyze their
progress and process, and then recycle the activity for further clarification and
understanding.

Diverger Teaching Methods and Strategies.   Divergers are imaginative
learners who are sensitive to people's feelings and values and need to integrate
their experience with the self. They learn by listening and sharing ideas and can

view direct experience from many perspectives. Teachers of these students should encourage their personal growth and insight and allow time for discussions and group work. These students need to be personally involved in their learning and seek authentic experiences. The arts and entertainment, literature, and social sciences are areas where these students excel.

Some strategies that encourage diverger learners are class discussions, small collaborative learning groups, simulations, role-plays (studying social behavior and values), debates, improvisations, and projects in art, music, and theater. They need to relate learning to personal experience and enjoy using technology to vary their learning such as videos, DVDs, tape recorders, laser discs, CDs, computers, and synthesizers. They prefer the teacher's role to be a facilitator, coach, or mentor. They respond well to brainstorming activities and creative assignments where personal involvement is the key.

A model that encourages and develops creativity in learning is the Synectics Model (Couch, 1993; Gordon, 1961, 1975). Using this model the teacher has students describe a situation or topic as they see it now. Then students suggest direct analogies to the situation, select one, and explore it further. In the third phase, students personalize the analogy by becoming the analogy they selected in phase two. Students next take their descriptions from phases two and three, suggest several compressed conflicts, and choose one. In phase five, students generate and select another direct analogy based on the compressed conflict. The final phase is a reexamination of the original task. The teacher has students move back to the original task or problem and use the last analogy and/or the entire Synectics experience. This model is designed to increase the creativity of individuals and groups—sharing this experience can build a feeling of community among students.

Another method useful for diverger students involves the use of divergent questioning. This involves the learner using opinion, judgment, and inference from the learner rather than recall of specific facts. Initially, the teacher probes to have the students restate, agree, or generate a different idea. Next the teacher extends the questions by having the students add additional information and elaborate. In the third step the teacher redirects questions. This refocuses the attention of the class should they lose focus. The last step is for students to justify their ideas and explain reasons.

As teachers of diverse student populations, our methods and strategies must meet the needs of our diverse learners. The twenty-first century's changing classroom demographics reveal the imperative to bring a variety of approaches to learning. Using Kolb's (1995) four categories of learning styles, teachers can meet the needs of a variety of learners within the classroom. Figure 2.3, the "Diverse Populations Teaching and Learning Observation Sheet" is a form that teachers can use to rate their ability to implement a variety of teaching styles to meet the needs of their diverse learners throughout a lesson presentation.

Lesson Title _____   **Standards** _____   **Grade** _____

1 Imaginative Learners 1 = emerging 5 = complete	Motivational introduction of content/gets students involved with learning.	Makes connections to the real world.	Is able to relate and build positive relationships with students.		Remarks
Lesson Plan **Presentation**	1 2 3 4 5 1 2 3 4 5	1 2 3 4 5 1 2 3 4 5			
2 Analytic Learners 1 = emerging 5 = complete	Relates science content to students' knowledge by providing concrete examples.	Provides basic facts, vocabulary, and scientific concepts using examples from students' frame of reference.	Maintains high expectations of all students/gives additional academic support for those having difficulty with concepts.	Recognizes confusion on the part of the learner	Gives adequate time for student responses	Remarks
Lesson Plan **Presentation**	1 2 3 4 5 1 2 3 4 5	1 2 3 4 5 1 2 3 4 5	1 2 3 4 5 1 2 3 4 5	1 2 3 4 5	1 2 3 4 5	
3 Common Sense Learners 1 = emerging 5 = complete	Provides opportunities for students to apply the knowledge they have received.	Keeps learners actively engaged in learning.	Provides guided practice for knowledge they have gained.		Remarks
Lesson Plan **Presentation**	1 2 3 4 5 1 2 3 4 5	1 2 3 4 5 1 2 3 4 5			
4 Dynamic Learners 1 = emerging 5 = complete	Allows students to plan and implement their own projects related to the lesson.	Evaluates completed projects and provides appropriate feedback.	Provides remediation where appropriate.		Remarks
Lesson Plan **Presentation**	1 2 3 4 5 1 2 3 4 5	1 2 3 4 5 1 2 3 4 5			

FIGURE 2.3   Diverse Populations Teaching and Learning Observation Sheet

Source: Model based on McCarthy, B. (1987). *The 4MAT System.* Barrington, IL: EXCEL, Inc.

SUMMARY

The twenty-first century classroom is rapidly changing from previous student populations. No longer can schools or teachers in the schools hide behind blaming the students and their environments for their lack of academic achievement. All educators are being called to account for the gap between the White, middle-class students and those who are in marginalized groups. A variety of federal policies have been passed to ensure that No Child Is Left Behind. Today educators must accept the challenge to provide instruction so that all students can succeed in school. Many teachers, schools, and states are beginning to show that this can indeed be accomplished. It is not just a dream; it is a reality.

Students preparing to be teachers must understand and be prepared to accept the demands of teaching in the twenty-first century classroom. In order to do this, students preparing to be teachers must examine their own attitudes, beliefs, and expectations regarding students of color. They must assess their own biases and assumptions about other ethnic groups and they must be willing to change those biases and assumptions. High expectations for all students must be maintained in order for changes in academic achievement to become a reality for diverse students. Individuals who intend to move into the teaching profession must ask themselves why they are interested in teaching and who they are interested in teaching. The colleges of education across the nation have a majority of English-speaking, White, middle-class, female students that go on to become teachers. Those beginning teachers must understand the needs of multicultural learners, English language learners, disabled learners, and low-socioeconomic learners that they will encounter in their classrooms. Star teachers, schools, and states are showing that these students can succeed when given high expectations, rigorous curricula, increased instructional time, funds to support professional development focused on changing instructional practice, focused efforts to involve parents on helping students meet standards, and state or district accountability systems in place that have real consequences for adults in the schools.

Sociocultural learning theory supports various learning styles for diverse ethnicity with the warning not to use learning styles to stereotype ethnic groups. Groups as a whole may exhibit certain learning or cognitive styles, but teachers need to remain aware that individuals may differ from the norm. Teaching that utilizes a variety of strategies to accommodate various learning and cognitive styles will benefit all learners in the classroom.

CHAPTER QUESTIONS

1. What is the most recent educational paradigm, and why has it occurred?

2. Describe several federal policies and how they respond to educational needs.

3. Write your own cultural autobiography. Describe the values and attitudes you hold based on your background and upbringing. What attitudes and beliefs do you hold about other cultures different from your own? What kinds of culturally diverse experiences have you had? At what stage do you place yourself in Helms' (1990) six-stage model and why?

4. Define a culturally relevant teacher. Do you consider you will be or are a culturally relevant teacher? Why or why not? If not, what are some things that you can do to become a culturally relevant teacher?

5. Answer the questions that Jenkins (2004) asks of those who would be teachers. Evaluate your answers. Are you the kind of teacher Jenkins describes? Why or why not?

6. What is your position on the learning styles debate? Is it important to teach to various students' learning styles? Why or why not?

SUGGESTED WEBSITES

Jerome Bruner: Concept Attainment Theory
www.infed.org/thinkers/bruner.htm

Education Trust, Inc.
www.edtrust.org

Cities Alliance
www.citiesalliance.org/citiesalliancehomepage.nsf

Haberman Foundation
www.habermanfoundation.org/

Hope for Urban Education
www.ed.gov/PDFDocs/urbaned.pdf

William Jenkins
http://jenkins.freehosting.net/pub.html

2005 San Diego County Office of Education Annual Report to the Community
www.sdcoe.k12.ca.us/pdf/anrep.pdf

2005 Association for Supervision and Curriculum Development
www.ascd.org/portal/site/ascd/index.jsp/

Synectics website: graphic organizers
www.writedesignonline.com/organizers/synectics.html

University of Kentucky Center for Poverty Research
www.ukcpr.org/RelatedLinks.html

REFERENCES

Abrahams, R. D. (1970). *"Can you dig it?" Aspects of the African esthetic in Afro-American.* Paper presented at African Folklore Institute, Indiana University.

Ausubel, D. P. (1980). Schemata, cognitive structure, and advance organizers: A reply to Anderson, Spiro, and Anderson. *American Educational Research Journal, 17,* 400–404.

Banks, J. A. (1988). *Multiethnic education: Theory and practice* (2nd ed.) Boston: Allyn & Bacon.

Bollin, G. G., & Finkel, J. (1995). White racial identity as a barrier to understanding diversity: A study of preservice teachers. *Equity and Excellence in Education, 28,* 25–30.

Bruner, J. (1990). *Acts of meaning.* Cambridge, MA: Harvard University Press.

Bruner, J., Goodnow, J. J., & Austin, G. A. (1967). *A study of thinking.* New York: Science Editions.

Chalmers, A. (1990). *Science and its fabrication.* Minneapolis: Minnesota Press.

Cohen, R. (1969). Conceptual styles, cultural conflict and nonverbal tests of intelligence. *American Anthropologist, 71,* 828–856.

Couch, R. (1993). Synectics and imagery: Developing creative thinking through images. *Art, Science & Visual Literacy: Selected Readings from the Annual Conference of the International Visual Literacy Association.* Pittsburgh, PA, September 30–October 4, 1992. ERIC No. ED 363 330.

Delpit, L. D. (1992). Acquisition of literate discourse. *Theory into Practice, 31,* 296–302.

Dewey, J. (1916). *Democracy and education.* New York: Macmillan.

Education Trust, Inc. (2003a). *Achievement in America.* Available: www2.edtrust.org/ NR/rdonlyres/14FB5D33-31EF-4A9C-B55F-33184998BDD8/0/8 (2005, February 18). Washington, DC: U.S. Department of Education, NCES, National Assessment of Education Progress.

Education Trust, Inc. (2003b). *Dispelling the myth online.* Available: www2.edtrust.org/edtrust/ dtm/ (2005, February 18). Washington, DC: U.S. Department of Education, NCES, National Assessment of Education Progress.

Gordon, W. J. J. (1961). *Synectics.* New York: Harper & Row.

Gordon, W. J. J. (1975). Training for creativity. *International handbook of management development and training.* London: McGraw-Hill.

Grant, C. (1991). Culture and teaching: What do teachers need to know? In M. Kennedy (ed.), *Teaching academic subjects to diverse learners* (pp. 237–256). New York: Teachers College Press.

Haberman, M. (1991). Can cultural awareness be taught in teacher education programs? *Teaching Education, 4*(1), 25–31.

Haberman, M. (1995). *Star teachers of children in poverty.* Indianapolis, IN: Kappa Delta Pi.

Hale, J. E. (1986). *Black children: Their roots, culture and learning styles* (Rev. ed.) Baltimore: Johns Hopkins University Press.

Hale, J. E. (1993). Rejoinder to ". . . myths of black cultural learning styles" in defense of afrocentric scholarship. *School Psychology Review, 22*(3), 558–561.

Heath, S. B., & McLaughlin, M. W. (1993). *Identity and inner-city youth: Beyond ethnicity and gender.* New York: Teachers College Press.

Helms, J. E. (1990). *Black and White racial identity: Theory, research and practice.* Westport, CT: Praeger.

Hilliard, A. G. III. (1976). Alternatives to IQ testing: An approach to the identification of gifted minority children. Final report to the California State Department of Education.

Hilliard, A. G. III. (1992). Behavioral style, culture, and teaching and learning. *Journal of Negro Education, 61*(3), 370–377.

Irvine, J. J. (2003). *Educating teachers for diversity: Seeing with a cultural eye*. New York: Teachers College Press.

Irvine, J. J., & York, D. E. (1995). Learning styles and culturally diverse students: A literature review. ERIC No. ED 382 722.

Jenkins, W. L. (2004). *Understanding and educating African American children* (12th rev. ed.) St. Louis, MO: William Jenkins Enterprises.

Jones, D. J. (1986). Cognitive styles: Sex and ethnic differences. ERIC No. ED 284 907.

Joyce, B., & Weil, M. (2000). *Models of teaching* (6th ed.). Boston: Allyn & Bacon.

Kidder, T. (1989). *Among schoolchildren*. New York: Avon Books.

Kolb, D. (1985). *Learning-style inventory: Self-scoring inventory and interpretation booklet*. Boston: McBer.

Kotlowitz, A. (1991). *There are no children here: The story of two boys growing up in the other America*. New York: Doubleday.

Ladson-Billings, G. (1994). *The dreamkeepers*. San Francisco: Jossey-Bass.

Ladson-Billings, G. (2000). Fighting for our lives: Preparing teachers to teach African-American students. *Journal of Teacher Education, 51*, 206–214.

Mikkelson, N. (1991). Building sociocentric classrooms: What ethnic minorities can teach us. ERIC No. ED 333 081.

More, A. J. (1990). Learning styles of Native Americans and Asians. ERIC No. ED 330 535.

Mortenson, T. (1997). *Research seminar on public policy analysis of opportunity for post secondary*. Available: www.edtrust.org (2004, March).

National Research Council (2000). *Inquiry and the national science education standards: A guide for teaching and learning*. Washington, DC: National Academy Press.

Nel, J. (1992). Preservice teacher resistance to diversity: Need to reconsider instructional methodologies. *Journal of Instructional Psychology, 19*, 23–27.

Perry, T., & Delpit, L. (eds.) (1998). *The real Ebonics debate: Power, language, and the education of African-American children*. Boston: Beacon.

Perry, T., Steele, A., & Hilliard, A. (1997). *Young, gifted, and black: Promoting high achievement among African-American students*. Boston: Beacon.

Serrell, B. G. (1983). A factor analytic comparison of four learning-style instruments. *Journal of Educational Psychology, 75*, 33–39.

Sleeter, C. E., & Grant, C. A. (1987). An analysis of multicultural education in the United States. *Harvard Educational Review, 57*, 421–444.

Taba, H., Durkin, M. C., Fraenkel, J. R., & McNaughton, A. H. (1971). *A teacher's handbook to elementary social studies: An inductive approach* (2nd ed.). Reading, MA: Addison-Wesley.

Tharp, R. G., & Gallimore, R. (1988). *Rousing minds to life: Teaching, learning, and schooling in social context*. Cambridge: Cambridge University Press.

Thelen, H. (1981). *The classroom society: The construction of education*. New York: Halsted.

U.S. Census Bureau. (March, 2003a). *Current population reports, educational attainment in the United States: Detailed tables No. 2*. Washington, DC: U.S. Census Bureau.

U.S. Census Bureau. (2003b). *Educational Attainment in the United States: 2003*. Washington, DC: U.S. Census Bureau.

U.S. Department of Commerce News: Economics and Statistics Administration: Bureau of the Census. (2003). *Poverty, income, see slight changes; Child poverty rate unchanged, census bureau reports*. Available: www.census,gov/Press-Release/www/2003/cb03-153.html (2003, November 7).

Webb, L. D., Metha, A., & Jordan, K. F. (2003). *Foundations of American education*. (4th ed.). Upper Saddle River, NJ: Merrill Prentice-Hall.

White, S. E. (1992). Factors that contribute to learning differences among African American and Caucasian students. ERIC No. ED 374 177.

CHAPTER 3

CHARACTERISTICS OF URBAN SCHOOLS

When one student is not a full participant in his or her community, then we are all "at-risk."

—*Mara Sapon-Shevin*, Educational Leadership, *61(10)*

URBAN PERSPECTIVES

Kathy Robertson and Lorelei Ward
Pre-Kindergarten Educators in an Urban Elementary School

It takes time to develop (parents') trust, so that the teacher can begin to make a difference in their lives. They have to understand that a teacher's skin color may be different from theirs, but the hearts are the same. —Kathy Robertson

Lorelei Ward, an urban pre-K teacher, expresses her desires to remain in urban schools by comparing her teaching experiences in schools: "In the suburban school setting, I felt that I was not needed. My heart remained with children in the urban setting. The urban students chose me. Further, I've received a lot of support from the principals in urban schools, which also has encouraged me to stay."

Kathy Robertson, another urban pre-K teacher, claims that her desire to teach in the urban setting is because "I have had community acceptance, and urban families have made me feel a part of their culture. I started (into teaching) as a director of a private suburban school; but when an opening in an inner-city school became available, I decided to try it. I have loved embracing the 'family feeling' that comes from working with urban students."

According to Robertson, "One of the key challenges in the urban school setting is that the parents may not understand the importance of reading and of getting an education. Most see their child as their possession. It takes time to develop their trust, so that the teacher can begin to make a difference in their lives. They have to understand that a teacher's skin color may be different from theirs, but the hearts are the same."

Ward identifies that what keeps her, along with fellow teachers, returning to urban schools are advantages offered in Title I schools, such as "informative and useful professional training opportunities that we find are not normally offered by suburban schools, since most suburban schools typically don't qualify as Title I schools, as do most urban schools. Also, teachers in urban schools welcome meeting and managing the continual challenges not evident in most suburban schools." In support of those ideas, Robertson finds that she and her colleagues return to urban schools year after year because of "the success of and growth we see in the children—and the fact that our urban teachers very much know that they are making a difference every school day."

From experiences she's gained in working with urban preschool children in their earliest stages of formal learning, Robertson sees varied differences in what children bring with them to school. "Urban children demonstrate diverse abilities, such that teachers must exercise flexibility, while striving to maintain high expectations for their students. These early learners benefit from our teaching them dynamics of caring, along with our upholding consistent behavior standards and modeling best behavior practices." To these points, Ward also agrees: "My fellow pre-K educators and I understand the need to spend the first month of school teaching and practicing the classroom rules and procedures expected of the children." Overall, both teachers concur that those who educate the early learners need to have a flexible mindset to be successful with the variety of situations they will commonly encounter in the urban school setting.

THE WORLD OF URBAN CHILDREN

Changing Urban Demographics

Anyone who would hope to achieve success teaching in urban schools must first understand urban environments that drive everyday life in the schoolhouse. There is little doubt that urban schools require highly skilled and committed teachers and administrators. These schools present the great challenge of educating children whose success represents a critical element in the survival of our society. Too often, children of color do not often receive the academic and intellectual knowledge base required to compete and perhaps to survive and participate in today's and certainly tomorrow's increasingly competitive workplace and in the life of the community.

The urban school picture has intensified over the past twenty years as a new wave of immigrants have come to America. The immigrants of the past—Irish, Italian, German, Poles—have mostly been replaced by Hispanics, Asians, and Middle Easterners. These newer immigrants bring with them significant challenges for schools. The immigrants of the past arrived in great numbers and essentially defined the culture. They were able to assimilate and find employment with minimal effort in a manufacturing economy seeking an unskilled labor pool.

The newer immigrants are attempting to fit into a more established American middle-class society that is far more complex than the American society of the 1920s and 1930s. In addition, they arrive from cultures that are considerably different than those of present-day Americans and, thus, assimilation on the social and economic (employment) level is more difficult.

One important consideration lies in the fact that the American economy now relies to a greater extent on a highly educated labor pool, as jobs take on a more technology-oriented nature. Finding steady and meaningful employment in this new environment is much more questionable than in the past, given the nature of the workplace. The economy requires a more highly educated worker, and today's immigrants most often do not possess the required educational levels to meet this need. Employees today are required to be adept with the thinking process, to make informed decisions about actions to be taken in varying circumstances, and to be problem solvers.

Those who are not highly educated are thus relegated to unskilled, low-wage employment. Prospects for the future would indicate an intensification of the need for high-skilled, technology-oriented employment.

The jobs readily available to these individuals are more likely to be found in and around our cities. This has caused a shift in demographics as the middle class has moved and continue to move to suburban areas, and as the poor, mostly immigrants, migrate into the cities. Here they join the poor who have little choice but to remain in the cities since they are financially unable to afford to move to suburban areas. Unfortunately, these are very often African Americans and now, to a greater extent, Hispanics. Thus, we find a melting pot of low-income families where once large numbers of White, middle-class families resided. The impact upon the schools in educating children from cultures vastly different than the dominant society, with language barriers to overcome and from the homes of the poor, has been and remains an extremely difficult challenge.

Wilson describes the dilemma present in daily homelife in poor families and its effect upon teachers and students:

> In such neighborhoods, the chances are overwhelming that children seldom interact on a sustained basis with people who are employed or with families that have a steady breadwinner. The net effect is that joblessness, as a way of life, takes on a different social meaning; the relationship between schooling and post-school employment takes on a different meaning. The development of cognitive, linguistic, and other educational and job-related skills necessary for the world of work in the mainstream economy is therefore adversely affected. In such neighborhoods, teachers become frustrated and do not teach, and children do not learn. It becomes a vicious cycle running throughout the family, community, and school. (Wilson, 1987, p. 57)

The result of this dilemma is that schools struggle to deliver instruction to meet the wide diversity of needs of the students. In order to cope, they more and more resort to more mechanical and rigid student sorting methods and ability grouping techniques that exacerbate the isolation of the economically disadvantaged. These children are offered instruction that is not real-world related and not pertinent to preparing them to live within the American social structure and find meaningful employment therein.

Burnett (1992) asserts that urban children who complete high school are not educated with the skills needed for the workplace. They are, therefore, not prepared to deal with the increasing cognitive requirements placed upon the workforce. Worse, these individuals are not sufficiently prepared to meet even minimum employability requirements.

Beyond cognitive skills, industry ranks teamwork ability, reliability, honesty, initiative, problem-solving ability, and decision-making skills as attributes most needed by the workforce (Goldenberg, Kunz, Hamburger, & Stevenson, 2003). These skills are not likely to be emphasized in the urban home and, therefore, fall within the realm of the school's responsibility. When the school does not succeed in meeting this responsibility, the cycle of poverty is transferred from parents to children, and continues unabated.

The results of the demographic shift described here have caused American cities to undergo a major transformation. Within the confines of urban areas, one now finds large concentrations of disadvantaged segments of the population. This has created an environment in which the social milieu is vastly different from that which existed several decades ago. These environments are home to mostly poor Blacks and, increasingly, to Hispanics.

Urban schools are heavily attended by children of color, and the likelihood is strong that those who teach in urban settings will experience, to a great extent, African American children. African American students represent 17 percent of the 47 million students attending public schools in the United States (National Center for Educational Statistics, 1999b), of these, 30 percent attend large central city public schools. In a number of urban areas, African American students represent well over 50 percent of the total student population. In 1999 in Detroit, for example, 81 percent of the students were African American. In other cities such as Philadelphia, the rate is 80 percent; Washington, DC, 88 percent; Atlanta, 92 percent; and in New York City, 86 percent (Lewis Mumford Center for Comparative Urban and Regional Research, 2002).

While African American children are found in urban schools in significant numbers, the neighborhoods and schools are becoming increasingly culturally diverse. Children of the poor are represented by various cultures, creating new challenges for educators. About 77 percent of the students in the Great City Schools, a coalition of sixty-five of the nation's largest urban public school systems, in 1999–2000 were African American, Hispanic, Asian American, and various other students of color, compared with 38 percent nationwide. Approximately 62 percent of these students are eligible for federal free lunch subsidies, compared to 38 percent nationwide (Casserly, 2002). There is a critical need to attract teachers to these schools who understand the urban culture, particularly African American, and to an increasing extent, Hispanic culture, and can successfully work within the parameters these cultures present.

According to the National Center for Educational Statistics (2003), the most rapidly growing culturally diverse group in schools today are Hispanics. In 2000, African American and ethnic enrollment reached 39 percent of public school students, of which 44 percent were Hispanic. Hispanics now represent 17 percent of total public school enrollment. From 1972 to 2000, African American and ethnic enrollments increased 1.7 percent; the percentage of Hispanic students increased by 11 percent while the percentage of African American students increased about 2 percent. The largest Hispanic enrollments are in the western United States, where they have reached 32 percent of students in 2000, representing a 16 percent increase since 1972. In the states of Arizona, California, Nevada, New Mexico, and Texas, Hispanic students make up one-quarter of public school enrollments.

In the ten largest school districts, Hispanics make up 41 percent of students. By comparison, Whites represented 19 percent, Blacks 31 percent, and Asian/Pacific Islanders 9 percent. Hispanics represent the largest ethnic group in the New York City, Los Angeles, Dade County, Florida, and Houston school districts.

Hispanics present a special challenge for educators because of the language barrier that exists. Added to this is the fact that the children are mostly from poor families. They attend schools where children of color make up the majority of the student enrollments. In 2000, in schools where children of color made up 90 percent of the enrollment, Hispanics represented 39 percent. Free and reduced-price lunch figures provided by the National Center for Educational Statistics attest to the poverty among Hispanic students. Fifty-nine percent of Hispanic fourth-grade students attended public schools where 50 percent of the students were eligible for free and reduced-price lunches, 26 percent in schools with 51 to 75 percent were eligible, 16 percent where 76 to 99 percent were eligible, and 17 percent where 100 percent of the children were eligible.

The challenges to educate children of color have been historically considered an African American issue. The growth of the Hispanic student population, however, is rapidly changing that dynamic. When schools plan for educating children of color, particularly the children of the poor, they would do well to seriously consider the education of Hispanics (National Center for Education Statistics, 2003).

The foregoing is not to suggest that African Americans or Hispanics or any other such groups pose problems for schools because of their culture. Indeed, their cultures are not deficient and are instead rich and must be valued. Teachers must not endeavor to change established and cherished cultural norms. Teachers should focus upon the positive experiences that children bring from their working-class families and communities. The issue is not one of culture but one of poverty. Unfortunately, the urban culture is an entity driven by poverty.

To understand that reality, teachers must understand the ugly face of poverty. Howey speaks of children "who live on the edge of poverty." Poverty is a distinguishing feature defining children in urban schools. More than 300,000 school-aged children are homeless in the United States. Roughly 300,000 newborns have had exposure to high levels of prenatal drugs and alcohol. Many of these children will be "non-compliant, aggressive, anti-social and unable to communicate or to understand effectively" (Howey, 2000). While Howey's commentary may represent an extreme, it should not be dismissed. Urban teachers are likely to find degrees of these behaviors to a greater or lesser extent. In spite of this, teachers in our classrooms exhaust their energies every day, attempting to educate all children so that they might enjoy useful and productive lives.

Urban Homes and Neighborhoods

A key to success in teaching urban children is to understand fully the conditions surrounding their lives. Individuals intending to teach urban children will not succeed and indeed will feel great frustration if they do not recognize the realities of urban life and build their teaching around those realities.

The children who come to school each day arrive carrying the burdens of the poor. Their homes are not bright and pleasant places, but often cramped, run down, and bleak environments. They do not enjoy the privacy of a personal bedroom, as do their suburban counterparts, where they can read or complete after-school assignments. They are more likely to share a bedroom with their parents or several siblings.

It is not uncommon to find living conditions that are not air-conditioned and, particularly in the South, stifling during the warm months and uncomfortably cold during the cold months. The family conversations are not encouraging or enriching as their parents, if indeed they have parents living in the household, are either focused upon survival or are too exhausted from working multiple jobs to give attention to their children. Further, parents or guardians may not be academically equipped to provide support for their children's learning.

The world of some urban children further deteriorates when they leave the confines of their places of living and enter their neighborhoods. Here they are exposed to horrendous conditions found in inner-city areas. Graffiti, vandalism, robbery, violence, and even killings are often regular occurrences. Children are exposed to gang activities, drug dealing, drug use, prostitution, and a myriad of negative situations that shape their lives.

Lederhouse indicates that the neighborhood gang influence holds great power over students and the "fears of being accosted by rival gang members or shot in their crossfire were real" (1998, p. 51). Children bring fears derived from their experiences, because in the early stages of their lives they cannot understand or control the circumstances around them (Forresi, 2003).

In *Always Running* (1993), Rodriguez writes emotionally about the fear he experienced growing up as a young Mexican boy in Los Angeles. He describes how he and a friend were constantly running from someone.

It never stopped, this running. We were constant prey, and the hunters soon became big blurs: the police, the gangs, the junkies, the dudes on Garvey Boulevard who took our money, all smudged into one. Sometimes they were teachers who jumped us Mexicans as if we were a hideous stain. We were always afraid. Always running. (p. 36)

These conditions, combined with urban demographics, bring great challenges to today's classrooms, increasing the difficult task of teaching effectively. These realities that are today weaved into the fabric of society have important implications for teaching. Today's classroom is likely to have children who:

- are living in a single-parent family;
- are not likely to go to college;
- have been born to unmarried parents;
- will be poor at some point in their childhood;
- are a year or more behind in school;
- are living with one parent or without biological parent(s);
- were born poor or are poor;
- have a parent (or parents) who did not graduate from high school;
- likely to be Hispanic or African American;
- living in a family receiving food stamps;

- have a foreign-born mother;
- have parents without health insurance;
- are living with a relative;
- were born to a teenage mother;
- speak a language at home other than English; and/or
- are not likely to graduate from high school. (Children's Defense Fund, 2001)

These characteristics result in an extremely difficult childhood experience. For children living in urban environments, this period is particularly challenging given the numerous stressful conditions that are ever-present. As a result, urban schools are plagued by high rates of behavior problems and academic failure. Gallay and Flanagan (2000) suggest that children carry the issues of their home and neighborhood environment into the school setting, resulting in low social and emotional competence, negative and stress-filled life events, psychiatric disorders, and behavioral problems.

Brouilette conducted research that involved interviewing school dropouts. She found that most students left school because of external circumstances and internal feelings of hopelessness. Many of these students were receiving average or even above-average grades, but left due to such circumstances as the necessity for another wage earner, a pregnancy, or situations involving violence. According to Brouilette, "The internal factors these students mentioned were also partly situational; they did not know where they could turn for help or felt that there was no way out of their predicament that would allow them to stay in school" (Brouilette, 1999, p. 316).

Home and Neighborhood Influence School

When students arrive at school, they do so carrying the burdens of young minds experiencing confusion and negative self-image. They experience difficulty attempting to satisfy the requirements of the school and the adult-type responsibilities in their homes and neighborhoods. This confusion and frustration dictates their vision of appropriate behavior that leads to serious consequences in school and with the legal system.

Emeral A. Crosby, principal of Pershing High School in Detroit, worries about gangs and the problems that stem from drugs (Crosby, 1999). He also worries about student behavior that threatens the learning environment:

> Delinquent behavior is too mild a term to describe a problem that can be devastating for urban schools. In the high schools, for example there is a kind of anarchy or civil war that is more serious than most people outside the schools realize. Students are angry young people, and they question every rule. Students commit acts of defiance that are astonishing in their destructive effect on the population and the institution. (Crosby, 1999, p. 301)

Crosby cites these conditions that contribute to delinquent behavior:

1. The education of urban youth is not related in a meaningful way to real-world employment and social conditions.
2. The school model does not represent a pluralistic society with students living grouped according to ability, race, and economic class.
3. The school does not prepare students for adult life by not providing models of behavior that will benefit them in the future. (Crosby, 1999)

Crosby's elements are instructive. Disruptive students are usually acting out as a magnification of frustration. Teachers and school leaders need to acknowledge that these elements are at the root of the frustrations. A recognition and acknowledgement that they are barriers to learning is a first step toward resolving to change the status quo and creating more positive conditions for learning. Students who are successful learners will not experience high levels of frustration and thus find less reason to engage in disruptive behavior.

As we have seen, the inner city environment of the poor, in which these children live, has a way of spilling over into the schoolhouse. In particular, when schools fail to address the needs of children and/or when children do not experience success in learning, they tend to become frustrated and even angry. The heartache of family and neighborhood living, with the added frustrations in school, are simply overwhelming. The result is an acting out that only serves to exacerbate the situation.

While the reality of this unfortunate scenario results in great frustration for teachers who need to focus upon creative, positive, and effective classroom learning environments, it is the students who suffer to the greatest extent. In urban schools where there is a need to maximize effective instruction and where children require much-needed attention, teachers are hard-pressed to meet these needs.

Ladson-Billings' article *Fighting for Our Lives* makes an impassioned statement regarding the struggle by African Americans to receive an education that might elevate them out of poverty. The statement can be generalized to all poor and minority students:

> Ultimately, the work of education in a democracy is to provide opportunities for all citizens to participate fully in the formation of the nation and its ideals. These ideals can never be fully realized if significant portions of our society are excluded from high-quality education and the opportunity to play public roles in the society. African American students are suffering in our schools at an alarming rate. They continue to experience high dropout, suspension, and expulsion rates. Although possessing a high school diploma is no guarantee of success in U.S. society, not having one spells certain economic and social failure. Thus when we fight about education, we indeed are fighting for our lives. (Ladson-Billings, 2000, p. 212)

If children are to learn at high levels, these issues must be resolved so as to allow teachers to maximize their time in the process of teaching and learning.

The only genuine hope for these children, given these conditions, then, is their school. They arrive at the schoolhouse often exhausted and confused. They need comfort and seek attention, love, and encouragement from the adults that is sorely lacking in their home and neighborhood experiences. Meanwhile, well-intentioned teachers are expected to provide them with intellectual stimulation in the form of instruction driven by the predesigned curriculum.

Teachers must recognize that providing instruction that results in genuine learning under these conditions cannot be approached as business as usual. New and unique strategies must be applied. It is imperative that teachers recognize the conditions with which their students arrive and consider these elements as they plan to deliver instruction. It is foolhardy and shortsighted not to meet the basic needs of children as one considers teaching and learning. Admittedly, this presents unique and complex challenges and requires high levels of understanding, patience, and great skill on the part of teachers. While daunting, successfully teaching these children should not be considered an impossible task.

Crosby, describes the result of the urban school dilemma:

> In the face of this multitude of problems, those in authority react with stricter punishments, armed hallway guards, metal detectors, and forms of repression meant to stem the tide. The rules becomes more mechanical, rigid, and impersonal. The students are known by their ID numbers, and personalities of teachers are affected by the need to maintain order at great cost to everyone in the school. (Crosby, 1999, p. 301)

The conditions that exist in urban schools demand greater measures to assure the security of students and school employees. When one visits an urban school, they will see evidence of these security measures. The level of security depends upon the intensity of demand, with inner-city schools in larger cities utilizing security measures to a greater extent. These measures divert funds sorely needed for instructional purposes to the utilization of mechanical and human means to secure schools. Security can be found in parking lots, school entranceways, corridors, lunchrooms, play areas, and other areas of student assembly. It is not uncommon to find uniformed and armed guards and/or police patrolling school areas.

Significantly, teachers and administrators become the first line of defense, as they are required to monitor school areas, particularly corridors and lunchrooms and outside areas during student arrival and dismissal times. Expecting teachers to expend energy in the monitoring effort represents a gross misuse of their professional time. More time and energy expended in monitoring activities equates to less time and energy devoted to the process of teaching and learning. While this seems an inefficient misuse of professional time, it is nevertheless a necessary evil in too many urban schools.

It is important for teachers to recognize the realities that exist in many urban homes and to understand the great influence and effect this has upon children. The images of the lives of their children must be constantly at the forefront of the thinking patterns of teachers as they approach decisions about instruction and general classroom management. High levels of patience, tolerance, understanding, warmth, and love must be the order of the day.

Lederhouse (1998) drives the message of patience, tolerance, and understanding home:

> When a 9-year-old student turned down a request to deliver a note to the school office, her teacher asked what could possibly make her so tired by 9:30 A.M. Expecting to hear that the student had stayed up too late the night before, the teacher instead learned that the girl had been up at 6:00 A.M. to take her family's clothes to a laundromat so that her siblings would have clean clothes for school that morning. After finishing the laundry, she had returned home to provide breakfast and supervise her brother and sister until they left for school. Her mother, who worked the night shift, was unable to see them off. (p. 53)

Teachers must be constantly aware of the burdens that children carry and the fact that they are young and often helpless. Teachers are in a unique position in which they can help children to shoulder these burdens. To be helpful, they must see the teaching of children of color in a positive light. According to Nieto:

> In the end, if teachers believe that students cannot achieve at higher levels, that their backgrounds are riddled with deficiencies, and that multicultural education is a frill that cannot help them to learn, the result will be school reform strategies that have little hope of success. (1999, p. 175)

When teachers adopt a belief system that children can succeed without regard to their color or the financial status of their families, they can have a powerful effect upon learning. While there is no silver bullet that will increase student learning, a proper belief system can make a positive beginning.

Nieto (1999) raises the question, "Who does the accommodating? Do students accommodate to the culture or do teachers accommodate to the lives of children?" She suggests that what is needed is "accommodation without acculturation" when dealing with students of color. Nieto draws upon the research of Margaret Gibson (1987) in which Gibson analyzed the learning of Punjabi Indian children in American schools. These students experienced academic success in spite of social class barriers, lack of educated parents, and lack of English language skills. They experienced racism from their peers and also from their teachers due to the fact that they were culturally different than the students in their school. The Punjabi students have maintained their native language and their cultural values and practices while experiencing success in school. Their success did not replace their culture and traditions but represented the learning of new skills. What occurred is that the students accommodated to the school culture while not acculturating. Total assimilation was not a requirement for success.

Urban teachers should not insist that students of color abandon their family cultures and traditions in order to succeed in school. Forcing accommodation

can create an undue burden upon the students and also their families. Teachers should consider accommodating to the lives of the children. This is best accomplished by meeting the children halfway. They should allow children to preserve their cultures, languages, and traditions. Children can maintain their identities while slowly assimilating the new culture. Nieto suggests that we view

> teaching and learning not as an accommodation—which inevitably implies loss rather than gain—but rather as a negotiation among students and their families, and teachers and schools. It must be, however, a negotiation that is mutually defined, constructed, and achieved. (Nieto, 1999, p. 76)

Accommodating to the lives of children by meeting them halfway and allowing them to enter our culture without losing their identities is an important requisite for success.

THE STATUS OF TEACHERS IN URBAN SCHOOLS

Urban Teacher Issues

There are a number of elements that characterize the status of the teaching entity in urban schools. These have a sharp affect upon the overall stability of the teaching staff and the potential for success or failure in attempts to educate children.

To begin, the teacher turnover rate in urban schools is considerably greater than in suburban areas. Schools with high concentrations of students receiving free or reduced-price lunches (50 percent or more) have a greater turnover rate than those with lower concentrations (National Center for Education Statistics, 1995). Ingersoll (2001) confirmed this condition in a study which found that schools with poverty levels of greater than 50 percent had markedly higher teacher turnover rates than those with low-poverty populations

Schools with 50 percent or more students of color experienced twice the turnover rate of schools with smaller populations (National Center for Education Statistics, 1995). Freeman, Scanfidi, and Sjoquist (2002), in a study of teacher turnover in Georgia, found that teachers who moved from schools serving large populations of low-income children, children of color, and low achieving students, moved to schools where the population of such students was less. In a study of the Philadelphia City Schools, Useem and Neild (2001) found a significantly higher teacher turnover rate in higher-poverty schools than those with lower rates.

It would appear that when teachers in low-achieving schools find an opportunity to move to schools serving children of higher social economic status they will often do so. In many cases, the rate of turnover is disturbingly high and results in teachers generally unprepared to accommodate the student population. Thus, in those schools with the greater need, the teacher turnover rates are at their worse levels. One can readily understand how teachers are drawn away from urban schools by higher pay and better and safer working conditions. Teaching in urban settings can be stressful and unsettling, leading to high levels of teacher burnout over a short period of time.

The result of this phenomenon is that the urban schools are more often staffed by uncertified and/or newly-hired teachers. Thus, the schools most needing experienced teachers have difficulty hiring those with experience needed and in keeping veteran teachers from moving to nonurban schools. In addition, the most experienced teachers tend to be assigned to higher-level curriculum and college preparation classes and not to the remedial and general classes where most of the so-called lower level children are placed.

In addition to the problem of a high degree of teacher turnover in urban schools, there are high levels of teacher absenteeism with its resultant reliance upon the need for substitute teachers. This ultimately has a detrimental effect upon classroom instruction. These symptoms reflect the challenges of urban teaching that can cause teacher stress and burnout. Student learning is colored by the qualifications, experience, and skill that teachers bring to the classroom. Ascher (1991) decries the fact that urban schools in need of the best qualified teachers often have difficulty hiring and retaining the best qualified. He indicates that schools serving children of the poor and children of color generally have limited funding, and thus are hard pressed to adequately fund teacher salaries, instructional materials, and the maintenance and upkeep of the educational environment.

On the other hand, those teachers who have long tenures in urban schools are in need of serious retraining efforts. The training that these teachers received was geared toward teaching students from a middle-class perspective, and they must now deal with children of color and children of the poor. Given the differences in cultures and social values of these children, their teachers are ill-equipped to understand the needs of their students and are subsequently in need of massive retraining efforts. Such retraining is generally not available due to lack of funding and time constraints.

Another influencing factor is that teachers who choose to remain in urban schools often desire to reside outside the urban area to enjoy suburban lifestyles. This results in teachers being disengaged from their students and communities. The obvious decreased interest in the community in which they teach further distances these teachers from their students and their families whose relationships are an important ingredient for success.

Finally, there is a considerable bureaucracy at play in urban school districts. The school systems do not seem to be invested in the classroom and seem not to provide adequate support or bonuses for teachers. There is little reward for the difficult work involved in teaching in an urban classroom. Thus, teaching in an urban setting can be a lonely and isolated profession. As the urban environments change, there remains an increased need for intensive teacher retraining. Yet, teachers too often lack access to training that would enable them to increase their effectiveness (Crosby, 1999).

These issues eventually find their way into the classroom instruction that involves the students. Teachers must be skilled in working in urban communities and with children of color and poor children. Failure to provide appropriate training or retraining can only bring failure to efforts to teach these children at high levels. Certainly suburban parents expect that their children will receive a top-notch education—do urban children not deserve similar expectations?

The urban situation is not hopeless—it is indeed challenging and often difficult, but there are many dedicated teachers in American city schools who are making a difference and causing children to learn at levels that will result in productive future citizens. There is great importance in placing the most effective teachers in our urban classrooms. According to Gordon:

> Find the right people, and two things happen: organizational performance improves, and the need for remedial programs decline. Finding the right teachers for urban schools is thus the first step in helping these schools improve. (Gordon, 1999, p. 305)

Teacher Beliefs

Urban schools that were originally home to White and middle-class students are now heavily populated by mostly children of color and children of the poor. We have been slow in acknowledging this factor. In recent years the migration of

Hispanics, Middle Easterners, and Asians has joined the inner-city African Americans, creating major educational issues that we are just beginning to recognize.

It is not surprising that this recognition has been so slow in coming. Unfortunately, the views of many Americans that African Americans are an inferior race have been slow to change. Although perceptions have improved greatly since the civil rights activities of the 1950s and 1960s, there continues to be apparent an underlying belief that these children cannot achieve at high academic levels. Thus, expectations among educators for the education of African American children have remained at a low level. These expectations have signaled to African Americans that they cannot achieve academically. This same belief has now been extended to Hispanic children. The result has been that the children are routinely placed in low-functioning groups where they achieve according to the low expectations of their teachers.

The expectations of teachers, therefore, have contributed to create the problem of African American, Hispanic, and other urban children's academic underachievement. Haberman (1989), speaking about African American children, indicates that on top of the belief that these children are inferior and incapable of learning is the attitude, on the part of many White teachers, that they would rather not teach African American children.

Unfortunately, these beliefs of inferiority and attitudes about the inability of African American children to learn at high levels have now carried over to Hispanic children. It is not surprising, then, to find urban schools where large numbers of African Americans and Hispanics attend struggling from seriously low levels of academic achievement.

Adding to teacher belief systems and attitudes about minority children lies the issue of inadequate teacher-training programs. Most teachers have not received training in teaching urban minority children, or their training in this area has been limited or inadequate. The result has been that the teaching of these children has been ineffective (Ladson-Billings, 2000).

Many students become so frustrated with their failure in school that they eventually drop out. They see life as hopeless and meaningless. Their consistent school failure together with their everyday living in impoverished neighborhoods has a cumulative effect resulting in feelings of meaningless, hopelessness, and loneliness. They see their situations as desperate with nowhere to find help or no one to whom they might turn for help. Faced with this predicament, they eventually leave school (West, 1993).

For urban children, school is the best means of escaping their impoverished lives. Thus, abandoning their education usually casts them into lives driven by unemployment, drugs, alcohol, crime, and imprisonment. For many it is not school failure that causes them to drop out, but the stresses of the everyday life situations of the poor.

Urban teachers need to understand the urban condition to be effective in their teaching. Understanding the general needs of children is an important fac-

tor as teachers struggle to find ways to motivate them for learning. This is particularly true for those who teach in urban areas. Recognition of children's backgrounds and/or home conditions is imperative if teachers are to succeed in their efforts to maximize student learning.

STUDENT ACHIEVEMENT

Influence of Culture and Social Class

There are a myriad of problems that teachers face in urban schools—achievement rates are low, disruptive behavior is high, and absenteeism is frequent. In addition there are issues related to a transient population and a lack of parent or guardian participation in the education of their children. Added to these issues, the children's personal, economic, and family situations are likely to have a negative impact upon students' learning. As a result, teachers find themselves involved in what Burnett (1994) has called a "vast web of interconnected social problems" (p. 16).

While these problems are real and ever-present, student achievement is often reflective of an attitude about persons of diverse cultures. Americans place greater or lesser degrees of value upon some races and cultures (Hacker, 1992).

It is this value system that influences attitudes about the ability of children to learn. These attitudes can be explained according to three instructive theories:

1. *Deficit Theory:* Students of certain races and/or cultures are at a disadvantage because of their cultural, social, or language backgrounds. These elements result in certain behaviors at home that clash with the culture of schools and society in general. These are the elements that lead to academic underachievement.
2. *Expectation Theory:* Teachers do not expect students from certain racial or ethnic backgrounds to succeed. Thus, they teach differently and hold lower expectations for these students. The result is a self-fulfilling prophecy in which academic performance suffers.
3. *Cultural Difference Theory:* This theory envisions cross-cultural understanding about students. Teachers can overcome underachievement issues through a recognition that they have the power to neutralize the cultural gap which exists between the home and the school. (Sadaker & Sadaker, 2003)

It is evident that attitudes drive the actions of individuals. It would appear from the actions of some educators and often the policies of schools that the deficit and expectation theory has a strong foothold. If teachers individually and schools collectively are to succeed in raising levels of student academic achievement, they must abandon the notion that race, culture, and social and language backgrounds block the ability of children to achieve and therefore expectations must be lowered. When teachers and schools embrace the cultural difference theory, they recognize that the cultural gap that exists between home and school can be breached. In such cases, they will hold higher expectations for their students, and with appropriate instruction, the students are likely to achieve at the higher levels.

Brantlinger asserts that there is a significant social class influence on schooling:

> Class distinctions and conflict are ever present in the on-going life of school, and there is a dominate/subordinate delineation in adolescents' thinking about social class. In addition, school is not a socially neutral setting. Low grades, tracking, special education placements, and humiliating interactions with teachers make school a source of stress for low-income participants. (Brantlinger, 1995, p. 4)

The Fallacy of Tracking

Considerable research and literature indicates that urban schools are often characterized by student-tracking patterns that create unequal access to favorable learning conditions. The inequality allows students, already advantaged by class or race, access to more enriched curriculum and positive learning conditions. It is common to find poor African American and Hispanic students in lower-level general or vocational courses, while their White counterparts enjoy access to higher-level, enriched educational opportunities (Wheelock, 1992).

The National Educational Longitudinal Survey found that African Americans, Hispanics, Native Americans, and other low-income students are twice as likely than upper-income White students to be in remedial math instruction. These already disadvantaged students receive a less demanding curriculum, creating a self-fulfilling prophecy of failure (National Center for Educational Statistics, 1991).

Wheelock describes the negative effects of tracking upon children of the poor and children of color, and defines tracking in this way:

> Tracking involves the categorizing of students according to particular measures of intelligence into distinct groups for purposes of teaching and learning. Once they have been sorted and classified, students are provided with curriculum and instruction deemed suited to their ability and matched to spoken or unspoken assessments of each student's future. Research has dramatically demonstrated, however, that this practice has created as many problems as it was designed to solve. (Wheelock, 1992)

Tracking creates particularly serious dilemmas in city schools where children of the poor and children of color are relegated to low tracks, and in the great majority of cases, remain there as long as they remain in school. Here students receive a watered-down curriculum based upon their supposed lesser ability to learn. In teaching situations, students who require the most creative and challenging instruction actually receive the lowest level of instruction, while the most challenging and enriching experiences are reserved for students who already enjoy economic, social, and environmental advantages. Thus, the issues of unequal class distinction are intensified (McDonnell, Burstein, & Ormseth, 1990).

The Association for Supervision and Curriculum Development (ASCD) has been critical of tracking practices and has urged schools to abandon the practice. According to ASCD, "Students should not be permanently grouped for instruction according to assumptions about their abilities to learn. Grouping should be for particular instructional purposes" (Association for Supervision and Curriculum Development, 1980, p. 1).

Course enrollment patterns in urban schools mark a clear picture of the tracking environments that exist. Poor African American and Hispanic students are placed in lower-level general or vocational classes in disproportionate numbers. According to Wheelock (1992), children of the poor and of color are twice as likely as White or upper-class-income students to be in remedial classes. Additionally, their teachers are less experienced. McDonnell found that teachers in 42 percent of the remedial, vocational, and general mathematics classes had five years or fewer teaching experience, while 19 percent of those in prealgebra and algebra I classes had five years or more (McDonnell, Burstein, & Ormseth, 1990).

Wheelock writes about the results of the tracking experience for children:

> Over time, students at the lower levels move so much more slowly than those at the higher ones that differences that may have been real but not profound in the earlier grades become gigantic gaps in terms of achievement, attitude, and self-esteem. Furthermore, the sorting of students into groups of "haves" and "have-nots" contradicts the American educational credo that schools are democratic communities of learners whose purpose is to offer equal educational opportunity to all. (Wheelock, 1992, p. 6)

The fact that our society has been built around racial, ethnic, and social class lines spills over into the schools. Tracking students stems from the influences of the society over time. Oakes, a foremost authority on the subject of academic tracking, confirms the historical perspective:

> The matching of students to different tracks carried with it racial, ethnic, and social-class overtones from the very beginning. Early on in this century, low-level academics and vocational training were thought to be more appropriate for immigrant, low-income, and minority youth, whereas rigorous academic preparation was seen as better meeting the needs of more affluent whites. Few questioned the rightness of this pattern, just as few questioned the many other social and economic barriers faced by African American and Latino minorities before the 1960s (in Wheelock, 1992, p. x).

Oakes goes on to state that

> sorting students into "high" and "low" tracks severely limits the educational and occupational futures of low-income, African American, and Latino students and, in racially mixed schools, perpetuates stereotypes of minority students as being less intelligent than White ones and constrains opportunities for meaningful interracial contact (in Wheelock, 1992, p. xi).

While some progress has been made in untracking schools, the practice remains prevalent today. Upper-class, mostly White parents pressure schools to ensure that their children are enrolled in the upper-level classes. Their children are best served in the current structure, and they are not above using their political influence to hold these conditions in place. School boards and administrators, feeling the pressure from parents, most often elect to leave tracking in place rather than to alienate those parents whose support they desire. Thus, those students already disadvantaged by economics, class, and race are exposed to the lesser curriculum and never achieve sufficient success to exit the lower tracks. This has serious implications for their ability to learn at levels that will allow them to ever achieve higher levels of income or improved class status in life.

Student achievement is negatively affected by instruction that lacks in interest or does not present academic challenge. The result is high incidents of student apathy and low academic performance. Montgomery and Rossi (1994) assert that poor school performance stems from students viewing schoolwork as dull, passive, and irrelevant. Boykin (1998) argues that urban students do not receive academically stimulating and interesting instruction due to their placement in lower tracks and remedial courses where they are exposed to an ongoing diet of repetitive work and drill and practice.

Best Urban Teacher Behavior

The Gallup Organization, utilizing the Urban Teacher Perceiver Interview, sought the best urban teacher traits, referred to as themes. Their research helps to define the best teachers according to recurring behavior. Eleven themes identified in the research prove to be instructive in describing their "best urban teacher behavior."

1. *Commitment:* Teachers with high commitment have made a very conscious decision to contribute to people through education and to work where there is the greatest need. Commitment means sticking with the students and teaching in spite of obstacles. Such teachers generate ideas about how to help students and other teachers.

2. *Dedication:* Dedicated teachers find satisfaction from each step forward in a student's life. Typically, such teachers have a history of investing in others and emotionally becoming part of their lives.

3. *Individualized Perception:* The urban teachers who are most valued by their students have a sense of the differences among their students and express regard for their individuality. It is natural for these teachers to personalize their teaching even when they see many students every day.

4. *Caring:* The best urban teachers show warmth and affection to their students and give priority to the development of their relationships with students as an avenue to student growth.

5. *Involver:* Effective urban teachers see life as a two-way street. These teachers want to be partners with their students, with parents, and with other teachers. Students have more say in their education when the teacher is an involver.

6. *Empathy:* Sensitivity and anticipation of student feelings mark teachers who bring empathy to the classroom. Students are more ready to accept themselves and to establish relationships when they work with teachers who acknowledge and understand their feelings.

7. *Positivity:* Teachers who rated high for positivity have hopeful attitudes toward their students. These teachers look for what is right and help others to feel better.

8. *Initiator:* An initiator is an advocate for students. These teachers are willing to speak up when doing so makes a difference for the students.

9. *Stimulator:* There is more emotion and excitement in a classroom when the teacher is a strong stimulator. Teachers who are stimulators can be personally dramatic as well as very receptive to the ideas and opinions of students.

10. *Input:* Teachers who rate high for input are intrigued with ideas and search constantly for ideas and activities that are applicable to the classroom. These teachers' own learning needs are met by creating new techniques and sharing them with others.

11. *Concept:* Teachers who rate high on the concept theme have developed a philosophy about what is best for students and are guided by a positive learning concept. (Gallup Organization, 1993)

The same Gallup study asserts that effective urban teachers have the courage and empathy to work in difficult environments and they are caring. Gordon agrees:

> All students need caring teachers and recent work suggests that, when students perceive a teacher as caring, both student behavior and academic performance improve. But it is the intensity of working for and caring about students in urban schools that makes effective urban teachers different from their counterparts in the suburbs. (Gordon, 1999, p. 306)

The research suggests that effective teachers maintain the above qualities while focusing their teaching upon subject content (Gallup Organization, 1993). Knowledge of subject content is often singled out as an important trait for all great teachers. A teacher who possesses a solid working knowledge of subject content and understands the science of learning has the potential for effectiveness and success. The importance of this combination cannot be underestimated. The importance of understanding of subject content in particular has been mentioned as a key to success by numerous researchers (Finn, 1997).

The model urban teacher, then, has a solid knowledge of subject content, understands the science of teaching and learning, and possesses many of the characteristics found in the Gallup research.

The NDEA National Institute for Advanced Study of Teaching Disadvantaged Youth conducted a study aimed at determining the type and extent of problems teachers perceive as they experience teaching in inner-city or so-called ghetto schools. There were forty-five significant areas reported by more than one-third of the respondents, which have been condensed into nine categories:

1. problems that seem to involve disruptive or disturbing student behavior;
2. problems that seem to arise out of students' home conditions;

3. problems of parent–school relationships;
4. problems of working with the exceptional child;
5. problems of providing for individual differences;
6. problems of child-to-child relationships;
7. problems of building skills in independent work;
8. problems of school conditions; and
9. problems of the child's self-worth and self-concept. (Cruickshank & Leonard, 2002)

There is no magic bullet that will resolve all of the problems indicated above. Skilled teachers, however, can neutralize the problems with appropriate strategies. Teachers cannot change the home conditions of their children but they can make inroads into addressing many of the expressed problems in the everyday life of their classrooms.

While there are numerous strategies that might be employed, there are three major strategies that must be employed:

1. Teachers must employ instruction that causes children to learn. This requires that instruction be at the level of the individual child. When the child can grasp the instruction given and build understanding, she will experience success. Everyone desires to succeed, and success breeds success. When children succeed, they seek further success—it feels good. Once a child is turned on to learning, issues of disruptive behavior and issues of self-worth dissipate. Providing instruction at the level of each child provides for individual differences and reaches the exceptional child.

2. Teachers must recognize that the job of educating children is very difficult and cannot be achieved in isolation. Partnership with the home is imperative. Parents are in an excellent position to help by reinforcing the work of the teachers at home. The challenge in urban areas is one of enticing parents to join with the teacher. (A discussion regarding parents as partners is presented later in this chapter). Teachers *must* be convinced of the benefits of bringing parents into partnerships and they *must* convince parents of the critical role they can serve. With those parents who are most resistant, teachers must work to build one-on-one relationships. They must be sincere in their approach and work to convince parents that their children have the best possibility of success by joining forces between the home and the school.

3. Last, urban teachers must see their responsibility to their children as a total commitment. They must develop a mindset in which they feel a deep sense of responsibility, love, and deep affection for their children. Children and parents will recognize the sincerity of their teacher and feel their caring and genuine love. In response, many of the problems expressed above by Cruickshank and Leonard can be overcome resulting in greater learning for the children.

The problems described herein are serious and pose an enormous challenge for teachers. It is encouraging that there are urban schools throughout America, many in extremely impoverished city neighborhoods, where children are performing at normal and even high academic levels. This fact should enlighten those individuals who plan to teach in urban areas with heavy concentrations of poor families.

The key to success in urban classrooms is best expressed by the Gallup Organization, as indicated earlier—teachers must possess a solid knowledge of subject content and understand the science of learning. To this combination, add the qualities of deep respect, concern, and commitment for children, and the need to view them as precious individuals. Teachers must prepare strategies to overcome the problems described by Cruickshank and Leonard as they experience teaching in inner-city or so-called ghetto schools. There are indeed many effective strategies that might be employed. A good beginning would be to review and employ the "best urban teacher behavior" themes also expressed earlier in this section.

Most importantly, teachers must never give children, particularly poor urban children, signals that they are inferior and that they are not capable of high levels of achievement. Urban students, in particular, need constant encouragement. Without encouragement to achieve, they work only to live up to this low expectation (Ladson-Billings, 2000). They will be victims of a self-fulfilling prophecy and be relegated to a continuous, vicious cycle of poverty.

THE ROLE OF PARENTS

Need for Family Relationships

The involvement of parents or guardians in the lives of their children cannot be underestimated, particularly in their academic lives. Research suggests that parental involvement with adolescent children may be supportive of positive academic achievement. The quality of that involvement has been associated with increased student competence (Mason, Cauce, Gonzales, & Hiraga, 1996).

Parents of urban children can make a positive contribution to the achievement levels of their children. When parents receive encouragement and adequate training, they can be effective. Disadvantaged children gain most when their parents are involved in their school lives; this is true of all children, including those identified as special education, gifted, and limited English proficient.

Results are impressive when parents are involved directly in their children's learning activities in the home. Programs involving parents in reading, homework support, and tutoring using teacher-provided materials and instructions are particularly powerful. Research indicates that the earlier the parental involvement begins, the more impressive the results (Cotton & Wikelund, 2001).

Of particular importance is the quality of the relationships between inner-city youth and their fathers. The well-being of these children is influenced by a positive relationship between the child and father. Zimmerman, Salem, and Maton (1995) conducted research around the relationship between African American fathers and their sons and found that the increased amount of time they spend together produced fewer incidents of anxiety and depression and higher levels of self-esteem. A study by Salem, Zimmerman and Notaro (1998) equated time spent with fathers with lower levels of drugs, alcohol, and cigarette use.

While research in this field has focused on the absence of parental relationships, the importance of close parent–student relationships has been established. The involvement and support of family can lead to strong personal adjustment and academic performance. Given this reality, it is easy to see the necessary and critical role of the family in the academic success of the child. It is also evident as to why, given the incidents of lack of support in urban families, children suffer in terms of academic achievement, self-esteem, and social connections.

Educators need to recognize when lack of family involvement is an issue for a child. Armed with an understanding of the functions of family relationships and how they can affect a child's academic performance, teachers may be in a position to help. They can help forge substitute supportive relationships between a child and counselors, support groups, fellow teachers, coaches, and peers. Helping students to find areas of interest in athletics, civic and religious groups, and various in-school and community activities can be positive steps in assisting students to find important, influential, and supportive relationships (Gallagher, Alvarez-Salvat, Silsby, & Kenny, 2002).

Need for Role Models

The effects of urban life markedly influence the attitudes and personal development of children. They observe behavior of the individuals around them, especially parents and guardians, and draw conclusions about behavior that in their eyes appears normal. Their understandings of appropriate behavior over time become engrained in their personal development.

Children are great imitators, and thus there is considerable influence stemming from the role models in their lives. Role models can affect children negatively or provide positive influences and these influences will carry over into the personal attitudes and overall emotional stability of the children. Children who are subjected to negative role models develop negative attitudes about everyday life situations that serve to block their desire to learn. The lack of positive role models in many urban homes has the potential to dictate a child's attitude and behavior, eventually affecting his learning.

Payne suggests that to understand the importance of role models, one must first consider *functional* and *dysfunctional systems*. She indicates that a "system is a group in which individuals have roles, rules, and relationships. Dysfunctional is the extent to which an individual cannot get his/her needs met within a system"

(Payne, 1998, p. 82). While not universal, it is somewhat common for urban homes to be devoid of rules, and for relationships to be weak or even nonexistent. In such cases, roles that are typically played by parents and children in suburban homes are distorted in urban homes, leaving children confused and often alone in attempting to understand or find meaning in everyday life.

Not all urban homes are dysfunctional; when they are, parents or guardians are engrossed with so many everyday issues that they find little or no time for their children. Parents often work long, hard hours in several jobs. Further, due to lack of funds or proper healthcare, they tend to abuse their health and are prone to contracting illnesses and diseases. They are also prone to excessive use of alcohol and drugs. Given these conditions, children are often left to their own decisions and forced to fend for themselves. At a time in their lives when they need love, attention, support, and direction, their needs go unmet.

To make matters worse, children must often bear adult-type responsibilities. In such cases, the children must forego their needs in order to address family needs. They may need to find employment to support family income, or they may be responsible for caring for family members who suffer from illness. The normal sequence is for a child to experience childhood followed by adolescence followed by adulthood. The need to take on adult responsibilities robs the child of normal emotional development (Payne, 1998).

As children mature, they should gravitate from dependence to independence to interdependence in a process which Covey (1989) calls the "maturity continuum." When children cannot be dependent upon their parents or guardians, they have lost the first phase of the continuum. During the first phase, role models are of great importance. The child observes the behavior of role models who are present and utilizes their behavior as a resource to build their own personalities. Without a wholesome dependency stage on which to draw, they are ill-equipped for the later stages of the continuum.

Without role models, the child is rarely exposed to proper behaviors in the home and thus finds role models elsewhere. Unfortunately, too often these role models are found on the streets of their neighborhoods where life may be grossly distorted.

One often hears the phrase, "children grow up fast on the streets." There is great meaning to that phrase. At a time when children should be enjoying childhood and developing their personalities and attitudes, they lack the proper role models on which to depend. Bradshaw (1988) sees these children as constantly moving from a child's role to an adult role—from being dependent to independent, referred to as *codependency*. That constant tug from one to another coming when a child has not reached a normal level of understanding of herself is devastating. It affects all that the child does and distorts emotional development. Teachers in urban settings must recognize that these conditions exist and apply appropriate emotional support for the children. In many cases, this places primary importance in teachers serving as the role models that are so sorely lacking in the home and neighborhood.

Payne suggests seven elements that teachers can apply to provide emotional resources when a student lacks access to positive role models:

1. Create support systems.
2. Use appropriate discipline strategies and approaches.
3. Establish long-term relationships (apprenticeships, mentorships) with adults who are appropriate.
4. Teach hidden rules.
5. Identify options.
6. Increase individuals' achievement levels through appropriate instruction.
7. Teach goal-settings. (Payne, 1998, p. 86)

While it is not the case in all urban homes, teachers must recognize that where urban homes are void of support systems for children, they must fill that void. Examples of how teachers can support children within the resources suggested by Payne follow:

■ Students need appropriate discipline. Where urban homes are lacking in discipline, or the discipline may be inappropriately severe, teachers should practice a tough-love approach mixing reasonable discipline with love and caring to be effective.

■ Teachers can take the lead in helping children build healthy relationships with individuals who can help children to understand how to cope with daily burdens. Coaches, counselors, psychologists, caring individuals, and potential employers are but a few examples of individuals with whom children can build long-term relationships. Teachers can also entice children to join worthwhile outside organizations, such as Boys and Girls Clubs, 4-H, Scouts, and YMCAs. They can also influence children to participate in in-school activities such as athletic teams, clubs, committees, and other worthwhile endeavors.

■ Rules are a fact of life in our society. Urban children may not recognize the need to live within the parameters established by rules. These can be "hidden" or foreign to children. Teachers can establish rules in their classrooms and develop a sense of responsibility on the part of their students. Classroom rules form a precursor to wider rules within society.

■ Urban children have options available to them. They struggle, however, to understand these options and with the decision-making process that helps them to filter the pros and cons of each option and that determine the best course of action. Decision making and selecting among options requires practice. Teachers can provide the practice by identifying options available for simple decisions, leading to more complex situations as children mature.

■ Perhaps the best support system for a child to crave learning and remain in school is that of achieving success. Through appropriate instruction offered to the level of students' understanding, teachers more than anyone can encourage children to learn. Students who succeed in learning crave greater knowledge. It is the responsibility of the teacher to provide appropriate instruction for children geared at their level of understanding.

- The ability to set goals is another arena that requires practice. Parents in suburban homes have achieved higher educational levels and hold employment positions in which they understand goal setting. These understandings are transferred to their children through normal interaction. This is not likely to be the case in urban homes. The responsibility to cause children to understand and practice goal setting then moves to the teacher. By providing various goal-setting exercises and activities imbedded in instruction, teachers can support children in gaining this skill.

Parents as Partners

Much has been said in this chapter about the home life of urban children. In some cases these children reside in homes where parents or guardians show little or no support for the school's efforts in providing academic instruction. There is ample evidence to suggest that when parents become involved in their child's education, the academic achievement of the child is positively affected (Finn & Rock, 1997). Educators have long struggled with finding effective strategies to involve urban parents in the education of their children.

Teachers need to be proactive if they hope to involve urban parents in their children's education. Waiting for parents to become involved is not effective. There is considerable evidence to suggest that the involvement of parents in the school life of the child is an essential ingredient in the academic success of the child. Yet, attempting strategies to involve parents can be very frustrating. Urban parents are so involved in dealing with everyday problems of survival that they are likely to think for the moment and leave the education of their children to the school. Also, many urban parents with low levels of education are intimidated by the school environment, generally, and by educators, specifically. Nevertheless, attempting to involve parents is a necessary exercise for educators who hope to achieve success in teaching urban children.

It would be instructive here to view the general attitudes of teachers and the perceptions of parents regarding parental involvement. McDermott and Rothenberg (2000) conducted focus groups with urban teachers and parents around the subject of family involvement in their school. They found that teachers were frustrated when parental involvement was lacking. Teachers assumed that parents would support their efforts for their children's learning.

Urban teachers sometimes have limited or no knowledge of the culture of their students. They have limited knowledge of whether parents help their children with schoolwork (Baker, Kessler-Sklar, Piotrokowski, & Parker, 1999). Research by Pianta, Cox, Taylor, and Early (1999) revealed that most communication from the teacher to the home of low-income families consisted of "low intensity" letters and flyers, while face-to-face interaction was limited or nonexistent. As African American and Hispanic enrollments increased, fewer contacts took place. Sadly, some teachers do not view parents as partners in their children's education and hold a we–them attitude (Linek, Rasinski, & Harkins, 1997).

The negative feelings of parents linked with the attitudes of teachers form a powerful mix of misunderstanding and distrust that prevents fruitful collaboration. According to McDermott and Rothenberg (2000), parents "expressed distrust toward the school because they felt the faculty had been biased against African Americans and Latino children and their families" (p. 55).

As a result, parents did not participate in their school, wishing to interact only with those teachers who "respected and valued their children."

The McDermott and Rothenberg focus-group sessions yielded the following perceptions from urban parents about their schools and teachers:

1. Parents feel uncomfortable in the school.
2. Teachers make parents feel dumb.
3. Many teachers speak down to them and "brush them off."
4. Parents feel excluded because of negative attitudes they perceived in teachers.
5. Teachers treat parents as "beggars."
6. Teachers have poor communication skills.
7. Teachers lack respect for Hispanics and African American people.
8. Parents generally perceive their schools as racist institutions.
9. Parents perceive public education as designed for middle-class children.

One interchange during the focus groups indicates the strong emotions involved in parents' perceptions. One parent shared her frustration with her daughter's school:

> She was "sick of hearing the word "immaturity" . . . this word was a code [word] to retain kids . . . it was used to retain children of color . . . they track my child by saying she is immature . . . it is the same negativity!

The parent told the other parents:

> You should not feel intimidated by the school. I know they don't make you feel comfortable. They throw language at you. It makes you feel uncomfortable. Teachers should communicate so you understand . . . teachers need to be creative . . . build on what my daughter knows. I had some fights with her teacher. Parents should not back off. I don't care what they [the teachers] think of me. (p. 58)

These perceptions, driven in large measure by the actions of some teachers, are most disturbing especially in light of the considerable research examining low-income urban parents and their schools. Parental involvement in most schools can help to foster improved psychological climate in the school and positively affect the academic performance of children (Comer, Haynes, Joyner, & Ben-Avie, 1996). Hoover-Dempsey and Sandler (1997) submit that teachers must maximize their efforts to make families feel welcome, understanding that urban parents often feel excluded due to the fact that they are poor and suffer from a difference in culture and ethnicity.

Comer and Haynes (1991) suggest three levels of involvement that allow parents to be involved according to their levels of comfort.

1. Have a small group of parents represent others on school planning councils.
2. Have parents become involved in daily school and classroom activities such as general volunteers, teaching assistants, or monitors.
3. Have parents become involved in events such as holiday programs and special school events.

Most teachers have not received training in the facilitation of parental involvement, and struggle to find strategies that are effective. Enticing urban parents to be more involved requires a mind-set on the part of the teacher. It is important to recognize that parents do not become involved because they do not know how and where to effectively help their child. Teachers should not mistake the lack of involvement for a lack of caring. Urban parents, particularly the poor, care deeply about their children and recognize the importance of success in school if their children are to function in a society that places a premium on education. Parents should not be faulted for this lack of involvement. The fault lies instead with teachers who either do not attempt to involve parents or who are unsuccessful in their efforts to bring about meaningful parental involvement. Teachers should touch the emotions of parents in their communications. They must cause parents to believe that they care deeply about the child's welfare and that they genuinely need the parent in partnership. The sincerity with which this is undertaken is critically important and will influence whether parents become dedicated partners.

Teachers must, through personal contacts, convince parents of the importance of the role they must play. Teachers must assist parents in recognizing the type and level of involvement in which the parent can best participate. It is the role of the teacher to convince parents of the belief that their involvement can be influential and improve their child's educational performance (Hoover-Dempsey & Sandler, 1997). Hoover-Dempsey and Sandler suggest that teachers should:

1. Maintain regular contact with parents.
2. Discuss the positive qualities of the child.

3. Share strategies and techniques that are planned during the school day and those in which the parent can engage.
4. Give parents the impression that their children have academic abilities and can achieve successfully.

The key to reaching urban students and parents lies not within the students and parents but within the teacher. Three ingredients are necessary: an understanding of the conditions under which the children live; the skill and patience to provide instruction at the level of each student; and a genuine demonstration of love for the children. Once a teacher fills the void in the life of a child with genuine attention, concern, and affection, she will be rewarded by children and parents who will demonstrate great affection in return and a surprising ability on the part of the children to crave learning. This is an emotion that is not readily present in suburban settings but is ever-present when teaching urban children. Once a teacher develops an understanding of these students and recognizes the desperate lives they live, the task of teaching the students can be seen clearly through the lens of understanding.

Those who contemplate teaching in urban settings must recognize and be sensitive to the conditions so prevalent in the lives of their students. At first blush, it would appear that teaching under these conditions would present a daunting, if not impossible task. The authors have worked in urban schools experiencing the burden of the poor, and also in suburbia with the children of the middle and wealthy classes. Given a choice, the authors would opt to teach the urban poor. In spite of the difficult conditions surrounding urban schools, there is an underlying warmth and genuineness residing with poor children. Those who teach these children can feel that emotion and recognize the desire on the part of the children to receive an education that can lift them from the poverty they have known. When teaching in an urban school, one soon learns that the students' parents hold this same desire.

SCHOOL BUILDING FACILITIES

A Problem of Major Magnitude

The deteriorating condition of school facilities in the United States presents a serious dilemma for educators. The American Association of School Administrators indicates that 74 percent of schools in the United States are in need of immediate replacement or repair, with 25 percent characterized as inadequate facilities for learning (National Center for Educational Statistics, 1999a).

Based upon General Accounting Office (GAO) estimates, $112 billion would be needed to renovate schools across the nation. Fifty billion dollars of the amount estimated as needed occurs in the major cities across the nation. The estimate of needs considers costs to meet aging and general deterioration, overcrowding conditions, retrofitting to accommodate technology, and repairs that have been deferred over the years. On top of these issues, funds are required to construct new facilities to accommodate enrollment issues.

The need to replace, repair, or renovate urban school infrastructure seems obvious given that the average city school has a life of more than fifty years and in 1999, according to the National Center for Education Statistics, the average age of a school building was forty years. Numerous schools do not meet current building codes and do not have wiring to accommodate today's fast-moving technology needs (Council for Great City Schools, 1997, p. 7).

School districts, in general, face serious funding problems that are magnified in urban environments due to the many pressing needs of city areas. When funds are short, maintenance budgets are often reduced based on the thinking that these costs can be deferred to a later date. Deferring maintenance ultimately leads to greater costs as buildings continue to deteriorate and repair and replacement costs increase. In addition, improperly maintained equipment ultimately affects the operating efficiency of the equipment. From 1983 to 1991, the cost of deferred maintenance of schools in the United States increased from $25 billion to $100 billion (Hansen, 1992).

In 1988, the Carnegie Foundation for the Advancement of Teaching suggested that our nation was in need of high levels of federal involvement in addressing school facilities issues. At that time they suggested that an effort similar to the Higher Education Facilities Act of the 1960s, which provided an influx of federal funds into colleges and universities following World War II, would be needed to address the problems of our nation's deteriorating school facilities. It would appear that their suggestion for a massive funding effort to support school facilities remains as relevant today as it was in 1988. Certainly, these deteriorating conditions appear to be most prevalent in urban facilities.

School Facilities Dilemma

Students in urban areas very often face significant inequalities with respect to their opportunities to learn. In *Savage Inequalities: Children in American Schools,* Kozol presents the hurdles students face in Washington, DC in poverty, discrimination, and in their personal lives. Further exacerbating their lives is the reality that every day they must attend schools that are intellectually demeaning and physically deteriorating (Kozol, 1991):

> There was a hole in the ceiling of a classroom on the third floor. . . they'd put a twenty gallon drum under the hole to catch the rain. The toilets at the school were downright unpleasant. But if you really want to see some filth, go down into the basement—to the women's toilet. I would not go to the bathroom in that building if my life depended on it. (p. 184)

Kozol describes schools in Washington, DC:

There are "two worlds of Washington," the *Wall Street Journal* writes. One is the Washington of "cherry blossoms, the sparkling white monuments, the magisterial buildings of the government of politics and power." In the Rayburn House Office Building, the *Journal* writes, "a harpist is playing Schumann's *Traumerei*, the bartenders are tipping the top brands of scotch, and two huge salmons sit on mirrored platters." Just over a mile away, the other world is known as Anacostia. In an elementary school in Anacostia, a little girl in the fifth grade tells me that the first thing she would do if somebody gave money to her school would be to plant a row of flowers by the street. "And I'd buy some curtains for my teacher. It's like this," she says. "The school is dirty. There isn't any playground. There's a hole in the wall behind the principal's desk. What we need to do is first rebuild the school. . . . build a playground. Plant a lot of flowers. Paint the classrooms. Fix the hole in the principal's office. Buy doors for the toilet stalls in the girls' bathroom. Fix the ceiling in this room. Make it a beautiful clean building. Make it pretty. Way it is, I feel ashamed." (1991, p. 181)

Overcrowding and Class Size Issues

Emeral A. Crosby, principal of Pershing High School in Detroit, criticizes the fact that the urban schools are frequently too small to house student enrollments. The schools were built at a time when enrollments were smaller and have not expanded over the years as enrollments increased. He describes elementary schools that cram students into buildings considerably above their enrollment capacities and high schools that must accommodate up to three thousand students, well beyond their capacities. According to Crosby, "Handling the volume of students entering, passing through the halls and exiting the building is a tremendous problem. What's more, the lack of campus means that many interscholastic and intramural activities—such as soccer, football, and tennis—cannot be offered" (Crosby, 1999, p. 299).

The overcrowding conditions in New York City can be used as an example of the situation in many cities. The New York City schools have faced a dramatic increase in immigration levels. Overcrowding there has presented a very serious problem where student enrollment was above one million students in 2004. The situation in New York is not unique but found in most cities. Cities are particularly hard hit because space for construction is at a premium and funding is not likely. City schools are utilizing spaces never intended as classrooms, such as libraries, gymnasiums, laboratories, band rooms, and even closets and hallways. Specialized classes, such as science, the arts, trades, and technology are particularly vulnerable and often not appropriately equipped (Burnett, 1995).

Overcrowding in any school situation is a serious dilemma. Burnett (1995) concludes from his studies that overcrowding in schools with a high proportion of students of poverty can have a dire impact on learning. Overcrowding effects instructional techniques, student concentration, classroom order, and school scheduling.

Overcrowding in a school usually results in large class sizes. A significant number of studies provide evidence that the reduction of class size in urban classrooms positively affects student achievement. This is especially true in the early grades. Jones (1998) conducted a study in which eleven thousand students were tracked in classes of twenty five students and also in classes of fifteen students. He found that children in the smaller classes outperformed their counterparts in larger classes and that the achievement gap persisted in the children's later school years.

Although there has not been a great deal of research on overcrowding, and much of the research available is inconclusive, there is some evidence that overcrowding can have detrimental effects on learning, particularly in schools with a high proportion of children living in poverty. A 1995 study on overcrowding in the New York City schools found that standardized test scores in mathematics and reading were significantly lower than schools that did not have overcrowded conditions. When asked, teachers agreed that overcrowding negatively impacted classroom activities, instruction in general, and innovative teaching methods. Teachers also stated that they had difficulty maintaining order in overcrowded classrooms (Burnett, 1995).

Burnett indicates that the following problems result from overcrowding:

1. Logistics are severely impacted for the school day.
2. Daily schedules are frequently disrupted.
3. Noise levels are high.
4. Extended lunch periods sometimes begin as early as 9 A.M.
5. Teachers must shuttle from one room to another transporting materials from classroom to classroom.
6. Locker space is insufficient.
7. Hallways are crowded, extending travel time between classes.
8. Electives (art, music, technology) are often eliminated.
9. Administrators and teachers devote an inordinate amount of energy to maintaining order.

Teachers should not be deterred by the fact that they do not control class size; they must employ effective strategies to overcome it. One such strategy is the use of cooperative learning within the classroom context. Small group instruction in a cooperative, problem-based environment can influence students' academic achievement in urban settings. Cooperative learning can address class size while allowing students to experience personal identification and involvement within a group, which students seem to need as a requisite for achievement (Slavin, Madden, Dolan, & Wasik, 1996).

While cooperative learning may be a means to deal with overcrowded classrooms, it should be considered beyond that objective. Johnson and Johnson indicate that:

Cooperative learning resulted in higher levels of reasoning, more frequent generation of new ideas and solutions (i.e., process gain) and greater transfer of what is learned within one situation to another (group-to-group individual transfer) than did competitive or individualistic learning. (Johnson & Johnson, 1994, p. 4)

They further assert that:

The fad that working together to achieve a common goal produces higher achievement and greater productivity than does working alone is so well confirmed by so much research that it stands as one of the strongest principles of social and organizational psychology. Cooperative learning is indicated whenever learning goals are highly important, mastery and retention are important, a task is complex or conceptual, problem solving is desired, divergent thinking or creativity is desired, quality of performance is expected, and higher-level reasoning strategies and critical thinking are needed. (Johnson & Johnson, 1994, p. 4).

Cooperative learning is only one strategy that can be effective in urban classrooms. While teaching conditions in urban schools can be problem-filled, there are numerous ways for these problems to be addressed. (See Chapter 4, The Urban Teacher, for further examples and explanations.)

Armed with a range of approaches, teachers can cause their students to succeed. In spite of the negative news about urban student academic achievement levels, there are numerous success stories and numerous teacher heroes or heroines who serve as bright lights in meeting the challenges which urban schools present.

Facilities Influence Learning

Urban schools suffer from a general lack of resources to raise them to a level that is commonly associated with high-achieving schools. Supplies such as children's literature, books, textbooks, and basic equipment such as desks and chalkboards are often inadequate. Higher-level equipment such as computers, calculators, and laboratory equipment are also seriously inadequate. The U.S. Department of Education has concluded that the condition of the school plant and the availability and quality of supplies and equipment are linked to achievement and students' behavior and the general morale of the teachers in urban schools (Bowers, 2000).

There is some evidence that individuals are influenced by their physical environment. In schools this influence is likely to be considerable. Following years of deferred maintenance, many urban schools show signs of serious deterioration resulting from years of neglect. It is not uncommon to find such conditions as dirty walls in need of painting, areas of peeling paint and plaster, toilets and sinks that are in poor working order, and inadequate lighting in urban schools. Problems of old and inefficient heating, cooling, and ventilation systems, which usually malfunction when not properly maintained, add to the overall deteriorated physical environment (Frazier, 1993).

Andrews and Neuroth (1988) feel that the problems of poor indoor air quality in schools represent a very adverse situation. They suggest that the performance of students and teachers is adversely affected by indoor air quality problems, since poor air quality may have a significant negative effect upon the ability of students to concentrate. They further assert that young children have greater vulnerability to air contaminants such as asbestos, radon, and formaldehyde, often found in schools.

Discussion around the condition of school facilities most often centers upon those conditions that are most visible. Schools are seen as part of the infrastructure of a community and are, therefore, thought of as a community capital investment that should be maintained and protected. Creating an environment that optimizes learning is usually not a major consideration. Unfortunately, there has been little research on the possible link between school building conditions and students' academic achievement.

Edwards (1991) conducted research in Washington, DC schools and found that as building conditions improved from poor to fair that students' achievement scores increased an average of 5.45 percent. When a school's improved condition moved from poor to excellent, the increase in achievement reached 10.9 percent. While these results are instructive, greater amounts of research regarding the possible link between building condition and achievement are needed to present convincing arguments for enhanced funding for school repair, renovation, and new construction.

Principal Emeral A. Crosby maintains that older buildings require frequent, ongoing renovation, "but they can never be properly updated to meet the needs of modern students" (Crosby, 1999, p. 299). It is important for teachers and administrators to work with facility planners to create educational environments to meet the needs of both the building inhabitants and programmatic needs. Too often this is not the case. When buildings are remodeled or replaced, they may not consider proper educational planning and educational needs remain unmet.

Education is so steeped in culture that it is difficult to change any aspect of that culture. When we think about educational change we often think about curriculum and instruction, which provoke great resistance when change is suggested. In spite of the fact that many urban schools are fifty or more years of age, they continue to house educational programs unable to meet modern-day educational needs.

Over time, curriculum and instruction have slowly undergone significant changes but school buildings have not changed significantly to keep pace and present obstacles to delivering positive educational programs:

> Often located in the oldest parts of the city, many of these buildings are in violation of modern fire codes and are hazards to safety. The plumbing is obsolete; asbestos insulation poses health problems; lead poisoning from paint and soil has a negative impact on student learning and brain development of young children. Furthermore, these buildings cannot accommodate the activities, the equipment, and the materials that new programs and modern technology demand. (Crosby, 1999, p. 299)

Descriptions of the conditions present in many urban school plants are discouraging and alarming. Teachers in these schools complain, often bitterly, about the lack of leadership and community support to rectify the problems. Yet these loyal and committed teachers continue day after day to deliver instruction to children in spite of the shortcomings in their schools' physical conditions. When asked about these conditions, they almost universally respond positively believing that it is their work and commitment that will ultimately cause their students to succeed. Thus, while unhappy with conditions, their attitudes about the potential for their students' academic progress are positive. They do not allow facility conditions to dampen their spirits or to affect their teaching.

SUMMARY

The problems of urban schools described in this chapter are overwhelming to anyone considering a teaching career in urban settings. A great many of the problems that plague urban schools with which teachers must deal are formed outside the school. Problems of poverty, unemployment, lack of intellect, crime, and racism are ever-present. The despair that pervades families and neighborhoods are deeply rooted. Yet teachers are meeting these challenges every day in their classrooms. There is much evidence around the nation that children are learning, test scores are rising, and dropout rates are decreasing. Where this is occurring, one will find bold leadership on the part of the administrators and teachers and extraordinary efforts by these individuals. For them, the challenges are formative, but the successes they are building are rewarding.

Successful teaching and learning in an urban school does not simply occur. It requires that a combination of knowledge, skill and commitment be brought into the classroom every day. Urban teachers must have an understanding of the conditions under which the children live, have the skills and patience to provide instruction at the level of each student, and must have an enormous amount of love for these very special children.

CHAPTER QUESTIONS

1. How have urban demographic shifts influenced education in urban areas?

2. How do urban home conditions and urban neighborhoods influence the school environment and how are teachers affected?

3. Discuss how culture and social class influence learning.

4. What are the major detrimental effects of student tracking upon student academic performance?

5. What is the value of forming partnerships with parents and what strategies can be employed to convince parents to participate in their children's education?

6. How do school facility problems, particularly overcrowding, influence learning in urban schools and what can teachers do to overcome the problems?

SUGGESTED WEBSITES

American Institutes for Research: *An Educators' Guide to Schoolwide Reform*
www.aasa.org/reform/

National Institute for Urban School Improvement
www.inclusiveschools.org/

The New Educator: College of Education at Michigan State University
ed-web3.educ.msu.edu/NEWEd/Fall04/urban.htm

U.S. Department of Education: The Center for Comprehensive School Reform and Improvement
www.csrclearinghouse.org/index.cgi

U.S. Department of Education, *Implementing Schoolwide Programs: An Idea Book on Planning*
www.ed.gov/pubs/Idea_Planning/index.html

U.S. Office of Elementary and Secondary Education (OESE)
www.ed.gov/about/offices/list/oese/index.html?src=mr

REFERENCES

Andrews, J. B., & Neuroth, R. (October 1988). *Environmentally-related Health Hazards in Schools*. Paper presented at the annual meeting of the Association of School Business Officials International, Detroit, Michigan.

Ascher, C. (1991). Retaining good teachers in urban schools. ERIC Clearinghouse on Urban Education, Digest No. 77. Available: www.edrs.com/members/sp.cfm?AN=ED341762 (2004, May 15).

Association for Supervision and Curriculum Development. (1980). *What we believe: Positions of the Association for Supervision and Curriculum Development: Ability grouping and tracking.* Available: www.ascd.org/cms/index.cfm?TheViewID=1369tophav=1 (2004, May 14).

Baker, A., Kessler-Sklar, S., Piotrokowski, C., & Parker, F. (1999). Kindergarten and first grade teachers' reported knowledge of parents' involvement in their children's education. *The Elementary School Journal, 99,* 367–379.

Bowers, R. S. (2000). A pedagogy of success: Meeting the challenge of urban middle schools. *Clearing House, 73,* 235–238.

Boykin, A. (1998). Reformulating educational reform: Toward the proactive schooling of African American children. In R. J. Rossi (ed.), *Educational reforms and students at risk.* New York: Teachers College Press.

Bradshaw, J. (1988). *Bradshaw on the family.* Deerfield, FL: Simon & Schuster.

Brantlinger, E. (1995). Social class in school: Student perspectives (Research Bulletin No. 14). *Phi Delta Kappan Center for Evaluation, Development, and Research,* 4.

Brouilette, L. (1999). Behind the statistics: Urban dropouts and the GED. *Phi Delta Kappan, 4,* 313–322.

Burnett, G. (1992). Career academics: Educating urban students for career success. ERIC No. ED 355 310.

Burnett, G. (1994). Urban teachers and collaborative school-linked services. ERIC No. ED 371 108.

Burnett, G. (1995). Overcrowding in urban schools. ERIC No. ED 384 682.

Carnegie Foundation for the Advancement of Teaching. (1988). *An imperiled generation: Saving urban schools.* Available: www.edrs.com/members/sp.cfm?AN=293940 (2004, May 17).

Casserly, M. (2002). *Beating the odds II: A city by city analysis of subject performance and achievement gaps on state assessments.* Washington, DC: Council of Great City Schools.

Children's Defense Fund. (2001). *The state of America's children yearbook: America's children: Key national indicators of well being.* Available: www.childrensdefense.org/ac2001/Acol.ASP (2004, April 18).

Comer, J., & Haynes, N. (1991). Involvement in schools: An ecological approach. *The Elementary School Journal, 91,* 271–278.

Comer, J., Haynes, N., Joyner, E., & Ben-Avie, M. (1996). *Rallying the whole village: The Comer process for reforming education.* New York: Teachers College Press.

Cotton, K., & Wikelund, K. R. (2001). Parent involvement in education: School improvement research series. *Regional Educational Laboratory.* Available: www.nwrel.org/scpd/sirs/3/cu6/html (2004, September 30).

Council for Great City Schools. (1997). *A marshall plan for urban schools.* Available: www.cgcs .org/about/onissues.html (2004, May 17).

Covey, S. R. (1989). *The seven habits of highly effective people: Powerful lessons in personal change.* New York: Simon & Schuster.

Crosby, E. A. (1999). Urban schools forced to fail. *Phi Delta Kappan, 81*(4), 298–303.

Cruickshank, D., & Leonard, J. (2002). *The identification and analysis of perceived problems of teachers in inner city schools.* Occasional paper one, NDEA National Institute for Advanced Study in Teaching Disadvantaged Youth. ERIC No. ED 026335.

Edwards, M. A. (1991). Building conditions, parental involvement, and student achievement. Unpublished Master's Thesis. Georgetown University, Washington, DC.

Erikson, E. (1987). The human life cycle. In S. Schlein (ed.), *A way of looking at things: Selected papers of Erik Erikson, 1930–1980.* New York: Norton.

Finn, C. E. (1997). The real teacher crisis. *Education Week.* Available: www.edweek.com/ ew/vol-17/09finn.h17 (2004, May 18).

Finn, J. D., & Rock, D. A. (1997). Academic success among students at risk for school failure. *Journal of Applied Psychology, 82,* 221–234.

Forresi, B. (ed). (2003). *Children and adolescents confronting fears.* Available: www .segretariatosociale.rai.it/INGLESE/codici/ bambani_adolesc_paureE/paureE.html (2005, February 9).

Frazier, L. M. (1993). Deteriorating school facilities and student learning. ERIC No. 82. Eugene: University of Oregon.

Freeman, C., Scafidi, B. C. & Sjoquist, D. L. (2002). *Racial segregation in Georgia public schools, 1994–2001: Trends, causes and impact on teacher quality.* Paper presented August 2002 at the Conference on Resegregation of Southern Schools, Chapel Hill, N. C.

Gallagher, L. A., Alvarez-Salvat, R., Silsby, J., & Kenny, M. A. (2002). Sources of support and psychological distress among academically successful inner-city youth. *Adolescents 45,* 161–183.

Gallay, L. S., & Flanagan, C. A. (2000). The well being of children in a changing economy: Time for a new social contract in America. In R. O. Taylor & M. C. Wang (eds.), *Resilience across contexts: Work, family, culture and community* (pp. 3–33). Mahwah, NJ: Lawrence Erlbaum.

Gallup Organization. (1993). *Urban teacher research: Summary of interview development study.* Lincoln, NE: Gallup Press.

Gibson, M. A. (1987). The school performance of immigrant minorities: A comparative view. *Anthropology & Education Quarterly, 18*(4), 262–275.

Goldenberg, I., Kunz, D., Hamburger, M., & Stevenson, J. (2003). Urban education: Connections between propaganda and prevailing views of education, *Education, 123*(7), 628–635.

Goode, A. (2002). *Leadership: What are the essential qualities of successful leaders?* Available: www.ocmetro.com/metro041802/business041802.html (2004, October 11).

Gordon, G. L. (1999). Teacher talent and urban schools. *Phi Delta Kappan, 81*(4), 304–307.

Haberman, M. (1989). More minority teachers. *Phi Delta Kappan, 70,* 771–776.

Hacker, A. (1992). *Two nations: Black, white, separate, hostile, unequal.* New York: Charles Scribner's.

Hansen, S. J. (1992). *Schoolhouse in the red: A guidebook for cutting our losses: Powerful recommendations for improving America's school facilities.* Arlington, VA: American Association of School Administrators.

Hoover-Dempsey, K., & Sandler, H. (1997). Why do parents become involved in their children's education. *Review of Educational Research, 67*(1), 3–42.

Hopkins, G. (2000). Principals identify top ten leadership traits. *Education World.* Available: www.educationworld.com/a_admin/admin/admin190.html (2004, October 11).

Howey, K. R. (2000). *A review of challenges and innovations in the preparation of teachers for urban contexts: Implications for state policy.* Milwaukee: University of Wisconsin–Milwaukee National Partnership on Excellence and Accountability in Education.

Ingersoll, R. M. (2001). *Teacher turnover, teacher shortages, and the organization of schools.* Seattle, WA: Center for the Study of Teaching and Policy.

Johnson, R. T., & Johnson, J. W. (1994). An overview of cooperative learning. In J. Thousand, A. Nevin, & V. Nevin (eds.), *Creativity and collaborative learning.* Baltimore: Brookes Press.

Jones, R. (1998). What works? *American School Board Journal, 184,* 28–33.

Kozol, J. (1991). *Savage inequalities: Children in America's schools.* New York: HarperCollins.

Ladson-Billings, G. (2000). Fighting for our lives: Preparing teachers to teach African American students. *Journal of Teacher Education, 51,* 206–214.

Lederhouse, J. N. (1998). You will be safe here. *Educational Leadership, 58,* 51–54.

Lewis Mumford Center for Comparative Urban and Regional Research. (2002). *Choosing segregation: Racial imbalance in American public schools, 1990–2000.* Albany: University of New York at Albany.

Linek, W., Rasinski, T., & Harkins, D. (1997). Teacher perceptions of parent involvement in literacy education. *Reading Horizons, 38,* 90–106.

Mason, C. A., Cauce, A. M., Gonzales, N., & Hiraga, Y. (1996). Neither too sweet or too sour: Problem peers, maternal control, and problem behavior in African American adolescents. *Child Development, 67,* 2115–2130.

McDermott, P., & Rothenberg, J. (2000). Why urban parents resist involvement in their children's elementary education. *The Qualitative Report.* Available: www.nova.edu/ssss/QR/QR5-3/mcdermott.html (2004, October 12).

McDonnell, L. M., Burstein, L., & Ormseth, T. (1990). *Discovering what schools really Teach: Designing improved coursework indicators.* Washington, DC: U.S. Department of Education, Office of Educational Research and Improvement.

Montgomery, A., & Rossi, R. (1994). Becoming at-risk of failure in America's schools. In A. Montgomery & R. Rossi (eds.), *Education reforms and students at risk: A review of the current state of the art.* Washington DC: American Institute of Research.

National Center for Educational Statistics. (1991). *National educational longitudinal survey.* Washington, DC: U.S. Department of Education. Nels: 88, NCES No. 91–460.

National Center for Educational Statistics. (1995). *Which types of schools have the highest teacher turnover.* Washington, DC: U.S. Department of Education. Available: http://nces.ed.gov/pubs95/web/95778.asp (2004, October 4).

National Center for Educational Statistics. (1999a). *Condition of America's public school facilities.* Washington, DC: U.S. Department of Education. Available: http://nces.ed.gov/surveys/trss/publications2000032/7.asp (2005, January 9).

National Center for Educational Statistics. (1999b). *The condition of education.* Washington, DC: U.S. Department of Education.

National Center for Educational Statistics. (2003). *Status and trends in the education of Hispanics.* Washington, DC: U.S. Department of Education. Available: http://nces.ed/gov/pubs2003/hispanics/section1.asp (2004, October 4).

Nieto, S. (1999). *The light in their eyes.* New York: Teachers College Press.

Payne, R. K. (1998). *A framework for understanding poverty.* Highlands, TX: RFT Publishing.

Pianta, R., Cox, M., Taylor, L., & Early, D. (1999). Kindergarten teachers' practice related to the transition to school: Results of a national survey. *Journal of Teachers Education, 100,* 71–86.

Rodriguez, L. (1993). *Always running: Gang days in L.A.* New York: Simon & Schuster.

Sadaker, M., & Sadaker, D. (2003). *Teachers, schools, and society* (6th ed.). Boston: McGraw-Hill.

Salem, D. A., Zimmerman, M. A., & Notaro, P. C. (1998). Effects of family structure, family process, and father involvement on psychosocial outcomes among African-American students. ERIC No. E J 589172.

Slavin, R., Madden, J., Dolan, L., & Wasik, B. (1996). Success for all: A summary of research. *Journal of Education for Students Placed At-Risk, 1,* 41–76.

Useem, E., & Neild, R. (2001). Teacher staffing in the district of Philadelphia: A report to the community. ERIC No. ED 454352.

West, C. (December 1993). *Race matters.* Paper presented at the meeting of the American Association of Higher Education National Conference on School/College Collaboration, Pittsburgh, PA.

Wheelock, A. (1992). *Crossing the tracks.* New York: New Press.

Wilson, W. J. (1987). *The truly disadvantaged: The inner city, the underclass, and public policy.* Chicago: University of Chicago Press.

Zimmerman, M. A., Salem, D. A., & Maton, K. I. (1995). Family structure and psychosocial correlates among urban African American adolescent males. *Child Development, 66,* 1598–1613.

Zimmerman, M. A., Salem, D. A, & Nataro, P. C. (2000). Make room for daddy II: The positive effects of fathers' role in adolescent development. In R. O. Taylor & M. C. Wang (eds.), *Resilience across contexts: Work, family, culture, and community* (pp. 233–253). Mahwah, NJ: Lawrence Erlbaum.

CHAPTER 4

THE URBAN TEACHER

*The real measurement of our teaching ability comes not
from the success of the eager beavers who are open and
receptive to learning, but in our ability to motivate the
unmotivated, to show care and understanding to those with
the greatest need, to cause the unreceptive to be more
receptive, and thereby promote a perception of school as a
worthwhile place to be, a place in which people care
and students learn.*

—Denyce S. Ford, Professor, Howard University

■ ■ ■ ■ ■ ▬▬▬▬▬▬▬▬▬▬▬▬▬▬▬▬▬▬▬▬▬▬▬▬▬▬▬▬▬▬

URBAN PERSPECTIVES

Rebecca Harper
Fourth-Grade Urban Teacher

*In that most of our students come from unstructured environments, this
classroom community proves very powerful in students' learning and
achieving grade-level standards and expectations.*

Rebecca Harper thoroughly enjoys teaching in the urban setting. "I feel that I am
giving back to this community," she elucidates, "and it's my contribution to these children to help them grow not only academically, but also spiritually, and emotionally, as
well."

Harper contends that "to best meet the challenges of teaching in urban schools,
teachers need to understand the culture of poverty. Urban teachers should know and
expect how their students will react to everyday situations. And further," she explains,
"along with the connections we make with our students, it is vital for teachers to understand the often complex, individual differences among urban students. To benefit
their learning, I find success in designing for each of my students a specific education
plan that creates goals for each student to achieve and, as achieved, for which they are
praised and rewarded. Understanding student differences helps the urban teacher decide with fairness how best to respond to a plethora of unique classroom situations that
arise every day."

With respect to teaching standards-based objectives to her students, Harper
finds that perceptiveness and recognition of students' strengths offer very satisfactory
results for best practices in the urban classroom. "It is important, for example, to balance attention given to respective students in class. Typical in most classrooms are the
academically high students demonstrating the most ideal behaviors, and benefiting

from the special, personal-growth opportunities and designated honor responsibilities. In contrast, students struggling with their academics more likely exhibit behavioral concerns, and they are less likely to receive positive recognitions in the classroom. However," she continues, "it is critical to the low achievers' self-esteem and general well-being to praise special moments for them, as well as it is to make available to them rewarding opportunities in the classroom and school. Every student must experience that shining moment!"

"Above all," explained Mrs. Harper, "we establish in my classroom a *community of learners* who trust and care for one another. The students know of my high expectations of them, and that I stand firm on those beliefs. With this family climate in place, the students will then open up and express their emotions. They have strong desires to please me," she further contends. "In that most of our students come from unstructured environments, this classroom community proves very powerful in students' learning and achieving grade-level standards and expectations."

Teachers stand at the center of the educational enterprise. They, more than any group, affect the overall success or failure of children in school. There is therefore great importance for teachers to understand their roles and to develop the attitudes and skills to function in urban classrooms. The heart and soul of any school is the classroom. At the helm of each is the classroom teacher, whose role is to guide the students' learning experiences. One cannot underestimate the dominant responsibility the teacher holds in assuring positive student achievement in the classroom. Considerable amounts of research support the fact that the single, most significant factor that determines whether students successfully achieve in school is the classroom teacher (Barth, 2003; Corbett & Wilson, 2002; Haycock, 2001; MSDEd., 1998; Rice, 2003; Wenglinsky, 2002).

Urban teachers must recognize the powerful influence they can leave upon the students they teach. Making such an impact upon the lives of the students inspires dedicated urban teachers. There is great satisfaction in successfully meeting students' needs that assist them toward achieving their academic goals. Haberman (1995) refers to teachers as "champs" at nurturing all students of any cultural or ethnic group. Importantly, successful urban educators fulfill the urban school students' sense of belonging to the school and to their classroom family that is a critical element and a necessary ingredient in positioning students for learning.

Effective urban teachers affirm students' basic desires to understand and to crave learning, motivating them to meet and stretch their learning both in the classroom and beyond (Ormrod, 2003; Shields, 2004). If the teacher is critically important in the learning process, as indicated above, then it follows that if students are to succeed, their teachers must be of the highest quality.

Teaching in urban classrooms is an exceptionally rewarding experience only when practitioners are prepared for teaching in an urban environment. They must be skilled in using pretested and reliable strategies and methods that are flexible and effective. When effective teaching strategies are utilized, teachers experience gratifying results from their students' academic, social, and emotional achievement gains. Most teachers in urban schools, particularly those with longevity, having proven effectiveness over years of teaching, are capable, motivated, and resilient professionals who welcome opportunities that build on their cultural awareness and pedagogical strengths. They firmly believe in their students' abilities to succeed and reject notions that their learners lack abilities and lack motivation to adequately perform to grade-level standards. Urban teachers pride themselves in the gains their students achieve and are strengthened by solid emotional connections with their students (Irvine, 2003; Williams & Woods, 1997).

Distinguished Professor of Education Martin Haberman (1995) commends urban educators, honoring their "basic decency" in their fields of expertise. Successful urban teachers demonstrate in daily classroom performance qualities that include:

- being nonjudgmental, and understanding their students' behaviors, without labeling them either *good* or *bad;*
- not being overly moralistic, but attempting to guide, influence, and persuade—and not preach;
- being focused, as objective problem solvers who reserve any show of emotional shock or dramatic display;
- being effective listeners, as they seek to gain full understanding of students from informative sources; and
- being tolerant, flexible facilitators. (Shaughnessy, 1999)

CHARACTERISTICS OF URBAN STUDENTS

Children learn what they live. Such is true in the urban city experience of school children. Highlighted throughout this text is the focus on better understanding of the urban population and its learners. Only when teachers open their hearts and minds to their students, and consider the circumstances they endure, can they effectively motivate each student to meet or exceed strong academic expectations.

Urban educators encounter daily the family and community concerns reflected by their students in school. The pressures and experiences that the children carry into their classroom are an outgrowth of the society and culture in which they live. Their lives are colored by everyday experience with the heartache of poverty, disintegrating home environments, child abuse, current violent culture, materialism, and pressures to achieve (Lindquist & Molnar, 1995). The urban lifestyle conditions enter the school and are manifested in students' misbehaviors, academic deficits, and negative and/or destructive attitudes. When teachers gain an understanding of the frustrations children carry into the classroom, they are better equipped to deal with those behaviors.

The behaviors are readily observable and teachers must be skilled in recognizing the outward signs that students display that indicate serious problems. By recognizing these problems, teachers take the first step in supporting and helping students to cope and engage their learning frame of mind. Signs of urban student concerns and problems that teachers in urban schools should be alert to observe are:

- antagonism toward school, rebelliousness
- resistance or demonstrated hostility to adult influences
- lack of respect for themselves and educators
- need for self-discipline
- high rates of absenteeism
- academic skill deficits
- lack of motivation and/or withdrawal from classroom challenges
- poor study skills
- demonstrations of test phobia
- feelings of inferiority and failure
- immature behaviors and poor adjustment actions
- lack of academic or vocational goals
- little or no interest in outside hobbies, sports, and other activities
- demonstrations of feelings of rejection, frustration, and/or victimization (Forte & Schurr, 2002; Irvine, 2003; Matus, 1999; SECTQ, 2003)

Observing these undesired characteristics of students deserves closer teacher investigation into students' needs and special circumstances to assist them in selecting better behavior choices or helping change student attitudes to more positive ones.

Most urban students will identify with some or many of these negative descriptions. It is no wonder that enlisting in gangs and engaging in violent acts that involve drugs and weapons are more commonly experienced in the urban school environment than among any other population of learners. Urban school educators must remain aware and attentive to students' acquiring any of the above-listed negative behaviors, and gain understanding of the special needs of their learners, and be prepared to address respective students' critical, and in some cases life-threatening, concerns (Forte & Schurr, 2002; Irvine, 2003; Matus, 1999; SECTQ, 2003).

What follows briefly describes lifestyle conditions that serve as catalysts to negative behavior and disinterest in learning:

1. *Poverty:* Simply defined, poverty is "the extent to which an individual does without resources" (Payne, 1998, p. 16). There are approximately twelve million children in the United States, or 16.7 percent of the entire nation's population, living in poverty (Lindquist & Molnar, 1995; U.S. Census Bureau, 2000). This results in the household provider's unemployment and families living in deplorable housing conditions (Haberman, 1995).

2. *Disintegrating home environments:* Many urban school students live in homes where their humanistic needs are not met (Payne, 1998). Due to the lack of stable and continuous adult supervision, care, and guidance in the home, many urban youngsters actually rear themselves. They live with serious problems of family relationships that render families dysfunctional. In lieu of a family support system, students often turn to gangs that provide what they perceive to be inclusive, supervisory, and caring protection (Lindquist & Molnar, 1995).

3. *Child abuse:* The extent of at-home treatment runs the scope and breadth from love to neglect to brutal and repeated assaults on urban children in their home environment. Poor inner-city students are seven times more susceptible to abuse or neglect than students of higher socioeconomic means (Payne, 1998). Parents are typically the children's attackers, and the children are most likely to be their victims (Lindquist & Molnar, 1995).

4. *Current violent culture:* Children in urban homes often live with family violence. Parents who live desperate lives often turn to drugs and alcohol, causing them to lose reasonable perspective. This results in parents physically attacking each other and attacking their children. In addition, with far less supervision in the home, urban students are most susceptible to the viewing and internalizing of content to which they are exposed in games, advertisements, television programs, videotapes or DVDs, theatres, and the Internet (Lindquist & Molnar, 1995). Many of these programs contain graphic sex, violence, and drug content.

5. *Materialism:* Unsupervised and curious, urban children are typically overly exposed to "what's cool" and to the "must-haves," consumables that are heavily advertised. Without the luxury of more varied and less-materialistic influences, children in urban environments, who are bombarded by the advertising media, possess an overwhelming need to fulfill their desires, which inevitably instills competition for best clothes, best jewelry, best cell phone, and so forth (Lindquist & Molnar, 1995).

6. *Pressures to achieve:* In many urban homes, there is little or no pressure to achieve in school. On the other side of the coin, pressure can be considerable—families who offer all they can financially afford to meet their children's material needs and desires sometimes expect much from their children in return for their monetary sacrifices. Wanting better than "just average" efforts, or the "average" label given their children, they can exert excessive or overly zealous school achievement expectations from home. For some students the response to pressures to achieve—in or out of school—may often lead to a variety of unfortunate, antisocial, or destructive acts (Lindquist & Molnar, 1995).

Urban students who grow up in poverty-stricken environments typically demonstrate behaviors that reflect ingrained thought processes that may include the following:

- *Suspicion of adults:* Urban students often lack trust in adults, due to their inconsistent treatment that often fluctuates from sincere kindness to neglect to brutal abuse. They will often demonstrate wariness of adults' motives

and actions. This uncertainty or mistrust is apparent in shyness, uneasiness, or withdrawal from adults.

- *Relationship avoidance:* Students from this population often refrain from interacting with other individuals, for fear that these individuals my subject them to harm or danger.
- *"No hope" life perception:* Often the older students and young adults see no chance for a better life, nor of escaping a continued life of poverty.
- *Tolerance for and accommodation of bureaucracy:* Impoverished families are forced to succumb to mandated bureaucratic and ritualistic procedures that enable them to collect subsidies that dictate where and how they live. For the income received, they may well compromise their true-life desires. Children observe this behavior and act in a similar manner.
- *Responsiveness to orders:* Likewise, families operate under orders and demands they must meet. They interpret *power* as the definition of oneself (Payne, 1998). This may well be the reason that urban children are so enamored with the power they perceive in gang membership.

Thus, urban students from poverty environments are likely to demonstrate frustration with their world. Pent-up anxieties often lead to anger and aggression, or to violence toward others. In turn, this population of learners often becomes socialized to violence, abuse, and even death. They may very well witness crime, the harboring of felons, drug deals, and neighborhood foul play or shootings. Chapter 6, "Classroom Management in the Urban Setting," reviews and offers considerations and best practices for better understanding these issues, and best practices to assist students troubled with disturbing issues outside of school that compete with maintaining academic focus. It must be emphasized that teachers in the urban setting, as well as those in any school environment, need to reflect sensitivity and compassion by treating their students with respect and courtesy. The students deserve to be understood and teachers are responsible for making them aware of verbal expression and behavioral expectations (Payne, 1998).

TEACHERS AND THE URBAN CULTURE

As the nation looks to its educational settings to close the so-called or identified achievement gap between White students and students of color, the urban education environment provides the most common battlefield on which this challenge is met and conquered by its teachers daily. The following are examples of the realities of urban school preservice and new teachers:

1. Preservice teachers often student teach in suburban schools, although the most available positions for novice, first-year teachers are in urban schools.

2. Preservice teachers generally do *not* have much experience with urban schools. Most did not attend urban schools. Many did not have the opportunity to student-teach in this type of educational environment.

3. First-year teachers are often placed in the most difficult urban schools with the most challenging students, while availed little or no support. This is one of critical reasons why most of them leave urban school employment within the first three years of teaching.

4. Preservice and novice teachers are unprepared for the vast sociocultural diversity of the children they encounter. They find themselves in need of much self-introspection and better knowledge of the children's backgrounds, learning circumstances, and learning strategies and styles.

5. New teachers often "blame the victims." They are also quickly acculturated into the worldview of their colleagues and the school—a culture that is unfortunately often one of negativity and hopelessness.

6. Most new teachers do not know much about their students' urban-based home/community, parents or guardians, and values of the culture that feeds the school. And many do not make an effort to learn this vital information (Haberman, 1995; Herrera, 2002; Irvine, 1999, 2003; Iverson, 2003; Jenkins, 2004; Langness, 1998).

In the urban environment, the school's culture and its expectations of the students will likely differ from what urban students intuitively know and think. Typically, the students' at-home culture, norms, beliefs, and traditions are vastly different from what they experience in the culture of the urban classroom. The transition of moving from the one setting (home and neighborhood) to another (school), can create student anxieties that are often manifested in inappropriate behavior or lack of interest in learning. In order to avoid this sort of cultural mismatch between the students' lives at home and at school, teachers in urban settings must attempt to gain familiarity with their students' families and at-home environments. This familiarity helps in placing faces with names, exchanging pleasantries and information, and constantly learning about the physical home environment. The insights gained are helpful in creating classroom conditions that are conducive to learning. Welcoming students to a classroom that features subtle relationships to the students' home environment eases them into a physically nonthreatening, learning environment. Students learn best in a pleasing and comfortable setting. Gaining knowledge of families' and students' homelives enhances the cultural match that will help teachers to know more about their students, as well as allowing them to offer familiar identities between home and school (Irvine, 2003). Chapter 3, which deals with the characteristics of urban schools, provides descriptive information about urban family and neighborhood conditions.

Establishing Relations between and among Home, School, and Community

Urban teachers can learn much about their students by understanding their family situations. This is important since cooperative support from parents is critical to engage parents in their childrens' education. Urban teachers who are effective demonstrate respect and dignity for the families they serve and encourage healthy family relations with the school. Engaging parents in volunteering at school, giving their time and attention to assist with classroom instruction or school or classroom projects, and accompanying classes on field trips, are examples of worthwhile parental involvement in the school.

Comfortable relations are apt to lessen parents' apprehensions about the school, and those relations also help to gain mutual respect and encourage dialogue necessary to establishing amicable, working partnerships between home and school. Effective communication practices (see Chapter 3) facilitate, support, and transmit the all-important messages that emphasize the importance of education to the lives and futures of urban school children. The building of partnerships and trusting relationships between and among the school, home, and community provide an effective template for communications that can significantly benefit urban learners (Irvine, 2003; Peterson and Hittie, 2003).

Undertaking the uniqueness of the urban school environment does not occur easily or quickly. The learning curve can be a difficult experience. Most of what urban teachers learn about the uniqueness of their professional assignments in urban settings is experienced through on-the-job training. Supervised student teaching in urban schools provides initial apprenticeship experience. Newly accredited teachers assigned to urban schools are often assigned informative, encouraging, and supportive mentors who are typically the more seasoned and knowledgeable teaching veterans with urban school experience. In addition, educators new to urban settings are provided population-specific workshops and seminars that offer vital, invaluable explanations and applicable urban classroom strategies to enhance instructional effectiveness. Allied assistance and support provided during student teaching with a dedicated mentor program helps maintain stability for teachers learning about their urban school and students during on-the-job training experiences. The help offered serves to guide appropriate pedagogical methods and should effectively minimize potential classroom problems (Haberman, 1995; Shaughnessy, 1999).

Most teachers in urban schools are White, monolingual females. Most self-profess their initial lack of preparation, or no preparation, to teach in the typical urban classroom (Chizhik, 2003). Without adequate preparation for teaching in urban classrooms, novice educators are likely to feel overwhelmed by the challenges they encounter that differ significantly from those experienced in other student population settings such as rural and suburban. In order for teachers to best prepare to work with the diverse learners typically found in the urban environment, it is important for them to develop a comfort level that allows them to build rapport with their students who are typically of diverse ethnic backgrounds and of low socioeconomic status. Prior teacher preparation field experiences in schools with urban children, or with urban students in out-of-school extra-curricular activities, is desirable. Effective urban educators find relationship-building interactions critical to gaining population-specific confidence. Coupled with and assisted by their own self-efficacy skills, a confident and easy comfort level with culturally and linguistically diverse students—who typically make up urban classroom demographics—greatly assists endeavors to work with students to help them meet grade-level objectives, goals, and expectations (Haberman, 1995).

Urban Teacher/Urban Student Bias or Prejudice

Keying in on strategies that prove to motivate their students to do their best work, effective urban teachers must accept and properly address cultural and linguistic diversity issues within their classrooms. From analyzing their own personal reflections, most will learn immensely about their own thought tendencies and biases toward students they teach or otherwise encounter in the urban school setting. Teachers new to the urban school should take the time to examine their own cultural backgrounds and attempt to understand what biases they each hold that may negatively impact their interactions with and understandings of their students.

In general, successful urban educators know themselves well and realize how their own cultural backgrounds and upbringing influence how they think and develop values. Due to teachers' differing cultural perceptions, it is prudent for them to acknowledge that their judgments of students, or reactions to student-related issues, may be biased. When urban teachers are aware of their own biases and thoughts from which their own ideas, beliefs, opinions, and understandings of others arise, they are much better equipped to help their students comprehend their individual or collective cultural or prejudicial biases (Irvine, 2003).

TEACHER CHARACTERISTICS

Teacher Understandings

Effective teachers in the urban school setting come to know, understand, and anticipate the array of student behaviors typically witnessed in the urban schools. These are not behaviors that can be expressed as "kids will be kids." As discussed previously, as teachers are made aware of the emotional baggage their students carry—observed more in urban schools than in others—they engage their perceptive skills to deal with resultant behaviors. For example, the teacher can provide a refreshed start to the school day, and thereby influence students to enter the learning climate void of outside-of-school problems. Another strategy would be to plan strategies to deliver varied instruction to capture student interest.

In order to successfully manage the multifaceted student academic and behavioral concerns that typically arise in urban school settings, teachers must acknowledge and take opportunities to better comprehend the students' world as it actually exists. To enable students in urban schools to function at their best, urban teachers must gain a comprehensive understanding of their students' hidden rules of conduct, many of which are culture-based, nonverbalized cues, thoughts, and/or habits. Teachers should respect and even celebrate the diversity of cultures, while weaving into their daily teaching the modeling of generally accepted rules of American societal norms, and at the same time allowing students to maintain their native cultural values and traditions. This well-meaning exposure, not meant to discount a students' native cultural mores, habits, or heritage, offers the students an opportunity to slowly gain respect for American norms while maintaining their cultural traditions. When students are allowed safe, in-class experimentation, they may develop an understanding and appreciation of the American culture in which they will live and ultimately work, and recognize that, in so doing, they are not required to abandon their native culture. Offering appropriate options, coupled with added support from school personnel, guidance from adult and peer mentors, and high expectations set for students, urban classroom teachers can positively impact their learners. That impact has the potential to lead students toward fulfillment of positive academic and life experiences and accomplishments (Payne, 1998, 2003).

Teachers need to be aware of hazardous and objectionable, or at best marginal, environmental conditions that are known to exist in highly populated urban communities. Damaging environmental problems include polluted air and drinking water, tainted soils, toxic paints on structures, and the like. Upon doctors' examinations, students may test positive to exposure to toxins (lead paint, harmful contaminants). Studies contend that these deplorable situations lead to disproportionate numbers of minority students who qualify for special education programs. In addition, other probable causes are likely: lack of proper medical care; poor prenatal and infant health and nutrition monitoring; the birth mother's addiction to drugs and/or alcohol while carrying the fetus; stressful and/or violent living conditions; little or no access to preschool programs; and/or severe, unattributed behavior problems (Irvine, 1999; Ormrod, 2003).

Unacceptable human circumstances are likely to come to the attention of teachers in urban environments. They are morally obligated to seek guidance and report any questionable or detrimental influence impacting their students. Urban teachers must take the lead, and as necessary voice their concerns on a student's behalf, to protect vulnerable youngsters from and deter adult-imposed or adult-influenced damage or harm. Classrooms must be designed as safe havens for the students—free of fear, tension, mistrust, or violence. Further, urban teachers should model peaceful problem-solving and curbing or offsetting displays of inappropriate, ineffective, or disturbing reactions amidst aggressive situations (Herrera, 2002; Irvine, 2003; Lindquist & Molnar, 1995).

Winning Features of Urban Teachers

Success in the urban classroom should be every teacher's goal. Undergraduate, preservice teacher education programs offer a substantial variety of courses that expose students to content, methods, and strategies helpful and necessary to know and practice in the classroom. Practice in the urban classroom greatly helps preservice teachers who expect to work with urban populations of learners. In addition, Haberman (1995) identifies seven features employed by teachers who excel in urban classroom settings.

Demonstrating Persistence.   Urban educators persist in their quests to locate, understand, and employ teaching methods that will engage all their students in the learning process. They do not accept the notion that their students are abnormal or in need of special assistance beyond that which they are possibly able to provide in the classroom.

They persist in their efforts to make the classroom interesting and engaging, striving to involve the students in all forms of learning. Further, they persist in their searches to find the best instruction for each student. Urban teachers continually reflect, by journaling, for example, to better apply the standards-based content, or knowledge that their students should acquire, and to enhance their abilities to provide the best instructional deliveries. They strive in their day-to-day efforts to get each student on par with high academic expectations, and in sync with a love of learning.

Sharing the Love of Learning.   Effective teachers prove to be excellent stewards or proficient managers of knowledge. They realize the importance of individuals receiving a valid education, and they typically exhibit an unending quest for learning. Likewise, effective urban teachers maintain ongoing interests that involve continued learning and sharpening of skills. Their endearment of and commitment to continued learning has an influence upon their students. For example, teachers may share with their students their interests in music or art or animal protection or learning about computers. When teachers demonstrate their desire for and enjoyment in varieties of learning, and similarly engage their students in means of active learning, the individual and collective motivation and zeal is indeed contagious.

Continuing the Desire to Learn.   Talented urban teachers practice and test learned philosophies, as well as practical and classroom-relevant strategies, directly benefiting their classes. They enthusiastically welcome new ideas that, when applied to their specific classroom practice, are likely to result in notable improvements in student learning and in students' achievement gains. Energized teachers are typically dissatisfied with stale or routine instructional approaches. They maintain a desire to know about the latest scientifically-proven teaching methods that they can apply with the objective of positively impacting their students' academic performance.

Learning Opens Doors to Possibilities and Opportunities.   Despite negative concerns often demonstrated by learners at risk of academic failure, effective urban teachers look to and incorporate ideas and implement proven strategies intended to better students' learning and their everyday lives. Responsible and caring urban teachers assume the responsibility of engaging their learners in grade-level content made relevant for students to use and understanding. Rather than point blame at the students' background or deplorable living conditions or cultural differences, these teachers take the initiative to keep *alive* their students' continued interests in learning. These teachers constantly encourage each student to continue his education. It is vital for urban students to understand the necessity of embracing new knowledge and skills that, ultimately, will enhance their ability to find meaningful employment and enjoy productive lives. Haberman (1995) asserts that "for the children and youth in poverty from diverse cultural backgrounds who attend urban schools, having effective teachers is a matter of life and death."

Student Respect.   Effective urban educators demonstrate care, respect, and concern not only for their students, but also for their professional colleagues and other adults. They realize, too, that they are responsible to teach those students who lack awareness or abilities to reciprocate those qualities. Many urban students, due to a myriad of possible reasons, have great difficulty or demonstrate no desire to exercise these values. Urban teachers must understand that, despite their very strong, affirmative compassion for their students, some students will likely express or exhibit their initial and continued dislike for the teacher, the instruction, the supervision, and the school, as a whole. Despite this unfortunate reality, above all else, astute urban teachers model respect for themselves, their students and families, and colleagues and other adults encountered during the school day. They continue to attempt to instill in and receive from all students genuine, deserved respect.

Positive Attitudes.   The typical school year in an urban setting can be a taxing event for teachers as they directly touch lives on a daily basis. The nature of the profession and its responsibilities affecting the lives of students necessitate that school personnel demonstrate and maintain supportive and positive attitudes in their daily service to the school and its constituents. Effective teachers in the urban setting learn how to remain emotionally buoyant in their chosen career. They strive to insulate themselves from the stresses of the job. They find that building and valuing relationships and collaborative time with like-minded educators, and networking with their colleagues, better enables them to maintain upbeat attitudes. Through teacher networks they share current information items and related successful classroom initiatives. Those who are fortunate to work within cooperative teaching teams learn about partnership instruction and access opportunities to resolve feelings of alienation or loneliness. It cannot be emphasized enough how important communication and collaboration with colleagues are in helping urban teachers learn how to excel and how to succeed in their chosen career. The networking, or connectedness, enables educators to gain better understandings of how the school's formal bureaucracy works, and ways to avoid its complications.

Acknowledging Imperfection.   Given the dynamics of the urban classroom, errors are inevitable. The classroom is an ecosystem of diverse interests, academic learning rates, learning styles, and maturity levels. It lends itself to continuous behavior interventions, trials, planning, and decisions (Kopetz, 2003). It is prudent for urban teachers to know, anticipate, and understand that amidst such a dynamic and changing environment of simultaneously occurring activities, errors in judgment are unavoidable. Urban classrooms should serve as safe grounds where—if and when they occur—errors are expected and accepted. What is important is an attitude that errors can be connected with understanding and patience. Teachers who demonstrate tolerance and acceptance of errors, self-made or otherwise, lead their students to acquire and display similar, nonaccusatory behaviors (Shaughnessy, 1999). Here again the teacher can, as the model, impact significantly how students choose to behave when faced with similar circumstances.

Attributes of Effective Urban Teachers

Some teachers excel in their profession, while others struggle to survive their school placements. It is reasonable to conclude that successful teaching entails qualities or attributes that help to explain the experiential differences. Given the variety of school populations, conditions, resources available, class sizes, personalities, school culture, community, and parental support, it is difficult to isolate a list of the model qualities or attributes that lead to success in teaching. No one type of teacher fits all classrooms. However, studies *do* suggest that there are powerful teacher attribute indicators that lead to success in the classroom.

On review and analysis of numerous empirical studies, Rice (2003) identified several key attributes of quality teachers. Those selected for study were teachers who demonstrated high-quality classroom instruction skills. Among the indicators of identified, effective teacher attributes were the teacher's experience, the teacher's preparation for the career, the teacher's coursework achievements, and the teacher's own test scores.

Teacher Experience. In the classroom, as the teacher's *learning by doing* experiences accumulate, the more effective the teacher becomes, as measured by evaluative observations and student achievement gains. Therefore, typically, the more classroom experience, the better able the educator is to meet standards-based, grade-level goals.

Teacher Preparation. The greater the academic and hands-on experiences learned in teacher preparation coursework, and its accompanying certifications, licensures, and advanced degrees, the stronger the students' academic achievements (especially in math and science at the secondary school levels). This means that when preservice teachers are exposed to and learn the strategies that best engage their students, academic goals are more likely to be met or exceeded.

Teacher Coursework. Instructional effectiveness occurs for teachers who are adept in both content knowledge and the accompanying pedagogical skills and strategies that aid in best instructional delivery practices. McCabe (2004) suggests that teachers are more likely to elicit considerable gains in student achievement when they have a comprehensive knowledge of the subject matter they teach. Further, their continued learning through additional college coursework of current, contemporary pedagogical practices demonstrates significant instructional improvements. Educators with a thorough understanding of teaching content, and the skill to package and teach the content, greatly benefit their students.

Teacher's Own Test Scores. Teachers who have demonstrated strong literacy achievement or superior verbal skills in their own assessment performances tend to garner demonstrated higher levels of achievement from their students. Therefore, teachers proving to be excellent readers and comprehenders of knowledge expect and are likely to bring to their students similar skill improvements and academic achievements (McCabe, 2004; Rice, 2003).

These effective teacher attributes can lead to strong student cooperation and student achievement, when linked with (1) fostering and nurturing the students' total development, (2) visiting with students' families (off-campus, in the community, or in the student's home), and (3) the practice of speaking Standard English in class and while on school grounds (Irvine, 2003; Payne, 1998; Shaughnessy, 1999).

Above all, urban teachers must have confidence in their ability to cause students to succeed. They must believe that all students *can* learn at high levels and they should offer students the atmosphere and structure in their classrooms that encourages their students to pursue lofty academic goals (Irvine, 2003; Izumi, 2002; Meyer, 1999).

The current impetus in educational reform includes engaging all students in schoolwork that is rigorous and intellectually challenging. It comes as no surprise that for some students, meeting learning goals will be difficult. However, urban school personnel should assume that they do not have to exempt struggling urban students from performance goals expected of them due to an unfortunate homelife, upbringing, or specific adverse circumstances. Teachers should abandon overanalysis of how various students' backgrounds prohibit learning from occurring and attitudes that justify students' poor achievement history. Years of research have concluded that schools have been, and continue to be, at fault for holding low expectations for students of color. Among features that matter most when considering student academic performance, according to Haycock (2001), is the setting and maintaining of higher academic standards for urban school children.

Educators in the urban school who find the greatest success from their instructional efforts are those who set their expectations for students to achieve; communicate well those expectations among all involved; and remain in step with students, with a *we're in this together* attitude, as they seek to meet academic standards and goals. A classroom thrives when it includes the following:

- meaningful assessments that offer valuable student data and information for better instruction;
- accountability, or teachers responsible for students' learning;
- better instruction that is varied, made relevant, and actively engages the students; and
- good teachers (Haycock, 2001) who make the greatest impact on and influence the students most powerfully.

Demonstrating Care and Concern for Students

Urban educators who teach with genuine interest in and concern for each of their students will likely reap tremendous benefits. Students are typically perceptive when adults demonstrate interest in their well-being. As with most human dynamics, when teachers demonstrate compassion for their students, not only do students want to please their teachers by attempting to fulfill the teacher's desires, but the overall classroom climate is likely to have an amicable and safe sense for the students. Such a setting is likely conducive to healthy academic, peer, and social acceptance, as well as relationship building. Additionally, effective urban teachers who really know and understand their students are less likely to take as personal affronts any uncharacteristic student behavior, outbursts, or other types of typically unacceptable classroom behaviors (Corbett & Wilson, 2002; Herrera, 2002).

Further, when teachers demonstrate respect for students' opinions and encourage their responses to real-life issues addressed in class discussions, they build into the classroom a constructive atmosphere that likely encourages students to participate. When students are encouraged to establish positive and personal relationships with their teachers who engage in safe and comfortable interactions with them, they are more likely to be motivated and extend themselves to pursue academic successes. Feel-good classroom relationships thus yield benefits for both students and their teachers.

Heron and Harris (2001) encourage that urban educators exercise culturally sensitive practices through instruction that observes important events that occur in various cultures. Their research emphasizes instruction that:

- incorporates resources from out-of-school experiences (e.g., home and community events);
- is built on students' strengths and interests;
- recognizes that language and dialect differences may result in differences in teacher and student interactions (Teachers must remain aware of these differences to correctly interpret interactions with their students.); and
- provides students with opportunities to learn and practice newly-acquired skills and concepts. (Heron & Harris, 2001, pp. 294–295)

The more urban teachers weave into the curriculum relevant cultural activities that encompass all learners, the greater the prospect for learning to take place.

Urban students' self-esteem is enhanced when they feel in control of their academic achievement. As they improve their academic successes, they develop greater confidence in themselves. The self-respect they gain in increased achievements creates within them a strong desire to learn. Likewise, students' poor performances in school negatively impact those students' psyche. Struggling through class assignments or continued academic failure results in lowered self-esteem. Failed attempts to achieve causes students frustration, and also leads to potential classroom disruptions and student discipline problems. Students who demonstrate patterns of poor academic performance are in immediate need of the teacher's attention (Izumi, 2002; Matus, 1999).

The student's desire to *continue* learning is linked to their self-esteem. When grades tumble and self-esteem heads downward and help is not offered, many urban students will elect to drop out of school prior to earning their high school diploma. Reasons for this may include the pressures of making adequate progress in schoolwork coupled with their receiving little or no academic support or encouragement from their parents or other family members. Many need to take jobs to support their family's needs, at the expense of pursuing their educational goals. Dropouts may lack adequate social skills and experience problematic peer relationships, distracting them from academic focus. Being constantly behind in school or faced with continued low grades is self-defeating, and students in frustration give up on hopes of surviving the academic climate of the school. Under the circumstances, they are likely to experience a major dislike for school. Also, deterring their quest to complete their education may be accumulated significant fears of the school environment itself, perceived—for reasons known only to them—as dangerous or threatening or restrictive or violent (Ormrod, 2003). Teachers should remain alert to and investigate these warning signs and attempt to help students overcome their issues to prevent them from leaving school for seemingly better ventures. Low-wage jobs, unlawful merchandise trading, and so forth can appear to be attractive alternatives when students experience constant frustration in school.

Students bring to the classroom their out-of-school literacy skills that help them to derive meaning from instruction. By relating to those skills the in-school instructional experience becomes real and vital to the students. This linkage, known as *applied learning*, between the institution and their life experiences are catalysts for them to achieve academic accomplishments. For example, students who love skateboarding and understand its accompanying motion and balance theories, along with knowledge about certain equipment pieces necessary for safety and agility, may read all they can find on the sport. In-class applications that incorporate the students' skateboarding knowledge may include freewriting compositions, or using its arena surfaces to apply mathematical or scientific principles, or observing spelling rules that relate to terms in the sport's jargon. Applying outside interests to classroom skills can serve as an excellent template for learning the necessary critical grade-level competency skills (Ben-Yosef, 2003).

Jenkins (2004) urges urban teachers to consider that, basically, all children are the same, except that they each reflect unique personalities and tastes. Typical urban schools represent extremely diverse student populations and cultures. Yet the students are similar in many ways while each brings individual uniqueness. When urban teachers can better recognize and appreciate those differences and variations, they can acquire and manage the effective strategies that lead to best teaching practices amidst the diverse urban school population and environment. Jenkins proclaims that urban educators gain success in their efforts when they exhibit the following qualities.

They:

- demonstrate high expectations
- promote education as a "cure-all"
- phone students' homes, as needed or necessary
- *lead* the class (as opposed to *following*)
- refrain at all costs from excusing students' failures
- pose a teacher-unified pledge to educate their students
- exercise patience for student (incremental) successes
- drop "endless discussions" concerning racial issues
- as White teachers, avoid instructional time devoted to attempts to convince students of their (the teacher's) nonracist stance
- operate as one's natural self (versus pretending to be someone else)

Jenkins' list presents several major elements—essentially, teachers must hold high expectations for their students' academic performance, and they must do so with an air of confidence and leadership, while respecting each child's culture in a sincere and open fashion.

STRATEGIES FOR URBAN CLASSROOMS

Varied Instruction

It is important for all teachers to learn about and implement varieties of instructional deliveries in their classrooms. Routine and predictable content presentation can be boring to students, and teachers' creativity suffers. Teaching methods and strategies range on a continuum between *teacher-centered* instruction and *student-centered* instruction. Those that are teacher-centered focus on teachers as the sources and transmitters of knowledge. Where research has proven these methods sound, extremes of the practice demonstrate that too much teacher-dominated instruction tends to inhibit students, and likely lessens their learning enthusiasm and potential to achieve. Alternatively, student-centered methods of instruction tend to encourage students as curious and eager seekers of knowledge. They receive guidance and encouragement from their teachers for their fact-finding efforts; and they are motivated to seek further enhancements and to pursue self-directed, learning quests (Izumi, 2002).

Effective urban teachers develop techniques, often by trial and error, to generate students' interest in lessons and motivation for lifelong learning. They can significantly influence and encourage students' desires to acquire knowledge, and they are mindful to ensure that they experience success in their inquisitiveness to learn. Further, students understand lessons when they are actively engaged in discussion, they can reflect upon and explain what they are learning, and model what they understand of the lesson. Educators who encourage student learning and achievement can expect positive academic performances from their students (Barth, 2003; Burden, 2003; Corbett & Wilson, 2002; Herrera, 2002).

Offering students various instructional strategies benefits students in many ways. Burden (2003) indicates that teachers who vary instruction will:

- challenge students' thinking and performance abilities by nudging their learning beyond their comfort zones;
- group students in structured fashion, mixing students frequently, and assigning students to groups with careful attention to culture and gender balance;
- differentiate assignments by altering length and difficulty or adding enhancements;
- individualize study by accommodating students' individual learning styles and encouraging creativity and problem-solving skills;
- involve all students in class activities;
- allow students to try different types of activities by challenging students' thinking and understanding;
- use authentic and culturally relevant instruction learning, which should build on previously learned concepts and should make sense to the learners; and
- assess fairly by using varieties of evaluation methods. (Burden, 2003)

Implementing instructional strategies is greatly enhanced when teachers consider added features that keep students involved in their learning. With careful balance for what they incorporate and present in varied instructional designs, teachers of diverse student populations are encouraged to consider these strategies:

- use visuals, such as overhead slides, PowerPoint displays, etc.
- incorporate groupwork
- involve parents
- build on what students have already learned and know
- supplement instruction with lecture outlines for students to follow
- make instruction relevant for students (Ingersoll, 1996; Irvine, 2003)

Excellent Teacher Strategies

Six strategies implemented in best teacher practices include:

1. communicating expectations and followup;
2. keeping the classroom under control;
3. assisting students in need of help;
4. clearly explaining assignments;
5. maintaining content and performance expectations; and
6. varying classroom activities.

Communicating Expectations and Followup.   Students feel secure in knowing their physical and behavioral boundaries in classrooms. Consider the following.

1. overall sound, classroom management practices;
2. communicating academic performance expectations and behavior expectations;
3. appropriate language usage; and
4. individual and group assignment fulfillment.

These expectations, instilled early, establish a climate of expectation for the school year. Teachers set the stage by being clear about expectations for students. It is helpful to students when teachers clearly define with consistency *what* assignments (products) are expected, as well as *when* they are due. Good communication further requires that teachers remain consistent in their grading and recording promptly each student's submission, as well as offering feedback to students regarding the satisfaction of their work. Important also is feedback that indicates how students can improve, with suggested skill-building exercises (Barth, 2003; Burden, 2003; Corbett & Wilson, 2002; Herrera, 2002).

Keeping the Classroom under Control.   With practiced consistency in implementing their classroom management rules and procedures (described in Chapter 6, "Classroom Management in the Urban Setting"), teachers should exercise measures that eliminate distractions, thus helping students to focus on their learning objectives. Teachers realize that when verbally disciplining those who refuse to comply with classroom rules, engaged learners are distracted from accomplishing the tasks at hand, and some may not return to their previous focus. Maintaining a safe and active learning environment requires the mind-set that students are considerate of their peers and of each others' learning efforts (Corbett & Wilson, 2002).

Assisting Students in Need of Help.   If unchallenged academically, students find school uninteresting. Where urban students are concerned, teachers especially should not allow their interest to wane. Students can learn and achieve at higher levels when instruction is pitched at those higher levels. Arguably, some students require greater assistance and/or compensatory, or remedial, instruction more than others. Effective urban teachers expect maximum academic efforts and cooperation from students. They understand, too, that not all of their students will learn at the same rate. Some students will excel at a rapid pace and will need supplemental enhancement activities, as opposed to some who will need additional time and assistance on particular concepts and skills to keep pace with the class and with expected proficiency in reaching grade-level objectives. When teachers provide needed assistance to all types of diverse learners, they send the message that they are interested in each student, that they support her learning, and that they embrace the opportunity to further engage and challenge students' thinking processes (Barth, 2003; Burden, 2003).

Assessing students' needs and progress should be an ongoing, daily procedure (discussed in greater depth in Chapter 8: "Assessment and Evaluation").

The continual assessment of what is being learned, and what requires more understanding, informs teachers of specific student grasps of learning objectives and needs regarding those objectives. When further clarification and help is needed, teachers must first consider *how* they offer the help and *when* to provide that needed assistance. The academic help may occur during optimal times of the day, such as during classtime, or before and/or after school, or on weekends, or during the summer months. Specific help can be offered during free periods of the school day, at recess, or at student-chosen periods of the school day. It is often necessary to increase more instructional time during the school day for low-performing students to assist them to gain needed academic skills. While some students respond best to help that is offered individually, others may be more receptive to support offered in small groups, and still others may benefit greatly from assistance provided by peer tutors (Corbett & Wilson, 2002; Haycock, 2003). Varied combinations of instructional assistance is highly recommended to meet the diversity of student needs.

Students report that teachers who demonstrate the most patience and offer extra assistance on a regular basis provide the best classroom experiences for students needing the special support. Students want their teachers to help them become successful achievers in school. In turn, students should be encouraged to identify and set goals for their own improvement, and teachers should stand ready to support them to learn strategies that lead to their successful achievement of individual goals (Heron & Harris, 2001).

Clearly Explaining Assignments, Content, and Expectations.   In order for teachers to communicate their expectations to students successfully, they must first gain students' attention. When students are attentive to messages, they are able to satisfactorily respond. Students need to hear, through a teacher's vocalized instructions, and see, through visuals, what the teacher expects of them. For example, a teacher may ask, "Is anyone unclear about this assignment?" If there is no response, the teacher may assume the students clearly know what to do to complete the assignment. A better question might be, "Who will explain or repeat the instructions for this assignment?"

Urban teachers should indicate that they expect the best efforts from their students. They should make all attempts, verbal and visual, necessary at the beginning of announced instructions to ensure that all students understand what is expected of them, prior to moving on to added expectations. For assignment completion, students should demonstrate proof to their teachers that they know what is expected, and when it is to be completed and submitted, to ensure full-circle communication (Corbett & Wilson, 2002; Herrera, 2002). Explicitly verbalizing and demonstrating an accurate description of the acceptable, finished product is a most important first step.

Further, assignments are often best communicated when they are presented in step-by-step increments. Teachers sometimes refer to this strategy as *chunking*. Visual illustrations or examples should define the look of what is expected, as opposed to that which is clearly unacceptable. As the assignment is articulated, teachers should exercise patience in providing repeated explanations or providing needed clarifications prior to releasing the students to begin their work. As indicated earlier, students may be called upon in class to retell given instructions or provide answers to peers' requests for further clarification. Care should be taken to avoid embarrassment or controversy (Corbett & Wilson, 2002). When expectations are clear and understood by students at the onset of the learning activity, both students and teachers save time and frustration and learning is enhanced.

Varying Classroom Activities.   Breaking out of routine instructional deliveries, such as teachers lecturing or dictating, or all classmates working in their seats on the same assignment at the same time, keeps the learning environment fresh. Students enjoy and benefit greatly from class activities that are arranged in numerous and flexible modes (for example, whole class, small groups, teams, individually, and so on). Teachers should involve students in varying activities such as general class discussions, special task completion per group, active engagement in hands-on assignments, games, role playing, computer tasks, simulations, and interviews (Corbett & Wilson, 2002). While still observing schedules, such as transitions to special classes and breaks throughout the day, students enjoy and benefit from new and different approaches to learning.

In most classrooms, teachers find wide variations in students' learning aptitudes and capabilities. Thus, presenting information in diverse ways will likely impact and reach most or all students in the class. Recent studies of students who were interviewed to identify their learning preferences regarding in-class instructional activities indicate that they prefer more personal involvement, or active learning, and less teacher-lecture formats, or passive learning. High on their learning style preferences were performing skits about controversial, or noncontroversial but interesting, topics; and opportunities for students to explore their feelings on various subjects via written reflections or arguments (Heron & Harris, 2001; Herrera, 2002). Creative weaving of relevant topics with grade-level state standards and academic expectations can easily hook students into the learning process (Williams & Woods, 1997).

Incorporating the Students' Out-of-School Experiences.   In all schools, students have opportunities to grow and develop through their interactions with the formal academic curriculum, as well as the norms, rules, values, and other aspects intertwined in school culture. Outside of school, they undertake daily life activities that, when recognized and then incorporated positively into the academic arena, create promising learning experiences for students. For example, outside-of-school experiences may include student-related events or issues, objects, people, and concerns that engage and excite students when their experiences are linked to instruction.

Further, in order for urban students to successfully connect their outside experiences with their learning, research findings strongly encourage teachers to identify, investigate, value, and incorporate students' experiences.

WAYS TO BETTER PRACTICE

Establishing the Classroom Environment

Classroom settings should reflect feelings of warmth and safety, and should be welcoming to students and guests. They should be protected environments where students demonstrate pride in their learning, in their relationships, and in their achievements. Regular, comfortable, and nonthreatening student and teacher exchanges and interactions occur frequently. An amenable climate is anchored by teachers who initiate and maintain trusting kindred with their students. The establishment of positive relationships offers a classroom climate that is robust, collegial, and class participatory, which is healthy and results in academic success. Schools where classrooms are safe and exciting places to learn offer venues for students to freely express and exchange ideas and opinions. Physical signs are apparent in urban classrooms that show students accept and enjoy participating and learning. When one visits these classrooms, energized students are often observed actively engaged in constructive learning activities, with obvious commitment to the task at hand (Damian & Herrera, 2002; Forte & Schurr, 2002; Herrera, 2002).

Urban teachers find great success when their classrooms take on a student-centered learning atmosphere. When this learning approach works best, there exists a viable trust factor between teacher and student and the instructional culture is primed for successful independent and group scholarship. To best create and maintain this type of classroom environment, teachers should implement strategies provided in Figure 4.1.

Effective student-centered learning, to any degree, is thoughtfully crafted and always monitored by the teacher. When successfully implemented and directed, it is arguably one of the best teaching strategies that effectively engages students in the learning process. Successful urban teachers endeavor to maintain with their students, from the beginning of the school year, mutual relationships of honesty and trust. They encourage students' confidence that they can learn and achieve academic goals. These teachers involve all students in active participation and engagement through discussions, hands-on tasks, and learning activities. Mostly they hold students responsible for meeting academic goals that are challenging and meet or exceed grade-level performance standards, which creates for students a secure and organized classroom environment (Forte & Schurr, 2002, Herrera, 2002).

Finally, teachers activate the student-centered philosophy when they develop and support a schoolwide effort that encourages each and every professional

1. Become aware of each student's unique needs, characteristics, and interests.

2. Balance academic goals with affective goals that underscore students' emotional health and focus holistically on their cognitive development.

3. Emphasize active learning experiences over passive learning experiences in teaching academic content and skills.

4. Encourage high levels of in-class interventions, using specific initiatives that:
   - arrange for special situations whereby students get better acquainted with each other and form new friendships;
   - diminish the existence of physical, language, or social obstructions;
   - encourage student participation in extracurricular activities;
   - emphasize the need for nondisabled students to understand and appreciate students with special needs;
   - provide guidance to those with bad reputations to change for the better and make improved choices; and
   - set a classroom environment of mutual respect for all individuals (Ormrod, 2003).

5. Promote and incorporate into the curriculum exploratory programs that include, for example, student service clubs and special interest activities (e.g., Scouting, 4-H, Junior Achievement, drama, or band) and other field and community experiences.

6. Openly exhibit in the classroom various items such as posters and notable quotations that promote antiviolence, anticrime, and antidrugs programs.

7. Foster among students a collaborative mind-set in which each classmate exerts his or her best effort and assists others to reciprocate. Discourage the competitive mind-set in which each classmate strives to outdo others by any means possible, regardless of others' abilities or performances.

8. Provide for cultural differences and differences in learning styles within the typical learning environment through careful and individualized instructional planning.

9. Maintain high expectations for all students among all cultures and of all ability levels.

10. Instill and effectively maintain an atmosphere that emphasizes health, safety, and wellness. (Forte & Schurr, 2002; Irvine, 2003).

FIGURE 4.1   Strategies for Establishing a Student-Centered Learning Atmosphere

working in the school to guide and counsel, as called upon and as necessary, all students in the school. This plan allows educators, as student advocates and advisors, to maintain genuine adult–student interactions and mutual strong, academic, and humanistic relationships. All school professionals, while vigorously supporting standards-based, grade-level expectations that show students' best academic efforts, must value and attend to students' development of sound social/emotional health. Such schoolwide compassion that permeates the structured learning environment as a whole builds a solid and comprehensive learning community (Forte & Schurr, 2002; Ormrod, 2003).

Fostering a Comprehensive Learning Community

Urban educators must take the responsibility to emphasize the importance and necessity of students getting along with one another, accepting each others' differences, and collaboratively working together. When teachers in the urban setting insist that students uphold and practice these virtues, they significantly influence the whole child and the affective domain. Affective education incorporates skills that support students' ethical and character development. By doing so teachers recognize that each child has a unique learning style and they engage in dedicated efforts to meet the students' individual needs and respective learning preferences (Steinberg, 1998). Further, a significant outcome of this thinking and attitude is that it positively contributes to the traditional three Rs—Reading, wRiting, and aRithmetic—by ardently supporting a fourth R: Relationships (Forte & Schurr, 2002).

Urban educators support the learning community as an inclusive, positive network among the school's student and professional personnel. Relationship building of the whole person includes helping students develop positive attitudes, strong self-esteem, supportive emotional and social adjustment, and healthy personal beliefs. Like the so-called character education programs that schools frequently add into their curricula, all teachers strive to enhance interpersonal relationships and strengthen the development of their students' social, emotional, physical, intellectual, psychological, and ethical thought processes. Urban teachers wisely and judiciously agree to confront and discuss moral and value issues and not leave these deliberations to chance. Successful urban learning communities exercise academic freedom and license to address even the most controversial issues relative to their students' daily life concerns (Forte & Schurr, 2002; Morrell, 2002).

Effective urban teachers support a positive learning community in their discussions and modeling of democratic and moral ideals. They promote respect for others, equality and justice for all individuals, the proper regard for and appreciation of others' views, and humane treatment of living creatures. They are open to discuss with students why some behaviors are not acceptable, why such behaviors and activities such as immorality, cheating, stealing, dishonesty, and harsh conflicts are inappropriate. They encourage students to be aware and considerate of others' feelings and others' emotional states. They validate the admirable characteristics of heroes and leaders, and relate those to student qualities that should be emulated. Further, the teachers solicit and support their students' participation in community service activities and volunteer functions that, in turn, inspire students' involvement in rewarding life opportunities (Ormrod, 2003).

Within cooperative classroom structures, effective urban teachers create learning environments that offer successful academic experiences for their students. As they work interdependently, student assignments and test score performances improve, along with their motivation levels and enjoyment in the education process. Because such an environment reduces competition, distrust, and stereotyping among its students, this established learning environment proves dramatic and powerful gains in urban students' grades, test scores, and engagement in learning (Aronson, 2004).

The ideal concept of the urban school evolving as a learning community empowers its students and school personnel with a feeling of unity, as well as feelings of shared responsibility and respect for one another. Due to the large bureaucracies that often operate urban schools, the school environment may likely feel impersonal. Successful urban teachers seek out collegial support by keeping open the lines of communication with other school faculty, staff, and administrators. They should, as frequently as necessary, inform their school administrators of any pressing or unfulfilled academic or collaborative need, requests for desired teacher mentorships, or suggestions for specialized training. Additional concerns may involve the need for further dialogue, for example, if the class sizes are too large or difficult to manage, or problems with textbook and supply shortages (Matus, 1999). Entire schools working toward goals that benefit everyone in the learning community provide an optimum, positive culture that nurtures all who positively participate.

Teaching in the Multicultural Environment

One of the major contemporary issues in education today is the initiative to address multicultural perspectives and equity in school systems nationwide. In the United States, most students in urban schools represent several diverse racial, cultural, and linguistic minority groups (Chizhik, 2003; Irvine, 2003).

No *one* universal teaching strategy will successfully prove applicable to all urban classrooms, in which a host of students with diverse cultural backgrounds and differences are found. Haberman (1995) proclaims, "It is not possible to take what [effective urban teachers] do, and create '*10 Easy Steps*' for all teachers to follow" (p. 21). Thus, to emphasize this one-size-fits-none theory, the urban classroom teacher should determine strategies that work best and suit his or her respective personality and makeup by experimenting with a variety of research-based and proven multicultural approaches that celebrate all urban learners. Effective, urban teachers enthusiastically collaborate with their peers schoolwide to share what they experience as successful strategies and techniques that best establish positive and supportive multicultural environments (Gordon, 2005). With that goal in mind, it must be emphasized that networking—teachers collaborating with other education professionals—is an important means for learning about and remaining contemporary with effective current practices that enhance learning opportunities among students of diverse home lives and cultures.

Young (2000) offers multicultural teaching strategies that prove successful in the urban classroom of diverse learners, and center on the following aspects:

1. First and foremost, teachers maintain and communicate their belief that all students can succeed. The multiculturally enhanced classroom is one where all students feel valued and capable of reaching the teacher's high expectations.

2. Teachers *scaffold*, offering needed assistance to help students learn about various cultures represented in the school, and value students' personal heritage and pride in their respective cultural backgrounds. Helping students to develop pride in their cultures results in students developing positive self-esteem and building a positive relationship with the school that should help to curb discipline problems and enhance an atmosphere conducive to learning.

3. What teachers know about child and adolescent development, in general, will influence their expectations for their students. The urban student population represents diverse socioeconomic circumstances, varied languages spoken in the home, and wide-ranging cultural backgrounds and practices. When urban teachers understand the many dynamics that affect their students, they are better equipped to consider individual needs and strengths that factor in establishing everyday student expectations.

4. Teaching strategies for culturally diverse ethnic- and language-minority students must emphasize that students gain meaning from and practical application of knowledge learned. Effective urban teachers create for their students opportunities to use, manipulate, and extrapolate from information the concepts that maximize their understanding classroom information.

5. Assessments that entail multiple informal and formal measurements of grade-level objectives should be recorded daily by way of logging observations, scores on quizzes, test grades, performance-based evaluations, rubric or grading scale or checklist results, and portfolio activity. Sharing assessment information with students will help them understand academic areas in need of improvement.

6. Finally, parent input and involvement serves to greatly enhance the multicultural classroom. Teachers must work to get better acquainted with their students' communities and their cultures (Young, 2000). Parent participation and their ongoing support of activities that teach cultural customs and styles of dress, varieties of food preparations, heroes and celebrated accomplishments of their societies, and so on, better inform teachers of ethnic and cultural differences. Teachers can help to create students' awareness, appreciation, and respect for the contributions diverse cultures make in society.

OVERALL INSTRUCTIONAL QUALITY

The nationwide legislative initiative known as the No Child Left Behind Act has established momentum to offer heightened quality classroom instruction in all schools for all students. To close the achievement gap between the higher academic performers (often White students) and lower academic performers (mostly lower-socioeconomic students and students of color), students in urban classrooms need elevated challenges and strong support (Haycock, 2003). Students agree that the quality of their school experiences depends on good teaching. In interviews of nearly four hundred students from low-income, urban schools, Corbett and Wilson (2002) recorded results that indicate six commonly identified student descriptors of the best teachers who provide sound instructional practices. The students observed characterized "superior" instructors as those who instituted in their overall high-quality professional mission instructional techniques that include:

1. Consistently hold and enforce expectations that students complete their work.
2. Effectivly manage the classroom.
3. Availabile to assist any student in need of help.
4. Offer to clearly explain content and subsequent assignments.
5. Provide varied classroom activities.
6. Demonstrate caring by getting to know students.

Incorporating such techniques as a mainstay in teachers' instructional repertoires greatly benefits or ensures success in urban classrooms.

Effective Instructional Delivery Choices

A continuing theme in this chapter is the notion that teachers must continue to support a positive learning community with emphasis upon keeping the urban classroom fresh and alive with students engaged in the learning process. This translates into the need to utilize varieties of instructional approaches. Some strategies that prove to successfully accommodate learners in urban schools are models that include:

> guided inquiry-based learning
>
> constructivist teaching
>
> direct instruction
>
> cooperative learning
>
> holistic instruction

A brief explanation of each instructional delivery method follows.

Guided Inquiry-Based Learning.   Students gain a greater sense of control of their learning when they immerse themselves in teacher-designed, guided, inquiry-based learning. This *active* instructional approach to learning opposes *passive* instruction that is typically initiated when teachers present facts, figures, and concept descriptions in a sage-on-the-stage instructional format. Inquiry-based learning is a superior method, as it requires that students, as determined and purposeful agents in the learning process, build their learning (Heron, 2003).

As they pursue projects that teachers design to support learning objectives related to topics that are of interest to them, urban school students find that guided inquiry-based learning offers them opportunities to make choices of what they will investigate, research, and report. On some days or on some projects, students may work alone, with one or two classmates, or with a small project team. They may elect getting involved in community activities, participating in field trip adventures, and inviting guest speakers to class. As a summary of their efforts, students take great pride in participating in opportunities to present findings and discoveries to audiences of peers, school personnel, parents, and community members (Hartman, DeCiccio, & Griffin, 1994). Local media welcome innovative student projects that express to native and regional citizenry that education is fun, interesting, exciting, and rewarding.

Further, to ensure student success in the guided inquiry-based teaching strategy, Hartman, DeCiccio, and Griffin (1994) recommend that teachers accept and consider the following seven principles that can lead to optimum student learning in the urban classroom.

1. Regard all class members as capable of learning to high expectations.
2. Allow for students to grasp in-depth, relative concepts to strengthen their gained knowledge.
3. Learning is accelerated when students collaborate on projects with peers.
4. Students, although at times lacking in certain basic skills, possess developmental abilities of critical thinking.
5. When learning is integrated among varied subject areas or disciplines, the knowledge gained is more meaningful.
6. Students are able to demonstrate enhanced efforts when adults continue to hold their best interests in mind.
7. Families and community members are indispensable in the learning process. (Hartman et al., 1994)

Guided inquiry-based learning benefits not only the students, but their teachers as well. Students strengthen their teamwork and peer relationships while developing their projects, and tend to depend to a great extent on each other for guidance and information. As a result, teachers find themselves better able to devote time among all working groups, facilitating and stimulating students' and groups' efforts, and assisting where needed. Also, fewer off-task behaviors result, due to the students' focused interest and engagement in their tasks. All students gain when their enthusiasm proliferates during student-discovered, hands-on, active learning lessons (Pisauro, 2002).

Inquiry-based learning can improve social acceptance and tolerance of personality differences among peers. The students' participation in group research and presentations creates a dynamic interplay between students as they experience conflict management, accept individual and group responsibility, and recognize the need for proven diligence and work ethic. Also, this instructional delivery encourages students' creative expression and their efforts represent and display varieties of academic and emotional strengths. Students make significant cognitive gains as they become experts in their studies and their research skills cross over to practice and learning in other academic disciplines. Students learn the importance of and benefits to persistence, which will aid in learning additional concepts and skills. As students become more engaged in their inquiry projects, often their families become involved. Teachers' roles thus change from information providers to lead and resource facilitators (Hartman, DeCiccio, & Griffin, 1994; Kopetz, 2003; Pisauro, 2002).

Constructivist Teaching.   Theorists such as Jean Piaget, Lev Vygotsky, and John Dewey proposed that learning occurs when new information acquires real meaning and significance for students. As students learn, they create (construct) their own meaning and understanding from resources and stimuli presented in their classrooms. According to the constructivist viewpoint, learning occurs when students link new knowledge with their current knowledge and what they understand to be true. As students' innate and conditioned (learned) capabilities interact with the immediate environment, they are constructing, and thereby acquiring, their knowledge. Constructivist teaching involves instructional delivery that connects new information to already-learned information. It is critical to urban teachers that they strive to introduce new ideas and concepts as they relate new content to previously learned information (Williams & Woods, 1997). This teaching model focuses on stimulating the student's cognitive, or thinking, abilities. Activities teachers design can improve students' memory, discrimination, language, concept formation, self-evaluation, problem solving, and overall comprehension (Smith et al., 2004).

Direct Instruction.   Another excellent teaching approach that urban educators find successful, especially when combined with other strategies, is direct instruction. Direct instruction involves task analyses that break apart into manageable, sequential lessons information that continues to build greater knowledge and comprehension of the standards-based content. Research supports its effectiveness to enable urban school students to meet high-performance academic goals and greatly improve their learning. As this type of pedagogy has historically proven successful in teaching basic skills, its format encourages and assists students to build initial cognitive structures for learning such as subject vocabulary, organization of events and occurrences, and connective concepts (Burden, 2003).

Direct instruction, as in the Open Court Series (a popular published reading program), establishes an easy to follow, scripted curriculum that guides teachers with carefully designed lesson plans that entail specific knowledge and cover well-defined skills. Correctly implemented, the direct instruction method engages students in lessons that include the following:

- logically sequenced information steps
- practice exercises that follow each information step
- teacher instructions for monitoring and assessing student skill acquisition
- teacher suggestions that provide students' immediate feedback
- frequent tests that monitor ongoing student progress

Used in conjunction with other teaching methods, direct instruction in the urban classroom provides the structure and disciplined approach that may prove best in academic areas, such as reading, math, and science. It clearly defines grade-level standards for students, and ensures that all teachers at the same grade levels are utilizing similar information at a relatively similar pace. The instruction tolerates few teaching variances such as revising the pace, resequencing stories or topics, and so forth, and keeps lessons focused and on target. It encourages teacher creativity that enhances skills and concepts, making them more realistic and relevant to learners. There are drawbacks to *too much* direct instruction, however. In following scripted lessons, teachers may be overly informing students of specific knowledge, as they present a more passive—rather than active—role in the learning process. Thus, combining direct instruction strategies with other more active instructional approaches that allow learners to discover or acquire the knowledge for themselves seems the most efficient overall pedagogy (Izumi, 2002).

Cooperative Learning.   Keeping the urban classroom of students of diverse backgrounds comfortable, challenged, and motivated, in a positively charged learning climate, can be achieved when cooperative learning activities are carefully planned, implemented, and managed by the teacher. A valuable strategy for use in urban school classrooms, cooperative learning involves student participation in structured activities that acknowledge each students' interests and ideas. During its process, teachers and students get better acquainted with one another, as they learn and problem solve together in prearranged student groups. As group participants collectively work through solving problems and assembling information that meets established lesson objectives, there is verbal interaction among them. Student perceptions of held differences begin to dissipate when ideas from each participant are unique and deserving of respect. This serves to enrich overall learning. As an active learning method of instruction, incorporating hands-on activities, for example, the direct experiences offered in cooperative learning activities can bring relevance and meaning to new knowledge and related concepts to further students' understanding of information they are required to learn to meet standards-based objectives (Ciani, 2002; Damian & Herrera, 2002).

Compared to competitive and individualistic learning, Iverson (2003) identifies research that credits cooperative learning as a superior instructional method that fosters in students greater efforts to achieve, positive interpersonal relationships, and greater psychological health. She points out that through cooperative learning, group work entails varieties of projects where students benefit in brainstorming ideas and in learning complex bodies of information. Well-organized learning activities yield group projects that are much more comprehensive than any one member can create, given the same amount of time (Iverson, 2003; Langness, 1998). Hence, for its proven benefits, cooperative learning is a method deserving of frequent use in urban classrooms.

Educators often cite that the essence of cooperative learning is positive interdependence—the student mentality that "We are all in this together." Educators also know that there are additional essential components of cooperative learning:

- individual accountability
- face-to-face interaction
- social skills
- processing group effectiveness (Iverson, 2003, p. 181)

In cooperative learning, structured tasks can be arranged among groups that encourage and require active participation and input from all students, especially the more quiet or the less-appreciated classmates. Cooperative learning techniques prove not only successful in urban classrooms with diverse learners, but also the applied strategy changes attitudes of nondisabled peers positively toward peers who have special learning needs. Creating a powerful and enthusiastic learning environment, this instructional method ranks among the best (Burden, 2003; Young, 2000).

Holistic Instruction.   Beyond test score accountability and quantitative measures of student achievement is the mission of schools to appreciate and encourage in young people positive moral, emotional, physical, and psychological development. Effective urban classroom teachers demonstrate this holistic concern for their students, not only for their learning and academic successes, but also for assessing and helping students' emotional readiness to learn. Skills introduced emphasize broad-spectrum and authentic, real world topics and associations that provide a meaningful basis to meet diverse student needs and interests. This integrated approach to learning directly engages students with their environment, encourages a love of learning, and nurtures in students a sense of wonder. The methodology was established by educator Maria Montessori in her mid-twentieth century teaching practice. Holistic learning engages students in multiple patterns of learning. There is no one best way of instruction, but many paths of learning that recognize each student's diverse, individual learning style (Irvine, 2003; Miller, 2004; Smith et al., 2004).

Holistic instructional methods may be implemented in particular classrooms, grade levels, or in an entire school. The Cincinnati public schools, a large urban school district, created an experimental holistic school program called "Project Succeed Academy" (PSA). These efforts proposed to raise students' academic success by making learning more meaningful and instilling in students motivation and the will to actively participate in their learning. With the support of public and private funding, PSA was established with a holistic education philosophy design to include collaborative initiatives between and among families, children, schools, and the community. The holistic philosophy was undertaken by faculty and administrators who considered and accepted the mostly unfortunate conditions each child faced, as well as the impoverished environment where most of the children lived. Researchers evaluating the results of the PSA program noted that, following the family, school is the major component in the context of the urban children's lives. The holistic education concept implemented the program's major components:

1. students' physical and mental well-being;
2. students' academic success; and
3. socialization.

Results of this experimental school program yielded in its first year significant drops in student school suspensions (dropping 23 percent) and expulsions (dropping 12 percent); attendance held steady at 96 percent—uncharacteristically high; and following the two-year study, student promotion rates averaged 89 percent (Brown, 2004). These encouraging results infer that when a holistic education philosophy brings such success, as adopted and implemented in an entire urban school district, holism can achieve equally positive results when likewise adopted and implemented in an urban classroom.

Lesson Infusion.   The lesson infusion process helps incorporate students' out-of-school experiences into teachers' lesson plans and instructional activities (Williams & Woods, 1997). To begin, the teacher will need to review the subject material to be taught, and determine how and in what ways the information can be presented in class as meaningful, interesting, and relevant to the students. In the next step, the teacher connects and weaves those ideas with the subject material, or standards-based curriculum content, thus making the information relevant to urban learners. Finding connections between nonschool literature—trade or pop magazine, song lyrics, Internet chat rooms, comics—and those required by schools—textbooks, computer-based instruction programs, lesson supplements—can be a challenging yet worthwhile endeavor. When readings incorporate experiences of current and nonschool-based examples, urban youth and their teachers together are participating in valuable learning experiences. Third, the teacher designs the lesson to begin with the high-interest connections and build with additional objective-based activities to which the students can re-late. This infusion of examples that enliven concepts and make the learning rel-evant and meaningful thus engages urban learners as part of the curriculum. Finally, the teacher reflects and notes at the end of the lessons or activities new insights and considerations for changes in future lesson plans designed to teach similar content. Infusing student experiences and interests into classroom in-struction gives the learning purpose and meaning in students' daily lives. This type of instruction demystifies the process of learning, and creates knowledge gains. Additionally, teachers discover and contemplate new and improved ideas for student practice in research and problem-solving skills (Morrell, 2002; Williams & Woods, 1997).

SUMMARY

Effective urban teachers must acknowledge the differences among their students without denying the richness offered by their communities. They must help stu-dents explore educational curriculum in safe, respectful school/classroom envi-ronments that strive to integrate new ideas in ways that make sense to their learners. Teachers must exhibit a basic humane and caring teaching ideology. The practical teaching behaviors they learn, exhibit, and apply must be built on the foundation of the teacher's genuine belief system. Urban teachers' dedication to causing children to achieve at high levels, along with a determined philosophy that all students can learn and meet established academic and behavior expecta-tions, can be highly successful. Teachers in urban schools throughout the nation have proven this to be true. Teaching in urban schools can be extremely chal-lenging; teachers can meet this challenge when they maintain an understanding and loving attitude toward their students and when they apply culture teaching methods in their daily classroom activities:

> Poor and minority children depend on their teachers like no others. In the hands of our best teachers, the effects of poverty and institutional racism melt away, allow-ing these students to soar to the same heights as young Americans from non-disadvantaged homes. (Haycock, 1998, p. 11)

CHAPTER QUESTIONS

1. Why are teachers so important in the lives of their urban learners?

2. Identify objectives that teacher preparation programs should strive to meet that de-velop culturally sensitive and urban-lifestyle-savvy teachers.

3. What factors make up the appropriate mind-set of promising teachers who enter educational careers based in urban settings?

4. Why is teacher collaboration vital within urban school systems?

5. How can the teacher's self-analysis of personal biases help students understand their own biases?

6. Why are collaboratives between and among the school, families, and community so important?

7. What factors about their students should teachers consider to optimize learning in the classroom environment?

8. What determines excellent urban teachers?

9. What types of instruction and instructional practices best fit urban learners?

SUGGESTED WEBSITES

Center for Urban School Improvement
usi.uchicago.edu/ntn/ntn-programming.shtml

Eisenhower National Clearinghouse for Mathematics and Science Education (ENC)
www.enc.org/?ls=bc

Hamline University Center for Excellence in Urban Teaching
urbanteaching.hamline.edu/Webpage%20test%201.htm

National Clearinghouse on Child Abuse and Neglect Information
nccanch.acf.hhs.gov/

National Clearinghouse on Family Violence
www.phac-aspc.gc.ca/ncfv-cnivf/familyviolence/nfntsnegl_e.html

North Central Regional Educational Laboratory (NCREL)
Critical Issue: Educating Teachers for Diversity
www.ncrel.org/sdrs/areas/issues/educatrs/presrvce/pe300.htm

Social Justice Advisory Committee: British Columbia Teachers' Federation.
www.bctf.ca/social/

UrbanClassroom.com
www.medill.northwestern.edu/journalism/magazine/urbanclassroom/features

REFERENCES

Aronson, J. (2004). The threat of stereotype. *Educational Leadership, 62*(3), 14–19.
Barth, P. (2003). What students need to succeed. *Thinking K–16, 7*(1), 26–30.
Ben-Yosef, E. (2003). Respecting students' cultural literacies. *Educational Leadership, 61*(2).
Brown, L. (2004). Project succeed academy: A public–private partnership to develop a holistic approach for serving students with behavior problems. *Urban Education, 39*(1), 5–32.
Burden, P. R. (2003). *Classroom management: Creating a successful learning community* (2nd ed.). New York: John Wiley.
Chizhik, E. W. (2003). Reflecting on the challenges of preparing suburban teachers for urban schools. *Education and Urban Society, 35*(4), 443–461.

Ciani, A. (2002). *Teacher education issues for urban middle schools.* Westerville, OH: National Middle School Association.

Corbett, D., & Wilson, B. (2002). What urban students say about good teaching. *Educational Leadership, 60*(1), 18–22.

Damian, C., & Herrera, T. (2002). Supporting success in the urban classroom. *Eisenhower National Clearinghouse, 9*(4), 50. Available: www.enc.org/print/features/focus/archive/urban/resources_v9n4/document.shtm?input.

Dilworth, M. E. (ed.). (1998). *Being responsive to cultural differences: How teachers learn.* Thousand Oaks, CA: Corwin Press.

Forte, J., & Schurr, S. (2002). *The definitive middle school guide: A handbook for success.* Nashville, TN: Incentive Publications.

Gordon, M. (2005). *Ten common myths in American Education.* Brandon, VT: Holistic Education Press.

Haberman, M. (1995). *Star teachers of children in poverty.* Indianapolis, IN: Kappa Delta Pi.

Hartman, J. A., DeCiccio, E. K., & Griffin, G. (1994). Urban students thrive as independent researchers. *Educational Leadership, 52*(3), *46*(2).

Haycock, K. (1998). Good teaching matters . . . a lot. *Thinking K–16, 3*(2), 3–14.

Haycock, K. (2001). Closing the achievement gap. *Educational Leadership, 58*(6), 6–11.

Haycock, K. (2003). A new core curriculum for all. *Thinking K–16, 7*(1), 1–2.

Heron, T. E., & Harris, K. D. (2001). *The educational consultant: Helping professionals, parents, and students in inclusive classrooms* (4th ed.). Austin, TX: Pro-Ed.

Herrera, T. (2002). You have to have the passion. *Eisenhower National Clearinghouse, 9*(4), 24–27.

Ingersoll, G. M. (1996). Teacher talk: Cultural diversity in the classrooms. *Center for Adolescent Studies, 2*(2). Available: www.education.indiana.edu/cas/tt/v2i2/cultural.html.

Irvine, J. J. (1999). The education of children whose nightmares come both day and night. *Journal of Negro Education, 68*(3).

Irvine, J. J. (2003). *Educating teachers for diversity: Seeing with a cultural eye.* New York: Teachers College Press.

Iverson, A. M. (2003). *Building competence in classroom management and discipline* (4th ed.). Upper Saddle River, NJ: Pearson.

Izumi, L. T. (2002). They have overcome: High-poverty, high-performing schools in California. Report to Pacific Research Institute for Public Policy. San Francisco, CA. ERIC ED No. 469 963.

Jenkins, W. L. (2004). *Understanding and educating African-American children.* (12th rev. ed.). St. Louis, MO: William Jenkins Enterprises.

Kopetz, P. B. (2003). Understanding the at-risk student: Vital teacher knowledge for successful classroom management and instruction. In *Fostering our youth's well-being: Healing the social disease of violence,* D. W. Rea & R. Stallworth-Clark, (eds.). New York: McGraw-Hill.

Langness, T. (1998). *First-class teacher: Success strategies for new teachers.* Los Angeles, CA: Canter and Associates.

Lindquist, B., & Molnar, A. (1995). Children learn what they live. *Educational Leadership, 52*(5), 50–52.

Maryland State Department of Education. (1998). *Minority achievement in Maryland: The State of the State, Final Report* (pp. 1–61).

Matus, D. E. (1999). An innovative strategy support: Student teachers in urban secondary schools. *The Clearinghouse, 73*(1), *37*(5).

McCabe, M. (2004). Teacher quality. *Education Week on the Web.* Available: www.edweek.org/context/topics/issuespage.cfm?id=50.

Meyer, J. (1999). It's a lot of hectic in middle school: Student-teaching in an urban classroom. *English Journal,* 45–51.

Miller, R. (2004). Holistic education. *Paths of Learning.* Available: www.PathsOfLearning.net.

Morrell, E. (2002). Toward a critical pedagogy of popular culture: Literacy development among urban youth. *Journal of Adolescent and Adult Literacy, 46*(1).

National Commission on Teaching and America's Future. (2003). *No dream denied: A pledge to America's children*. Washington, DC: National Commission on Teaching and America's Future.

Nieto, S. M. (2003). Profoundly multicultural questions. *The Best of Educational Leadership,* 16–19.

North Central Regional Educational Laboratory. (2003a). *Constructivist Teaching and Learning Models*. Available: www.ncrel.org/sdrs/areas/issues/envrnmnt/drugfree/sa3const.htm.

North Central Regional Educational Laboratory. (2003b). *Constructivist View of Learning*. Available: www.ncrel.org/sdrs/areas/issues/students/atrisk/at7lk6.htm.

Ormrod, J. (2003). *Educational psychology: Developing learners* (4th ed.). Upper Saddle River, NJ: Pearson.

Payne, R. K. (1998). *A framework for understanding poverty* (rev. ed.). Highlands, TX: RFT.

Payne, R. K. (2003). *Understanding and working with students and adults from poverty*. Available: www.ahaprocess.com.

Peterson, J. M., & Hittie, M. M. (2003). *Inclusive teaching: Creating effective schools for all learners*. Boston, MA: Pearson.

Pisauro, J. A. (2002). I catch the pattern! *ENC, 9*(4), 22–24.

Rice, J. K. (2003). Teacher quality: Understanding the effectiveness of teacher attributes. *Economic Policy Institute*. Available: www.epinet.org.

SECTQ. (2003). Southeast Center for Teaching Quality. Available: www.teachingquality.org.

Senge, P. (1990). *The fifth discipline: The art and practice of the learning organization*. New York: Currency Doubleday.

Shaughnessy, M. (1999). An interview with Martin Haberman. *Journal for a Just and Caring Education, 3*(2).

Shields, C. M. (2004). Creating a community of differences. *Educational Leadership, 61*(7), 38–41.

Singer, A. (1996). *"Star teachers" and "Dreamkeepers": Can teacher educators prepare successful urban educators?* Paper presented at the Annual Meeting of the American Association of Colleges for Teacher Education, Chicago, IL. ERIC ED No. 395 898.

Smith, T. E. C., Palloway, E., Patton, J. R., & Dowdy, C. A. (2004). *Teaching students with special needs in inclusive settings* (4th ed.). Boston, MA: Pearson.

Southeast Center for Teaching Quality. (2003). NCLB teaching quality mandates: Findings and themes from the field. *Teaching Quality in the Southeast Best Practices and Policies, 3*(4).

Steinberg, S. (1998). Social science and the legitimation of racial hierarchy. *Race & Society, 1*(1), 5–14.

U.S. Census Bureau. (2000). Washington, DC: U.S. Government Printing Office.

U.S. Department of Education, Office of Policy Planning and Innovation (2003). *Meeting the highly qualified teacher's challenge: The secretary's second annual report on teacher quality*. Washington, DC: U.S. Government Printing Office.

Wenglinsky, H. (2002). How schools matter: The link between teacher classroom practices and student academic performance. *Education Policy Analysis Archives, 10*(12). Available: http://epaa.asu.edu/epaa/v10n12/.

Williams, B., & Woods, M. (1997). Building on urban leaders' experiences. *Educational Leadership, 54*(7).

Young, L. J. (2000). *Culturally relevant pedagogy in contextual teaching and learning*. Paper prepared at Michigan State University (pp. 166–168).

CHAPTER 5

URBAN TEACHERS AS LEADERS

Education should focus more on where kids are
going than where they came from.
—W. L. Jenkins, 2002

URBAN PERSPECTIVES

Linda Blazek
Exceptional Education Urban Teacher

The harsh reality is that too many people, sometimes students' own parents, tell them that they will not amount to anything. My hope is that I can be the agent of change in their lives. Perhaps I can influence my colleagues to be the same for them, also.

"The thing that keeps me coming back to work in urban schools," explained Linda Blazek, a twenty-plus year veteran of teaching in urban schools, "is the knowledge that my students are making gains, and that I can see those accomplishments bettering their lives. Rather than to persuade them to become like me, I encourage them to grow to become better than me. I want to instill in my students that they can learn to do anything, and inspire them to develop dreams of their own." She continued, "The harsh reality is that too many people, sometimes students' own parents, tell them that they will not amount to anything. My hope is that I can be the agent of change in their lives. Perhaps I can influence my colleagues to be the same for them, also."

Blazek is genuinely compassionate about her teaching experiences in urban schools: "After graduating from college with my teaching credentials, I decided to substitute teach in urban schools, which led to an interim position for me in that setting. I fell in love with the urban students during my first-year placement, and found that I could truly make positive differences in their lives."

Blazek is determined to convince not only her urban students with special needs that they can excel in academics. "Our urban students come to school transporting diverse issues, albeit they can learn anything. We all must realize their benefits gained from grasping new knowledge—despite their adversities—rather than make excuses for their lack of understanding what's taught them in school," she emphasized. "I expect my students with special needs to learn beyond basic, functional skills, to also gain in learning higher-order thinking skills. Consequently, having set those high achievement levels for them, we see our students rise to those expectations."

Teachers of the urban students who receive "exceptional or special education" programming in their schools must be equipped to provide students not only standards-based instruction, but varieties of cognitive strategies that best fit each student's learning strengths and style of learning, according to Blazek. "As I reflect on preservice teachers who are preparing to educate students in the urban setting," she explains, "I recommend that they understand how to teach their students to think. It is especially important that our students are taught how to take information and use it creatively for their own purposes."

Blazek expressed skeptical perceptions of teacher preparation programs' effectiveness in orienting their preservice educators to the student and classroom circumstances found typical in urban schools. She expressed, "All too often, students in teacher preparation programs never see the inside of an urban classroom, or school, for that matter. And, following their program completion and college graduation, many are placed in urban schools while critically lacking the understandings necessary to teach the socioeconomic group located in most urban settings." Veteran teachers of urban or any school setting should be willing to mentor new teachers and prepare to lead in schools, as welcomed and as necessary.

"Thus," she concluded, "I find it of paramount importance for preservice teachers, or those making the change to urban settings, to acquire as much knowledge as they can about cultural differences as well as an essential exposure to the urban classroom. Learning as much about the urban setting *prior* to service here is key to a richly rewarding teaching experience."

A CASE FOR TEACHER LEADERS

Leadership and School Reform

It is clear that urban schools are struggling in their efforts to assure that all children learn at high levels and to improve overall academic achievement. There is little doubt that these schools cry out for massive reform. Indeed, the society in which we live, and our American way of life, are jeopardized unless there is serious reform. Minority and poor populations, in great numbers, face the prospect of not being able to find meaningful work and being unprepared to function in our society due to a lack of appropriate levels of learning. Students in our schools today will be called upon to provide the leadership necessary to carry on our democratic society. There is concern that they will not be prepared to take on that responsibility.

There is a great imperative to reform schools across the United States. This imperative is most crucial in urban schools. Reform most often translates into changing the status quo, a process that is filled with peril. Effective reform requires highly skilled leadership in which teachers must play a role. Reform efforts that do not engage teachers are likely to be doomed to failure.

Reform saps a great deal of an organization's energy. When attempted in unskilled fashion, and reform falters, then a great deal of time and personal energy is lost. We cannot afford to fail in our reform efforts. The consequences for our children and their future as citizens of our great nation cannot be tolerated. This chapter deals with the issues surrounding leadership in schools and the challenges of providing skilled leadership for reform efforts, with particular emphasis upon teachers as leaders.

Unfortunately, the reform process is too often driven by an individual, such as a principal or superintendent of schools, with little or no consultation with stakeholders. Also, too often, the bureaucracy that thrives in organizations drives school reform. These ill-conceived reform initiatives are top-driven where decisions are made in a vacuum, and consultation with teachers and parents is either insignificant or nonexistent.

Bureaucracy in Schools

Much has been written concerning the attitudes of central office administrators and school principals about sharing decision making with teachers. While not universal, in too many cases these individuals lead their schools based upon a Weberian model. This model, advocated by Max Weber in the early 1900s, is built upon the notion of bureaucracy that stresses specialization, impersonality, hierarchy of authority, and rules and regulations. Hoy and Miskel (1996) indicate that Weberian type models and their components are predominantly found in school organizations today that are characteristically bureaucratic in nature.

The issue here is that a top-down bureaucratic model does not consider the basic complexities at work in schools. The model is unworkable in schools that represent highly complex social organizations. To complicate the issue further, the individual notion of leadership that is commonly held connotes an attitude of controlling and directing and a feeling that leaders know what is best for others (Block, 1996). Under this circumstance, top-down management moves its goals and objectives with a limited view. According to Block, to reach common goals in an organization, individuals at the top of the hierarchy must maintain control, consistency, and predictability. The sad fact is that without their involvement in decision making, teachers lack a sense of purpose in reaching school goals.

Bureaucracy in public schools, particularly in urban schools, presents a major impediment to the success of teacher leadership. Bureaucracy is often a force at the root of the decision-making process in schools. Challenging the bureaucracy can endanger the professional status of an individual, and thus teachers are often reluctant to question direction from high-level dictates of the system.

Urban systems are typically large and impersonal, having greater bureaucratic tendencies. Wahlberg (1999) suggests that bureaucracy is particularly detrimental in communities of lower socioeconomic status. Urban areas suffer from a low level of community collaboration that is reflected in the schools. The ability for the education community to work collaboratively for improvements is necessary for collective decision making and dealing with reform issues.

In recent years, urban school districts have become more bureaucratic in their efforts to meet the challenges of increasing state- and federally mandated programs. As a result, schools have experienced greater numbers of rules and regulations diverting attention from their efforts to improve academic performance.

The nature of urban schools may be a contributing factor in fostering greater bureaucratization. Teachers and administrators in urban schools have little time to be reflective practitioners. They tend to be constantly harried, interrupted, and harassed, leading them to focus upon short term fixes to solve immediate problems. These same issues cause teachers to escape to the isolation of their classrooms. Weick (1978) refers to this isolation and lack of schoolwide perspective as schools being "loosely coupled." The notion of loose coupling suggests that faculty in a school go about their daily teaching in isolated fashion, without regard to the school's vision or mission and without professional connection to their fellow teachers. There may be some benefits from loose coupling in terms of respecting individuality, however, when considering school reform issues, loose coupling may hamper efforts to develop consensus (Louis & Miles, 1990; Westoby, 1988).

In bureaucratic organizations, information moves through a bureaucratic hierarchy that is quite removed from the everyday experiences of classroom teachers. Information is utilized by the bureaucrats to make decisions that drive the organization—the schools. Thus, the bureaucracy is in a position of considerable power and influence. Crosby sees the bureaucracy as "an anonymous and faceless collective, it is difficult to control, sidestep, or subvert. Because it seeks to perpetuate itself and its processes, it frequently serves as the brakes that bring

innovation and change to a halt" (Crosby, 1999, p. 299). Crosby sees bureaucracy as a major obstacle in efforts for urban school reform:

> Urban schools must change in response to the growing complexities and demands of our society that have made the existing networks and organizational structures obsolete. When the bureaucracy blocks meaningful change, it is inevitable that the urban schools will fail a large number of their clients, the students. (1999, p. 299)

Teacher leaders may find their efforts stifled by the bureaucracy in schools and school districts. Their attempts to be effective agents for change are hampered by the school district's policy makers and school-level administrators. Paulu and Winters (1998) see the following as major barriers that leave teachers feeling powerless:

- too little time for reflection;
- rigid school schedules;
- unrelated instructional tasks;
- jealousies within the school;
- lack of support from peer teachers and administrators; and
- overemphasis on state mandated high-stakes testing.

In spite of the barriers present from administrators who are unwilling to involve teacher leaders in collaborative decision making and bureaucratic realities, most school reform studies continue to advocate "for teacher empowerment, shared governance, collegial collaboration, professional development, and more time for reflection. They see teacher leadership qualities as necessary elements for redesigning schools for success" (Wynne, 2002a, p. 3).

Principals as Leaders

School reform requires major decisions to be made and significant changes to be instituted. The means by which school decisions are made, however, may not accommodate the imperative for reform. Crosby asserts that "the decision making process in urban schools contributes to their failure" (Crosby, 1999, p. 298). He suggests that the *decision process* in American organizations is a *group process*. Crosby states that, "It is not individual ability that determines success in our society; it is the efficient operation of the decision-making process, which is the sum of accumulated information and the skills of a group" (Crosby, 1999, p. 298). Attempts for an individual, such as a principal, or small group of administrators to steer the process of school reform are doomed to failure. Schools are simply too complex to attempt to reform without involving all stakeholders in the process. According to Mulford, "One of the most consistent findings from studies of effective school leadership is that authority to lead must not be located in the person of the leader but can be dispersed within the school system and among people" (Mulford, 2003, p. 2).

Troen and Bales (in Allen, 2003, p. 3) believe that when traditional hierarchies are employed by principals, that a "culture of isolation" is fostered. They state that, "principals have to make an attitudinal shift. They tend to believe that power, or what they think of power, is a sum zero game. Often principals worry that teacher leadership will take power away from them." Troen and Bales suggest that principals work so that teachers do not become isolated by involving them in team activities to assist with the decisions made in the school. Baker (in Reagon, 2001), believes that what is needed are people who are not interested in being leaders, but those who would develop leadership in others. This represents an attitude of change on the part of the principals that would allow teacher leadership to flourish.

Teachers seem willing and even eager to be part of a collaborative decision-making process. The reality is that when their eagerness is not encouraged and cultivated by the principal, teachers become disenfranchised with the system and become increasingly isolated. Further, they become to a large extent dependent on the principal to make the decisions, give answers, and to direct all aspects of the schools' existence (Lambert, 2003). When teacher leadership occurs in a school, it is because it is valued by the principal. By that same token, teachers must be ready to participate when the offer is presented.

In the 1980s, shared decision-making began to be implemented in school reform efforts. Since that time, it has been a growing trend. While not as yet a part of the culture of educational institutions, more and more schools are exercising some form of shared decision making that engages teachers in playing a greater role in school governance.

Principals who agree to share leadership of the school with faculty work with teachers collaboratively and bring them into the decision-making process by devising new leadership strategies based upon facilitation and trust and the abandonment of hierarchal authority. Letting go of authority and leaving behind the role of director may be a fearful venture for some principals. Teachers can assist by participating willingly and demonstrating an ability to be productive team members while providing expertise (Liontos, 1994).

What is needed is a leadership approach that empowers teachers to share the leadership function with the principal. Goode (2002) presents a series of quotes from leaders that encourage shared leadership:

> Leaders empower rather than dictate. In my view, a leader's critical responsibility is to surround oneself with talent and then allow the creative energy of others to flourish.—Craig Ritter, Principal, University Park Elementary School, Irvine, California

> A leader demonstrates his or her enthusiasm by performing in the same manner that he expects others to perform. He leads by example rather than instruction . . . and delegates to each subordinate at a level whereby they can achieve success . . . a leader also promotes the entire team, not just himself.—Nick Yocca, partner, Stradling, Yocca, Carlson, and Rauth, Newport Beach, California

A leader should not make herself indispensable, she should encourage others inside the organization to grow and to prepare for new roles.—Ralph J. Cicerose, Chancellor, University of California, Irvine

A good leader allows others to shine that they too will develop a deeper commitment to the organization and strengthen the team.—Magie Wakeham, Executive Director, Families Forward, Irvine, California

These leaders encourage a shared leadership environment. Teachers cannot be assured that they will work in a school where the principal will be so forward looking. In such cases they can exercise teacher leadership to a lesser extent, at least to the extent that the principal will allow. Modern-day leadership preparation programs stress the need for shared leadership. Therefore, more and more, teachers today are likely to find principals who embrace the concept. In such instances, it is extremely important for teachers to participate fully. This can present a considerable challenge since teacher education programs usually do not include leadership training. This chapter should be helpful to teachers as they embark into the leadership arena.

Hopkins (2003), reporting on a survey of forty-three principals on the successful traits of school leaders, points out that principals ranked "the ability to involve others in decision making in the school" in the top ten traits necessary to lead successfully. Principals stressed the need to rely on others in the decision-making process, and to empower others to carry out the vision for the school.

There is one additional feature regarding the notion of shared leadership. It extends the sharing to parents and other shareholders. Principals and teachers must be ever-cognizant of the fact that the school exists within the wider community. They must recognize and understand the complex ways in which the schools are embedded in the neighborhood. This is especially critical in urban areas given the diverse nature of urban communities. There is not a question of whether to involve stakeholders, but rather a question of the best strategies as to how to achieve that objective.

It may be that teachers will need to take the lead in this endeavor since principals are not always forthcoming. Goldring's (1990) study of the attitudes of principals toward stakeholder involvement suggests that bureaucracy impedes efforts to build community mentality. The study found that principals working in low socioeconomic settings were more bureaucratic and had less positive attitudes toward stakeholders than those in higher socioeconomic areas.

Teachers as Leaders

Teachers are at the heart of the efforts to reform our schools. Our nation has entered a time in education when society is demanding, with increased intensity, that all students achieve high levels of academic performance. Until now we have been satisfied with and expected just select students to reach these high levels. The reform efforts suggest that teachers be actively involved in decision making surrounding the strategies within the schoolhouse to achieve these much-needed reforms.

Teacher leadership is not a new phenomenon. However, the leadership roles that teachers have traditionally played have been limited in scope, and are often insignificant when viewed from the overall school perspective. Teachers are most involved in decisions connected with curriculum development and academic program development. Leadership roles, which are limited in scope, such as grade chairpersons, department heads, and team leaders have also been commonplace for teachers. These are roles in which teachers serve as representatives rather than leaders (Livingston, 1992).

As the pressure to restructure schools intensifies, teachers will increasingly be expected to play major leadership roles in their schools. The representative roles described above by Livingston will not suffice. In the past and indeed currently, teachers with leadership potential, or a desire to lead, have moved into administrative positions. The Carnegie Forum on Education and the Economy (1986) and the Holmes Group (1990), strongly suggest that teachers must be leadership partners in their schools. This will require teachers to begin thinking beyond their individual classrooms, from a schoolwide perspective.

Howey (1988) and Livingston (1992) have advocated for higher levels of teacher leadership roles in their schools. They base this on the premise that teachers, whose responsibilities are directly involved in the classroom, are best qualified to influence decisions in the school, especially decisions concerning curriculum and instruction. It is suggested that teachers must be empowered and

supported to take on stronger leadership roles. Failure to do so places in jeopardy the ability for schools to sustain efforts for school reform.

To describe teacher leadership, one must recognize that the notion of teachers as leaders differs from what we have come to recognize as the traditional view of administrative or management-level leadership. Teacher leadership concentrates on shared decision making, teamwork, and community building, and moves away from the top-down bureaucratic practices of traditional modes of leadership (Alvaredo, 1997; Coyle, 1997).

Teachers seem to focus principally on providing services to others and assuring that their students receive a quality education (McLaughlin & Yee, 1998). They do not view leadership from a hierarchical perspective in the organization. They see a level playing field in which collaboration and teamwork are the main ingredients (Troen & Boles, 1992).

A number of behaviors and qualities are evident in teacher leaders. They:

- demonstrate expertise in their instruction and share that knowledge with other professionals;
- remain consistently developing on a professional learning curve;
- frequently reflect on their work to stay on the cutting edge of what is best for children;
- engage in continuous action research projects that examine their effectiveness;
- collaborate with their peers, parents, and communities, engaging them in dialogues of open inquiry/action/assessment models of change;
- become socially conscious and politically involved;
- mentor new teachers;
- become more involved at universities in the preparation of preservice teachers; and
- present themselves as risk takers who participate in school decisions. (Alvaredo, 1997; Crowther, 1997; O'Hair & Reitzug, 1997; Paulu & Winters, 1998; Wynne, 2002b)

The qualities indicated above carry with them a sincerity of purpose revolving around means to improve education for students in collaboration with parents, peers, and so forth. This is contrary to the bureaucratic model, which is usually politically motivated and self-serving.

The opportunity for teachers to exercise leadership does not simply occur. Palmer asserts that discussion about school direction is not likely to happen if leaders with position status (for example, superintendents and principals) do not *expect* it or *invite* it into being. Those verbs are important in establishing that coerced conversation will fail. "Conversation must be a free choice . . . conversation begins only as leaders invite us out of isolation. . . . This kind of leadership can be defined with some precision; it involves offering people excuses and permission to do things they want to do but cannot initiate themselves" (Palmer, 1998, p. 156).

New Leadership Paradigm

Truly involving teachers as leaders involves a major paradigm shift—a new way to view leadership. Rost argues that "our values are changing radically" (1993, p. 100). We must now leave behind the industrial paradigm of leadership, dependent on rules and regulations, and move to a postindustrial model. This important paradigm shift is just beginning. Rost states that "a profound transformation of leadership thought and practice must take place . . . if the needs of the people living in . . . the twenty-first century are to be well-served" (1993, p. 100). Much of the thought and practice in education is undergoing considerable transformation, while leadership continues to function in an industrial paradigm. What is needed now is to guide relationships and transform how leadership occurs within the school environment.

Rost defines the new leadership as: "An influence relationship among leaders and followers who intend real changes that reflect their mutual purposes" (1993, p. 102). This definition of leadership, if exercised, represents a powerful impetus for teacher leadership in school reform. Note that the definition is based upon four essential elements:

1. The Relationship Is Based on Influence.   This suggests that individuals in the leadership relationship use persuasion to influence others. This influence uses individual behavior to persuade others in the relationship. It is not coercive, authoritarian, dictatorial, or steeped in power. It may involve reputation, prestige, personality, status, message content, perception, and other persuasive resources. Rost defines influence as:

> Leadership as an influence relationship has two characteristics: (1) is it multidirectional, in that influence flows in all directions and not just from the top down; and (2) it is non-coercive, meaning that it is not based on authority, power, or dictatorial actions but is based on persuasive behaviors, thus allowing anyone in the relationship to freely agree or disagree and ultimately to drop into or out of the relationship." (1993, p. 107)

Thus, teachers are free to persuade and influence others who share the leadership relationship. Leadership then becomes an act of multidirectional sharing. Teachers are advantaged in this sharing environment. They can wield powerful influence due to their expertise in and knowledge of the instructional process which they experience daily in their classrooms. Their points of view then can be very influential.

2. Leaders and Followers Are the People in the Relationship.   Since leadership is shared and collaborative, there is a constant shifting of individuals from leaders to followers and vice versa. The leadership relationship requires active participation. Passive people cannot influence, and are, therefore, not involved—neither are passive people followers. At any time, followers can become leaders and leaders can become followers. The dynamic is constantly shifting based on the influence relationship at any particular time. Teacher leadership can flourish since leadership is constantly shared as the role of leaders and followers shifts based upon the influence exerted by any person.

3. Leaders and Followers Intend Real Changes.   There is a need to define the purpose of the organization and to agree upon its future direction. Later in this chapter we deal with the process of developing an agreed-upon vision for the school. According to Rost:

> The word *intend* means that the leaders and followers purposefully desire certain changes in an organization. . . . The desire is not accidental or developed by chance. The intention is deliberate and initiated on purpose. . . . The word *real* means that the changes the leaders and followers intend must be substantive and transforming. Real means that leaders and followers intend change in people's lives, attitudes, behaviors, and basic assumptions . . . in the groups . . . they are trying to lead. (1993, p. 114–115)

Teacher leaders must be prepared to make their intentions known and be prepared to influence others. It is through the process of attempting to exert influence and to persuade that leaders and followers reveal their intentions. The leadership relationship requires sharing, which ultimately leads to agreement about the mission of the organization and the "real" changes needed to achieve the mission. Again, Rost's words are instructive:

> The intention is in the present, and the leaders and followers give solid evidence of their intentions by their words and actions. The intention is part of the glue that holds the relationship together. Real means that the change the leaders and followers intend are substantive and transforming, not pseudo change or sham. (1993, p. 117)

Collective experiences of the textbook authors bring concurrence that bureaucrats (individuals in hierarchal leadership positions) are "game players," and it is difficult to determine whether their intentions as expressed are real and sincerely motivated. Teachers, on the other hand, can usually be counted on to approach relationships with sincerity and their real intentions are expressed. This type of leadership relationship would be very natural and comfortable for teachers.

4. Leaders and Followers Develop Mutual Purposes.   As a result of frequent and meaningful interactions, leaders and followers reflect their understandings of their mutual purpose. This understanding is important, since "leaders and followers are engaged in a common enterprise; they are dependent upon each other, their fortunes rise and fall together" (Burns, 1978, p. 426). Rost describes *mutual purposes* in the following quote.

To reflect their mutual purposes, leaders and followers must come to some agreement about their purposes. This agreement must be consciously achieved by the interaction of leaders and followers. It must be developed using non-coercive methods. It must be forged in the relationship that leaders and followers have, one that allows followers to influence leaders (and other followers) as well as leaders to influence followers (and other leaders). (1993, p. 120)

Under the Rost concept of leadership, the relationship is shared. At any time any teacher can play a leadership role or a follower role. Decisions are not autonomous, but collaborative ventures in which all participants have value. Under this concept, teachers may choose whether to enter the leadership relationship without sacrificing their beliefs or integrity. Participants freely agree to intentions and mutual purposes through an interactive process.

School reform is about leadership. As we attempt reform, an understanding of leadership is essential. Leading requires knowledge about how individuals react in an organizational setting. As teachers become more and more involved in leadership relationships, they must develop realistic expectations of the leadership process in organizations. Leadership does not occur easily and teacher leaders must understand the process and develop the skill to be successful in their efforts.

It must be stated here that while teachers may have the desire to share in the leadership of the school and in reform efforts, their efforts to do so may be frustrating. Bureaucracies and the individuals who benefit by them are powerful and bent upon preventing the sharing of the leadership enterprise. The model presented by Rost is sensible and, if implemented, could be an effective road map in successful school reform efforts. It is presented here together with other elements of leadership under the premise that if urban teachers are knowledgeable about skillful leadership, they are more likely to influence the nature of leadership in their schools and to be skillful and effective when given the opportunity to exercise teacher leadership.

Throughout the remainder of this chapter, references to *leaders* will mean principals and teacher leaders sharing the leadership relationship as defined by Rost. *Leaders* does not refer to the principal alone, but to principals and teachers in a collaborative effort to provide leadership for the school.

COMPONENTS OF EFFECTIVE LEADERSHIP

The Need for Organizational Vision

Vision plays a crucial role in setting direction for an organization—especially a complex social organization, such as a school. Effective leadership in a school setting begins with the establishment of vision for the organization, sometimes referred to as *mission*.

The development of a vision should not be haphazard. There is too much importance in all stakeholders sharing a sense of direction. Effective planning and decision making must fit into that direction. Organizations need vision around which to plan and around which decisions can be made. Agreeing on a vision and planning around the vision, as well as making decisions to achieve the vision, is best achieved as a team effort. Principals and teachers, including stakeholders, mainly parents, need to be involved together and must build ownership in the process and the results of that process. Discussed further is the building of a vision for the school involving a team approach, with emphasis on the involvement of teachers as leaders.

Teachers should be deeply involved in setting the vision for their school, working with the principal, and involving parents and other stakeholders. Developing a vision should not be the sole domain of the principal, but a matter of shared leadership. It may, however, and often does, originate with the principal. The successful leaders that the authors have known seem to have an image of the organization they desire in the future which they readily share with their faculty.

There are a variety of definitions for vision that suggest that a vision creates a mental image or picture, allowing one to see future orientation and direction of an organization. It provides direction for an organization by articulating what it desires to attain. It allows employees and other stakeholders a means to understand the organization and what it intends (Nanus, 1992). By providing a picture, vision not only describes an organization's direction, but also a basis for accomplishing the vision, as it guides the work of the organization. Vision provides a mental construct that serves to guide individual and group behavior and to provide a picture of the future for which all are willing to work. A vision must inspire a level of commitment encouraging all to work for its attainment.

Nanus (1992) maintains that a vision has five characteristics; it

1. attracts commitment and energizes people;
2. creates meaning in workers' lives;
3. establishes a standard of excellence;
4. bridges the present to the future; and
5. transcends the status quo.

According to Westley and Mintzberg (1989), creating a vision involves a three-stage continuum:

1. an image of the desired future for the organization's (vision) is
2. communicated (shared), which serves to
3. empower followers so that they can enact the vision

Chrispeels (1990), in his unpublished report on effective schools, indicates that there is a commitment to change when a school staff has a shared vision. The concerted efforts of members of an organization increase the possibilities of the vision's accomplishments. Vision is little more than an empty dream until is it shared widely and accepted (Boyd, 1992).

While a vision may begin with a principal's personal concept, it must ultimately be a group's consensual image for the future. It is, therefore, important that there be a sense of ownership by all stakeholders. Teachers, of necessity, play an important leadership role in the development of the vision. The vision needs to be shared by those who will be involved in its realization. The shared vision becomes a "shared covenant that bonds together leader and follower in a moral commitment" (Sergiovanni, 1990, p. 24). The vision of the school, developed collaboratively and influenced by teacher leaders, ultimately becomes the common ground that compels all involved to realize the vision.

The relationship between teachers and the principal is an important one. Principals tend to encompass the whole school in their thinking; their vision is organizational. Teachers' visions appear to focus primarily on the individual or personal actions in the school academic environment. The likelihood is that the two are attending to different aspects of the same vision. It is this difference in teachers' and principals' perspectives that make the development of a shared vision so powerful.

The process of developing a shared vision is time-consuming and teachers may shy away from full participation. This would be shortsighted. When teachers share in the leadership in the school, they can exert considerable influence. The result is that the realization of the school's vision provides a reward for the time and energy invested in a collaborative process.

Establishing the Vision

There are various approaches to the development of a shared vision. The following four steps suggested by Mendez-Morse (1993) can be employed to facilitate the conceptualization of the vision:

1. Define the Organization.   In formulating a vision, a critical first step is to determine, as much as possible, what is known about the organization as it currently exists and how its various components are interrelated. Boyd (1992) suggests that there is importance in understanding the role of the school in the community. Items such as school size, the school's overall culture, and the attitudes, beliefs, norms, and relationships that exist, all play an important role. According to Nanus (1992), an organization can be defined by an understanding of its purpose and its value to society. The first step, then, in developing a vision, is a full understanding of the school as it presently exists.

2. Involve Critical Constituencies.   The individuals or groups identified as constituencies include those that are both inside and outside the school. These individuals should be significant stakeholders such as parents, students, business representatives, community representatives, and so forth. Consideration of the major expectations and interests of all stakeholders should help forge a realistic vision. The involvement of varied constituencies often presents challenges to the collaborative effort needed in the development of a shared vision. Teachers and principals must be skilled in extracting consensus among the variety of interests. This requires a commitment of time and patience. The ultimate good would be to bring the group to consensus without serious disagreement stalling the process.

3. Explore the Possibilities. Planners suggest that consideration must be given to future developments and trends that may influence the school in a process known as environmental scanning. There must be a scan of possible major changes in the economical, social, political, and technological environments and how they impact the school presently and in the future. Examples of specific issues educators should consider are student enrollment trends, employment trends, trends in technology, and social, economic, and political trends.

4. Committing the Vision to Writing. Upon completion and agreement of the vision, it should be committed to writing clearly and concisely. Rogus (1990) suggests using the consensus statements as a beginning point in writing the vision statement and securing faculty reactions so that the faculty will determine the final form representing a united vision.

Educators are being challenged to meet the present needs of students to prepare them to successfully function in the twenty-first century. They must meet this challenge first with a vision. They ensure its attainment by continuously collaborating with others to develop a shared vision. When educators invest time and energy in developing a vision and preparing a written statement reflecting that vision, they provide an inspiring image of the future for themselves, their colleagues, constituents, and most importantly, their students.

The leadership of teachers in this endeavor cannot be underestimated. It must be viewed as a necessary ingredient in forming a successful school. It should be noted that while vision may never be reached, having a vision will make the journey worthwhile. A vision is neither a beginning nor an end; it serves as a reminder of the image of the future for the school.

The Effectiveness of Teams

Making school environments and programs successful takes more than just an individual effort—it takes teamwork. Schools are more and more using teams to accomplish many tasks. Teams may work on varied projects, such as site-based management, curricular reform, the implementation of new programs, or restructuring. For teamwork to be successful, teams and individual team members must have clear, shared goals, a sense of commitment, the ability to work together, and access to needed resources and skills.

In many schools, teachers work in isolation, administrators try to accomplish tasks single-handedly, and the responsibility for implementing new ideas falls to certain individuals. Barwick (1990) believes that our society has progressed too far for an organization to be guided by the vision of only one person. Barwick describes a team as a "very special designation awarded to a group of people who feel energized by their ability to work together, who are fully committed to a high level of output and who care about how each member feels during the work process" (Barwick, 1990, p. 33).

Working together in teams is a more effective way to accomplish important tasks. If teachers are to be considered as a viable part of the leadership of a school, they must understand the value of working in a team atmosphere. Success in working as part of a team is dependent on an understanding of the nature of teams in the workplace. Teams tend to be better at solving problems, have a higher level of commitment, and include more people who can help implement an idea or plan. Furthermore, teams are able to generate energy and interest in new projects.

Teams have many advantages over individuals working in isolation. Maeroff (1993) notes that experts who support the use of teams make the following statements:

- Those closest to the work know best how to perform and improve their jobs.
- Most employees want to feel that they "own" their jobs and are making meaningful contributions to the effectiveness of their organizations.
- Teams provide possibilities for empowerment that are not available to individual employees.
- Teams tend to be more successful in implementing complex plans.
- Teams develop more creative solutions to difficult problems.
- Teams build commitment and support for new ideas among staff and community members.
- Teams become part of the learning process of professionals in schools.

Many corporations such as General Electric, Boeing, and Federal Express have employed the team concept to make daunting tasks more manageable. They have been able to streamline processes to make everyone's efforts more productive. Lombardi (1996) has observed that by employing the team concept, organizations will: (1) improve employee involvement and managerial support; (2) give employees a sense of ownership and increase their level of commitment; (3) increase focus on the customer and subsequent customer satisfaction; and (4) reduce labor costs while improving quality. While his writings are aimed at corporate United States organizations, parallels can be drawn and are instructive for today's educational organizations.

Lombardi believes that progress and productivity are enhanced when teams are employed because people do not like the idea of being "managed." He believes good leadership in the twenty-first century workplace will be more like a coach and embrace the team concept. He states that the downfall of many leaders is the concept of "if you want it done right, then do it yourself." This attitude will decrease productivity partly because the leader is solving all of the problems. The people in the work group cease to think on their own and let the leader do all of the thinking.

As principals are better trained to employ a team approach to decision making, they will seek to involve their teachers in the team process. Teachers, therefore, need to understand the process and be prepared to function within it and to participate fully. The move toward team decision making represents a golden opportunity for teachers to demonstrate their abilities to engage in leadership and to contribute to school reform plans.

Teams work well together because they are striving for a common goal or purpose that has strong meaning for all of the team members. Kelly gives an example of the power of teamwork: "Snowflakes are one of nature's most fragile things, but just look at what they can do when they stick together!" (Kelly, 2003). Lombardi believes there are five characteristics of a team, including: (1) the team collectively determines what end result it wants to achieve and how it will be achieved; (2) team members will understand how accomplishing the team's goals will help them achieve their individual goals; (3) team members can see how their individual efforts contribute to the overall success of the team; (4) the team is mentally tough, able to rise each time it falls; and (5) the team makes its vision an absolute part of its belief system.

Teams can give a powerful boost to the spirit and effectiveness of any organization. In addition, teams increase the ability of people to work together and can lead to better understanding, clearer alignment, and much stronger motivation (Kaufman, 2002). When people work in teams they better understand that they are greater collectively than individually (Grazier, 1999). Collaborative teammates do more than just work with one another. Each person contributes something to the discussion that adds value to the overall relationship and synergy of the team.

Building the Team

According to Maddux (1992), teams are most productive when all members understand their common purpose. Teams must be viewed as people united in a need to collaborate toward common goals. Teaming is not something to do to simply create harmonious work groups—the purpose reaches far beyond that objective. Teams provide a way to formalize the power of collaboration among individuals. They provide a means to blend the talents, skills, and creativity of diverse individuals and varied attitudes, opinions, and beliefs. Teams use collaboration so that the work group leverages its skills, time, and resources for its own benefit and that of the overall organization.

The welcoming and acceptance of each team member is imperative. Team members are like puzzle pieces of many sizes and shapes. We must learn the strengths and the shortcomings of the pieces to discover how they best fit together (Hendrickson, 1996). According to Blair (2002), teams move through four distinct development stages:

- forming;
- storming;
- norming; and
- performing.

Forming occurs when the group initially comes together. Conflict is seldom voiced directly, because it is likely personal and often destructive. The members will usually be guarded in their opinions and generally reserved. *Storming* is the second stage, where division can be expected to form and personality clashes will often occur. If not managed correctly, very little communication occurs, since individuals tend not to listen and some continue to be unwilling to talk openly.

During the *norming* stage, the group begins to recognize the merits of working together and the conflicts subside. A new spirit of cooperation is evident, and members begin to feel secure in expressing their viewpoints and to discuss these openly with the group. Work methods become established and recognized by the group. Lastly, the *performing* stage is the culminating point that occurs when the group has settled upon a system that allows for a free and frank exchange of views and a high degree of support by the group for each other and for group decisions.

During the early stages of teambuilding, members may become frustrated by what appears to be a lack of progress. Understanding that the early stages of teambuilding can be awkward, patience must be exercised allowing each stage to run its course on the way to a mature and productive team.

Weiss (2002) suggests several tips on how to allow teachers to develop and work as a winning team.

- *Find or create a team leader.* Great teams don't just happen; a team leader carefully and purposefully builds them. This person is one interested in group leadership, or has talent for working with people.

It must be remembered that shared leadership means that leadership is fluid with different members filling the leader role at different times, depending on circumstances and the influence of relationships at play. The leader described here is the person who most influences the building of the team and the general functioning of the team—not one who makes the team's decisions.

- *Develop good communications with your team.* Build an imperative for teamwork with an understanding that by working together both personal as well as organizational goals can be best accomplished. Once the team leader is acknowledged, she should assume that communications are enhanced within the team framework.

- *Figure out what your organization needs to be successful.* Successful organizations begin with a plan. That plan is almost always purposeful, both short-term and long-range. This is called a *strategic plan*, and it begins with the team deciding on the organization's goals.

- *Assess the strengths, weaknesses, and needs of the team.* Once strengths and weaknesses of team members are known, it will be fairly easy to assign tasks to team members in order to reach team goals.

- *Agree on team rules.* All groups, whether teams or mobs, have rules. Most often they are unwritten. Successful teams have written rules that they develop themselves.

■ *Support the team—even when there is conflict.* Support is relatively easy when everyone gets along. The real test of a team is when there is a disagreement. This is when conflict negotiation is crucial. Team members must learn to mediate differences of opinion, listen to them, accept them, or reject them without resentment.

■ *Encourage creativity and risk taking.* People learn and grow from their mistakes. Only those who are allowed to fail will be willing to try new endeavors. Team members need to support creative ideas and attempts, learn from those that do not succeed the first, second, or even the tenth time, and continue to try again.

■ *Give positive and constructive feedback.* Almost every person has a desire to be liked and accepted. People will want to be part of a team that recognizes their strengths, and offers to help with weaknesses.

■ *Motivate the team.* People are motivated by the prospect of having their needs met. Appreciation and recognition are certainly high-level motivators.

Developing an effective team from an existing group of individuals, with a wide range of skills, roles, and educational levels, in a fast-paced environment filled with challenges and critical decision-making requirements, can be an intimidating task (Weymeyer, 2004). Building the team requires time, commitment, objectivity, and the willingness to make hard decisions. In order to accomplish this in a successful manner, the team needs a plan to follow. Katzenbach and Smith (1993) offer the following requirements and guidelines for building effective teams:

■ Teams must be small enough in the number of members.
■ Members must have adequate levels of complementary skills.
■ The team must have a truly meaningful purpose.
■ The team must have a specific goal or goals.
■ The team and its members must establish a clear approach to their work.
■ Members must have a sense of mutual accountability.

Frustrating Elements of Teams

There are some frustrations that may surface as teachers participate in team efforts. The assumption of leadership activities usually carries no remuneration and little time earmarked for teachers involved. The time factor is particularly frustrating, as carrying a teaching load and participating in leadership activities represents a double-duty situation.

An additional frustration in working with teams is that teams require cohesion and one will occasionally find those who are resistant to working in teams. According to Katzenbach and Smith (1993), resistance to working in teams is often the result of:

■ lack of conviction that teams are worth the effort;
■ discomfort and risk for individuals; and/or
■ a school that lacks clear focus of performance and success.

Each of these sources of resistance can be overcome. Lack of conviction can be eliminated as the group develops common goals and begins to work together. Discomfort in a team setting can be reduced when individuals are encouraged to speak up and feel safe and comfortable in the group. (Refer to page 158 regarding vision.) Having a clear vision for the organization is critical to guide the team and to focus its efforts.

Shared decision making can often create conflict and disagreements among teachers as they attempt to reach a consensus. Issues that might ordinarily be ignored must now be resolved. There may also be issues of power when novice teachers with a great deal of enthusiasm attempt to influence veteran teachers. Learning to work together in a new way could take years of resolving conflicts until a smoothly functioning team matures (Weiss, Cambone, & Wyeth, 1992).

According to Liontos (1994), studies of shared decision making indicate a tendency for teams to focus on trivial problems such as bus supervision, parking, smoking, faculty lounges, coffee breaks, and so on. This could be frustrating for teachers who prefer to tackle core issues dealing with teaching and learning.

Great teams do not simply occur. They mature in effectiveness as team members participate in activities that engage and challenge them. Every team gathering is an opportunity for powerful teaching and learning. Effective teams provide trusting and supportive relationships where participants engage collaboratively in committing to and reaching common goals.

Successful team building for the purpose of school decision making is reliant on the attitude of the school's principal. She must believe in shared decision making and resolve to make it a part of the overall culture of the school. Modern programs of principal preparation stress the power of shared decision making and the team approach to school leadership. Teachers may not find this attitude exercised in all schools. They will often decry the situation that exists in their schools in which they are not consulted and decisions are made at the top in arbitrary fashion. Clearly, in this kind of environment, teachers will encounter great difficulty in attempting to share the leadership necessary for effective school reform.

There is also the possibility that a principal may articulate support for shared leadership and decision making and continue to act according to an authoritative style of leadership. Spalding (1994) studied a principal who expressed sharing but regularly manipulated the process to satisfy his agenda. He used such tactics as planting ideas, creating pressure on opponents, and bestowing favoritism on supporters. Clearly, he played at sharing leadership but continued to see himself as the decision maker. Blase, Blase, Anderson, and Dungan (1995) in their study of principals, discovered that even when principals enthusiastically supported sharing leadership, they would on occasion become directive and even exercise vetoes when they perceived that teacher-led decisions were not appropriate or might be harmful to students.

Research suggests that the bureaucracy at play in schools and the attitudes of designated school leaders often stifle the ability for teachers to exercise leadership. Wynne asserts that barriers such as too little time during the work day for reflection, rigid school schedules, unrelated instructional tasks, jealousies/lack of support from peer teachers and administrators, and overemphasis on state mandated high-stakes testing hamper the effectiveness of many teachers who, while teaching, step beyond their classroom to lead. All of these barriers leave too many teachers feeling powerless. (Wynne, 2002b, p. 3)

Wynne further asserts that "despite these impediments, most school reform studies continue to advocate for teacher empowerment, shared governance, collegial collaboration . . . and more time for reflection" (Wynne, 2002b, p. 3).

In spite of these constraints, teachers must recognize that they have the ability to provide powerful influences in their school. Teachers are most directly involved in the classroom, and thus in the best position to help in making decisions regarding school programmatic and curricular direction. It is in this arena that they should most attempt to concentrate their influence.

Weiss, Cambone, and Wyeth (1992) studied schools where shared decision making was in place. They observed that teachers complained about the issues and frustration they sometimes faced in the team process. In spite of this, they almost universally indicated that they did not wish to return to the way things were in the past.

The value of teams and sharing that occurs within teams brings individuals together and, when this process occurs, there is great power and strength in decisions made and actions taken. Rudyard Kipling likened this to the strength in a pack of wolves: "The strength of the pack is the wolf, and the strength of the wolf is the pack." The single strength of any principal or teacher in a school is multiplied greatly in a team effort, thereby ultimately benefitting the children who are to be educated.

IMPLEMENTING REFORMS

Understanding Resistance to Change

School reform and school decision making, whether applied skillfully or haphazardly, will eventually lead to change, and change frequently leads to conflict situations. If teachers are to share in the leadership of a school, they must recognize this reality and be prepared to deal with it skillfully. This section discusses the change process and resistance to change, as well as means to resolve conflict.

Change is an inevitable byproduct of school reform. Educators do not easily accept change and are often resistant to any suggestion that some element of curriculum, instructional delivery, or general school policy must change. Teachers are often adverse to any suggestion that they participate in the change process. Palmer describes the teachers' dilemma well:

I am a teacher at heart, and I am not naturally drawn to the rough-and-tumble of social change. I would sooner teach then spend my energies helping a movement along and taking the hits that come with it. Yet if I care about teaching, I must care not only for my students and my subject matter but also for the conditions, inner and outer, that bear on the work teachers do. Finding a place in the movement for educational reform is one way to exercise that larger caring. (Palmer, 1998, p. 182)

Resistance to change is natural, and attempts to change the status quo in a school should expect to encounter resistance. The key in instituting change is not whether to expect resistance but to plan around how it will be overcome.

There is an old saying that there is one thing in life that is certain besides death and taxes and that is *change*. Change is a fact of life everywhere, including schools. We cannot run from it, ignore it, or hide from it—but we must come to terms with it. The leadership that principals and teachers exercise together provides the pivot point for the change process and the counsel for those who are having difficulty in dealing with change (Ladew, 1998).

Change usually produces stress, uncertainty, confusion, and fear. It can be a time of great confusion in which individuals are affected both physically and emotionally. Teachers who become involved in leading change must understand the change process and the importance of creating a climate for successful change and the steps in the process.

There are three major elements involved when change is attempted that inhibit one's ability to change: (1) fear of the unknown—the feeling of a loss of control; (2) fear of failing—new responsibilities may bring failure; and (3) fear of new relationships—professional and personal relationships may be affected.

Individuals typically move through a series of stages of change involving shock or denial, anger, procrastination, depression, and acceptance. They often react by engaging in fight-or-flight mentality or total disassociation with the situation altogether. In choosing to embrace change, they may resurrect opportunities for success that have previously met with failure (Sammon, 2001).

Fullan and Stiegelbauer (1991) present several reasons for resistance to change that occur in an organization.

- The purpose is not clear.
- The participants are not involved in the planning (they do not have ownership).
- The change is based on personal reasons.
- The habit patterns of the work group are ignored.
- There is poor communication regarding change.
- There is fear of failure.
- Excessive work pressure is involved.
- The cost is too high, or the reward for making changes is inadequate.
- The present situation seems satisfactory.
- There is a lack of respect and trust in the change initiator.

Milstein (1993), in discussing change, writes that change means loss and destabilization. He also indicates that change means taking risks, learning new roles, and demands faith to function in the unknown. Marshak adds that "change involves a perceived loss; this creates grief and generates resistance. Loss and uncertainty create an environment of fear, anxiety, and frustration" (1996, p. 2).

Norman analyzes how changes affect teachers. She submits that the confidence teachers have in their ability, or self-efficacy, plays a large role in how well they adapt to changes. If they are confident about their ability to positively affect student achievement, then they will usually be willing to take risks and accept change. Additionally, Norman states that "teachers who possess low self-efficacy usually resist change efforts for fear of disrupting what is already in place" (Norman, 2003, p. 4).

Fullan (1998) believes that teachers attach meaning to change by utilizing criteria in assessing any given change. These pertain to the balance of rewards and costs, or, more simply, "Why should I put my efforts into this particular change?" Research shows that teachers use four main criteria:

1. Does the change potentially address a need? Will students be interested? Will they learn? Is there evidence that the change works, in other words, that it will produce claimed results?
2. How clear is the change in terms of what the teacher will have to do?
3. How will the change affect the teacher personally or in terms of time, energy, new skills, sense of excitement, and competence, or interfere with existing priorities?
4. How rewarding will the experience be in terms of interaction with peers or others?

When teachers perceive negative responses to these questions, they can oppose change rather strongly. Since change cannot be avoided, preparation must be made to deal with resistance. A first step is to understand that the resistance is normal. In some ways, it may be beneficial in preventing change from occurring without having fully thought out all aspects and consequences of proposed changes. Understanding the varying forms in which resistance presents itself is instructive and attempting up front, to respond to the criteria that Fullan suggests teachers utilize in assessing change are important strategies in possibly limiting the impact of resistance.

Dealing with Change

How principals and teachers provide leadership is the defining factor in the change process. Effective leadership understands that change is not an event, but a process. The literature on leadership and change consistently indicates that strong and effective leadership is not only "critical for initiating change, but also to sustaining the gains won by the process" (Sammon, 2001, p. 35). An agreed-upon vision is a key issue in any consideration of change. All stakeholders must create and communicate a vision for growth and translate that vision into action steps that can be agreed upon by all stakeholders in the school (Sammon, 2001).

Instituting change in an organization such as a school is a difficult proposition. It involves a struggle to seek strategies that others will accept and adapt to. This presents a universal problem, in that "finding the right blend of diplomacy, chiding, professional development, empowerment, top-down delivery, or delegation are a handful of issues that leaders must consider as they move their school toward change" (Hopkins, 2003). As we have seen, change is a fact of life in attempts to reform schools, and change encounters resistances.

Much has been written here regarding the change process in schools. If teachers are to share in school leadership, they must understand the process. Only with full understanding will they be armed to deal with the issues associated with any organizational change. How change is approached is a critical element in whether it will be successful.

One important element is the matter of sensitivity. Understanding why individuals resist change is not enough—there must be sensitivity to their needs and attempts to meet natural human needs. Reaching out and helping others to see the need for change and the benefits that may accrue is imperative.

Bolman and Deal, who have written widely in the area of organizational change, suggest that those seeking change be sensitive to the following:

Human resources. Change causes people to feel incompetent, needy, and powerless. Developing new skills, creating opportunities for involvement, and providing psychological support is essential.

Structure. Change alters the clarity and stability of roles and relationships, creating confusion and chaos. This requires attention to realigning and renegotiating formal patterns and policies.

Politics. Change generates conflicts and creates new winners and losers. Avoiding or smoothing over those issues drives conflict underground. Managing change effectively requires the creation of arenas where issues can be negotiated.

Symbolism. Change creates loss of meaning and purpose. People form attachments to symbols and symbolic activity. When the attachments are severed, people experience difficulty in letting go. Existential wounds require symbolic healing. (Bolman & Deal, 1991)

Again, there must be an agreed-upon vision for the school prior to any attempt for planning and decision making and ultimately any attempt to institute change in the organization. Any discussion of dealing with change must begin with the importance of sharing a vision.

The need to articulate and agree upon a vision for the school cannot be underestimated in reducing the barriers to change. Vision provides guidance for the organization and articulates what the stakeholders wish to attain. It serves as a "signpost pointing the way for all who need to understand what the organization is and where it intends to go" (Nanus, 1992, p. 9).

Once an organization agrees upon a vision, they must agree upon the means for its accomplishment. If the means requires change, which is usually the case, the initial justification for change is evident. Hord (1994), writing for the Southwest Educational Development Laboratory, lists a number of components necessary to achieve successful change. She lists first the articulation of a vision and its expectations. Attempting any substantive change prior to stakeholders agreeing upon a vision—a direction for the organization—is indeed foolhardy.

As our nation continues to seek new ways to address the educational needs of students, educators must embrace change. School leaders—teacher leaders included—will be faced with the challenges of changing the culture and climate of schools in order to produce results. Educators will be challenged to guide parents, community partners, and students through the change process.

One of the most important aspects of change is building relationships. Principals and teachers must be willing to listen to stakeholders and respond to their concerns by creating an atmosphere of collaboration. Collaborative decision making is a crucial ingredient for reform and occurs more often in schools where trust is engendered. "Strong trusting relationships make it more likely that reform initiatives will diffuse broadly across the school because trust reduces the sense of risk associated with change" (Bryk & Schneider, 2003).

Shared decision making, discussed earlier in this chapter, tends to have a strong motivational impact on the stakeholders (Lloyd, 2002). Norman reflects on the human element in the educational change process:

> The human element of the reform process focuses on the relationships, the interactions, and the dynamics of people. It is only when the people in this process are

considered first and their needs and wants met that the educational reform has much chance for success.

    Even though the school's structure is a major target of change, the people within the structure must have their own self-interests resolved before they can truly show concern for the organization. (Norman, 2003, p. 1)

Regardless of whether change is positive, there must be preparation for individual or group resistance. Resistance must be confronted by understanding the nature of its occurrence, responding in ways that are forthcoming, and preparing stakeholders to adapt (Ladew, 1998). When people are allowed to participate in the decision-making process, resistance levels drop. When stakeholders are allowed to play a role in the change process, they are more likely to accept and support the effort. When they develop a sense of ownership in the change, along with a vested interest, it is more likely to succeed.

It appears to be human nature to resist change. It has already been stated that a primary reason for resistance to change stems from a fear of the unknown. Without any advance information or input, most people assume worst-case scenarios. One of the most powerful ways to reduce resistance to change is to remove as much of the unknown as possible. People respond more positively if they are aware that the change is coming and prepare themselves in advance (Lloyd, 2002).

Change is an ongoing process that should not require an atmosphere of revolution in the school. A prudent beginning might be to survey the teachers and assess the strengths and weaknesses of the school. Invite all stakeholders (administrators, teachers, parents, students, business partners, and community leaders) to help evaluate the things that are positive in the school, what makes it successful, and what needs changing. This helps to build a collaborative effort. Look at the data for the school and determine, as a collaborative effort, what needs changing. Set clear realistic goals and find the needed financial resources to help make the changes possible (Sammon, 2001). This can be followed by an assessment plan that validates and identifies those areas in need of change and provides a guideline for understanding why there is the need for change (Snowden & Gorton, 2002).

Teachers, parents, community partners, and students must be guided through the change process. In *The Dance of Change*, Senge (1999) identifies strategies necessary in creating a climate for successful change. According to Senge, change must be approached with enthusiasm and a willingness to commit to the change. Those who least change must demonstrate a personal investment in the need for change and foster an atmosphere that encourages and supports personal learning with the creation of teams and professional development opportunities. All stakeholders must see direct benefits to them and to their students and see increases in areas defined by the change process as needing improvement. Finally, a climate must be created in which the change practices become institutionalized.

Senge goes on to say that failure to sustain the change process occurs again and again despite all the resources committed to the effort. He observed that organizations that fail to sustain changes in the end face crises in their organization. Sammon agrees on the need to initially create the climate for change. According to Sammon, there are three goals to consider in order for organizational change to occur: (1) "adopt and encourage an attitude of increased expectations; (2) allow for comprehensive and meaningful planning; and (3) commit to a process of continual improvement" (Sammon, 2001, p. 34).

The need to create a climate for change is well established. The creation of an appropriate climate is followed by taking skillful steps to institute the change.

Kotter suggests an eight step process to change, indicating that for change to take place the following must be addressed.

1. *Establish a sense of urgency.* People need to recognize urgency and require motivation for effort to be sustained. Organizations fail to recognize how difficult it is to move people out of their comfort zones. Change is needed when 75 percent of the organization recognizes that business as usual is no longer acceptable.

2. *Form a powerful coalition.* Usually the change process will begin with a small number of people and then grow when others recognize the need for change. No one single individual can accomplish this—it requires a coalition that enjoys trust. Regardless of size of the organization, usually a small number of individuals lead the efforts.

3. *Develop a vision and strategy.* A vision helps to guide the direction in which the group needs to move. Vision helps spark motivation, keeps projects aligned, and provides a way to evaluate the progress.

4. *Communicate that vision.* The vision of the school must be transformed into a movement for change. To be successful, those who advocate change must walk the walk and communicate through their actions. Every possible communication effort must be used to be effective.

5. *Empower employees and others to act on the vision.* Remove obstacles that inhibit change from taking place. Not all obstacles will be eliminated, but it is important to deal with the most onerous obstacles.

6. *Plan for and create short-term wins.* Real transformation takes time to implement, so it is important to achieve short-term goals so as to not lose momentum. Baby steps will keep the team from being discouraged.

7. *Consolidate improvements and keep momentum for change moving.* This process can be time-consuming. The process and progress is fragile and there are likely to be setbacks. It is important to maintain momentum and to realize that change involves a slow process that may take years to accomplish.

8. *Anchor new approaches.* Change will survive if it becomes embedded into the norms and values of the school. Two factors will help with this approach. First, show others how the new changes improved the system. Second, assure that the new process will continue to be supported. (Kotter, 1996)

Successful change requires collaborative leadership in which teachers are heavily involved. Most individuals need some sense of what to expect and what direction to take. All stakeholders must be allowed the opportunity to participate in the change process. If they are not allowed to participate in the process they will experience feelings of dissatisfaction, distrust, distress, and resentment. Teacher leaders must be "change agents" who facilitate the change process in order for schools to continually improve (Gupton, 2002). The plea here is for teachers to participate fully in the leadership in their schools and to serve as change agents. These teachers must be invested in the involvement of all stakeholders in the change process with the ultimate goal of leading their school in producing students who are prepared to be tomorrow's leaders.

When individuals work in teams and attempt to make collaborative decisions, conflicts are certain to arise. Change, in particular, serves as a magnet for conflict. Understanding the conflict phenomenon and developing skills to deal with it is critical if teachers are to succeed in the leadership arena.

Understanding Conflict

Conflict is inevitable. It is a regular occurrence in all aspects of life. The opportunity for conflict is intensified in an organizational setting. Left unattended, it can be a destructible force within the organization. Conflict is universally present in a change environment.

As teachers endeavor to share leadership in a school, they will almost surely face conflict situations. These situations can be extremely stressful and can blur the focus needed to deal with the real issues in a school. Worse, the frustration that conflict brings might cause teachers to shrink from participation in the leadership process. This can be avoided when teachers understand the conflict phenomenon and are able to deal with it confidently.

It should be emphasized here that conflict is not unique to school organizations. People experience conflict in their personal and professional lives daily. Before engaging in any discussion related to dealing with conflict, it is important to define and understand conflict. Webster's dictionary defines conflict as "(a) competitive or opposing action of incompatibles: antagonistic state or action [as of divergent ideas, interest, or persons] (b) mental struggle resulting from incompatible or opposing needs, drives, wishes, or external or internal demands." These "incompatibles" are expanding with an ever-increasing diverse workforce and structural changes within organizations. Conflict resolution skills have become as important in leaders' skill sets as technical ability and job knowledge. Thus, teachers who would become involved in leadership relationships need to understand conflict and be skilled in dealing with it confidentially.

In schools, as in other organizations where a number of people work together, there will most likely be conflict. Conflicts between people may be a result of differences in knowledge, beliefs or values; or competition for a position, power, recognition, or personal dislike and/or varying perceptions or attitudes often in relation to the structure of the organization (Weider-Hatfield & Hatfield, 1995). Individuals in leadership situations often become involved with others who are negatively affected by conflicting situations. It is not uncommon for this to occur when individuals are required to perform certain tasks, activities, or roles that do not match their expertise, interests, goals, or values.

Because each individual perceives the world differently than someone else, disagreement is a normal occurrence (Texas Center for Women's Business Enterprise, 1997). Two people who agree all of the time are telling each other what they want to hear and not what they really feel. "Manage conflict—don't suppress it" (Barrier, 1998, p. 35). Conflict is inevitable and should be resolved. It is not an evil to be destroyed. Conflict can be seen as a chance to grow and learn. It is a basic part of the growth and development of any group. Working through conflict is a bonding and growing exercise. The strength of social systems depends on how they prevent conflict and deal with it when it does occur (Mayer, 2000).

Conflict can be "unnerving and unexpected, and involves such issues as trust, commitment, acceptance, career security, and professional esteem" (Stockwell, 1997, p. 6). When conflict is perceived as negative, it is because the disagreement concerns interests or ideas that are personal and meaningful to the conflicting parties. Resolving conflict requires a great deal of skill (Texas Center for Women's Business Enterprise, 1997).

In a perfect world, a collaborative negotiation would be the result of thorough communication and understanding by each person (Deutsch & Coleman, 2000). In the real world, two people may know each other well, and yet not understand each other. This misunderstanding is exaggerated by conflict. In order to resolve conflict, one must understand its basic nature.

The traditional view of conflict management prior to the 1940s was that it was harmful and should be avoided. Furthermore those generating conflict were viewed as troublemakers who were negative influences in the organization. During the 1950s, dealing with conflict evolved into a behaviorist approach. Conflict was accepted in the workforce by taking an authoritarian stance where management solved all conflict issues. By the 1970s, management theorists recognized conflict as essential for both people and organizations to adapt and grow within a changing environment (Kathman & Kathman, 1990).

Not all conflict is negative in an organization. If energy is harnessed and directed toward problem solving and organizational improvement, the results can be positive. Bacal (2004) in an article on organizational conflict, refers to positive conflicts as "The Good" and negative conflicts as "The Bad." When situations reach extreme conflicting levels, they are referred to as "The Ugly." When situations reach an ugly stage, the organization ceases in attempts to resolve or address the issues. In such situations negativity rises, there are no actions to resolve the issues, and there is little interest on the part of those involved to work toward a resolution. In the end, this can lead to the breakdown of team cohesiveness and productivity, to the detriment of the group. When bad or ugly types of conflicts arise, it is imperative for effective conflict resolution techniques to be applied.

Conflict is a universal part of human interaction. In today's fast-changing, diverse workplace, conflicts between managers and employees, with new employees, and within teams arise daily. Conflicts should not be viewed as a threat to working relationships or to the productivity of school personnel. Rather, resolving conflicts satisfactorily can actually strengthen the school and improve results. School leadership can optimize performance by empowering employees to resolve differences and implement effective solutions. Further, conflict can be a positive force when teams understand how to channel their ideas toward a common outcome.

Utilizing a skillful approach to resolving conflict requires an understanding of the sources of the conflict. There are many sources of conflict, including individual differences, interdepartmental relations (a department defines other departments in terms of its own operation), job ambiguity, poor communication, and environmental stresses (for example, limited resources). The results of conflict include stress, decreased productivity and work quality, diminished job satisfaction, lowered morale, higher absenteeism, poor communication among departments, and a climate of distrust (Kathman & Kathman, 1990).

Assessing Conflict Situations

"Conflict resolution is a process—a means to an end" (Masters & Albright, 2002, p. 74). We all experience conflict in our daily lives, both personal and professional. We can all think of a time when we wished we had handled conflict differently. "When one mishandles conflict, he/she will suffer consequences—broken relationships, distrust, vengeance, squandered time, divisive meetings" (Masters & Albright, 2002, p. 69).

During the initial stages in which conflict is analyzed, a number of factors must be considered. Issues such as needs, desires, perceptions, power, values, and emotions must be determined in order to gain a true representation of the conflict. When managing conflict, it is important to understand the real problem. Many problems are secondary and unless the real problem is uncovered, it will reoccur. We have all experienced coworkers who seem to argue about the smallest things, when the real concern is something larger than they are unwilling to communicate. The real issue is often disguised in different forms (Masters & Albright, 2002). Hoban (2004) suggests that conflict usually results from one or more of the following elements:

- *Needs*—essential things or a desire—wants. These are more easily resolved. They usually involve items wanted but not essential.
- *Perceptions*—interpretations of reality. These are more complex, involving the need to change someone's perception, which can be difficult.
- *Power*—influence over others. These are also complex and often involve a compromise to deal with power situations.

- *Values*—principles that are important to oneself. These are the most challenging since convincing someone to change her value system is difficult and often not possible. Some compromise must be sought.
- *Emotions*—personal feelings toward a subject. These are very difficult, requiring a great deal of patience in order to settle a person's emotional mind-set.

Conflict Resolution

The first step in resolving conflict is understanding the source of the conflict. Hoban's elements described above can be very instructive and form an important first step in conflict resolution. Having determined the source of the conflict or the element driving the conflict, one must then decide upon the appropriate conflict resolution style. In so doing, it is important to keep in mind that conflict cannot be avoided. At least one can attempt to keep it from getting out of control. Each individual handles conflict differently based upon how she chooses to react. That reaction should be mindful of the element driving the conflict. The following five styles for approaching conflict are generally supported by research (Culbertson, 2001; Kathman & Kathman, 1990):

1. *Competing.* An individual pursues her own concerns at the other person's expense. In employing competing techniques, one person uses power to win in a conflict. It is described as a *win-lose* situation in which one's power is used to overrule another person. It is not a preferred method since it can potentially damage relationships, but useful in situations of conflicting values or in the presence of time constraints (Kathman & Kathman, 1990). Competing techniques are generally used when goals are highly important and there is less regard for other members in the conflict (Culbertson, 2001). Caution is advised here since allowing force to resolve conflict can actually escalate the conflict and make it worse.

2. *Accommodating.* The opposite of competing; an individual neglects her own concerns to satisfy the concerns of the other person. It is described as a *lose/win* situation. This approach is most effective when maintaining a good working relationship is most important. It involves one party giving in to another to avoid confrontation. Usually accommodating techniques are used when confronting differences that may damage relationships (Culbertson, 2001). Allowing others to satisfy themselves and neglecting your own concerns sometimes helps protect valuable relationships.

3. *Avoiding.* The individual does not immediately pursue her own concerns or those of the other person. She does not address the conflict. The conflict is recognized but resolution might be postponed or completely disregarded. This approach is appropriate when the issues are insignificant or not critical but the "potential for damaging an important working relationship is significant" (Kathman & Kathman, 1990).

Postponement is acceptable when seeking better timing for resolution. Sometimes a cool-down period is wise before tackling a conflict, but the issues should not generally be avoided. Avoidance represents a *lose/lose* situation and is detrimental to relationships as well as the health of the organization. Avoidance can worsen the conflict needing to be resolved and it should not be allowed to continue without resolution. Culbertson (2001) suggests that avoidance techniques are typical when emotions are too involved.

4. *Compromising.* Compromising techniques require all parties to give up a little in order to serve the common good, yet allow individuals to keep aspects of their original position (Culbertson, 2001). Compromising techniques work best when all members are equally committed to the goals. With compromising, the parties seek some expedient, mutually acceptable solution that partially satisfies both parties. It is considered a *no-win, no-lose* situation. Compromising involves finding the middle ground for both parties when they receive some, but not all of their wants. This method is useful when limited resources cause the conflict. It seeks a middle ground involving a give-and-take on the part of both parties.

5. *Collaborating.* The opposite of avoiding; collaboration involves an attempt to work with the other person to find some solution that fully satisfies the concerns of both parties. It represents a *win/win* resolution that seeks to find the best possible solution to satisfy the needs of all involved. It involves open communication between the parties with honest levels of collaboration, cooperation, and problem solving. Collaborating is the most desirable means to settle conflicts and the ultimate goal in managing conflict. Collaboration allows creative solutions that will satisfy all parties. During the collaboration process, teamwork, cooperation, and trust must be very high. Collaborative decisions are those that are mutually satisfying for all parties (Culbertson, 2001). The collaborative process allows all individuals to have ownership in the solution.

One important point to consider in deciding the style to be used for conflict resolution is the level of concern for the relationship with the other party. The question to ask is whether meeting personal goals outweighs the need to maintain relationships, or vice versa. Figure 5.1 reviews each style in terms of its value for relationships or meeting goals and the relationship desired.

The final step in the process involves the process of resolving the conflict. This is the point at which the parties engage in discussion of the issues. It is possible for an individual to approach discussion according to a particular style and as a result of the discussion change course and seek another settlement. For example, one may enter the discussion utilizing a competing *win/lose* approach and determine that it is best to shift to a compromise *no win/no lose* resolution.

The Texas Center for Women's Business Enterprise (1997) suggests means to resolve conflicts and maintain important relationships with coworkers. When one senses an interpersonal conflict with a coworker, she should initially try to

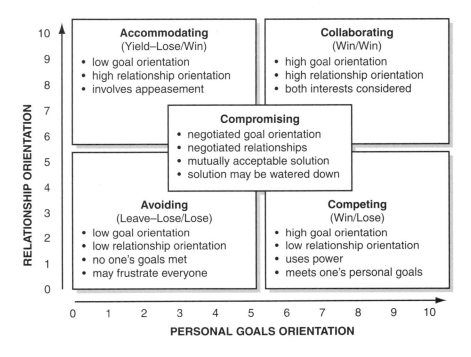

FIGURE 5.1   Conflict Resolution Styles

decide upon the source of the problem. The parties should establish a time to discuss the problem privately and without interruptions. It is important to understand the skills described herein and to act as nonconfrontational as possible. Ask the coworker to define the problem, and if he or she insists that there is not a problem, which is often the case, describe what you think is the problem. Ask the other person for feedback without attacking or accusing and listen to him or her with an open mind. Show respect for what he or she has to say, review the position, and try to understand how he or she feels. Do not point a finger of blame even if the issue appears to be the other's fault. Conflict is hardly ever a one-way street. Try to generate a mutually beneficial compromise to help save the relationship (Texas Center for Women's Business Enterprise, 1997).

Successful negotiations are based on several principles, which if applied encourage resolution. These principles, according to the Texas Center for Women's Business Enterprise (1997), are:

1. Defend–attack interactions are always nonproductive.
2. Ask many questions to gain information.
3. Summarize and repeat what you understand to be true to assure that you are concentrating on the important points.
4. Try to see the other person's perspective.

The Importance of Listening

There will always be disagreement, but it is possible to disagree diplomatically. It is best for the listener to communicate to the other person that she has heard and comprehended the message before stating an opinion. This allows the person to know that the other party is truly listening, that she understands their opinion, and that it will be considered when offering a response. It is also important for the other person to know that she is valued even if there is disagreement with her position. This can be accomplished by saying, "I can see how you might feel that way, and this is how I feel." This also allows the other person know that there is disagreement but it is not a superiority contest (Texas Center for Women's Business Enterprise, 1997).

Resolving a conflict involves moving through the steps of conflict resolution and finding a solution to the problem. Additionally, emotional conflict resolution is necessary to place feelings in perspective. Although everyone deals with conflict emotions differently, there are several fundamentals that are common as listed by Mayer (2000, pp. 103–104):

- feeling that they are accepted as individuals and their personalities and not their values are under attack (or no longer under attack);
- feeling they can maintain their dignity, or "face," as they move to resolution;
- feeling their core needs are respected and addressed;
- having enough time to gain perspective and experience healing;
- having others accept their feelings as valid and values as legitimate; and
- feeling genuinely and nonjudgmentally heard.

Listening, acknowledging, responding, and resolving remaining differences are the four steps to alleviating conflicts during team meetings (Weiss, 1997). Listening and hearing are not one and the same. In order to listen, one must clear her mind of outside distractions and concentrate on verbal and nonverbal communication. Nonverbal communication includes gestures, posture, and how a person speaks. Acknowledging does not mean one must agree with the other party. Individuals need to know that they have been heard. A skilled way to respond would be, "Let me be certain that I understand. You are saying that you . . ." (Weiss, 1997). This will help to clarify any misconceptions. After one has heard what the other party has to say, and has acknowledged their position, it is time to tell your side. A good way to transition into that is by saying, "I understand your position, and now I'd like you to listen to mine—okay?" (Weiss, 1997, p. 7). Most conflicts represent a buildup of multiple issues. Break the disagreement into parts that can be managed, then discuss solutions for each issue. This will resolve any remaining differences and assure that the conflict will not reoccur.

Deutsch and Coleman (2000) present several skills necessary in the process of conflict resolution:

- effectively distinguish positions from needs;
- reframe a conflict so that it can be seen as a mutual problem to be resolved collaboratively;
- distinguish threats, justifications, positions, needs, and feelings, and communicate one's perspective using these distinctions;
- ask open-ended questions in a manner that elicits the needs, rather than the defenses, of the other and, by so doing, communicate a desire to engage in a process of mutual need satisfaction;
- when under attack listen to the other person and reflect back on her needs or interests behind the attack; and
- create a collaborative climate through the use of informing, opening, and uniting behaviors. (Deutsch & Coleman, 2000, p. 503)

Skillful Brainstorming

The final step in conflict resolution is brainstorming possible solutions. Developing solutions can be another seemingly impossible task. Brainstorm for possible solutions even when a compromise seems out of the question. If one acts quickly and appears open to suggestions, they might succeed in diffusing the situation (Masters & Albright, 2002).

Building relationships may not be at the forefront when involved in a conflict, but one can learn a great deal about a person's real character during disagreements. Dealing with conflict effectively, one can gain the trust and respect of the person with whom she is engaging (Masters & Albright, 2002).

The skill of listening is perhaps the most important ingredient in the conflict resolution process. Listening gives the other party permission to disagree, express strong opinions, and reveal passion from her ideas. Listening does not try to resolve the conflict hastily, or even to resolve the conflict at all. Listening helps achieve a true winwin situation by aiding the other party in defining her win. The relationship formed and trust gained will be of great benefit to the school overall (Van Slyke, 1999). Listening has several goals: to prevent escalation of the problem; to resolve not only the obvious problems but the real issue as well; to depersonalize the argument; to develop solutions; and to build relationships (Masters & Albright, 2002).

It is important to prevent escalation of the problem because a shouting match is useless, as is holding in anger and resentment. These only cloud judgment and cause conflict to intensify. Thomas Jefferson reportedly counted to ten—and depending on the severity of the situation, to one hundred—to avoid reacting in anger (Masters & Albright, 2002).

Depersonalizing in a conflict is not always an easy task. When being criticized or if someone is acting stubborn, try to stay in control and not take comments personally. This is also a good time to try Jefferson's logic of counting to ten, or even counting to one hundred might be appropriate. It is important to try to concentrate on the situation and not on personal feelings. This will produce a better chance of a useful exchange (Masters & Albright, 2002).

Much of the foregoing has concentrated on one-on-one conflicts. The conditions and processes are similar cases of group conflict. Conflict resolution for school teams must be viewed in the context of its benefits to team building. Much has been written here about the necessity and importance of a team approach to school leadership. Conflict unchecked will be detrimental to the effectiveness and perhaps even to the survival of the team.

The key to a good team is mutual respect between all members (Weiss, 1997). If the members truly respect each other, discussions and disagreements can be resolved without fights or major conflicts. Teacher leaders will be involved in meetings with fellow teachers, administrators, and other professionals on a frequent basis. It will be important to reach decisions as well as form a team that is working toward the overall goal, which is what is best for the students. A prudent goal for the team would be for each member to agree to do what is best for the students, even if his or her ideas or wishes are not implemented.

"A conflict culture must be anchored by leaders who learn how to see through the haze of disaffected behavior and to listen and accept different points of view" (Van Slyke, 1999, p. 134). The first step in creating the ideal balance in conflict is to model behaviors that encourage constructive disagreement and collaborative solutions. Persons in this environment must demonstrate the ability to listen, confront, and collaborate (Van Slyke, 1999).

According to Barrier (1998), conflict resolution is not deciding who is the winner and who is the loser, but deciding which outcome is better for the group as a whole. Conflicts that occur during meetings can greatly disrupt the flow of the meeting, but at the same time they can bring to light very important issues (Texas Center for Women's Business Enterprise, 1997). When there is conflict in a meeting, those involved may gain insight into the functioning of the group by the questions being raised. Encouraging team members to conceal their feelings of disagreement only causes the issues to emerge in odd places, times, and forms (Barrier, 1998).

When conflict is properly handled there can be many benefits to the team. Conflict causes the underlying issues to surface, inducing motivation and strength to deal with difficult problems. People's understanding of real interests, goals, and needs increase while continuous communication around those issues is stimulated. Conflict, handled skillfully and when not allowed to intensify, can enhance decisions and consensus that will eventually increase flexibility, innovation, and improvement (Van Slyke, 1999).

Fullan states "reform often misfires because we fail to learn from those who disagree with us" (Fullan, 1998, p. 6). Being a teacher leader is not about trying to avoid conflict, but eliciting constructive comments that might lead to powerful reform and change. Resistance and conflict can often stem from people who have valuable contributions to share with the group and have powerful insights (Fullan, 1998). Most individuals resist for very good reasons. Principals and teacher leaders must value those differences and allow all members to contribute to finding alternatives and solutions to the thorny issues surrounding school reform.

Any attempt to reform schools must involve shared leadership and collaborative decision making. Teachers as leaders must share a seat at the decision table. This inevitably will involve dealing with conflict situations. Their skills in dealing with conflict will, in large measure, enhance their effectiveness. Teachers must learn how to resolve conflict for these reasons:

- Conflict is unsettling and unpredictable. If poorly handled, it can become negative and destructive.
- Confrontation causes people to react in an unpleasant, defensive, and emotionally intense manner. They may break down, flee, or counterattack.
- Conflict often raises fundamental personal concerns about trust, commitment, and acceptance in one's relationship to another. In superior-subordinate relationships, it also raises concerns for career security and professional esteem. (Stockwell, 1997, p. 6)

It is difficult to go through a day without encountering some form of conflict. Today it might be the cashier who overcharges or the spouse who forgot to take out the trash. Tomorrow it may be a professional colleague who opposes a new initiative. How one manages daily conflict can have an impact on an individual's attitude and demeanor. Those who do not resolve the conflicts they encounter usually can maintain anger and frustration that is stressful and unhealthy. This is true in everyday life situations, and for teacher leaders it can be the margin of difference between professional success and frustration.

SUMMARY

Urban schools cry out for massive reform. Too many reform efforts are bureaucratically top-down driven, resulting in failure. Teachers who are involved on a daily basis in our classrooms are in the best position to lend expertise to reform efforts and yet they are usually not consulted in a meaningful way. The time has come for teachers to play a greater role in the way we have traditionally thought about school leadership.

The leadership definition advanced by Rost (1993) earlier in this chapter holds great promise for teacher leadership possibilities. As teachers become involved in an influence relationship they essentially take on leadership roles for which they must be prepared.

Leadership can be very stressful and often frustrating. If teachers are to engage in leadership they must develop an understanding of the process and thus gain confidence in its undertaking. This chapter suggests that they must develop in the following elements of leadership.

- *Vision.* Vision sets the direction for an organization. Leading the reform effort is enhanced when stakeholders agree upon a vision. Setting vision must be the first step in any reform effort.

- *Team building.* Bringing a vision to reality must involve the work of many individuals who are united in teamwork. Teams blend the talents, skills, and creativity of diverse individuals, benefitting the entire organization.

- *Decision Making.* Efforts for reform require numerous decisions to be made. Decision making is not a one-person task. The best decisions are those in which stakeholders are involved in shared decision making.

- *Change.* School reform will surely require change that produces stress, uncertainty, and confusion. Change should be viewed as a process, not an event. It may not be possible to totally avoid resistance to change, but developing vision and utilizing team building and shared decision making may lessen resistance as stakeholders build ownership in the direction of the school.

- *Conflict.* Conflict, when not understood, can be extremely stressful and can be destructive to a team or an entire organization. Conflict is ever-present and teacher leaders must develop the skill to resolve conflicts as they arise. Developing conflict resolution skills is imperative for teacher leaders.

If teachers are to succeed as leaders, they must understand the leadership process. Only with full understanding will they develop the confidence to accept and deal with the issues that confront leadership on an almost constant basis. Teacher leadership cannot and should not be viewed as an option in urban settings. It must be viewed as an imperative.

CHAPTER QUESTIONS

1. Why is there importance in teachers being involved as leaders in educational reform?

2. How does bureaucracy in schools hamper teacher leadership efforts?

3. What are the elements of leadership as defined by Rost (1993)? Discuss the role of teachers within that definition.

4. How does leadership establish vision for the school, and assure that it is shared by all stakeholders?

5. What are the benefits of leadership and decision making being shared in teams and what are some negative aspects?

6. What are some reasons for resistance to change and how can leadership deal with that resistance?

7. Discuss the pros and cons of the five styles for approaching conflict, including the benefits and negative aspects of each.

SUGGESTED WEBSITES

2005 Association for Supervision and Curriculum Development
www.ascd.org/portal/site/ascd/index.jsp/

2005 International Reading Association
www.readingonline.org

2005 San Diego County Office of Education Annual Report to the Community
www.sdcoe.k12.ca.us/pdf/anrep.pdf

Consortium for Policy Research in Education (CPRE)
www.cpre.org/index_js.htm

Northwest Regional Educational Laboratory
www.nwrel.org/index.html

U.S. Department of Education, *Implementing Schoolwide Programs: An Idea Book on Planning*
www.ed.gov/pubs/Idea_Planning/index.html

WestEd
www.Wested.org/

REFERENCES

Allen, R. (2003). Building school culture in an age of accountability: Principals lead through sharing tasks. *ASCD Education Update, 45*(7), 1–8.

Alvaredo, C. (1997). *If leadership is everyone's domain, I'm taking the lead: Investing in early childhood leadership for the 21st century.* Boston, MA: Wheelock College.

Bacal, R. (2004). *Organizational conflict: The good, the bad, and the ugly.* Available: www.conflict 911.com (2004, June 28).

Barrier, M. (1998). Putting a lid on conflicts. *Nation's Business,* 86, 34–35. Available: http:// web6.infotrac.galegroup.com (2004, July 2).

Barwick, J. (1990). Team building: A faculty perspective. *Community College Review, 17*(4), 32–39.

Blair, G. (2002). Groups that work. *IEE Engineering Management Journal.* University of Edinburgh: School of Engineering and Electronics. Available: www.see.ed.ac.uk~gerald/Management/art0.html (2004, July 7).

Blase, J., Blase, J., Anderson, G. L., & Dungan, S. (1995). *Democratic principals in action: Eight pioneers.* Thousand Oaks, CA: Corwin Press.

Block, P. (1996). *Stewardship: Choosing service over self-interest.* San Francisco: Barrett-Koehler.

Bolman, L. G., & Deal, T. E. (1991). *Reframing organizations: Artistry, choice, and leadership.* San Francisco: Jossey-Bass.

Boyd, M. (1992). *School context: Bridge or barrier for change.* Austin, TX: Southwest Educational Development Laboratories.

Bryk, A. S., & Schneider, B. (2003). Trust in schools: A core resource for school reform. *Educational Leadership,* 60, 40–45. Available: www.ascd.org/publications/edlead/2003 .bryk.html (2004, July 10).

Burns, J. M. (1978). *Leadership.* New York: Harper & Row.

Carnegie Forum on Education and the Economy. (1986). *A national proposal: Teachers for the twenty-first century.* New York: Carnegie Forum on Education and the Economy.

Chrispeels, J. A. (1990). *Achieving and sustaining school effectiveness: A five year study of change in elementary schools*. Paper presented at the Annual Meeting of the American Educational Research Association, Boston, MA.

Coyle, M. (1997). Teacher leadership vs. school management: Flatten the hierarchies. *Clearing House, 70*(5), 236–240.

Crosby, E. A. (1999). Urban schools forced to fail. *Phi Delta Kappan, 81*(4), 298–303.

Crowther, F. (1997). Unsung heroes: The leaders in our classrooms. *Journal of Educational Administration, 35*(1), 5–17.

Culbertson, H. (2001). *Conflict management strategies and styles*. Available: www.snu.edu/~hculbert.fs/conflict.htm (2004, June 27).

Deutsch, M., & Coleman, P. T. (2000). *The handbook of conflict resolution: Theory and practice*. San Francisco: Jossey-Bass.

Fullan, M. (1998). Leadership for the twenty-first century: Breaking the bonds of dependency. *Educational Leadership, 55*(7), 6–10.

Fullan, M., & Stiegelbauer, S. (1991*). The meaning of educational change*. New York: Teachers College Press.

Goldring, E. (1990). The district context and principals sentiments toward parents. *Urban Education, 24*, 391–403.

Goode, A. (2002). *Leadership: What are the essential qualities of successful leaders?* Available: www.ocmetro.com/metro 041802/business 041802.html (2004, October 11).

Grazier, P. (1999). *What is team building, really?* Available: www.teambuilding.com/article_teambuilding.htm (2004, July 9).

Gupton, S. L. (2002). *The instructional leadership toolbox: A handbook for improving practice*. Thousand Oaks, CA: Sage.

Hendrickson, P. (1996). The toolbox for teams. *Speakers Platform*. Available: www.speaking.com/articlehtmPattyHendrickson/60.html (2004, July 8).

Hoban, T. (2004). *Managing conflict: A guide for watershed partnership*. Conservation Technology Informative Center. Available: www.ctic.purdue.edu/KYW/Brochures/ManageConflict.html (2004, June 24).

Holmes Group. (1990). *Tomorrows teachers*. East Lansing, MI: The Holmes Group.

Hopkins, G. (2003). Principals share lessons learned: Staffing decisions, bringing about school change. *Education World*. Available: www.education-world.com/a_admin/admin305.shtml (2004, July 10).

Hord, S. M. (1994). *Staff development and change process: Cut from the same cloth*. Austin, TX: Southwest Educational Development Laboratory. Available: http://sedl.org/change/issues/issues42.html (2004, July 10).

Howey, D. (1988). Why teacher leadership? *Journal of Teacher Education, 39*, 28–31.

Hoy, W. K., & Miskel, C. G. (1996). *Educational administration: Theory research and practice*. New York: McGraw-Hill.

Kathman, J., & Kathman, M. (1990). Conflict management in the academic library. *Journal of Academic Librarianship, 16*(3), 145–149.

Katzenbach, J., & Smith, D. (1993). *The wisdom of teams: Creating the high performance organization*. Boston, MA: Harvard Business School Press.

Kaufman, R. (2002). *Ten innovative ideas for successful team building events*. Ron Kaufman Active Learning. Available: www.ronkaufman.com/articles/article.team.html (2004, July 5).

Kelly, V. (2003). *Luken and May MMM Archive*. Available: www.lukenmay.com (2004, July 9).

Kotter, J. P. (1996). *Leading change*. Boston, MA: Harvard Business School Press.

Ladew, D. P. (1998). *How to supervise people*. Franklin Lakes, NJ: Career Press.

Lambert, L. (2003). *Leadership capacity for lasting school improvement*. ASCD. Available: www.ascd.org/cms/objectlib/ascdframeset/index.cfm?publication=http://www.ascd.org/publications/books/2003lambert/foreword.html (2004, July 7).

Liontos, L. B. (1994). *Shared decision-making.* Eugene, OR: ERIC ED No. 368 034.

Livingston, C. (1992). Teacher leadership for restructured schools. In C. Livingston (ed.), *Teachers as leaders: Evaluating roles* (NEA School Restructuring Series). Washington, DC: National Education Association.

Lloyd, K. (2002). *Be the boss your employees deserve.* Finger Lakes, NJ: Career Press.

Lombardi, V. (1996). *Coaching for teamwork: Winning concepts for business in the twenty-first century.* Bellevue, WA: Reinforcement Press.

Louis, K. S., & Miles, M. (1990). *Reforming the urban high school: What works and why.* New York: Teachers College Press.

Maddux, R. (1992). *Team building: An exercise in leadership.* Menlo Park, CA: Crisp Publications.

Maeroff, G. (1993). *Team building for school change: Equipping teachers for new roles.* New York: Teachers College Press.

Marshak, D. (1996). The emotional experience of school change: Resistance, loss, and grief. *NASSP Bulletin, 80*(577), 72–77.

Masters, M. F., & Albright, R. R. (2002). *The complete guide to conflict resolution in the workplace.* New York: American Management Association.

Mayer, B. (2000). *The dynamics of conflict resolution: A practitioner's guide.* San Francisco: Jossey-Bass.

McLaughlin, M. W., & Yee, S. M. (1998). School as a place to have a career. In A. Lieberman (ed.), *Building a professional culture in schools.* New York: Teachers College Press.

Mendez-Morse, S. (1993). *Vision, leadership, and change.* Southwest Educational Development Laboratory. Available: www.sedl.org/change/issues/issues23.html (2004, May 20).

Milstein, M. M. (1993). *Restructuring schools: Doing it right.* New York: Corwin Press.

Mulford, B. (April 2003). *School leaders: Changing roles and impact on teacher and school effectiveness.* A paper commissioned by the Education and Training Policy Division, Organisation for Economic Cooperation and Development (OECD), for the Activity Attracting, Developing, and Retraining Effective Teachers (pp. 1–65).

Nanus, B. (1992). *Visionary leadership: Creating a compelling sense of direction for your organization.* San Francisco: Jossey-Bass.

Norman, S. J. (2003). *The human face of school reform.* Indiana University–Purdue University–Fort Wayne. Available: www.nationalforum.com/12norman.html (2004, July 9).

O'Hair, M., & Reitzug, V. (1997). Teacher leadership: In what ways? For what purposes? *Action in Teacher Education, 19*(3), 65–76.

Palmer, P. J. (1998). *The courage to teach: Exploring the inner landscapes of a teacher's life.* San Francisco: Jossey-Bass.

Paulu, N., & Winters, K. (eds.). (1998). *Teachers leading the way: Voices from the national teachers forum.* Washington, DC: ERIC ED No. 462 376.

Reagon, B. (2001). Fund for Southern Communities Award Ceremony. Atlanta, GA: Spelman College. Available: www.ericdigests.org/2002-4/teachers.html (2004, July 8).

Rogus, J. F. (1990). Developing a vision statement: Some consideration for principals. *NASSP Bulletin, 74*(523), 6–12.

Rost, J. C. (1993). *Leadership for the twenty-first century.* Westport, CT: Praeger.

Sammon, G. (2001). The challenge of change. *The High School Magazine, 7*(9), 32–36.

Senge, P. (1999). *The dance of change: The challenges of sustaining momentum in learning organizations.* New York: Doubleday.

Sergiovanni, T. J. (1990). Adding value to leadership gets extraordinary results. *Educational Leadership, 47*(8), 23–27.

Snowden, P. E., & Gorton, R. A. (2002). *School leadership and administration.* New York: McGraw-Hill.

Spaulding, A. M. (1994). *The politics of the principal: Influencing teachers' school-based decision making.* Paper presented at the annual meeting of the American Educational Research Association. New Orleans, LA: ERIC ED No. 374 542.

Stockwell, R. G. (1997). Effective communication in managing conflict. *CMA: The Management Accounting Magazine, 71,* 6. Info Trac One File. Available: http://web6.infotrac.gale group.com (2004, June 29).

Texas Center for Women's Business Enterprise. (1997). *How to resolve conflicts without offending anyone.* Available: www.onlinewbc.gov/Docs/manage/conflicts.html (2004, July 6).

Troen, V., & Boles, K. (April 1992). *Leadership in the classroom: Women teachers as a key to school reform.* Paper presented at the annual meeting of the American Education Research Association, San Francisco, CA.

Van Slyke, E. J. (1999). Resolve conflict, boost creativity. *HR Magazine, 44*(12), 132–135. Info Trac One File. Available: http://web6.infotrac.galegroup.com (2004, July 5).

Wahlberg, H. (1989). District size and learning. *Education and Urban Society, 21,* 154–163.

Weick, K. (1978). Educational organizations as loosely coupled systems. *Administrative Science Quarterly, 21,* 1–19.

Weider-Hatfield, D., & Hatfield, J. D. (1995). Relationships among conflict management styles, levels of conflict, and reactions to work. *Journal of School Psychology, 135*(6), 687–700.

Weiss, C. H. (1993). Shared decision making about what? A comparison of schools with and without teacher participation. *Teachers College Record, 95,* 69–72.

Weiss, C. H., Cambone, J., & Wyeth, A. (1992). Trouble in paradise: Teacher conflicts in shared decision making. *Educational Administrative Quarterly, 28*(3), 350–367.

Weiss, D. H. (1997). Four steps for managing team storms. *Getting Results, 42,* 7. Info Trac One File. Available: http://webb.infotrac.galegroup.com (2004, June 26).

Weiss, J. (2002). *Team building.* Prometheon Online Library. Available: www.speaking.com/ articles.html/JoyceWeiss,M.A.CESP325.html (2004, July 4).

Westley, F., & Mintzberg, H. (1989). Visionary leadership and strategic management. *Strategic Management Journal, 10,* 17–32.

Westoby, A. (ed.). (1988). *Culture and power in educational organizations.* Milton Keynes, U.K.: Open Systems Press. Available: www.arasite.org/westoby.htm (2005, January 8).

Weymeyer, R. (2004). Eliminating office politics through team building. *The Physician Executive, 301*(1), 64–67.

Wynne, J. (2002a). *Teachers as leaders in education reform.* ERIC ED No. 462 376.

Wynne, J. (2002b). *Urban teacher leaders: Testimonies of transformation.* Unpublished paper presented at AACTE Conference, Dallas, TX.

CHAPTER 6

CLASSROOM MANAGEMENT IN THE URBAN SETTING

Students want to be accepted as learners,
not counted as problems.
—Damian and Herrara, 2002

■ ■ ■ ■ ■

URBAN PERSPECTIVES

Gilda Lyon
Urban High School Chemistry Teacher

I believe that I've developed over the years a true understanding of my students' needs, and I very much accept their cultural values and differences. I make it a point to create initiatives to connect with each of my students. Also, I know that students in our urban classes will exhibit behaviors to the extent that teachers allow them.

Gilda Lyon *knows* the ins and outs, as well as challenges and successes, of effective classroom management in urban classrooms. She has spent twenty-eight of her thirty years of teaching in the urban high school setting. "The personal rewards from teaching these students are great," reflected the five-foot-one, small-framed urban educator extraordinaire. "Most days I *know* that I have made a significant difference in the lives of my students. This can be gauged by what I call the 'awe factor,' which is measurement of my students' enthusiasm expressed and evident during our classroom hands-on and minds-on activities. When the concepts that I teach are tied to relevant ideas—such as the chemical interactions and physical transformations that occur as we make ice cream from basic ingredients—student enthusiasm for what they experience hands-on fuels the reasoning and learning of standards-based, scientific principles."

Although Lyon is petite in stature, she is long and strong in her classroom management of students in her chemistry classes. "I believe that I've developed over the years a true understanding of my students' needs, and I very much accept their cultural values and differences," she contends. "I make it a point to create initiatives to connect with each of my students. Also, I know that students in our urban classes will exhibit behaviors to the extent that teachers allow them."

To further her students' respect for her classroom standards and procedures, Lyon emphasizes the importance of collaborating with her students' parents or guardians. "I strongly believe in positive partnerships among those at home who are responsible for my students," she purported. In that those partnerships serve to productively support her associations with and expectations of students in her classes, she contends, "It's vitally beneficial to my teacher-to-student relationships to make contact with parents or guardians at home as *early* in the new school year as possible, via phone calls or home visits. Also, I find that it's important to know where your students live. Continued communication throughout the school year, by way of multiple media sources (e.g., notes home, email, general and school-based radio and/or TV announcements), and repetition of notifications, greatly helps busy parents learn about, remember, and make arrangements for parent-teacher meetings, conferences, and other important school-related events."

In sum, Lyon is convinced of the potential of her urban students. "Every child is a 'gifted' child," she justified. "It is up to teachers to find ways that extrapolate those gifts for use in classroom activities. No student can be in my class—and NOT learn!"

CULTURALLY SENSITIVE URBAN CLASSROOM MANAGEMENT

Understanding Urban Culture

Americans seem to be enamored with finding the proverbial silver bullet to solve their most difficult problems. Managing the urban classroom, indeed challenging, requires *three* silver bullets. Essentially, urban classroom management must be approached by exercising three elements:

1. an understanding of and sensitivity to the needs of urban students;
2. skill in establishing the classroom setting; and
3. effective teaching practice.

Taken together, these elements can form a powerful front in managing the classroom environment with the overall objective of improved student academic achievement.

As a requisite for effective urban teaching, the teacher must fully recognize the home and neighborhood conditions under which children live. Once recognized and acknowledged, teachers must employ sensitivity to meet the needs of their students in recognition of the everyday life conditions the students face. They must primarily understand that many of these children come to school both academically and socially unprepared.

Social, emotional, and/or behavioral problems are likely to surface among students in the urban classroom. Chapter 3 indicates that students' classroom performance is strongly influenced by the families' low socioeconomic status, and accumulated research findings report that most children from poor backgrounds start school already deficient in skills from those children of more privileged means. When family income falls short of meeting its basic needs of food, housing, healthcare, childcare, transportation, taxes, and so forth, student well-being is greatly jeopardized. Effected is the student's cognitive development, as well as his physical development (NCCP, 2003; Snowman & Bichler, 2003).

Socioeconomic status has been shown to link to a student's achievement test scores, grades, truancy, and school failure or dropout rate. Many students living in poverty will work to support themselves and their families, and, consequently, become disengaged with their formal education. Fifty percent or more of students who live in poverty eventually drop out of school (Burden, 2003). The National Center for Children in Poverty (2003), through extensive research accumulations and findings, reports that a strong pattern exists between family income and its students' development, as it relates to their health, social and emotional functioning, and cognitive skills. They conclude that the more income a family has, the better children perform in school (NCCP, 2003; Snowman & Bichler, 2003).

Urban students' school performances reflect numerous complex situations that involve race, poverty, family, neighborhood conditions, and peer pressure, all of which challenge the urban teacher's application of classroom instructional delivery. Upon arrival to formal schooling (for example, kindergarten), students of low-income families demonstrate a significant achievement lag behind their peers who are from more affluent means (Kopetz, 2003; Ormrod, 2003; Thompson, Grandgenett, & Grandgenett, 1999). Students who fall behind academically may be retained at a certain grade level, and will subsequently repeat the grade. Forty percent of students who are retained will eventually drop out of school. Studies concur that, if retained to repeat a grade for a *second* year, the possibility of those students dropping out of school rises to 90 percent (Thompson, 2003).

Effective urban teachers show genuine interest and sincere sensitivity to their students' needs. Their warmth and concern reflective in their management philosophy of the classroom demonstrates that they sincerely care for their students. Research supports that teachers who make an effort to really know their students, and support them with encouragement and guidance, are best equipped to motivate and engage them in formal classroom learning and continued academic achievements (Matus, 1999; Williams & Woods, 1997). Alienated students *need* attention from interested adults who will motivate them to succeed. The students often drop out of school simply because no one cared (NCREL, 2004).

Successful teachers in urban settings learn all they can about their respective students. They gain as much knowledge as possible about the daily routines and influences present in their students' homelives and in their respective neighborhood associations, as well. Urban educators become acquainted with the students' daily living environment, as culturally familiar references presented in the classroom give relevance to the students' learning and can add a sense of comfort to the classroom for students of various ethnic origins. Teachers' familiarity with each student and his background thus better connects them to their students, and enables them to share in their classrooms acknowledgement and acceptance of practices and relevant situations that occur in students' home environments (West Education, 2004).

Teaching in culturally diverse, urban settings with students from varieties of ethnic backgrounds requires that educators remain sensitive to students' instilled beliefs, values, and customs. They need to understand their students' styles of learning, communication, and discipline and, as it applies to typical urban populations, they need to acknowledge and understand the effects of poverty on students' learning and behavior.

Knowing well the student and his living conditions help teachers to justly interpret certain student behaviors to which they might not otherwise respond appropriately (Grossman, 1995; Irvine, 2003; Nakamura, 2000). When teachers attempt to consider and understand the cultural realities of their students, they are best able to incorporate into their classroom management strategies various cautious, prevention and intervention techniques.

Further, realities of children from urban populations who struggle academically in school are commonly due to conditions for which they have little or no control, such as low birth weight, the possibility of lead poisoning, hunger and malnourishment, makeup of the family, frequent school changes, school safety, and homelife that likely includes above-average or heavy television watching, less parent availability, little or no reading to young children, and general lack of parent participation in children's education (Barton, 2004). In brief, the following sections explain such conditions that very likely lead to instructional barriers or challenges to the urban teacher.

Low Birth Weight.   Infants of such condition are typically at risk of delayed motor and social development and are more likely to fail or repeat grades. Children of color experience higher rates of low birth weight than White children.

Lead Poisoining.   Current data identify children of color under the age of 6 as two to three times more at risk of lead poisoning from their immediate environment than White children.

Hunger and Malnourishment.   If children are hungry or malnourished, it impacts their cognitive development. Black and Hispanic children under the age of 18 are nearly three times more likely to be hungry and unsure of their food supply than are White children.

Makeup of the Family.   Trends are discouraging, as two-parent families are becoming less existent in the United States as well as in all developing countries. Figure 6.1 illustrates that only 36 percent of African American children live in two-parent households; 65 percent of Hispanic children live in two-parent households; and 74 percent of White children live in two-parent households (U.S. Census Bureau, 2003). Thus, since 6.4 of every ten African American children reside in non-two-parent environments—in fact, it is estimated that almost one in ten

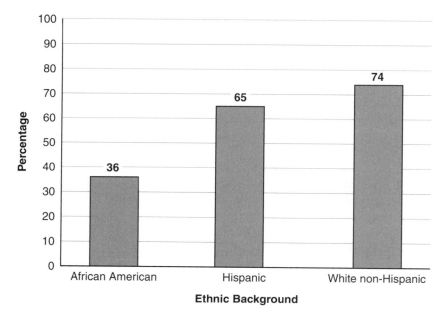

FIGURE 6.1   United States Children in Living in Two-Parent Homes

Source: Table C3. *Living arrangements of children under 18 years and marital status of parents by age, gender, race, and hispanic origin of the child for all children: March 2003.*
Available: www.census.gov.pop.www.socdemo/hh-fam/cps 2003.html.

Black children lives with neither parent—and 3.5 of every ten Hispanic children reside in non-two-parent environments, and 2.5 of every ten White children reside in non-two-parent environments, children of struggling, single-parent mothers, and sometimes fathers, are concentrated more among families of color than among the White population. From their communities and schools, it is apparent that these children of color, in general, need all the help they can get (Barton, 2004). These conditions are inherent in urban communities.

Frequent School Changes.   Regarding the effects of mobility, for example, a recent study conducted in Jefferson City, Kentucky identified "frequent school changers" as having scored poorest on tests. The highest population of "frequent school changers" were students from economically poor and single-parent households (Barton, 2004), a combination of factors, affecting children in urban environments.

School Safety.   Fear and disruption impede learning. Unsafe schools affect negatively the classroom climate, demonstrating a range of student behaviors that include disrespect for teachers, absenteeism, the prevalence of alcohol and drugs, violence, and possession of firearms. The percentage of students of color who fear an attack at school is double that of White students.

Less Parent Availability. Research conducted and summarized by the Child Trends Data Bank (www.childtrendsdatabank.org) concludes that students' parent participation—that is, strong interaction between parents and the school—yields students who demonstrate few behavior problems and better academic performance, who are more likely to go on to complete their high school studies (Barton, 2004).

Effective urban teachers are sensitive to and knowledgeable of the diverse cultures of urban communities brought by the children into the classroom. Due to cultural differences, some student behaviors demonstrated in the home are deemed inappropriate if exhibited in the classroom or at school, in general. Some student behaviors based upon family cultural differences might go unnoticed, but should alert teachers of students' learning needs; for example, Hispanic students may not request academic assistance when they actually do need the help. Teachers are liable to misconstrue other culturally ingrained student behaviors that suggest disinterest or even disrespect, such as students of other countries who may offer no or only limited eye contact with their teachers. Thus, the better the teachers' comprehensive understanding of their students' culturally-relevant behaviors, and those that are learned and practiced in their home environment, the more acceptance and guidance they can provide. Further, keeping open lines of communication with students' parents or guardians helps to offset misunderstandings that may be the cause of student discipline problems in the school or classroom.

At-Risk Student Classroom Behavior

From a label made prominent as a result of the 1983 report *A Nation at Risk* (see Chapter 1), the at-risk student originates from all ethnic and socioeconomic backgrounds. In urban settings, these students are more likely to be from minority families, specifically of African American, Asian American, Hispanic, and Native American origins. Disproportionate numbers of students who drop out of school are minority students; many live among families who speak little or no English in the home. They are the students most likely to drop out of high school, not having completed the coursework necessary to earn their high school diplomas (Maryland State Department of Education, 1998; U.S. Department of Education, 2004).

To gain a better understanding of the academic achievement gaps that exist among high school students, and demonstrating the percentages of at-risk students who do not complete high school, Figure 6.2 identifies, by race, percentages of high school students graduating in the spring of 2003. While White and Asian American students are close in number of students graduating, the gap present between African American graduates is significant, as is the alarmingly lower graduation rate of Hispanic students.

Urban schools teach the greatest concentrations of minority students considered at risk. There is no simple answer or single strategy to "cure" these students of their at-risk liability (Ormrod, 2003). Typically, students at risk are children and adolescents who have not acquired, and are ill-equipped to use, skills necessary to develop and mature into productive citizens in our society. Critically affecting students' attitudes, behaviors, and potential to progress academically and into secure employment are their less-than-adequate living conditions, lack of attention from home, and scarce community support (Burden, 2003).

The design of classroom management practices in urban schools should take into consideration that urban students are typically among the neediest of youngsters. Urban students are prone to facing adverse living conditions daily (Quality Counts, 1998). Very likely to leave school prior to high school graduation, the at-risk student population will display some or many of the following personal at-risk indicators:

- low self-esteem
- lack of adequate attention span; highly distractible
- poverty
- health problems
- teenage pregnancy, sexual activity
- abuse and neglect
- alcohol and/or drug abuse
- suicide attempts
- show little or no motivation

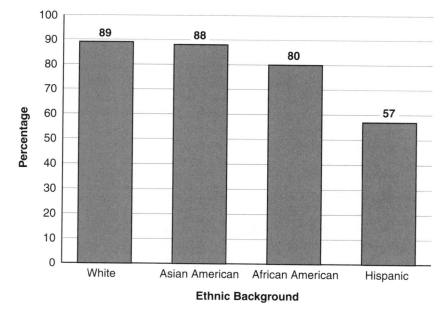

FIGURE 6.2   High School Graduates in United States, 2003
Source: U.S. Census Bureau Educational Attainment Survey, 2/03–4/03.

- void of family support
- gang violence
- overall poor quality of life
- juvenile delinquency
- eating disorder and/or self-abuse

Students may exhibit in school behaviors that demonstrate the noteworthy indicators. The characteristics may be demonstrated by students who display personal at-risk indicators in school that often include:

- academic difficulties and/or grade repeats
- poor study skills and/or incomplete or no homework
- bored with school; unchallenged by schoolwork
- detached from academics and school overall
- truancy, excessive absenteeism
- feelings of failure (threatened by learning)
- lacking in social skills; failure to get along well with teachers or peers
- deficient English language skills
- quick to join peers in alternative education settings
- not feeling safe (Burden, 2003; Forte & Schurr, 2002; Ormrod, 2003; Quality Counts, 1998)

"Achievement gaps mirror inequalities in those aspects of schooling, early life, and home circumstances that research has linked to school achievement" (Barton, 2004, p. 13). This statement offers a clear indication of how complex the challenges are to succeed in closing the current achievement gap. Since the implementation of the accountability movement in the No Child Left Behind legislation, reports are surfacing that demonstrate incremental growth toward this achievement.

Impact of At-Risk Variables on Students in the Classroom

Urban educators should understand that many of these conditions develop and exacerbate each other. For example, low self-esteem likely leads to behavior problems that may lead to drug and/or alcohol abuse that may lead to violent or criminal activities. Further, when young students have difficulties in relating to others, such as exhibiting aggression or defiance, or appear anxious or withdrawn, these feelings typically continue within them through adolescence, and lead to delinquency or other risky actions (NCCP, 2003). Students from low socioeconomic backgrounds are suspended from school far more frequently than students of high socioeconomic levels (Maryland State Department of Education, 1998). Effective classroom teachers in the urban setting flex their creative, problem-solving strategies to offer specific assistance to help meet their learners' vast and scattered needs. Educators present to students better options to consider and use, rather than their current repertoire of negative or irresponsible behaviors. Teachers' consistent modeling and recognizing appropriate behavior in school rewards students' acceptable and admirable qualities that they themselves choose to demonstrate.

Classroom management in urban settings can influence, educate, and lead students who are receptive to accepting better behavior choices. Where student attitudes stem from culturally prevalent social factors—namely, intense bias, racism, and or sexism, the positive, organized learning atmosphere established by effective urban teachers can help students discover new identities outside of what they currently know. In this pleasant, predictable learning environment, students are availed opportunities to grasp visions of better or new ways to conduct their behavior in responsible manners (Burden, 2003; The Condition of Education, 2003; Jones & Jones, 2001; Kopetz, 2003; Maryland State Department of Education, 1998; Nakamura, 2000; Ormrod, 2003; Thompson, Grandgenett, & Grandgenett, 1999).

Seasoned, more experienced educators claim that the key to helping potentially at-risk students achieve their potential is to early identify students with a proclivity to inappropriate behavior choices—and not give up on them. Teachers can lead with beneficial interventions and encourage positive peer relations. Further, prevention, along with early intervention, is much more effective than offering late assistance that seeks to fix resulting student problems. Remaining vigilant in the drive to leave no child behind, urban educators and parents assist struggling learners early in their preschool and elementary years. They can nurture and guide these students to maintain honest and earnest efforts to better themselves and achieve academic goals, as opposed to accessing poor behavior choices, or falling behind in their advancement from grade to grade (The Condition of Education, 2003; Thompson 2003).

ATTITUDES OF EFFECTIVE URBAN TEACHERS

Successful urban teachers recognize that each student contributes to the richness of ideas and actions present in the learning environment. They recognize the magnitude and the degree of influence they have on their students, as they aspire to guide students to achieve to their fullest potential. They understand students' varied differences in cognitive abilities, language, interests, home environments, socioeconomic status, and so on. Ethnic and cultural differences may create achievement barriers for students, however, and their situations are further exacerbated when they come from poor backgrounds or live in poverty. As opposed to only acknowledging certain students for their proven abilities, effective teachers manage their classroom with attitudes that encourage and positively reinforce all students for their demonstrated efforts and unique abilities. Their genuinely expressed can-do attitudes set the supportive educational milieu that moves stu-

dents to improve their grade-level academic skills and assist them to reach instructional goals (Maryland State Department of Education, 1998).

When learning about their students, teachers' attitudes demonstrate their value of individual differences. Effective teachers understand that their students are children or adolescents *first*, who demonstrate acquired, unique learning styles. Students are more alike than different and they deserve respect for their shared needs, concerns, and goals. Effective educators focus on each student's abilities amidst a nonthreatening classroom environment that encourages teachers and students to learn from one another, as well as from existent, printed knowledge. Students, in turn, are availed opportunities to mirror the teachers' enthusiasm, as each student is treated as though he is the most important student in the class (Burden, 2003; Taylor, Pressley, & Pearson, 2000).

RECOGNIZING URBAN DIVERSITY

In order to best meet the educational needs of diverse populations of students in our classrooms, educators are charged to create positive, supportive, and caring classroom learning environments that offer relevant and responsive curricula and instructional strategies with representing its students' different cultures and communities. Further, rather than ignoring, tolerating, or mildly accepting students' cultural differences, effective urban teachers celebrate their students' diversity. They build heritage connections for students that fit numerous grade-level subject areas. Achievement is boosted by school climates that celebrate diversity and stress zero tolerance for inequality among individuals. They create the most pleasant of learning environments (Ben-Yosef, 2003; Burden, 2003).

Effective urban educators take opportunities to demonstrate the value of variations in student learning styles, behaviors, physical attributes, languages, and family backgrounds. The multicultural mix of knowledges and talents lends itself to fascinating stories, interesting discussions, and demonstrations of culture-based practices such as foods, clothing, and traditions. Scheduling invited class guests— such as local or regional role models, heroes, and mentors—from the community can enrich student understandings, and visits to museums or special area events can reinforce and support what students learn in their class lessons (McBee, 1998; U.S. Department of Education, 2004; West Education, 2004).

Accommodating Diverse Learners' Needs

Urban teachers must be sensitive to the unique needs of their learners who represent diverse backgrounds. Organized and prepared, they must make sound, quick decisions to contend with unanticipated occurrences. Healthy in-class communication and collaboration, practiced and encouraged in the classroom, is essential for urban children in order to nurture them and to benefit their capability as successful learners (Ormrod, 2003; Tinzmann et al., 1990).

Sound classroom management practices effectively create the learning environment that encourages urban students to engage in a cooperative and collaborative manner, as opposed to a climate of competitiveness and rivalry. Key to the urban teacher's success in the classroom is not only engaging students in active learning, but also his focus on sound and consistent classroom management practices (Burden, 2003; Nakamura, 2000; Ormrod, 2003; Zirpoli, 2005). For urban children this is imperative.

Urban teachers' successful management of their classrooms of students with diverse ethnic and cultural backgrounds challenges them to adopt strategies and techniques that best accommodate this special population of learners to achieve academically, behave appropriately, and interact well with their peers. Again, although differences and variability between and among ethnic groups may be strong and wide, these students are more alike than different. Teachers are cautioned not to overgeneralize their thoughts and ideas about individuals of particular cultures. Student cultural characteristics they may read and learn about do not exist in all cases for all students of that ethnicity. For example, individuals of different cultures (including Whites) hold varying criteria for "success." They respond to different types and deliveries of praise and recognition, as well as variations in how they receive criticism, acceptance, or rejection. Understanding that students of various cultures think and behave in different ways, and awareness that educators, themselves, uniquely interpret students' behaviors based upon their own frames of reference, encourages teachers to cautiously examine their accommodative responses to students in urban settings. Expectations of all learners must always remain high. Understanding and awareness of their students' individual challenges or personal circumstances helps urban teachers to learn and practice culturally appropriate, accommodative educational approaches from their classroom management skills repertoire (Grossman, 1995).

The teachers' concern for all students to achieve at high levels aligns with their sensitivity to students' needs for acceptance and value as important members of the class and important members of their neighborhood communities, as well. Effective teachers demonstrate appreciation for their students' differing qualities that greatly enhance the classroom climate and feelings of recognition and favorable reception from peers in their learning community. Effective classroom management, practiced in an environment among students of mixed cultures, is based upon an atmosphere that remains receptive to the views of all participants, yet prohibits any show of prejudice, oppression, rejection, or abuse. Urban educators appreciate that students' needs will vary and remain open to assisting them (Burden, 2003; Grossman, 1995; Maryland State Department of Education, 1998; Taylor, Pressley, & Pearson, 2000).

Modeling Appropriate Behavior

Students in the urban school environment acquire a wealth of opportunities to learn gentle, moderate, and socially acceptable patterns of communication from their teachers and other school personnel. Teachers model their values and beliefs in their self-expression, dress, interests, and so on. In schools and classrooms, students learn from the manner in which teachers respond to their peers' appropriate, or sometimes inappropriate, verbal statements, or to unexpected classroom occurrences. Students are exposed to their teachers' skills of offering temperate responses to a peer's anger or aggressive actions, or to rare occurrences if students engage in aggressive behaviors in the urban classroom or school. Exposed to teachers' modeling moral reasoning and empathy in their decision-making tasks, students learn skills of fair and just negotiations and appropriate expressions of feelings. Students will scrutinize the interpersonal relations they witness at play between and among faculty and administrators and other school personnel that impacts their view of how positive associations and friendships are welcomed and valued as they exist in an amicable workplace (Canter and Associates, 1998; Ormrod, 2003).

Further, teachers influence their students when they model appropriate skills by thinking aloud their ideas or demonstrating procedures in step-by-step fashion. They may verbalize their hypothesized predictions to situations or experiments. They may summarize ideas in passages to provide examples of thought continuity. They problem solve with students ideas that think through tough group situations and problems. Students are presented multiple opportunities daily to learn from their teachers effective negotiation skills that help them achieve their desires (Tinzmann et al., 1990).

In addition, through educators' positive role modeling, students are exposed to proper and socially acceptable conduct. Educators help in students' relationship-building skills when they encourage and conduct informal chats with them. When adults in the school environment allow the time for students to adequately express themselves and to interact positively with them, these collective and strong in-school communication experiences pave the way to improved student efficacy; that is, students gain opportunities to express their learning accomplishments, as well as their desire to learn more. Enabling students to model and practice effective verbal interaction skills provides them valuable communication benefits, academically and for life experiences ahead (Heron, 2003; Matus, 1999).

Teaching in an urban setting represents a unique opportunity to influence the lives of children that is not present in suburban areas. These are the children of minority families and the children of the poor, and therefore require extraordinary efforts on the part of their teachers. Managing the classroom so that it is conducive to learning is one of the most important skills the teacher must employ. How the teacher plans classroom management begins with an understanding of urban conditions and a sensitivity to work within those conditions.

CLASSROOM SETTING AND ENVIRONMENT

Establishing the Basics

Given the challenges that urban areas present for schools, it is imperative that teachers establish a comfortable, yet very organized, classroom setting. This cannot be left to chance, but must be strategically planned. This section will focus upon establishing a classroom environment that positions children for learning.

Motivating Urban Students in the Classroom

It is important to instill in students the desire to learn and gain greater knowledge about the world and its specific novelties, interesting facts, and trends. Urban teachers have a responsibility to students to incorporate in the classroom a purpose for learning and an understanding for the need for knowledge. To create in the classroom this attraction and contagious motivation, teachers should consider establishing a classroom climate that holds true the following tenets:

- All students can succeed in school.
- Students' interests are high priority in instruction; they are encouraged to share their own experiences.
- Praise, reinforcement, encouragement, and guidance reap rewarding student gains and benefits.
- Enthusiasm for and value of students and their ideas boost students' aspirations.
- Social connections and relationships are coveted.
- Care and concern are genuine, even when discipline is rendered.

- Teachers and students demonstrate a willingness to empathize with students' expressions of feelings.
- Students' ideas are heard and valued in the classroom.
- Students' or teachers' raised voices in the classroom are unbecoming and inappropriate.
- Classroom activities offer success to students, which encourages further effort.
- Opportunities are created that encourage all students to participate.
- Continual and consistent efforts to commend admirable student performance is standard in classrooms.
- Students' privacy is respected and can be shared with the teacher nonpublicly and confidentially.
- Students are encouraged to be active and identified with the school, instilling the sense of belonging.
- School members attend community cultural events to learn more about the students.
- Capitalizing on students' strengths promotes strong self-esteem.
- Parents are respected, as exhibited in the students' presence. (Burden, 2003; Haberman, 1995; Nakamura, 2000; Ormrod, 2003; Teacher Talk, 2004; Wong & Wong, 1998).

Educators who supervise the classroom are managers who create positive learning environments and empower their students to understand and get actively involved in their instruction and learning. Classroom management, proven to be scientific since it is based upon behavior research, remains an art that can be learned. Techniques of successful classroom management are refined with on-the-job experience. Effective urban educators, as astute classroom managers, are goal-driven, very much in control of the learning environment, and know what is going on amidst an established, supportive classroom atmosphere. They seek to maintain positive relationships with their students, satisfy students' basic needs for best focus on academic matters, model behaviors and attitudes that students should wish to emulate, promote group cohesiveness, and enhance students' belief in the value of school. Necessary to a successfully run class with optimal conditions for learning is a teacher's expertise in highly developed instructional skills, which include areas of planning, teaching, and evaluating, as well as skills of group management and organization. These skills also include the expertise to establish an overall program recognizing the students' wide range of abilities and needs (Blair, 2003; Grossman, 1995; Jones & Jones, 2001).

Effective teachers design and practice classroom management strategies that establish and enhance a pleasant learning environment—an atmosphere that demonstrates class compatibility, academic time, and purpose for achieving grade-level, standards-based goals. Effective classroom management entails several considerations and factors that teachers contemplate, design, implement, tweak, and reflect upon for use in their classrooms as necessary (Blair, 2003;

Grossman, 1995). The following segments contain key elements of classroom management, beginning with the classroom's physical arrangement, classroom climate, maintaining and respecting order, student behavior, planned class activities, monitoring achievement, assignment modifications and accommodations, and prosocial encouragers. These elements are important in any teaching situation, but they are of critical importance in urban classrooms.

Physical Arrangement.   The desks, tables, learning and computer centers, and so forth, represent a well-planned design that allows for adequate flow between the teacher and students for valuable and meaningful interactions. The design keeps distractions to a minimum and the teacher has full viewing range of her students that enhances individual and group monitoring (Burden, 2003; Ormrod, 2003).

Classroom Climate.   The ambiance or classroom atmosphere demonstrates respect, acceptance, and compassion for all individuals. This is particularly important in urban classrooms since these qualities are often not resident in the home. The classroom is pervasively positive, achieving an amicable environment that enhances students' personal growth. Though somewhat businesslike, it transmits comfortable and nonthreatening feelings. Effective urban teachers endeavor to make the students feel that they are special. Student work and projects are displayed in the classroom and throughout the school, as well. Posters reflecting cultural differences or foreign language phrases add multicultural enhancements that encourage and strengthen students' self-esteem and enthusiasm for learning. The students enjoy the sense of belonging that these efforts create in the school and in their classrooms. Their obvious comfort level in the setting helps them maintain interest in learning. Along with varied assignments and teacher instructional formats that have relevance to real-world tasks, the focused and respectful classroom climate heightens student motivation levels and gives class participants good feelings about attending school (Burden, 2003; McBee, 1998; Nakamura, 2000; Ormrod, 2003).

Maintaining and Respecting Order.   An effective learning environment is structured, and boasts a system of order that enables its students to achieve successfully. When students have an understanding of the teacher's expectations for an orderly classroom, and are hence focused on instructional activities and not on inappropriate behaviors, all class participants are more likely to engage in their own learning and project satisfaction with the established order and organization of classroom procedures (Burden, 2003). The need for order cannot be overemphasized for the urban classrooms. Many urban children have no order in their lives, and this often carries over into the classroom. It is critically important for the teacher to establish and maintain an orderly environment.

Student Behavior.   Behavior limits set are comfortable and appropriate, yet not too restrictive. Students are allowed certain curricular, supervisory, and/or decision-making powers, such as input into resolving how completed tasks appear acceptable per grade level standards, or setting mutually agreed-upon assignment deadlines. The focus of sound and consistent appropriate student behavior is on prevention, rather than correction, of unacceptable or indifferent behavior. There is no one magic formula for handling discipline problems once they surface. Effective teachers will choose their battles by prioritizing the severity of student behavior problems and dealing with or redirecting student misconduct toward quality options that make the best sense. More than "dodging bullets," or seeking "avoidance of problems," effective teachers will learn specific techniques that will help particular students who needing greater self-control and who do not respond to techniques that keep the class functioning and that keep most students on task in productive academic activities.

Boundaries are set and incorporated by way of classroom rules and procedures (see page 205). Established boundaries allow for student input, detail of appropriate consequences if boundaries are violated, and are honored and sustain consistent respect and enforcement by the teacher and students. Holding to these limits reduces fear, distrust, and threats—deterring components that are sure to interfere with and threaten the learning environment (Blair, 2003; Haberman, 1995; Nakamura, 2000; Ormrod, 2003).

Planned Class Activities.   True to the adage that "if you fail to plan, you plan to fail," effective teachers, to improve their classroom management skills, spend time before the school year, or at least prior to actual teaching, collecting and organizing materials needed for their class lesson activities. Having achieved this preparation gives them greater confidence in their daily interactions with the students, as well as more efforts concentrated on actual teaching. Teachers implement class activities with mutual dignity, respect, and trust as students participate in the instructional procedures and methods that encourage their continued, on-task behaviors and engagement in the learning process (Blair, 2003; Nakamura, 2000; Ormrod, 2003).

Monitoring Achievement.   Teachers continue surveillance and supervision of the classroom to keep the environment convivial and productive, while focused on achievement of instructional objectives (Blair, 2003; Ormrod, 2003). As educators plan students' learning tasks and activities, students can be led to take charge in planning their own learning activities. This type of self-regulated and self-motivating scholarship, monitored by the classroom teacher, allows students to adjust their learning, to self-question their perceptions and knowledge gained, and to engage in subject-related inquiry among their peers. Sharing of ideas and feedback, monitored by the teacher, affords students' personal responsibility for what and how they choose to learn. Effectively monitoring students' progress in the classroom demonstrates how measurement and students' instructional concerns are very much interdependent (Blair, 2003; Tinzmann et al., 1990).

Assignment Modifications and Accommodations.   As effective educators adjust their teaching strategies so that their instruction is paced and explained well to the class, students demonstrate individual differences in their understanding and completion of classwork or assignments. Some students are engaged at a steady pace, while others are in need of receiving additional time and practice. There are other students in need of lesson enhancements (for example, computer software, physical gadgetry, additional readings) to supplement the current assignment with additional learning challenges (Ormrod, 2003). In keeping student expectations high, yet fair to meet students' individual learning differences, teachers modify assignments to best accommodate their classroom of varied learning styles represented.

Prosocial Encouragers.   The classroom emphasizes prosocial values such as sharing and cooperation, listening with empathy, demonstrating concern for others, and praising students as a positive reinforcer. Students benefit when they collaborate on ideas and assignment efforts. This allows them to practice their prosocialness, as opposed to focus on self-regulated, competitive completion or response time, or grading. For encouragement that leads to academic success, educators should recognize students for their individual and group accomplishments. For urban children, teacher encouragement and recognition may represent the only positives they receive. Teachers are cautioned that when praising students using positive feedback, they do so with the intention to reinforce and motivate students' learning. However, for some students, a teacher's praise may negatively reinforce them. Praise offered that is indeed meaningful, genuine, and immediate encourages students most and develops intrinsic motivation to learn (Blair, 2003; Ormrod, 2003).

Classroom Rules and Procedures

A well-managed classroom is a predictable, task-oriented environment where students actively engage in learning activities and strive to meet their academic expectations. There is little wasting of time or confusion, and students enjoy a work-oriented, but relaxed and pleasing, structured class setting. Urban educators who effectively manage their classrooms rely less on disciplining, or correcting, their students (McBee, 1998; Wong & Wong, 1998).

It is desirable in the urban classroom that, instead of plans for punishing the wrongdoers, the teacher guides the class to establish goals for considerate behavior and logical consequences that advise and encourage students' appropriate conduct. However, when the teaching and content of study are made interesting, relevant, and meaningful, the students are far more apt to be engaged in the learning and less into misbehavior or rule violations (Haberman, 1995; Wong & Wong, 1998).

For students to begin their classroom experiences knowledgeable of teacher expectations and classroom rules and procedures, urban teachers proactively establish with the students these conventions and understandings at the beginning of the school year. Classroom rules can be established and posted as two sets of expectations, general and specific. General class rules, discussed and endorsed by the students and teacher, are designed as flexible desires that cover major behavioral values, such as

- respecting others,
- respecting school property, and
- being kind and polite to others.

Likewise agreed upon by students and their teacher, respected, and implemented consistently, are specific rules that target particular behavior expectations, such as

- arrive to class on time,
- keep hands and feet to oneself, and
- no vulgar or offensive language. (McBee, 1998; Wong & Wong, 1998)

General and specific rules, procedures, and expectations, as guided by the teacher, will differ from one class to another, and from one grade level to another, depending upon the age level and maturity of students in the class.

In addition to classroom rules and procedures, schools must have a schoolwide discipline plan. It should be developed by teachers and administrators working together to design disciplinary measures and consequences that both can agree to, abide by, and implement. Under the circumstances, there can be concurrence of "how the punishment fits the crime," and how behavior reprimands are carried out. Typically, schoolwide discipline plans necessitate policy for considering students referred to the office due to misbehavior that occurs in the classroom, and for handling student problems that occur outside the classroom boundaries (Edwards,

2004). As a set of standards consistently upheld and valued by school personnel and students, the posted schoolwide discipline plan should be explained and understood by both the faculty and students, and families of students, also. School personnel should support the plan, as well as one another, in upholding its stipulations and procedures. Its strength and effectiveness depend on its schoolwide, universal, and consistent support and implementation (Wong & Wong, 1998).

Daily Classroom Strategies

Teachers in urban school settings can best maintain classroom control when they organize and prepare ahead of class for what they anticipate to occur throughout the day. Effective classroom management requires that educators research and establish prepared "housekeeping" systems that easily facilitate basic routine tasks that are integral to daily school life. Skillful educators arrange and systemize where possible the daily learning activities, not only to anticipate the everyday responsibilities, but also to ensure that necessary instructional materials and supplies are on hand and available, as needed (Haberman, 1995). Urban educators should have their plans set and tools ready to go. General responsibilities also include:

> handling administrative procedures, for example, daily lunch and attendance counts;
>
> devising, explaining, and disseminating classroom rules and procedures, for example, posts and copies;
>
> clarifying and circulating to all parties concerned (students, families, and the community) the schoolwide discipline plan; and
>
> designing stipulations regarding students' transitions from activity to activity, for example, quiet in halls.

These good "housekeeping" plans, which provide preplanning and organized daily facilitating of class priorities, anchor and substantially benefit teachers' overall class management agenda.

Presented throughout this chapter is the need for urban teachers to design plans that follow with consistency their management strategies, due to the likelihood of unexpected classroom situations or changes that often occur. Effective teachers establish procedures to facilitate daily operations in their classrooms, accountability methods that track student achievements, and other assigned tasks that align with the schools' efforts to serve its mission in the community. These classroom procedures, as established and followed, expedite swiftly the classroom duties, taking least amounts of time away from academic instruction. Tasks that need efficient and systematic attention are:

- role-taking
- lunch counts

- collecting fund-raising monies and forms
- taking up homework assignments
- grading assignments (Wong & Wong, 1998)

Effective teachers, having planned the sequence and procedures of these daily operations, demonstrate efficient classroom routine maintenance that minimizes distractions to the academic and instructional focus.

Positive Interventions

Getting students involved in the class challenges urban teachers to develop positive approaches to engage students and help them feel part of the active learning environment. As possible interventions to accomplish that end, urban teachers should consider:

- providing opportunities for students to be class leaders and to contribute to classroom operations; in the elementary grades, for example, students are given responsibilities to empty shavings from the pencil sharpener, feed the goldfish, or change the weather icon on the calendar. In high school, students may take charge of drafting the homeroom attendance count or distributing beakers for the science project;

- assigning students a mentor or buddy who offers cosupport for the class projects and encourages teamwork;

- offering a physical outlet for certain students to let off steam, such as allowing a student to be the lunch-count runner to the cafeteria, or asking a middle school student to help carry books to the library;

- designing for individual students a personalized behavior-management contract, which helps particular students monitor their own progress toward achieving academic and/or behavior goals;

- shortening or modifying assignments, without lowering acceptable achievement standards for those students or jeopardizing their accomplishing skill objectives;

- offering more one-on-one attention from the teacher, aides, peers, tutors, or volunteer helpers, which often provides just the right amount of encouragement and guidance to keep students from struggling and to remain on task with their assignment;

- investigating and offering tangible and age-level appropriate (no- or low-cost) rewards that can motivate students to engage in learning activities and to reach their academic and behavior goals;

- setting up quiet time or places to withdraw for reading, meditating, or relaxation, considered a treat from the busy schoolday;

- involving parents, and encouraging their support, which heightens learning value and interest;

■ giving students choices of classroom assignments and activities, which offer students greater control of their learning and instructional choices that align with their interests;

■ offering conflict resolution skills training at any school-aged level, which gives students the negotiation tools that benefit their peer relations, general persuasive powers, and appreciation for others' ideas and solutions to problems. (Forte & Schurr, 2002)

Teachers Guiding Students for Self-Management

One of the chief goals of classroom management is for students to learn and exhibit best choices of self-control that monitors their own behavior management. There are a number of suggestions for educators as they monitor classroom activities, and, as importantly, guide students self-management skills. These include teachers' offering students limited choices, encouraging classroom activities, focus on problem-solving skills, providing kind and firm action, asking versus telling, actions versus words, and offering time-out.

Teachers Offer Students Limited Choices.   Educators guide student input in decision making when they offer students limited, appropriate choices. For example, given two acceptable options, students make an appropriate choice. If

there is extra time left from reading instruction, students may elect to fill the remaining time by finding a story from the bookshelf to read silently, or by completing a vocabulary enhancing software program on the classroom computer. A cooperation-rich experience offers students the option to first collaborate and discuss their choices. From such discussions, students are to readily engage in situations that employ their group decision-making input.

Teachers Encourage Classroom Responsibilities. Students contribute to class operations by fulfilling weekly or monthly assigned classroom tasks. This promotes their sense of belonging and fosters their feelings of significance and importance. Completing these assignments likely boosts their self-esteem, confidence, and self-efficacy, as well as assists the teacher in meeting classroom responsibilities.

Teachers Focus on Problem-Solving Skills. Effective urban teachers teach their students to be aware of four basic problem-solving options:

- ignore the problem or problematic situation;
- converse and sort out the problem with those involved, discussing possible solutions;
- agree on a solution that allows both ideas to win; or
- rather than resolve the matter immediately, set a later meeting time to discuss further and select solutions after sharing and brainstorming ideas with others to get additional perspectives for a just and fair resolution.

The teachers' classroom discipline issues are curtailed greatly when they take the time to teach these and additional types of peer mediation skills.

Teachers Provide Kind and Firm Action. Effective teachers make decisions, render them, and follow through, kindly and fairly, and with respect and dignity. Most often, the fewer words spoken to do this the better, avoiding a superfluous lecture. It must be remembered that urban students are likely to not be accustomed to kindness or respect, and therefore will react in like fashion.

Teachers' Asking versus Telling. To gain students' perceptions of problems, and in helping them to think through ideas to resolve the problems, such as involving their using good judgment and realizing consequences, the teacher who asks, rather than tells, students about strategies to solve concerns provides them opportunities to learn from mistakes. This provides lifelong, usable skills that students internalize and remember (Burden, 2003; Tinzmann et al., 1990).

Teachers' Actions versus Words. Sometimes a simple "no" response, with no follow-up explanation, is very much in order. It is often unnecessary for teachers to explain the "no," since the students typically understand the reason why that decision rules. During instructional delivery, effective teachers refrain from using profuse and ineffectual verbiage throughout the day, preferring to communicate by listening and by offering frank and succinct instructions. Teachers demonstrate their care and sense of humor by using nonverbal and understood gestures. These gestures, or *cueing*, allow teachers the advantages of controlling noise or attention levels *nonverbally* in the classroom. For example, they may raise a hand into the air, finger to the lips, or point to the posted classroom rules and consequences to get students' attention without uttering a word (McBee, 1998; Wong & Wong, 1998).

Classrooms Offering Time-Out.   Total class instruction suffers when the class or certain students in the class are in need of cooling off or a change of pace or scene. Students may wish to help with suggestions for a creating a classroom area designated for those who need to calm down and get refocused. This action is best initiated discretely with as little attention drawn to the student as possible (Nelson, 1998).

Facilitating Smooth Transitions.   Behavior expectations for what the school personnel and teachers expect when transitions take place should be communicated and practiced in each classroom. Transitions occur when class activities change within the classroom, or from the classroom to other school locations. In order to prevent confusion or misunderstandings that may occur, and to protect students and peers during transitions, rules and procedures are established, explained well, and practiced, indicating acceptable and appropriate behaviors expected to accompany various transitions occurring throughout the class day. For example, transition procedures to consider and implement may include:

- students exiting the regular classroom to pass to special classes;
- students coming in from the playground to class;
- the class exiting for recess, and later returning to their classroom;
- restroom procedures; and
- filing to and returning from the school cafeteria and library. (Wong & Wong, 1998)

Advantages to planning strategies to manage the learning environment include:

- reducing transition time from one classroom activity to the next;
- preventing discipline problems by implementing routines and expectations;
- heading off possible crises by recognizing signs of potential misbehaviors;
- monitoring students for safety and efficiency;
- segmenting different tasks that promote responsibility; and
- establishing student expectations and mutual respect. (Matus, 1999)

The Safe Classroom

The school grounds, supervised settings with physical boundaries where children and adults interact, respect each other, and encourage and enjoy their learning experiences, should offer a safe environment, free from harm. The school's culture is one that demonstrates positive regard for others and for property; thus, safety is manifested in mutual respect and cooperation, establishing a psychologically secure place for learning. Effective urban teachers find ways to create safe havens where students are active in a learning-motivated environment that is nonthreatening and peaceful (Haberman, 1995).

A classroom that students regard as safe from danger is one that experiences preventive maintenance procedures, considerations and commonly advised measures to ensure students free of verbal or physical abuse. Safe classroom feelings in the learning climate yield more meaningful learning for students. Teachers endure fewer distractions or situations requiring on-the-spot decisions. Important to implementing these elements is that

- the teacher has direct control over the physical classroom areas; and
- teachers' practice and self-monitoring of their own growth in developing the management skills improve supervising of students and potential misbehaviors and the entire class with each lesson experienced.

Thus, teachers leading the instructional environment and deputizing all students as peacekeepers and solution finders encourages safe relations in the classroom. Effective teachers manage the class safely when they think ahead and thereby avoid problems, sense the class's pulse and energy level, and maintain a continuous grasp of the total classroom situation (Blair, 2003).

A safe learning environment, as a basic necessity of sound classroom management, is everyone's responsibility. As emphasized earlier in this chapter, in order to meet basic goals of effective classroom management that stipulates providing a safe learning environment, students must take responsibility for managing their self-control, insisting that their classmates do likewise. Teachers foster and encourage the practice of consideration and respect within the classroom from the first day of class and forward. The teacher may initiate brainstorming discussions among the students to devise a list of what determines a classroom as safe. The list would include attributes that create a nurturing school environment and classroom. These descriptors, when displayed on classroom walls, envelope students in positive values and serve as reminders of respectful behavior. Student-solicited suggestions that lead to a safe classroom atmosphere are:

- Eliminate peer pressure.
- Give forgiveness freely.
- Students respect students.
- Zero tolerance for verbal abuse.
- No talking behind someone's back.
- Halt gossiping, bullying, constant putdowns, and lying. (Dyck, 2004)

Urban students often demonstrate skill deficits in their abilities to resolve conflict, to communicate well, and to remain attentive as the class proceeds through daily academic instruction. These suggestions are valuable and necessary in an urban classroom that encourages students' new ideas, freedom of self-expression, and acceptance of others' opinions, to provide the basis for healthy, optimum learning experiences.

Conflict, Aggression, and Violence.   Teachers should encourage discussions concerning behaviors that are not appropriate in school. In-school altercations should be analyzed and resolved. Never are students allowed to hurt each other, either physically or emotionally (Ormrod, 2003). Two examples that assist resolving student conflict in schools are (1) the use of student study teams, where administrators, teachers, and parents meet to discuss and learn why a child is acting inappropriately and (2) introducing incentives that encourage appropriate student behavior, such as for good behavior or for good attendance. Examples are week- or month-end pizza or popcorn or ice cream parties, or students may earn "dollars" as part of an all-grade-level or all-school raffle for age-appropriate, desired prizes (Izumi, 2002).

The National Center for Children in Poverty (2003) showcased a program that was introduced in schools that endeavored to prevent violent and aggressive behavior in youths. The largest and longest-running of its kind in schools, the Resolving Conflict Creatively Program (RCCP) trained and coached the members of the schools' faculty to help students resolve conflicts and better their relationships with peers. Students who attended the programs self-reported their changes in attitudes and their greater understanding of others' behaviors. Most especially, they perceived those behaviors as less hostile or provoking and not directly aimed at them, personally. In addition, program participants subsequently learned to solve problems in a more passive fashion and were less likely to use violence.

From this important study are findings that indicate the following as skills that teachers should promote and support as effective classroom managers:

active listening

expressing feelings

dealing with anger

assertiveness

collaborative problem-solving (using negotiation and mediation)

appreciating diversity

countering discrimination

Currently, approximately two out of three schools incorporate some type of violence prevention program to reduce factors that lead to violence and to reduce violent and aggressive student behaviors. Woven throughout the daily curriculum, a focus on the list of skills has significant value to the lives of rising urban youngsters (National Center for Children in Poverty, 2003).

Urban classrooms require teachers to plan for managing their classrooms. The students typically experience lives in their homes and neighborhoods that are disorganized and devoid of rules of behavior. The children are also often lacking in acceptable social skills. If the teacher does not manage the classroom environment, bedlam will result. The principal objective of any classroom and the responsibility of the teacher is to cause learning to occur. Learning occurs

best when there is an orderly atmosphere in the classroom. Order does not occur naturally with urban students. It must be designed, monitored, and gauged by the teacher, ideally with student input.

GOOD TEACHER PRACTICES

Establishing the Educational Environment

Effective teaching begins with the creation of an environment that is conducive to maximizing learning. For many urban students, the classrooms in schools provide the only stability in their lives. Likewise, the urban teacher offers to them access to a stable adult. Where many students are concerned, the classroom teacher is their only hope for anticipating a brighter future ahead (Wong & Wong, 1998). No matter the age of students or the grade levels taught, teachers have expectations that determine how they efficiently and effectively operate their classrooms to produce learning. Good teacher practices build upon the educators' classroom management that incorporates teacher leadership capabilities that create and maintain a positive learning environment. Educational settings that demonstrate healthy communications and interactions between and among students and their teacher(s) encourages the student enthusiasm that sets the stage for valued instruction and students' engaged learning (Burden, 2003).

Best teaching practices occur in a classroom setting that creates an extended-family feel to the learning environment. Having established in learning an atmosphere where the students are relaxed and yet energized with momentum sets the stage for productive academic activity and rising achievement levels (Haberman, 1995; Ormrod, 2003). The instructional backdrop is the preconstructed classroom management plan in operation, where there is order and procedures guide student participation, individually and in groups. Maintaining acceptable classroom behavior practices and promotes student confidence in the teacher's leadership, and prepares them to concentrate upon learning.

Effective urban educators establish a classroom learning atmosphere that demands respect among fellow classmates and teachers (see also, "Learning Communities" in Chapter 4). Building this type of learning environment is a matter of taking small and often repetitive steps that instill as routine what is expected of learners. From there, the teacher moves students forward toward goals of students' productive and positive self-managed behavior. To best achieve this, effective urban teachers focus on students' strengths, and not their deficits. Prevalent in their practice is the underlying expectation that *all persons deserve to be treated with respect and courtesy*. Through modeling and reinforcing kind and considerate behavior in the classroom environment, students are provided opportunities to solve problems peacefully and collaboratively, and benefit greatly from working in a friendly, welcoming academic setting (Ormrod, 2003).

Effective urban teachers establish in their classrooms learning-collaborative communities, active, constructive learning occurring through varieties of methods and among varieties of classroom member combinations. Research supports that successful educators typically strive to establish in their classrooms positive learning-collaborative environments that encourage teacher–student and student–student interactions, spirited student engagement in class lessons and activities, and meaningful, student-generated initiatives and motivation. The communities are successful in their instilling in students the responsibility for learning (Taylor, Pressley, & Pearson, 2000).

Effective classroom management in the urban setting is demonstrated by a consistent, expected atmosphere conducive to optimal learning and achievement. Students anticipate involvement in productive learning activities that transition smoothly throughout the school day. They expect that in-class misbehaviors rarely interfere with their striving to achieve instructional objectives. The physical arrangement of the classroom, the established and posted rules and expectations, and varied instruction in the curriculum are established, and welcome students to a secure and planned climate for learning (Forte & Schurr, 2002).

Effective urban teachers practice in their classrooms skills and competencies that best help students at risk of school failure. Categories of concern fall into five areas, including personal, professional, materials, methods, and learning environment. To best assist students at risk or otherwise struggling academically, the following suggestions deserve comprehensive attention in classrooms.

- Use varieties of learning techniques, strategies, and materials.
- Reteach skills and allow for practice.
- Be positive and patient.
- Demonstrate care, concern, empathy, love, and respect.
- Be humanistic; acknowledge others' dignity and self-worth.
- Set high expectations for students.
- Work for best communication with students and their families.
- Be firm, consistent, and fair. (Burden, 2003)

Along with teaching students skills that reinforce curricular emphases, including practices in classroom management and during instruction offers at-risk students greater chances for sound development and to succeed in school (Burden, 2003).

Effective teachers introduce and continually reinforce social skills that enable better relations among urban school students, teachers, and administrators. Discussed in class and modeled by the adults, social initiatives, practiced and honed in the school setting include:

using quiet voices;

taking turns;

accepting and offering constructive criticism;

clarifying ideas;

expressing feelings;

using time wisely; and

listening closely to others.

Maintaining a positive social atmosphere where the above are practiced creates a respectful environment where all children are valued, their opinions are respected, and all have an opportunity to learn.

Establishing Effective Classroom Collaboration

Urban classrooms engage students in learning when they can be collaborative in nature and practice. According to Tinzmann et al. (1990), the collaborative classroom is composed of an environment where shared knowledge among teachers and students abounds. It exists where teachers and students value and strengthen their knowledge, personal experiences, language, strategies, and the cultural awareness that all students bring to the learning environment. Also, in the following explanations, the researchers emphasize additional features of the collaborative classroom that include shared authority, teachers who serve as mediators, and heterogeneous grouping of students.

Shared Authority.   Students provide input into the activities and assignments and classroom rules and procedures that most appeal to them, and decide how they wish to be assessed about what they've learned. Teachers get a direct read on better ways to incorporate students' interests into the curriculum and classroom management. This collaboration encourages students to interact respectfully among themselves, and engages them in high levels of understanding and compromise.

Teachers as Mediators.   The teacher coaches students as they discuss and work through situations that apply new information to their experiences, or to learning in other areas. Significant student problem solving is guided by the teacher.

Heterogeneous Grouping of Students.   All class participants learn from one another. All are encouraged to make contributions to discussions, ideas, and resolutions; and all ability, achievement, and interest levels are easily represented in all classroom activities. Although noisier than most classrooms, class control is maintained when students have discussed the classroom's rules and procedures, and limits have been defined and are understood by all.

VARYING INSTRUCTION FOR BEST OVERALL LEARNING AND BEHAVIOR MANAGEMENT

Students learn best when they actively participate in the learning process. When teachers manage the urban classroom by incorporating any of the following active learning methods, students are most likely to remain on task with attention focused on new knowledge:

- sharing related experiences and news;
- role-playing to learn and reinforce concepts;
- videotaping class events, such as debates, spelling bees, or class participation in plays or musicals, for student and teacher reflection; and
- peer tutoring. (Matus, 1999)

Effective and varied classroom management strategies can improve students' abilities to attend to tasks and engage in the learning process. Additionally, teachers can better maintain order in an energized classroom environment. This type of fluid management makes school an enjoyable place to learn, as students achieve academic and social goals, positive accomplishments in their classroom, and comfort and satisfaction in their efforts (Matus, 1999).

If students are engaged in learning, and immersed and engrossed in their classroom activities, their teachers spend less time on and give less attention to discipline issues (Haberman, 1995). A study by Wenglinsky (2002) concluded that the effects of teachers' classroom management practices, along with their other personal characteristics, influence student achievement as much as the students' urban-living background. Important to student achievement is their exposure to active teaching that engages students in challenging, hands-on learning, rather than passive teaching, instruction where the teachers perform and students sit and respond or work independently at their desks. Active teaching helps students achieve higher levels of performance that they would not otherwise reach.

Conducting student-centered lessons guides collaborative learning and individual students who seek to enhance their knowledge independently, as well. The teachers' handling of instruction content, time, materials, complexity of learning tasks, expected outcomes, and assessment data navigates student-centered lessons, helping to keep classroom learning fresh and stimulating. Also, teachers who maintain computer literacy skills, and incorporate technology into the teaching of content, will generate student enthusiasm that enriches instruction, as well as the entire student learning process. In groups, supportive and enthusiastic teamwork permeates educational approaches, encouraging spirited interaction between and among students, their teachers, and other school personnel (McBee, 1998).

Teachers who practice their profession in *any* school setting should avoid ability grouping (NCREL, 2004). They should use varieties of teaching methods that seek to meet all students' learning styles and strong receptive modalities, for example, individual visual, auditory, or tactile strengths. They should mix into group work varieties of students. Since students respond well to hands-on, active learning, teachers who use cooperative learning methods meet with great success among mixed cultures of students (Teacher Talk, 2004). A classroom climate that incorporates the teaching strategies listed below proves to *increase* student learning.

- Increase the pace of instruction.
- Increase the amount of time actively engaged in learning.
- Provide incentives for effort.
- Provide challenging learning goals that students are taught to reinforce themselves for effort and achievement. (Maryland State Department of Education, 1998)
- Use lecture, discussion, cooperative learning, learning stations, role plays, case studies, games, simulations, and independent study projects.
- Use multiple materials in instruction.
- Use cooperative learning frequently. (Forte & Shurr, 2002; Haberman, 1995)

The results from instituting these types of suggestions in the urban classroom better develops the teacher's physical/emotional stamina, management and teaching style, and students' academic readiness skills, as discussed:

1. *Physical/Emotional stamina.* Despite disconcerting events that occur (for example, behavior problems in class, or students' experiencing violence or abuse), teachers carry on their instructional responsibilities, respecting all learners in the class.

2. *Teaching style.* Teachers engage students in learning by using coaching and guidance skills, versus teacher-directed lecture with little or no student interaction.

3. *Readiness.* Offering students prerequisite knowledge enables them to make appropriate and desired academic gains. (Haberman, 1995)

Teaching Students Learning Strategies: Metacognitive Skills

Teachers should not take for granted that students enter school and advance through grade levels unknowing of how, where, what, or when to study, or what is the best route to reach their achievement goals. Most urban students are in need of learning these metacognitive skills. Metacognition theory suggests that learners benefit by thoughtfully and reflectively considering the things that they learn and the ways in which they learn them (Forte & Shurr, 2002).

Students will exhibit frustration, sometimes to the point of becoming classroom behavior problems, when they cannot learn or respond adequately to meet their desired achievement goals. These students likely lack metacognitive skills, or the ability to know best how they learn and apply that knowledge appropriately and effectively. Metacognitive skills help students in their active monitoring and regulation and orchestration of learning tasks and processes. Teachers can assist students to explore their thoughts about academic tasks and make them aware of how their thoughts about learning activities influence or control what they eventually accomplish. Further, students learn that metacognition requires them to assess their current state of knowledge and understanding before, during, and following completion of the task, and prior to and during their completing the task. The students plan how best to accurately and successfully accomplish the goal; and while completing the task, they monitor and regulate their progress toward accurately and successfully accomplishing the goal (Nitko, 2004).

The following are types of skills that introduce students to varieties of strategies that develop their metacognitive efforts.

- Teachers encourage student interaction, such as expressing their ideas, paraphrasing, and summarizing.
- Rewards are given for student participation; teachers compliment class and individual efforts.
- Teachers ask open-ended questions.
- Teachers develop *wait time* for student responses; wait until at least one-half of the students' hands are raised before calling on them.
- Foster a positive classroom learning climate.
- Encourage student participation. (Forte & Shurr, 2002; Ormrod, 2003)

Improving Communication via Teaching Listening Skills

In a world that places great emphasis on communicating between and among others, there exists a void of good listeners. Developing superior listening skills would be pertinent to a student's ability to function in the classroom environment. Thompson, Grandgenett, and Grandgenett (1999) studied existing literature and, incorporated with their own observations and expertise, developed listening steps to practice in class, including demonstrations of:

1. receiving the message (hearing it);
2. understanding the message's content (comprehending it);
3. remembering the message in a positive light (coding it in the brain for future recall); and
4. evaluating the message's content (deciding how it is useful knowledge).

Further, Thompson, Grandgenett, and Grandgenett (1999) suggest twelve classroom tips for developing listening skills that would increase student listening skills in any learning environment, but particularly fitting to urban school settings. In that most often urban teachers work among students who struggle academically, or among disadvantaged learners, the following suggestions provide guidance for urban teachers to achieve better communication with their classes.

1. Prior to giving students directions to follow, establish a *listening environment*. Ensure the students appear ready to listen.

2. Teach listening skills as well as study skills. Since these competencies are rarely taught in the urban home or community, teachers have a welcomed opportunity to establish these important skills.

3. Slow the speed at which verbal messages are spoken to allow listeners to process information given. Disadvantaged learners appreciate time to hear the words and phrases and then to decode and analyze those concepts.

4. Emphasize the most important points of a verbal message for the listeners. This includes providing clear examples, highlighting, and numbering essential steps, helping disadvantaged learners to gain clearer understandings.

5. Repeat and clarify important points of a verbal message for the listeners. Most students in the class, including the most academically able, benefit when hearing the message repeated, perhaps in a different manner, or redefined.

6. Encourage listeners to visualize the verbal message being given. When students are encouraged to "picture this . . ." or are given examples, analogies, or metaphors for a concept, the more concrete become abstract ideas.

7. While encouraging students to keep an open mind when delivering to them a message loaded with controversial words or phrases, steer clear of words that may distract their thoughts. If shocking words or ideas are to be offered in a message or discussion query, teachers encourage good listening skills when they prepare students for the words and ideas, and ask that they pay close attention to understand the entire block of information given.

8. Acknowledge and reward good listening regularly. Teachers who exhibit their satisfaction and praise, or otherwise reward students for good listening, are demonstrating the high priority listening plays in learning as well as in life.

9. If extrinsic rewards are offered to students who demonstrate good listening skills, teachers should begin to slowly ease up on those types of rewards, to allow students to experience intrinsic rewards from their paying close attention to instructions.

10. When visual or graphic aids support the verbal message, students are more likely to pay attention and focus on the information given. Combining visual modes of learning with the auditory approach strengthens information for all learners.

11. Scrutinize any physical or emotional factors existing in the class that may discourage students from listening. Teachers who consider where students sit in class, or investigate individual students' listening difficulties, may provide simple changes in the class, or for the student(s), that make significant positive impacts upon their listening skills.

12. Summarize—review highlights of the discussion, lecture, or activity for the students. This has proven helpful particularly for disadvantaged learners to better understand new concepts that are featured and explored in schools. (Thompson, Grandgenett, & Grandgenett, 1999)

SUMMARY

When schools today are challenged as never before to assure that children achieve academically, there are many situations that must be brought together in order for this objective to be accomplished. One of the most powerful goals, and a considerable requirement, is to provide for children a well-organized and efficiently managed classroom environment. This does not occur by happenstance—it requires a teacher who is knowledgeable and skilled in the art of teaching in urban settings.

At the onset of this chapter, there was a notion of silver bullets as elements that generate effective classroom management. They are:

1. Teachers must understand and be sensitive to the unique needs of urban students.
2. Teachers must be skilled in planning and establishing the classroom setting.
3. Teachers must utilize effective, proven teaching practices designed around urban children and their unique needs.

The message of this chapter is clear for those who would teach urban children with the objective of high-level academic performance for all. The urban situation can be difficult, and it must be understood by the teacher. Teachers must feel the daily heartache of many of their children and plan the management of their class with that at the forefront. Issues of self-esteem, poverty, health, abuse, drugs and alcohol, family support, and so many others come together when children assemble in the classroom. Classroom management cries out for the recognition of the serious needs of the children. Teachers are in a pivotal position to meet students' needs in many ways—a major way being the atmosphere they create in their classrooms.

The main objective of the teacher is to cause learning to occur. This can best be achieved in an organized, structured, well-managed classroom. Within that environment, the teacher must be highly skilled in instructional delivery. When instruction is interesting and challenging, and students are involved, students have little time for mischief. It is the responsibility of the teacher to deliver the instruction in dynamic fashion, so as to keep the children interested and thoroughly engaged. Children with idle time—not engaged—will likely use the time in misbehavior. Teaching strategies are powerfully effective in urban classrooms and are a key ingredient in a well-managed classroom, when learning is maximized.

Finally, as teachers realize, recognize, and consider the at-risk factors that so heavily influence the urban students' beliefs, values, and behaviors, the better able they are to instill in students comprehensive and intrinsic appreciation and motivation for learning, better communication, and greater understanding of their world. Through sound classroom management practices and effective teaching strategies, academic teachers are entrusted to establish the optimum learning environment that best achieves academic goals.

CHAPTER QUESTIONS

1. How do the three elements of urban classroom management ultimately help students learn?

2. How does a student's socioeconomic status link to his performance in school?

3. What are three suggestions that will help urban teachers better know their students' culture?

4. Offer two examples of how at-risk behaviors of students challenge the urban teacher.

5. What are attributes of effective urban classroom managers?

6. Why should teachers understand the importance of the behaviors they model?

7. What school situations offer teachers opportunities to motivate their students?

8. Explain classroom rules and procedures, and how they keep classroom management in check.

SUGGESTED WEBSITES

How the Social Context of Urban Schools Influences Classroom Management
www.findarticles.com/p/articles/mi_m0NQM/is_4_42/ai_111506827

National Clearinghouse on Child Abuse and Neglect Information
nccanch.acf.hhs.gov/

No Child Left Behind: *The Achiever*
www.ed.gov/policy/landing.html

Public Education Foundation of Chattanooga
www.pefchattanooga.org/www/docs/3/new_society/

Urban Academy
www.urbanacademy.org/learn/urbanstand.html

REFERENCES

Ben-Yosef, E. (2003). Respecting students' cultural literacies. *Educational Leadership, 61*(2).
Barton, P. E. (2004). Why does the achievement gap exist? *Educational Leadership, 62*(3), 9–13.
Blair, T. R. (2003). New teachers' performance-based guide to culturally diverse classrooms. Boston, MA: Pearson.

Burden, P. R. (2003). *Classroom management: Creating a successful learning community* (2nd ed.). New York: John Wiley.

Canter and Associates. (ed.). (1998). *First-class teacher: Success strategies for new teachers.* Los Angeles, CA: Canter and Associates.

The Condition of Education. (2003). U.S. Department of Education, Office of Educational Research and Improvement. Washington, DC: National Center of Educational Statistics.

Dyck, B. A. (2004). Teaching for diversity: Valuing students for who they are. *Middle Ground,* 7(4), 27.

Edwards, C. H. (2004). *Classroom discipline and management* (4th ed.). New York: John Wiley.

Forte, J., & Schurr, S. (2002). *The definitive middle school guide: A handbook for success.* Nashville, TN: Incentive Publications.

Grossman, H. (1995). *Classroom behavior management in a diverse society* (2nd ed.). Mountain View, CA: Mayfield.

Haberman, M. (1995). *Star teachers of children in poverty.* Indianapolis, IN: Kappa Delta Pi.

Heron, A. H. (2003). A study of agency: Multiple constructions of choice and decision making in an inquiry-based summer school program for struggling readers. *Journal of Adolescent and Adult Literacy, 46*(7); 568(12).

Irvine, J. J. (2003). *Education teachers for diversity: Seeing with a cultural eye.* New York: Teachers College Press.

Izumi, L. T. (2002). *They have overcome: High-poverty, high-performing schools in California.* Report to Pacific Research Institute for Public Policy. San Francisco, CA: ERIC ED No. 469 963.

Jenkins, W. L. (2004). *Understanding and educating African American children* (12th rev. ed.). St. Louis, MO: William Jenkins.

Jones, V. F., & Jones, L. S. (2001). *Comprehensive classroom management: Creating communities of support and solving problems* (6th ed.). Boston: Allyn & Bacon.

Kopetz, P. B. (2003). Understanding the at-risk student: Vital teacher knowledge for successful classroom management and instruction. In D. N. Rea & R. Stallworth-Clark, (eds.), *Fostering our youth's well-being, healing the social disease of violence.* New York: McGraw-Hill.

Maryland State Department of Education. (1998). *Minority achievement in Maryland: The state of the state.* Final report (pp. 1–61).

Matus, D. E. (1999). An innovative strategy support student teachers in urban secondary schools. *The Clearinghouse, 73*(1); 37(5).

McBee, R. H. (1998). Readying teachers for real classrooms. *Educational Leadership, 55*(5), 56–58.

Nakamura, R. M. (2000). *Healthy classroom management: Motivation, communication, and discipline.* Belmont, CA: Wadsworth/Thomson Learning.

National Center for Children in Poverty (2003). *Low income and the development of America's kindergartners.* New York: Columbia University Mailman School of Public Health.

Nelson, M. D. (1998). Professional development schools: An implementation model. *NAASP Bulletin,* 93–100.

Nitko, A. S. (2004). *Educational assessment of students* (4th ed.). Upper Saddle River, NJ: Pearson.

North Central Regional Educational Laboratory. (2004). Available: www.ncrel.org/sdrs.

Ormrod, J. (2003). *Educational psychology, developing learners* (4th ed.). Upper Saddle River, NJ: Pearson.

Quality Counts. (1998). Urban education. *Education Week on the Web, 18*(16), 10. Available: www.edweek.org/ew/articles/1998.

Snowman, J., & Bichler, R. (2003). *Psychology applied to teaching.* Boston: Houghton Mifflin.

Taylor, B. M., Pressley, M., & Pearson, D. (2000). *Effective teachers and schools: Trends across recent studies.* Paper prepared for the National Education Association, Center for the Improvement of Early Reading Achievement, Ann Arbor, MI.

Teacher Talk. (2004). Available: www.drugstats.org/tt/v2i2/table.html.

Thompson, F. T. (2003). The affirmative action and social policy views of a select group of white male private high school students. *Education and Urban Society, 36*(1), 16–43.

Thompson, F. T., Grandgenett, D. J., & Grandgenett, N. F. (1999). Helping disadvantaged learners build effective listening skills. *Education, 120*(1).

Tinzmann, M. B., Jones, B. F., Fennimore, T. F., Bakker, J., Fine, C., & Pierce, J. (1990). *What is the collaborative classroom?* Oak Brook, IL: North Central Regional Education Library. Available: www.ncrel.org/sdrs/areas/rpl_esys/collab.htm.

U.S. Census Bureau (2003). Living arrangements of children under 18 years and marital status of parents by age, gender, race, and Hispanic origin of the child for all children. Available: www.census.gov.pop.www.socdemo/hh-fam/cps 2003.html.

U.S. Department of Education. (2004). Washington, DC. Available: www.ed.gov/index.html.

Wenglinsky, H. (2002). How schools matter: The link between teacher classroom practices and student academic performance. *Education Policy Analysis Archives, 10*(12). Available: http://epaa.asu.edu/epaa/v10n12/.

West Education. (2004). *Center for Educational Equity.* Available: www.WestEd.org/cs/wew.

Williams, B., & Woods, M. (1997). Building on urban leaders' experiences. *Educational Leadership, 54*(7).

Wong, H. K., & Wong, R. T. (1998). *How to be an effective teacher: The first days of school.* Mountain View, CA: Harry K. Wong.

Zirpoli, T. J. (2005). *Behavior management: Applications for teachers* (4th ed.). Upper Saddle River, NJ: Pearson Prentice-Hall.

CHAPTER 7

INSTRUCTION FOR URBAN SETTINGS

Failure to understand differences in learning styles, differences in cultural styles of language use and interaction patterns, and differences between classroom culture and children's out-of-school environment, can lead to teachers misreading students' aptitudes and abilities and to misattributions of student deficiency.

—Lisa Delpit, 1992

URBAN PERSPECTIVES

Buddy Sullivan
Math Teacher, Middle School

If students don't understand why they need to learn math, I feel it is my responsibility to motivate students and help them understand what an education can do for them. I take responsibility for student learning in my classes.

"I chose to teach and stay with the middle school urban setting, because I like the challenges! They keep me interested. I continue to find ways that I can make an academic difference in the lives of my students. I love the excitement I feel when I hear from former students about their academic and career successes when they come by and visit, or when I run into them in the community. It is exciting to hear that they are pursuing higher education and are in the process of preparing for a great productive career. All of these experiences go to make up the reasons for remaining in teaching in an urban setting—a genuine feeling that what I am doing is making a difference in the lives of students."

Intertwined with Sullivan's proven successful classroom instruction is a firm set of pedagogical values. "My philosophy of teaching is this: All (students) can learn at higher levels if they are taught at higher levels. I look at the potential that students have and begin to build from there. I don't just choose the students at the top of the academic ladder to be in an Algebra I class in eighth grade. American schools tend to base the courses students take on what they have taken in the past. Interesting that, in contrast, the Japanese base their choice of courses for students on *how willing* or *receptive* the student is to putting forth the necessary effort."

"If students don't understand why they need to learn math, I feel it is my responsibility to motivate students and help them understand what an education can do for them. I take responsibility for student learning in my classes. Some of the things that I do to motivate my eighth-grade students is to invite business leaders from the community into the classroom to talk with small groups of students during lunch about jobs and careers and the importance of math on the job. As opposed to taking my students to visit the jails to see where they might end up, I take them to visit the offices of CEOs and show them what they can become. I take them to see various businesses, where math is used on a daily basis, such as in banks, accounting firms, hospitals, and on construction sites. I bring in former middle school graduates to share their career stories, and what they might have done differently when they were the students' age. I connect what they are learning to the real world."

"I feel that it is important to redo the mind-set of urban students and show the importance of academic achievement over athletics and entertainment. Education is their ticket to success. I show them how learning Algebra I helps to prepare them for college. I take them on trips to colleges in the Tennessee area to show them what it is like and where they might go to college."

"When I have student teachers in my classroom, I show them the value of maintaining high expectations for the urban students. They often come with stereotypes of urban kids, and I show them what these kids can do when excellence is expected of them. I have them read about successful urban teachers, and share the research about what works with urban students. I show them how to be innovative and creative in presenting math information to the students. I connect the math to their world, and find ways to help them be successful in learning math."

"As I work with the parents of my students, I find that they want their children to be successful and go to college. I make positive connections with the parents, and encourage a partnership of us working together to make their children successful in school. Then, they will, in turn, help their children at home to turn off the TV and study in a quiet place. When they know that I am not against them, but am working with them and for their children, then together we can accomplish successes. I meet with the parents several times each semester to share how they can support their children at home. I go over the types of math that they will be studying and give them my phone number to call me if their child is struggling with an assignment, and they are not able to help them. We build a working relationship together."

CULTURAL CONSCIOUSNESS AND EFFECTIVE TEACHING

Positive Views of Student Learning

When we look at the student achievement data for students of color and low socioeconomic students, overwhelmingly we see that they achieve at a much lower level than do majority White middle-class students. This fact has been substantiated nationally and across ethnic groups. Blaming the students and their backgrounds is no longer an option. Urban students can learn as well as others, but they need additional assistance and ways of teaching that teachers must provide for them. As educators we must take full responsibility for the success of these students. We must be prepared to give these students the support they need to be able to succeed in the academic environment and thus succeed in the broader economic world as well. Therefore, curriculum and instruction must be different if we are to achieve different results than we have in the past. As professional educators we must change the way we think, the attitudes we have and the way we train our preservice teachers in order to make a difference in children's lives. We cannot be content with the status quo and past failures. We can no longer seek excuses for failure. We must commit ourselves to working for the success of all children who enter our schools. We must hold very high expectations for all our students.

Educating Everybody's Children (Cole, 1995) exemplifies good research practices for the achievement of all students and in particular addresses the needs of students from diverse economic, ethnic, racial, cultural, and linguistic backgrounds. The results of this research revealed that differences in achievement between students of mainstream and diverse backgrounds were not the result of differences in their ability to learn, but rather of differences in the quality of instruction they had received in school. Therefore, if teachers put into practice effective instructional strategies, they too will be able to improve the performance of all students.

Zeichner (1996) outlines five areas that contribute to teaching effectiveness from the literature on successful teaching for poor students of color:

1. *High expectations.* Believe that students of color can learn and learn well.
2. *Scaffolding.* Build bridges to make connections between the cultures of school and home, between where students are and where they need to be.
3. *Sociocultural knowledge.* Understand how ethnicity, second-language acquisition, and poverty drive school performance and achievement.
4. *Teaching strategies.* Make subject content relevant to the lives of diverse students by providing examples and illustrations from their cultures to explain subject content.
5. *Authentic assessment and parent involvement.* Provide student portfolios, checklists, inventories, and teacher observations in addition to creatively engaging parents in their children's education. (pp. 140–148)

To become a successful teacher of urban students, preservice teachers must develop a knowledge base and cultural understandings along with effective practices such as culturally relevant teaching that meet the needs of urban learners. Maintaining high expectations, scaffolding new subject matter content, and implementing appropriate instructional strategies such as authentic assessments will enable preservice teachers to be successful with urban students. Preservice teachers need to understand and be proficient in each of Zeichner's areas in order to effectively teach in the urban setting.

THE ROLE OF TEACHER EXPECTATIONS

Teacher Beliefs Affect Student Achievement

The attitudes and beliefs of teachers lie at the core of their ability to assist in the academic achievement and success of urban students (Brophy & Good, 1970; Grant, 1991; Grant & Sleeter, 1986; Pajares, 1992; Wiest, 1998). When teachers believe that marginalized students have the ability to succeed and hold them to high levels of academic achievement, then these students will indeed succeed at high levels. If teachers do not hold that fundamental belief about urban students, then urban students will continue to fail in the academic arena. It is imperative that as we train preservice teachers to be successful in the urban setting that we also address this foundational issue of attitudes and beliefs about the ability of urban students to achieve.

According to Pajares (1992), "beliefs are stronger predictors of behavior" than knowledge (p. 311). Just acquiring intellectual knowledge in isolated courses about other cultures is not enough. We must understand the attitudes and beliefs with which we have been raised, because our belief systems filter our understanding of reality. The earlier in life that we developed a belief, the more difficult it is to change it. We gain our beliefs through interaction with our culture, and thus our culture acts as a lens to interpret all that we see and understand about life. If we have had limited engagement with another culture, we will have developed stereotypes and biases that interfere with our effectiveness as teachers within the cultures that are represented in our classes. Many teachers currently teaching in urban schools, as well as those preparing to teach, have had little experience with cultures other than their own. The majority of students graduating from our colleges across America are White, middle class, and female. In order for colleges and universities to adequately prepare these students to work effectively with urban students, they must guide preservice students to first examine and understand their own cultural backgrounds and belief systems.

Brophy and Good's (1970) research on teacher expectations reveals the need to address the underlying attitudes and beliefs that teachers hold concerning children of color. In their research, they verify that when teachers hold high expectations for students, those students produce at high levels. On the other hand, when teachers hold low expectations for students, those students produce at low levels regardless of their potential. If teachers' belief systems are ignored in teacher training, then teachers will continue to misunderstand and misinterpret diverse children and their behaviors and be ineffective in raising the academic achievement of these students.

Grant (1991) agrees with Brophy and Good concerning the need for teachers to examine their own enculturation to understand how their upbringing affects their understanding and responses to other cultures and in turn their expectations or lack of expectations for students of color. Grant and Sleeter

(1986) reported in their three-year ethnographers' study of junior high students that it was the teachers' lack of understanding of how their own backgrounds affected their ability to teach diverse students that kept them from being effective with their students of color.

Wiest (1998) concludes from her research with preservice teachers that teacher attitudes and beliefs influence teaching behaviors that in turn affect student learning and behavior. She describes an informal cultural immersion project for preservice students where students apply what they have learned during the immersion experience to educational instruction. Students wrote that they had gained new information about specific cultures, had been challenged about their beliefs and understandings, and enhanced their personal and professional skills related to understanding and teaching diverse cultures. This was a brief immersion experience for the students, but they profited by it because they were asked to reflect on what had occurred, what they had learned, and then how they would teach differently in the classroom because of this experience. As we train education students to be effective in urban settings, we need to be guided by the types of field placements and experiences that show positive gains for students in understanding and teaching diverse students.

In *Educating Everybody's Children* (Cole, 1995), the second chapter focuses on "Barriers to Good Instruction"—that teachers' attitudes and beliefs about poor and marginalized students impact their expectations for these students. If they do not believe that these students can succeed, then their attitudes and beliefs become a self-fulfilling prophecy that then set in place a cycle of failure for these students. The Urban Middle Grades Network developed a model for success called the Three-High Achievement Model (Cole, 1995). This model emphasized high content, high expectations, and a highly supportive school environment as an effective approach to increase student achievement and retention.

One of the major issues in urban education stems from the attitude of too many teachers that students of color and students of the poor cannot reach acceptable levels of achievement. This attitude leads to presenting instruction at a low level. (See Chapter 3 for more on the ill effects of student tracking.)

Urban students can achieve at higher levels when teachers develop a no-nonsense attitude and hold students accountable for academic excellence. Teachers, armed with a positive attitude, and understanding of learning needs and well-planned relevant instruction, can cause students to work hard to reach learning objectives.

IMPROVING STUDENT PERFORMANCE

Scaffolding in Student Achievement

The term *scaffolding* can be used in a broad sense to include various kinds of support systems within the teaching and learning environment. Scaffolding for urban and/or poor and multicultural children includes many different kinds of support systems that bridge the gaps between the students' current knowledge and new knowledge to be gained. It can include peer or other types of tutoring, cooperative learning situations, or culturally relevant teaching that connects the child's environment meaningfully to the concepts to be learned. Scaffolding can also be in the form of graphic organizers that assist in identifying main ideas or text organization, the use of self-questioning strategies to guide a reader through the text, or the use of rubrics to help students assess their own progress. More recently scaffolding has been used to support the concept of problem-based learning. Bruner (1990) describes scaffolding as support in solving a problem that is beyond the capacity of one person through the assistance of another more advanced or skilled individual. In both discovery learning and problem-based learning, the learner relies on scaffolding to solve the problem.

One of the advantages of scaffolding is that it allows close interaction with students who have low self-esteem or a learning disability. This interaction provides immediate, positive feedback concerning the students' efforts and builds confidence in the student's ability to succeed with this task. One of the disadvantages of the method is that although the individualized nature of scaffolding meets the learning needs of each student, it can be time-consuming for the teacher. Another drawback is the measure of skill needed by the teacher to become effective in scaffolding. Training in this method is recommended to receive the full advantage of teaching and learning in this manner (Pressley, Hogan, Wharton-McDonald, Mistretta, & Ettenberger, 1996).

Effective Teaching Strategies That Accommodate Diverse Learners (Kame'enui, Carnine, Dixon, Simmons, & Coyne, 2002) presents scaffolding as a powerful tool for meeting individual, diverse learners' needs that produces, when properly

implemented, academically successful students. Hogan and Pressley (1997) reviewed the literature on scaffolding and determined several essential elements for scaffolding instruction, which can be used as general guidelines for effective implementation of scaffolding in the classroom.

1. Assess the student and curriculum in order to select appropriate tasks, interests, and levels to begin the scaffolding process.
2. Work with the student to establish shared instructional goals and evaluate the student's current needs and understandings.
3. As the instructional process proceeds, provide guidance and feedback to the student in the form of prompting, modeling, telling, questioning, or discussion.
4. Continue to assist students in maintaining their focus on their goals through praise, encouragement, and feedback on their current progress, encouraging them to monitor their own growth in learning.
5. Create a safe environment where the students are free to take risks and try alternatives.
6. Gradually release control of the learning to the students to perform the learning tasks independently.

Ellis and Larkin (1998) provide a helpful framework for scaffolding throughout the lesson. First, the teacher models how to perform the new or difficult task by using think-alouds or read-alouds. Second, the class practices the skill or task together with support from the teacher as in shared reading. Third, the students work together with a partner or small group to complete the task. Finally, the students are given independent practice where they can demonstrate individual mastery of the skill or task. For additional support in becoming a skilled teacher in scaffolding, see: *How to Scaffold Instruction for Student Success* (ASCD, 2002) and Beed, Hawkins, and Roller, 1991 for examples of student-teacher interaction during scaffolding.

Vygotsky (1978) used the term *scaffolding* more specifically to define the role of assisting others in their learning. He believed in the powerful interaction of the social and cultural contexts to influence intellectual development. Vygotsky espoused what he called the zone of proximal development (ZPD), an area within which a person has the ability to comprehend and grow intellectually with the aid of another more advanced person.

Students have a smaller zone of intellectual development when they work in isolation without the benefit of help from others. There is a contrast in the student's ability to grow intellectually between the proximal zone and the developmental level, between the student's assisted and unassisted performance. According to Vygotsky, teaching is effective only when it brings to life those latent abilities that are on the verge of maturing. Those latent abilities are those that lie in the zone of proximal development where the student needs assistance to move forward (Tharp & Gallimore, 1988). Assistance from older peers, adults, or experts is viewed by Vygotsky as vital to intellectual development. As teachers or more advanced peers work with other students to assist them in understanding a concept, they are scaffolding the learning for the students. Tharp and Gallimore call the method for bringing these latent abilities to life "instructional conversation" (p. 109). Instructional conversation involves the interaction of text, memory, conversation, and imagination between the person being taught and the person teaching.

Instructional conversation is at the heart of the Kamehameha Elementary Education Program (KEEP), a program for marginalized children as previously discussed in Chapter 2. For more than ten years this program assisted children of color to perform "at national-norm levels in reading achievement" (Tharp & Gallimore, 1988, p. 116). Utilizing a small-group format, the teacher engages the children in an instructional conversation. The teacher and students are involved in a give-and-take conversation about the text they are reading. Learning takes place as teacher and student mutually interact and contribute to the discussion. Conversation is shared, not dominated by the teacher. Instruction in comprehension follows a certain sequence called E (experiences), T (text), R (relationship). First, the teacher uses the child's (E) experiences to introduce content. Next, the teacher introduces the (T) text to be read, and last, establishes a (R) relationship between the text and the child's experiences. The teacher builds on the responses of the children to create a lively exchange of ideas.

Irvine (2003) gives examples of scaffolding as she talks about effective teachers of children of color that are skilled in connecting new knowledge to students' prior knowledge. She states, "Transfer involves finding pertinent examples and multiple representations of knowledge, comparing and contrasting, and

bridging the gap between the known (students' personal cultural knowledge) and the unknown (materials and concepts to be mastered)" (p. 58).

Ladson-Billings (1994) compares culturally relevant teaching to assimilationist teaching. Culturally relevant teaching views knowledge as something that is alive and changing—the constructivist point of view—versus knowledge that is static—the traditional view that a specific body of knowledge is imparted to the learner. She compares the two perspectives on gaining knowledge. A culturally relevant view will enable a teacher to present the concepts and material to various cultures in a manner that is passionate, critical, and meaningful. An assimilationist view sees knowledge as infallible with the teacher detached and neutral about the content. A culturally relevant view sees excellence as a complex standard that takes student diversity into account. Preservice teachers must gain knowledge of other cultures during their training both through texts and through experiences in the urban environment that will enable them to effectively translate information from the learning environment to the urban environment and thus make learning relevant to the urban learner. (See Chapter 6.)

THE ROLE OF CRITICAL PEDAGOGY

Teachers as Change Agents

It is important for preservice teachers to expand in their understanding of sociocultural knowledge and critical pedagogy. This knowledge is critical in enhancing teachers' ability to meet the needs of multicultural students effectively. The majority of new teachers coming into the workforce are from White, middle class, monolingual backgrounds; they will be teaching students whose backgrounds and experiences are considerably different from theirs. Preservice urban teachers need to be prepared differently than their predecessors. Principally, they need greater knowledge about the students they will be educating. "They need general sociocultural knowledge about child and adolescent development, about second-language acquisition, and about the ways that socioeconomic circumstances, language, and culture shape school performance and educational achievement" (Zeichner, 1996, p. 142).

America's teachers traditionally have been prepared in state-sponsored colleges and universities that grant bachelor's and master's degrees and serve a state region. Teacher education programs have required education students to take liberal arts as well as education courses. In the past, education courses taught social and psychological foundations, curriculum courses, instructional strategies, and student teaching (AACTE, 1988).

Ladson-Billings (2000) states in "Fighting for Our Lives: Preparing Teachers to Teach African American Students" that many educational institutions use specific coursework and diverse field placements to prepare preservice teachers to be effective with diverse students.

> However, no single course or set of field experiences is capable of preparing pre-service students to meet the needs of diverse learners. Rather, a more systemic, comprehensive approach is needed. Work that uses autobiography, restructured field experiences, situated pedagogies, and returning to the classrooms of experts can each provide new opportunities for improving teaching. (Ladson-Billings, 2000, p. 209)

Many prospective teachers do not wish to be part of an educational agenda that addresses the sociopolitical dimensions of teaching (Zeichner, 1996). They prefer not to be part of a critical pedagogy that encourages them to become social activists on the part of the urban children they teach. They are not interested in working with multicultural, multilingual, impoverished students with whom they have very little in common. They do not want to face the challenges that teacher educators who are social reconstructionists attempt to raise concerning social injustices. Successful teachers of urban and diverse students must be willing to become change agents in their school and community. They need to be aware of the issues of inequality and racism in schools and school systems and accept their part in standing against the status quo:

> The teachers I studied work in opposition to the system that employs them. They are critical of the way that the school system treats employees, students, parents, and activists in the community. However, they cannot let their critique reside solely in words. They must turn it into action by challenging the system. What they do is both their lives and their livelihoods. In their classrooms they practice a subversive pedagogy. Even in the face of the most mundane curricular decisions these teachers make a stand. I'm not a textbook teacher. I use the texts as resources but I have to teach what the children need, not what the district wants. The students come first. (Ladson-Billings, 1994, p. 128–129)

In *Educating Teachers for Diversity*, Irvine (2003) calls for teachers to initiate whole-school systemic reform where the teachers are involved in the instructional design of programs and in allocating staff and budgets. Most teachers are not prepared for this type of activist role in schools and need professional development in several areas to equip them for instructional leadership roles and in becoming agents for change (Fullan, 2003; Joyce, Wolf, & Calhoun, 1993). As part of this leadership role in the schools, teachers are to be mentors and coaches to other teachers in their building, especially those who are new to the profession and new to urban school settings. (For a full discussion of teachers as leaders, see Chapter 5.)

There is a growing body of literature seeking to address these concerns in urban education. Delpit, Howey, Irvine, Ladson-Billings, Zeichner, and others are adding to this knowledge base. The Holmes Partnership and its subsidiary, Urban Network to Improve Teacher Education (UNITE), have taken a leading role in addressing these issues. One such program has been developed at the University of California, Los Angeles in the Graduate School of Education and

Information Studies under the guidance of Oakes and Beck. Known as Center X, Where Research and Practice Intersect for Urban School Professionals (Center X Mission Statement, n.d.), the Center focuses upon preparing and supporting preservice, inservice, and graduate level teachers to be effective in urban schools. The Center combines the scholarship of UCLA faculty with the experience of urban school professionals to test and create new approaches to effectively teach in urban schools. One of the key values of Center X is that of preparing teachers to become social advocates for justice in urban school communities. Center X is committed to preparing teachers to be social change agents. The candidates in this program are trained to create curricula that integrate learning goals with students' homes and communities to make learning relevant to urban students' lives. (For further information, see the Center X website at the end of the chapter.)

Another program that emphasizes training teachers in culturally relevant pedagogy is the Boettcher Teachers Program in Denver, Colorado (Boettcher Teachers Program, n.d.). This alternative teacher licensing program is a partnership among the Boettcher Foundation, the Public Education and Business Coalition, the University of Denver's College of Education, the Rocky Mountain School of Expeditionary Learning, and two local school districts. Students in the program have their four-year degree and are trained in high-needs schools with course work that integrates theory and practice.

The students receive coaching and mentoring from district induction staff as well as ongoing seminars within a student cohort. One of the main goals of the program is to aid students to become effective teachers of diverse students through culturally relevant pedagogy in the areas of academic achievement (where all students are presumed capable of learning), cultural competence (the role of culture in education and learning about students' culture and community), and sociopolitical consciousness (the larger sociopolitical context of the school/community/nation/world). At the conclusion of the program, students are committed to working in high-needs schools for a total of four years. The goal is to improve the academic performance of diverse students in a high-need setting. (For further information, see the Boettcher Program Teacher website at the end of this chapter.)

In *Common Sense about Uncommon Knowledge: The Knowledge Bases for Diversity*, Smith (1998) discusses the necessary knowledge that preservice and inservice teachers should possess in order to be culturally responsible and responsive and defines thirteen areas of knowledge. These thirteen areas are:

1. foundations of multicultural education
2. sociocultural contexts of human growth and psychological development in marginalized ethnic and racial cultures
3. cultural and cognitive learning style theory and research
4. language, communication, and interactional styles of marginalized cultures
5. essential elements of cultures

6. principles of culturally responsive teaching and culturally responsive curriculum development
7. effective strategies for teaching minority students
8. foundations of racism
9. effects of policy and practice on culture, race, gender, and other categories of diversity
10. culturally responsive diagnosis, measurement, and assessment
11. sociocultural influences on subject-specific learning
12. gender and sexual orientation
13. experiential knowledge.

The authors feel that there is considerable importance in urban teachers' developing an in-depth understanding of cultures and diversity and related issues. See the end of the chapter for additional readings to increase teachers' knowledge of diverse cultures.

Teachers as Social Justice Advocates

Irvine (2003) also indicates that teachers must be advocates for social justice by becoming involved with issues of racism, sexism, and classism. She points to the difficulties that many White teachers have in addressing racist issues. (The subject of White teacher resistance to multicultural training is treated more thoroughly in Chapter 2.)

According to Gay (1995), many of the concerns of multicultural education are comparable to those of critical pedagogy in relation to issues of educational access, equity, and excellence in a culturally pluralistic society. Successful teachers of diverse students bring with them political perspectives through which they address the injustices in school and society that they see affecting their students. Biased social, organizational, and financial systems of schooling perpetuate dominance and oppression (Darling-Hammond, 1995; Kozol, 1991).

Zeichner (1993) and Sleeter and Grant (1987) use the term *social reconstructionist educators* that calls for teachers to use pedagogies that transform the structures of inequities and injustices in society by addressing them in the classroom and preparing students to address them in society. Cochran-Smith (1997) lists three important pedagogies of successful urban teachers that exemplify transformational teaching. These are:

1. Enable significant work and rigorous academic learning within groups of students who function as communities of learners.
2. Construct new knowledge with students by building on the knowledge, interests, cultural resources, and linguistic abilities students bring to school with them.
3. Make activism, power, and inequity explicit parts of the curriculum for students of all ages. (p. 49)

CULTURAL RELEVANCY

Ladson-Billings (1994) discusses the need for culturally relevant teachers to oppose the inequality, racism and injustice in the school systems where they are employed. These teachers must be certain of what is right for their children and take steps to do what is right despite opposition. Teachers and systems resist change. In order to develop teachers who are equipped to challenge inequities in the system, Ladson-Billings proposes six strategies:

1. Recruit teacher candidates who have expressed an interest and desire to work with African American students.
2. Provide educational experiences that help teachers understand the central role of culture.
3. Provide teacher candidates with opportunities to critique the system in ways that will help them choose a role as either agent of change or defender of the status quo.
4. Systematically require teacher candidates to have prolonged immersion in African American culture.
5. Provide opportunities for observation of culturally relevant teaching.
6. Conduct student teaching over a longer period of time and in a more controlled environment. (pp. 131–136)

Ladson-Billings goes on to provide a vision of a culturally relevant school. She cites three main areas in her vision: (1) provide educational self-determination so that parents, teachers, and community members can have a voice in and decide the direction of their schools; (2) honor and respect the students' home culture by bringing the richness of other cultures into the classroom experiences so that all children's cultures are represented and respected; and (3) help African American students understand the world as it is and equip them to change it for the better. Ladson-Billings states, "If students are to be equipped to struggle against racism they need excellent skills from the basics of reading, writing, and math, to understanding history, thinking critically, solving problems, and making decisions: they must go beyond merely filling in test sheet bubbles with Number 2 pencils" (pp. 139–140).

Instructional Implications

Some examples of instruction using critical thinking involve assisting students in their natural ability as problem solvers and thinkers. Instead of presenting information didactically to students with all questions already answered, the teacher should pose a problem for students to solve that involves all of the information that normally would have been given to students. In this way they become actively involved in finding the information for themselves. This method of teaching and learning is highly motivational for students (Bransford et al., 1986; Lambert, 1990; Onosko, 1992).

The use of alternative assessments to evaluate students' achievement and behavior such as building a model, drawing a picture, making a presentation, and discussing the concepts are all ways of assessing student knowledge and understandings and should be included in assessment strategies. Not all students learn in the same way and not all students test in the same way. Students must be given the opportunity to demonstrate what they have learned. Quizzes and objective tests have their place but should not be used exclusively when determining the information that students have grasped (Grace, 1992; Hewitt, 1993).

Having students generate their own questions and lead discussions is a highly effective motivational strategy for students (Adams, 1986; Carlsen, 1991; Goatley & Raphael, 1992). When students can generate the questions instead of the teacher, they become engaged and begin to own the learning in the classroom. They are pursuing information that they have some interest in and control over. Students having control over their learning is a foundational theme that Glasser (1998) uses to develop his highly effective high-poverty schools.

Choice Theory

Glasser (2000) proposes criteria for becoming a Glasser Quality School (GQS):

> Essentially, this is a school in which all students are doing competent work and many are doing quality work. Discipline problems have disappeared, state test scores are significantly higher—above the 80th percentile is common—and it is obvious to anyone who enters the school that it is filled with joy.

One of these schools is Aikman Elementary in Hereford, Texas. It is a high-poverty school and has students achieving at high levels.

Glasser bases his work on a concept called *choice theory*, described in *Choice Theory* (1998). A main theme, for which he provides guidelines to achieve, is the importance of having and maintaining good relationships with students, colleagues, and supervisors. Glasser advocates the Competence Based Classroom (CBC). Characteristics of the CBC classroom include students learning *why* they need to learn what they are being taught. He advocates that they also need to learn they have much more control over what they do than they have had in the past. He states, "This way of teaching will reduce the present educational gap between the rich and the poor, which eventually may reduce the widening economic gap between the haves and the have-nots" (p. 13).

Language and Student Achievement

The role that language plays in urban schools is another area of controversy in the cultural arena. As immigrants continue to stream into the United States, students are coming to school without competent knowledge of the English language. Our preservice teachers must be prepared to instruct these students using effective practices. Urban children come to school with a variety of dialects that are not Standard English, such as Black English (Ebonics), Hawaiian Creole, and Spanglish. However, these dialects should be understood as distinct languages with their own complexity and rules, not as a substandard form of language. Teachers should be aware of some of the rules of their diverse students' languages in order to respect their languages and assist them with translating languages or dialects into Standard English. Quite often the response to non-Standard English is for the teacher to assume that the student is not intellectual enough to succeed in school based on their speech. Teachers walk a thin line in needing to validate their students' language while at the same time teaching them Standard English.

Several types of support for English as a second language (ESL) and limited English proficiency (LEP) learners are legally required based on the Bilingual Act of 1974 and the 1974 Supreme Court ruling in *Lau v. Nichols*. One type of support is that of the pull-out program that allows for special English instruction. Another approach is the transitional bilingual program where students who speak no English are provided with their native language and are gradually transitioned until the student is proficient in English. A third approach is that of the full bilingual program where students are taught to become proficient in both their native language and in English (Webb, Metha, & Jordan, 2003).

The debate over bilingualism and English immersion continues. The impact on the students' culture, community, and native tongue are often forgotten as students learn to become proficient in English. Bilingualism supports, respects, and preserves the native language and culture of immigrant peoples. However, on the other hand it is also imperative for immigrant peoples to learn the English language in order to survive in the U.S. culture. Several states in the past few years have passed laws that restrict bilingual programs in schools in order to replace them with programs that contain more English and less transition time.

The Education Trust Online (2003) has documented the national achievement gaps among White, African American, Hispanic, and American Indian groups. In "Improving Achievement and Closing Gaps Between Groups," Haycock (2005) presents the current National Assessment of Educational Progress (NAEP) comparisons between White and Hispanic students in fourth-grade reading and math. Thirty-nine percent of White students performed at the proficient level, compared with 14 percent of Hispanic students, while 35 percent of White students performed at the basic level, compared to 29 percent of Hispanic students. At the below-basic reading level, 26 percent of White students compared to 57 percent of Hispanic students performed at this level. Math levels showed similar disparities. Thirty-six percent of White students performed at the proficient level, compared with 11 percent of Hispanic students, and 43 percent of White students performed at the basic level, compared with 36 percent of Hispanic students. Fifty-three percent of Hispanic students performed below basic math, while only 21 percent of White students performed below basic math.

A long-term study by NAEP in 1999 (Haycock, 2005) revealed that African American and Hispanic students were working with math and reading at the same levels as White 13 year olds. When percentages were compared among White, African American, and Hispanic graduation rates according to the Manhattan Institute for Policy Research in 2003, 72 percent of Whites graduated from high school compared with 52 percent of Hispanics and 51 percent of African Americans.

Hispanic Families and Education. In *English Learners: Reaching the Highest Level of English Literacy,* (Garcia, 2003) details educational information concerning Hispanic families. A three-year study was conducted on the effectiveness of the book loan program in the Los Angeles Latino community (Yaden, Madrigal, & Tam, 2003). The insights gained concerning Hispanic families reveal the strength and determination that Hispanics have to help their children become academically successful in school. As the program provided more books to their homes, parents were able to read more frequently to their children. The research found that Hispanic parents went to great lengths to have books available to their children and showed that they highly valued the books that they were loaned. In spite of many difficulties such as language barriers and economic pressures that face these immigrants in America, they decide to remain in the United States for the sake of their children's future. They understand the value of their children becoming proficient in English in order to succeed in American society and overcome many hardships to ensure that their children will be successful.

The parents would draw on their own experiences in learning to read in their native country in order to assist their children with reading. All of the parents in this study recognized the importance of reading aloud to their children. Even when they could not read all of the English words themselves, the parents would make up stories based on the pictures in the books. They would dramatize the stories to make them more interesting to their children. They would retell, reread, or translate the story as they read. Interacting with the children as they read to them was their most important focus.

The book loan program also had a positive effect on building relationships among teachers, teacher assistants, students, and parents. The program provided duplicate copies of the books for classroom use. Workshops of book reading and home literacy activities for parents were planned in the afternoon, providing time for parents to use public transportation to get home. Handouts and presentations were provided in both languages, as well as presentations in Spanish with translations provided for English speakers. One of the workshops invited parents to write down folklore, poems, rhymes, or songs that they shared at home in their family. The families received help with writing and dictation was taken by the researchers. These pages were then incorporated into a book that could be checked out of the lending library.

The parents reported that the reading activities at home created positive family time together. As the researchers worked regularly with the parents and gained their confidence, they became aware of the nature of home and literacy environments. They became aware of the importance of the bilingual books in connecting to students' background experiences while reinforcing a sense of pride. It was difficult to obtain children's literature in Spanish as well as alphabet, counting, and other informational books for young Hispanic children. However, these were the books that the parents requested. The program provided books that included both parent and child interests. The program also encouraged a variety of strategies for parents to use while reading with their children. Despite long working hours, the parents in this urban community had a strong desire for their children to succeed in school and become proficient readers.

Reading and English Language Learners.   *Teaching Vocabulary in All Classrooms* (Blachowicz & Fisher, 2002) provides a variety of methods for assisting English language learners in gaining vocabulary and comprehending text. Some strategies for teaching English to nonnative speakers of English in regular literacy classrooms involve activating and using prior knowledge. One such strategy, called the *in/out* strategy, in which before reading a book or passage, students decide which words will most likely be in the text and which will be out of the text (the teacher places a list on the board). Another strategy is called *knowledge rating* (Blachowicz, 1986), which asks students to examine teacher-selected words prior to reading a text. It draws on students' prior knowledge and addresses partial knowledge of words. The teacher selects some easy and difficult words that appear in the passage. On a chart the students choose if they can define the word, know about it, or never heard it.

Other ways that the teacher can assist is to scaffold the use of English by reading aloud to students followed by choral, partner, or paired reading and by providing an oral meaning of words. Teachers can aid students in understanding extended text by presenting words and phrases from a story about to be read and having students try to construct the story line themselves before reading the original story. Also, incorporating various media in lessons assists students in understanding the text. Some examples include providing pictures and charts as visuals to better understand text, labeling items around the room when appropriate, using audiotapes and videotapes to help process the information in a variety of formats, and providing computer vocabulary programs aimed at the appropriate age and interest level for the students (Blachowicz & Fisher, 2002).

The use of multiple modalities in teaching English language learners allows them greater involvement in the learning process and thus greater gains in improving their English. Some examples involve having students respond to text through art, drama, and music. Teachers can ask students to act out the meanings of words found in their readings or to draw a picture, mural, or three-dimensional display describing the action or setting of a story. Teachers can use songs from the popular culture that relate to the content of the lesson, or songs with repetitive lyrics or with a chorus to aid understanding and retention (Blachowicz & Fisher, 2002).

Four rules for native speakers of English who help English language learners (Buehler & Meltesen, 1983) are: (1) speak in short, simple sentences; (2) speak naturally, but slowly, and leave pauses after each sentence; (3) use gestures and act out meanings of words, and don't hesitate to draw pictures and use props; and (4) don't try to teach too much. Check to see that the student understands two or three items thoroughly before going on to teach more.

DIFFERENTIATING INSTRUCTION

One Size Does Not Fit All

Ladson-Billings (2000) argues that specific strategies and methodologies for understanding and teaching African American students are absent from the educational literature. She proposes that this is largely due to the adherence to a pedagogy that one size fits all, but in reality supports the academic achievement of mainstream U.S. Differentiating instruction addresses the argument that one size does *not* fit all.

In *How to Differentiate Instruction in Mixed-Ability Classrooms*, Tomlinson (2001) discusses methods and procedures that classroom teachers can use to reach all of the students in their classrooms, not just teach to those students in the middle. With the inclusion model becoming the national norm in many schools today as well as the increasing numbers of second-language learners, teachers—in particular those teachers in diverse urban settings—need to know how to instruct to meet the learning needs of all of their diverse students. Students vary in the way they acquire information, process information, and apply that information to new situations.

Differentiating instruction is different than individualizing instruction in that each student is not tested, diagnosed, and placed in an individualized text. Each learner is not separate from all the other learners in the classroom. Differentiated instruction means that the classroom environment supports a variety of learning options. At times the teacher may need to work with the class as a whole, as in choral or echo reading. At other times, the teacher addresses small groups with similar learning needs, or the teacher works as needed with a student one-on-one, as in individual conferencing during independent reading or writing. This concept uses flexible grouping according to the needs of the students at any particular time. Reading groups, math groups, or other groups are not static, and are able to change as the needs of the students change. Assignments are changed to meet the needs of students, not so much to lengthen or shorten the assignment, but to change the nature of the assignment to meet the particular student's interests and abilities. The teacher is the skilled conductor and coach of the class and monitors the needs of the students over time, changing the content, mode, and pace of instruction to meet the changing needs of the students.

Providing opportunities for students to work together in cooperative and collaborative learning settings (Johnson & Johnson, 1990), small-group participation, teaming students with others at varying levels, peer conferencing and peer collaboration (Herrmann, 1989) is conducive to African American, Hispanic, and Native American learning styles (Banks, 1988 More, 1990; White, 1992). When students are able to discuss subject matter with each other, rather than in isolation, learning is enhanced.

An excellent example of this concept in practice is the use of reading and writing workshops that have been developed over the past decade to engage students in taking ownership of their learning to read and write (Harvey & Goudvis, 2000 Keene & Zimmermann, 1997). Whole group, small group, and individual reading and writing and conferencing take place within this model, which utilizes the concepts of motivating student learning through building on background knowledge, experiences and interest levels, teaching slightly above the student's independent level, and scaffolding instruction to bridge the gaps to assist student learning.

Teachers in training need to keep in mind the needs of advanced learners as well as those who are struggling in their learning. Preservice teachers need to become expert observers of their students to know when they are bored or frustrated in their learning and when they need to be encouraged or challenged. Differentiated lessons are based on the readiness of students, varied interests of students, or on their learning styles.

Areas that a teacher can utilize to differentiate the readiness of students include presenting the material first initially at the simpler concrete level and then moving on to the more complex abstract level. For example, students first gain a concrete understanding of facts related to William the Conqueror arriving from France and conquering England in 1066 AD. The students would first understand the reasons why he came and how he was able to conquer England at that time. The more abstract level would be understanding and applying that knowledge to the long-term effects the event had on the English language. For three hundred years, the French language was dominant in England. However, after that period, the English language reemerged as the predominant language in England when Chaucer began writing *Canterbury Tales* in English. Students could explore how that occurred given that the French were the conquerors of the English-speaking peoples. Students must first grasp concepts at the concrete level before they can then move on to the abstract level.

Another example of differentiating through readiness involves moving students from a more dependent environment to an independent environment by giving students more choice and more freedom. For instance, when students begin to learn about using the scientific method to solve problems, they must first be guided and controlled during each step in the process. However, once they understand the process, then they can be given more freedom to apply the scientific method to other problems on their own. They are not observed as closely and are given more independence because they have demonstrated that they understand and can apply the process.

A third example of differentiating instruction according to readiness is assisting a student in moving from a structured environment to a more open-ended environment. When a student is learning a skill, such as music, math, or writing, she begins at the foundational level and practices the skills over and over again until they become automatic. Once that occurs, the teacher is willing to allow the student to become more creative with those foundational skills. They are allowed to move from the basic skills into more complex and unstructured forms of music, mathematics, or writing.

In differentiating by interest, teachers enhance student motivation to learn by being aware of the various interests of students in their classrooms. As content for study is chosen, teachers keep the interests of their students in mind. For example, in a study on the Civil War, students read supplementary and primary source materials about this period of time and apply their area of interest to that time frame. Students could work in isolation or in pairs. As the class discusses various aspects of the Civil War, students add information based upon their outside readings and insights creating a sense of excitement in bringing this time period alive to the students as they connected their learning to their everyday lives and interests.

As another way of building on students' interests, teachers can encourage students with similar interests to create an interest group around a subject area and develop an interest center based on their additional readings and investigations. As students study animal habitats, a group of students might choose to design and create an interest center that focuses on an animal habitat about which the students want additional learning. Some guidelines suggested for use in interest-based differentiation are linking interest-based exploration with key curriculum content, providing structure for students to succeed, developing efficient ways to share interest-based findings, and keeping an open mind for students with serious passions.

In differentiating lessons by learning style, there are several areas to consider: the sensory modalities of visual, auditory, kinesthetic, and tactile. Often students favor one area over another area. Some students need to see visuals in order to learn and not just hear instructions or directions. Other students are quite auditory and can listen to a lecture and learn best in that manner. Others, such as athletes, need to have movement and touch, hands-on learning, in order for them to learn at their peak potential. They cannot just see and hear in order to learn, they need to utilize their bodies to learn.

Another category of learning involves the global versus the analytic learner. The global learner sees the big picture and needs to be taught how to consider the details of the content being learned and how these fit into the big picture in a sensible way. The analytic learner focuses upon analyzing details to an extent that she does not see the big picture.

Students' learning and reading styles should be taken into consideration in designing and recommending appropriate instructional methods and materials (Boyatzis & Kolb, 1991; Gardner, 1983; Gregorc, 1982; Lewis & Steinberger, 1991). When teachers take students various learning styles into consideration in preparing lessons, students become more engaged, interested, and successful in their learning.

Incorporating Visual, Auditory, Tactile, and Kinesthetic Modalities of Learning

The teacher is a key player in determining how students achieve in their classes. The learning environment of the classroom should be accepting and nonthreatening to the students. They should feel safe when asking questions. When they feel accepted and encouraged in their learning, then they develop the confidence to achieve. Students have differences in learning styles and, therefore, need information presented in a variety of ways to meet all the needs of the learners. Some categories of learners include visual, auditory, and kinesthetic. As well as the teaching and learning environment, assessment should include a variety of domains so that the different learners have an opportunity to excel in their area of expertise.

Visual Learners.   Visual students learn by seeing and watching demonstrations. They like descriptions, remember faces, not names, and frequently take numerous notes. They tend to visualize in pictures, they are generally unaware of sounds, distracted by visual disorder, and the appearance of things is important. These students tend to plan in advance, stare, doodle, find something to watch, use plain language; they are neat and like order. These learners do well when presented with charts, diagrams, graphs, pictures, and symbols to use as they learn. During a lecture, they need to be supported by printed information such as an outline, overhead, PowerPoint demonstration, or writing on the board. They tend to do poorly with lecture and the use of audiotapes, as occurs in foreign language learning. They need to supplement with creating charts, diagrams, and graphs to understand material, reading the text chapters before coming to lecture, and creating an outline of chapter information referred to during a lecture.

Auditory Learners.   Auditory students learn through verbal instruction and enjoy dialogue and plays. They avoid lengthy descriptions and tend not to focus on illustrations that are given. They remember names, not faces, and think in sounds. These students remember by auditory repetition, are easily distracted by sounds, and like to talk out their problems. They tend to talk themselves through a problem and express emotion verbally. They enjoy listening, but also prefer to talk.

Auditory learners do well with lectures, audiotapes as in learning a foreign language, and verbal instructions. They do poorly with reading text information, dealing with charts, diagrams, and graphs, and following written directions. It is helpful when they can supplement their learning with listening to taped lectures or information. Reading questions and answers to text material out loud and discussing text and lecture information with another student is helpful for them. Working in small study groups and discussing questions and answers with other students about the material allows them to focus and learn the information.

Kinesthetic/Tactile Learners.   Kinesthetic/tactile students learn by doing and prefer reading action-packed information. They are not avid readers and remember best what they have done, not what they have seen or heard. To them, images are not important and they are distractible during oral and visual presentations. They are impulsive and tend to fidget as they are sitting. They need to touch, feel, and manipulate in order to learn. They use gestures when speaking, display emotions physically, and lose interest in detailed verbal discourse. They do well with lab situations, experiments, doing things with their hands, computer science, engineering, sports, situations that require good hand-eye coordination, and they excel with do-it-yourself situations.

These learners do poorly with sitting and listening to a lecture, reading a textbook, or reading directions. They like to be shown how to do something. They need to supplement with notecards to learn formulas, terms, and definitions. This gives them a sense of movement and is portable. They are encouraged in learning by computer programs to enhance learning and doing. If they can tape lectures and text notes, and then use headphones to listen while exercising or just walking around, they can better absorb the information. Having teachers think aloud as they demonstrate a concept or idea is helpful to them. Also, allowing these students to explore, manipulate, and experience the concepts and principles that have been relayed during a lecture session aids their comprehension.

The teacher's role is to provide the materials and encouragement necessary for the students to explore, manipulate, and build on the concepts given. Lab situations, writing exercises, researching ideas, building, and creating something with the information all enhance these students learning abilities. Reality-based learning approaches such as providing authentic purposes and audiences for reading, writing, speaking, and presenting mathematical and scientific hypotheses or calculations aids these students in making connections with what they are learning (Hollins,1993; Marzano, Pickering, & McTighe, 1993; Palincsar and Klenk, 1991). When students are provided real purposes for learning in the classroom, their interest grows and their involvement and learning increases.

Students actively learn by applying their subject areas to everyday life (Atkins, 1993; Cohen, 1992; Hodges, 1994). The research is clear that students show greater achievement gains when they can see the connections of what they are learning to their everyday lives. Please note the additional information in the Suggested Websites section at the end of this chapter.

GLOBAL LEARNING STYLE

The global learning style student is holistic; the student sees the whole instead of the parts, deals with the total situation, and tends to be perceptive and intuitive. Students with this learning style have difficulty analyzing and organizing unstructured materials and presentations. They are sensitive to what others are doing, thinking, and saying. They tend to conform, are socially aware, make favorable first impressions, and are tactful and well-liked. They are people-oriented, extrinsically oriented, affected by stress, tend to use repression and denial of unfavorable events and are less critical when evaluating others.

Some examples of strategies to support students who are global learners include class discussion and intergroup interactions, small collaborative learning groups, and paired group learning. Other methods that teachers can provide for these students are using outlines in presenting materials, providing close supervision and more direction. Use of simulations, role-plays, and projects involving, art, music, theatre, architecture, and models will motivate and aid the learning of these students. Brainstorming ideas and then helping students to organize those ideas for papers is a useful teaching method.

Global learners are not as effective at expressing ideas "on their feet," and need to prepare for questions and class discussions before class. Ways to encourage these types of learners include having students formulate outlines on text chapters and lecture notes, relating learning to personal experiences, and using videos, tape recordings, laser discs, CDs, DVDs, and computer programs to aid their learning.

Suggestions for a global learner in an analytical class include working with a tutor or a study partner, joining a study group, and learning to use structured study skills techniques such as Robinson's (1970) SQ3R (Survey, Question, Read, Review, Recite). These students should be well-prepared prior to class discussions, use planners in managing their time, submit assignments on time, ask questions only after having made an effort to find the answer first, and relate course content to personal experiences whenever possible.

Interdisciplinary teaching through the thematic connections of a variety of content areas allows students to see the connections among various content areas and thus learn in a more holistic manner to understand and retain information gained (Jacobs, 1991)

ANALYTICAL LEARNING STYLE

These students are logical, can separate elements from the background, deal with elements in isolation, and impose their own structure on unorganized situations. They are autonomous, have a highly developed sense of their own identity and are less sensitive to the feelings of others. They are often seen as impersonal, distant, individualistic and self-reliant. These students tend to be more concerned with ideas, principles, and theories than with people. They are task- and achievement-oriented, less likely to request help, innerdirected and motivated, and less affected by stress. They are more critical when evaluating others.

These students do well with lectures and learning through discovery. They tend to be neutral about films, videos, CDs, impose their own structure, and do not need outlines to help them organize information. They prefer distant supervision and less direction with the teacher's role as facilitator, coach, or mentor, and they prefer participant-controlled, unstructured learning activities. The use of divergent questioning that calls for opinion, judgment, and inference from the learner rather than recall of specific facts is more meaningful for them. Questions that probe for a different idea, extend to gain additional information, redirect to refocus the attention of the class, or develop reasons that challenge their thinking develops their critical thinking abilities.

Teachers should allow these students to explore, manipulate, and experience concepts and principles that have been relayed during a lecture session with the teacher's role to provide the materials and encouragement necessary for the students to explore, manipulate, and build on the concepts given. Lab situations, writing exercises, researching, building, and creating something with information are all activities that are motivational and challenging for these students. They enjoy impromptu questioning and effective at expressing ideas spontaneously. If an analytical learner finds herself in a class with a global teacher, she can extend outside reading and research related to class topics, volunteer to lead group activities, and relate course content to personal experiences whenever possible.

There is great power in instruction when teachers recognize the different learning needs of their students and differentiate instruction in recognition of those needs. Truly, "one size does not fit all," and force-fitting instruction will surely result in failure.

CONCEPT ATTAINMENT AS A KEY TO HIGHER LEARNING LEVELS

Moving beyond Facts and Details

Traditionally in the United States, curriculum has been taught using a topical focus containing numerous facts and skills to be learned by students. Because of the expanding rate of information increasing daily, we can no longer adhere to this methodology. In *Stirring the Head, Heart, and Soul* (2001) and in *Concept-Based Curriculum Instruction* (2002) Erickson disparages this curricular stance in favor of teaching concepts and generalizable principles as a means of making sense of subject matter and applying it to the real world. We can teach history with specific events, but those events need to be applicable to events throughout history and to our society today. Otherwise, we are only teaching discrete facts that have no relationship to each other and, therefore, cannot add increased understanding and meaning to today's fast-paced, information-driven lives. Erickson builds a case for a concept-based curriculum. She draws on Taba's (1966, 1971) research that found students who were taught concept formation strategies such as identifying, labeling, and subsuming items in an organized manner revealed a greater number of thought units than that of the control groups. Also, the treatment group test results showed that they also were able to make advances in learning the fact-based information.

Erickson (2002) defines concept as "a mental construct that is timeless, universal, and abstract" (p. 25). She suggests questions to ask in defining a higher-level concept: "Is it broad and abstract?" "Can it be represented in one or two words?" "Is it universal in application?" "Is it timeless and can carry through the ages?" and "Is it represented by different examples that share common attributes?"

Some examples of concepts when studying science are *cause and effect, order, organism, system, cycle,* and *equilibrium.* When studying the visual arts, some concepts include *rhythm, line, color, value,* and *space.* When studying math, some overriding concepts are *ratio, proportion, scale, symmetry,* and *probability.* Organizing subject matter by concepts encourages students to transfer those concepts to other subject areas and make sense of new information using those conceptual connections.

Going beyond the facts and details to embrace deeper conceptual understandings of subject areas allows students to transfer knowledge across time and cultures. Curriculum documents can and should be designed to facilitate this teaching and learning process. Throughout *A Mosaic of Thought* (1997), Keene and Zimmermann highlight the importance of teaching students to grasp the essentials of a piece of literature that they are reading. They model their own thinking processes out loud as they ask questions about the text they are reading, so that students can understand the thinking that takes place as a proficient reader reads. They model questioning strategies that ask students to go beyond the surface meanings of the text and go deeper by determining what is the essential, the most important part of the text that the author wants the reader to understand about what she has written. Some of the questions asked are: "Why do you think that the author used those particular words?" "What pictures come to your mind as you read this description of a character or setting?" and "Why might this action by a character be important to the essence of the text?"

Children of all levels can be taught to think in this manner. As we teach students to think deeper about the content areas they are studying by organizing the curriculum around concepts and principles instead of topics and facts and by teaching them thinking and questioning strategies as they read text, students will begin to exhibit higher levels of thinking, reading, and writing. Students from pre-K to elementary, middle, and high school, as well as diverse and urban students, can begin to think and learn at higher levels. They can begin to understand the bigger picture of concepts and principles and then apply the facts and details within that framework to make sense of the whole. All students can then begin to learn at higher levels. We cannot afford to keep English language learners, children of color, and children of the poor at a disadvantage by only teaching them the basic skills in the content areas. They, like their mainstream counterparts, need to be challenged and need to be taught at higher levels of thinking and learning in order to attain higher levels of academic achievement.

SUMMARY

The urban teacher's expectations and beliefs about urban students guides their behaviors and influences the academic achievement of the children of color, poverty, and English language learners in the urban classroom. It is imperative that preservice teachers address their own biases and assumptions about other cultures and, through this awareness, develop a balanced view of their own culture as well as a knowledgable respect for other cultures. Preservice teachers who are culturally aware can become powerful advocates for children of color and other marginalized students in their classrooms. They can also become agents for change in their schools and communities.

In order to become a successful teacher of urban, diverse, multicultural, multilingual children, teachers need to understand the role of scaffolding in helping students achieve in their classrooms. Through the practices of culturally relevant teaching strategies, instructional conversations, and critical pedagogy, teachers will begin to make a positive difference in the academic lives of urban students.

The strategy of differentiating instruction by readiness, interest, and learner styles will enable preservice teachers to match the curriculum to the various needs of their students in the classroom. As curriculum is developed by concept attainment instead of through organization and memorization of details and facts, students will be able to relate the generalizations and principles of the different disciplines to knowledge about the world and their everyday lives. Relevant, well-planned instruction that motivates student interest and learning will lead to the improved academic performance so desperately needed in urban schools.

CHAPTER QUESTIONS

1. How have teacher beliefs impacted their behavior and students' academic achievement?

2. Define scaffolding, according to Vygotsky; and explain how you would apply this method in teaching students who were below grade level in reading. What kinds of specific strategies would you employ?

3. How do Irvine's and Ladson-Billings' use of scaffolding differ from that of Vygotsky's? Compare and contrast these views.

4. Describe a teacher who is a change agent for social inequities found within the school and school system where he or she teaches. Are you willing to become a change agent?

5. Describe and then respond to the vision of a culturally relevant school that Ladson-Billings presents. Do you agree or disagree with this vision? Why or why not?

6. Describe specific methods you would use to apply differentiated instruction in your classroom of culturally diverse and ESL students, and students with disabilities.

SUGGESTED WEBSITES

2005 International Reading Association
www.readingonline.org

Boettcher Teachers Program
www.pebc.org/ourwork/schools/boettcher.html

Center X Mission Statement
http://centerx.gseis.ucla.edu/mission.php

Differentiated Instruction
www.cast.org/ncac/index.cfm?i=2876
www.teach-nology.com/tutorials/teaching/differentiate/planning/

Education Reform Network
equity.edreform.net/portal/equity/general

English as a Second Language
www.rong-chang.com/
esl.about.com/
owl.english.purdue.edu/handouts/esl/

Learning Styles
www.ldpride.net/learningstyles.MI.htm
www.chaminade.org/inspire/learnstl.htm
www.engr.ncsu.edu/learningstyles/ilsweb.html

North Central Regional Educational Laboratory (NCREL)
Critical Issue: Educating Teachers for Diversity
www.ncrel.org/sdrs/areas/issues/educatrs/presrvce/pe300.htm

Social Justice Advocates
www.socialjusticeeducation.org/
www.umass.edu/sje/
www.concernamerica.org/SocJusticeNews.html
www.emory.edu/EDUCATION/irvine/publications.html

www.aeispeakers.com/Ladson-Billings-Gloria.htm

U.S. Department of Education Publications
www.ed.gov/about/pubs/intro/index.html

Web-Based Education Commission (WBEC) Final Report
www.ed.gov/offices/AC/WBEC/FinalReport/

REFERENCES

Adams, M. J. (1986). Teaching thinking to Chapter I students. In Williams, B. I., et al. (eds.), *Compensatory education: Conference proceedings and papers* (Washington, DC: June 17, 18). Chapel Hill, NC: Research and Evaluation Associates.

American Association of Colleges for Teacher Education. (1988). *RATE II: Teaching teachers: Facts and figures.* Washington, DC: AACTE.

Association for Supervision and Curriculum Development (prod.). (2002). *How to scaffold instruction for student success.* [videotape]. Available: Association for Supervision and Curriculum Development, 1703 North Beauregard Street, Alexandria, VA 22311–1714.

Atkins, A. (1993). New ways to learn. *Better Homes and Gardens, 71,* 35–36.

Banks. J. A. (1988). *Multiethnic education: Theory and practice* (2nd ed.). Boston: Allyn & Bacon.

Beed, P. L., Hawkins, E. M., & Roller, C. M. (1991). Moving learners toward independence: The power of scaffolded instruction. *The Reading Teacher, 44,* 648–655.

Blachowicz, C. L. Z. (1986). Making connections: Alternatives to the vocabulary notebook. *Journal of Reading, 29,* 643–649.

Blachowicz, C. L. Z., & Fisher, P. J. (2002). *Teaching vocabulary in all classrooms.* (2nd ed.). Columbus, OH: Merrill Prentice Hall.

Boettcher Teachers Program. (n.d.). Available: www.pebc.org/ourwork/schools/boettcher.html (2005, February 18).

Boyatzis, R. E., & Kolb, D. A. (1991). Assessing individuality in learning: The learning skills profile. *Educational Psychology: An International Journal of Experimental Educational Psychology, 11,* 279–295.

Bransford, J. D., Sherwood, R. S., Vye, N. J., & Rieser, J. (1986). Teaching thinking and problem-solving: Research foundations. *American Psychologist, 41,* 1078–1089.

Brophy, J. E., & Good, T. L. (1970). Teachers' communication of differential expectations for children's classroom performance: Some behavioral data. *Journal of Educational Psychology, 61,* 365–374.

Bruner, J. (1990). *Acts of meaning.* Cambridge, MA: Harvard University Press.

Buehler, E. C., & Meltesen, D. (1983). ESL Buddies. *Instructor, 93,* 120–124.

Carlsen, W. S. (1991). Questioning in classrooms: A psycholinguistic perspective. *Review of Educational Research, 61,* 157–178.

Center X Mission Statement. (n.d.). Available: http://centerx.gseis.ucla.edu/mission.php (2005, February 18).

Cochran-Smith, M. (1997). Knowledge, skills and experiences for teaching culturally diverse learners: A perspective for practicing teachers. In Irvine, J. J. (ed.), *Critical knowledge for diverse teachers and learners* (pp. 27–87). Washington, DC: American Association of Colleges for Teacher Education.

Cohen, H. G. (1992). Two teaching strategies: Their effectiveness with students of varying cognitive abilities. *School, Science, and Mathematics, 92,* 126–132.

Cole, R. W. (ed.). (1995). *Educating everybody's children.* Alexandria, VA: Association for Supervision and Curriculum Development.

Darling-Hammond, L. (1995). Inequality and access to knowledge. In Banks, J. A., & Banks, C. A. M. (eds.), *Handbook of research on multicultural education* (pp. 465–483). New York: Macmillan.

Education Trust, Inc. (2003). *Achievement in America.* Washington, DC: U.S. Department of Education, NCES, National Assessment of Education Progress. Available: www2.edtrust .org/NR/rdonlyres/14FB5D33-31EF-4A9C-B55F-33184998BDD8/0/8 (2005, February 18).

Ellis, E. S., & Larkin, M. J. (1998). Strategic instruction for adolescents with learning disabilities. In B. Y. L. Wong (ed.), *Learning about learning disabilities,* (2nd ed.). (pp. 585–656). San Diego, CA: Academic Press.

Erickson, H. L. (2001). *Stirring the head, heart, and soul.* (2nd ed.). Thousand Oaks, CA: Corwin Press.

Erickson, H. L. (2002). *Concept-based curriculum and instruction.* Thousand Oaks, CA: Corwin Press.

Fullan, M. (2003). *Change forces with a vengeance.* New York: Routledge-Falmer.

Garcia, G. G. (2003). *English language learners: Reaching the highest level of English literacy.* Newark, DE: International Reading Association.

Gardner, H. (1983). *Frames of Mind: The theory of multiple intelligences.* New York: Basic Books.

Gay, G. (1995). Mirror images on common issues: Parallels between multicultural education and critical pedagogy. In Sleeter, C. E., & McLaren, P. L. (eds.), *Multicutural education, critical pedagogy, and the politics of difference* (pp. 155–189). Albany: State University of New York Press.

Glasser, W. (1998). *Choice Theory: A new psychology of personal freedom.* Chatsworth, CA: William Glasser.

Glasser, W. (2000). *Every student can succeed.* Chatsworth, CA: William Glasser.

Goatley, V. J., & Raphael, T. E. (1992). Nontraditional learners written and dialogic response to literature. In Kinzer, C. K., & Leu, D. K. (eds.). *Literacy research, theory and practice: Views from many perspectives.* 41st Yearbook of the National Reading Conference. Chicago: National Reading Conference.

Grace, C. (1992). The portfolio and its use: Developmentally appropriate assessment of young children. Urbana, IL: ERIC ED No. 351 150.

Grant, C. (1991). Culture and teaching: What do teachers need to know? In M. Kennedy (ed.), *Teaching academic subjects to diverse learners* (pp. 237–256), New York: Teachers College Press.

Grant, C., & Sleeter, C. (1986). *After the school bell rings.* Philadelphia: Falmer.

Gregorc, A. E. (1982). *An adult's guide to style.* Columbia, CT: Gregorc Associates.

Harvey, S., & Goudvis, A. (2000). *Strategies that work.* Portland, ME: Stenhouse.

Haycock, K. (2005). *Improving achievement and closing gaps between groups.* Education Trust, Inc. Available: www2.edtrust.org/EdTrust/Product+Catalog/recent+presentations.htm (2005, February 10).

Herrmann, A. W. (1989, May). Teaching writing with peer response groups. Bloomington, IN: ERIC ED No. 307 616.

Hewitt, G. (1993). Vermont's portfolio-based writing assessment program: A brief history. *Teachers and Writers, 24,* 1–6.

Hodges, H. (1994). A consumer's guide to learning styles programs: An expert's advice on selecting and implementing various models in the classroom. *The School Administrator, 51,* 14–18.

Hogan, K., & Pressley, M. (eds.). (1997). *Scaffolding student learning: Instructional approaches and issues.* Cambridge, MA: Brookline Books.

Hollins, E. R. (1993). Assessing teacher competence for diverse populations. *Theory into Practice, 32,* 93–99.

Irvine, J. J. (2003). *Educating teachers for diversity: Seeing with a cultural eye.* New York: Teachers College Press.

Jacobs, H. H. (1991). Planning for curriculum integration. *Educational Leadership, 49,* 27–28.

Johnson, D. W., & Johnson, R. T. (1990). Social skills for successful group work. *Educational Leadership, 47,* 29–33.

Joyce, B., Wolf, J., & Calhoun, E. (1993). *The self-renewing school.* Alexandria, VA: Association for Supervision and Curriculum Development.

Kame'enui, E. J., Carnine, D. W., Dixon, R. C., Simmons, D. C., & Coyne, M. D. (2002). *Effective teaching strategies that accommodate diverse learners* (2nd ed.). Upper Saddle River, NJ: Merrill Prentice-Hall.

Keene, E. O., & Zimmermann, S. (1997). *Mosaic of thought.* Portsmouth, NH: Heinemann.

Kozol, J. (1991). *Savage Inequalities.* New York: Harper.

Ladson-Billings, G. (1994). *The Dreamkeepers.* San Francisco: Jossey-Bass.

Ladson-Billings, G. (2000). Fighting for our lives: Preparing teachers to teach African American students. *Journal of Teacher Education, 51,* 206–214.

Lambert, M. (1990). When the problem is not the question and the solution is not the answer: Mathematical knowing and teaching. *American Educational Research Journal, 27,* 29–63.

Lewis, A., & Steinberger, E. (1991). *Learning styles: Putting research and common sense into practice.* Arlington, VA: AASA.

Lytle, S., & Cochran-Smith, M. (1997). Teacher research: Some questions that persist. In Irvine, J. J. (ed.), *Critical knowledge for diverse teachers and learners* (pp. 27–87).

Marzano, R. J., Pickering, D., & McTighe, J. (1993). *Assessing student outcomes: Performance assessment using the dimensions of learning model.* Alexandria, VA: ASCD.

More, A. J. (1990). Learning styles of Native Americans and Asians. ERIC ED No. 330 535.

Onosko, J. J. (1992). Exploring the thinking of thoughtful teachers. *Educational Leadership, 49,* 40–43.

Pajares, M. (1992). Teachers' beliefs and educational research: Cleaning up a messy construct. *Review of Educational Research, 62*(3).

Palinscar, A. S., & Klenk, L. J. (1991). Learning dialogues to promote text comprehension. Washington, DC: National Institute of Child Health and Human Development, PHS Grant 059.

Pressley, M., Hogan, K., Wharton-McDonald, R., Mistretta, J., & Ettenberger, S. (1996). The challenges of instructional scaffolding: The challenges of instruction that supports student thinking. *Learning Disabilities Research and Practice, 11*(3), 138–146.

Robinson, F. P. (1970). *Effective study* (4th ed.). New York: Harper & Row.

Sleeter, C. E., & Grant, C. A. (1987). An analysis of multicultural education in the United States. *Harvard Educational Review, 57,* 421–444.

Smith, G. P. (1998). *Common sense about uncommon knowledge: The knowledge bases for diversity.* Washington, DC: American Association of Colleges for Teacher Education.

Taba, H. (1966). *Teaching strategies and cognitive functioning in elementary school children: Cooperative research project 2404.* San Francisco: San Francisco State College.

Taba, H., Durkin, M. C., Fraenkel, J. R., & McNaughton, A. H. (1971). *A teacher's handbook to elementary social studies: An inductive approach* (2nd ed.). Reading, MA: Addison-Wesley.

Tharp, R. G., & Gallimore, R. (1988). *Rousing minds to life: Teaching, learning, and schooling in social context.* Cambridge: Cambridge University Press.

Tomlinson, C. A. (2001). *How to differentiate instruction in mixed-ability classrooms* (2nd ed.). Alexandria, VA: Association for Supervision and Curriculum Development.

Vygotsky, L. S. (1978). *Mind in society: The development of higher mental process.* Cambridge, MA: Harvard University Press.

Webb, L. D., Metha, A., & Jordan, K. F. (2003). *Foundations of American education.* Upper Saddle River, NJ: Merrill Prentice-Hall.

Wiest, L. R. (1998). Using immersion experiences to shake up preservice teachers' views about cultural differences. *Journal of Teacher Education, 49,* 358–365.

White, S. E. (1992). Factors that contribute to learning differences among African American and Caucasian students. ERIC ED No. 374 177.

Yaden, D. B., Madrigal, P., & Tam, A. (2003). Access to books and beyond: Creating and learning from a book lending program for Latino families in the inner city. In Garcia, G. G. (ed.), *English learners: Reaching the highest level of English literacy* (pp. 357–386). Newark, DE: International Reading Association.

Zeichner, K. M. (1993). *Educating teachers for cultural diversity.* East Lansing: Michigan State University.

Zeichner, K. (1996). Educating teachers for cultural diversity. In Zeichner, K., Melnick, S. S., & Gomez, M. L. (eds.), *Currents of reform in preservice teacher education* (pp. 140–142). New York: Teachers College Press.

ANNOTATED BIBLIOGRAPHY ON SOCIOCULTURAL KNOWLEDGE

Smith, G. P. (1998). *Common sense about uncommon knowledge: The knowledge bases for diversity.* Washington, DC: American Association of Colleges for Teacher Education.

Smith's publication exemplifies knowledge about diverse language learners and is suitable for teacher education programs. Information presented in this document involves bidialectism, bilingualism, sociolinguistic characteristics of non-Standard English systems, and the assessment of nonstandard language (Smith, 1998).

ETHNIC IDENTITY LITERATURE

Bernal, M. E., & Knight, G. P. (eds.). (1993). *Ethnic identity: Formation and transmission among Hispanics and other minorities.* Albany: State University of New York Press.

Phinney, J. S., & Rotheram, M. J. (eds.). (1993). A three-stage model of ethnic identity development in adolescence. In M. E. Bernal & G. P. Knight (eds.), *Ethnic identity: Formation and transmission among Hispanics and other minorities* (pp. 61–79). Albany: State University of New York Press.

Since culture exerts a significant influence on family structure, childrearing practices, and the other processes of cognitive, physical, and social development such as self-concept and motivation, preservice and inservice teachers need to understand these varying processes and apply this information to teaching and learning. Phinney and Rotheram and Bernal and Knight are two foundational publications that synthesize much of the theory and research in these areas.

RESILIENCE LITERATURE

Bernard, B. (1991). *Fostering resilience in kids: Protective factors in the family, school, and community.* Portland, OR: Northwest Regional Educational Laboratory.

Winfield, L. (1991). Resilience, schooling, and development in African American youth. *Education and Urban Society, 24,* 5–14.

Another concept concerning marginalized ethnic and racial cultures involves the literature of resilience. Resiliency literature can be found in Bernard (1991) and Winfield (1991). A study of this research reveals the ability of urban and minority youth to overcome adversity and become responsible, self-supporting, industrious, and creative citizens who do not give in to the negative influences in their lives. Having knowledge of this literature opens the eyes of preservice and inservice teachers to the strengths of urban and minority students. When educators think negatively about these students and feel that nothing can overcome the obstacles that these children face, this literature defies that perspective.

SOCIOPOLITICAL PERSPECTIVES ON HUMAN DEVELOPMENT

Mallory, B. L., & New, R. S. (eds.). (1994). *Diversity and developmentally appropriate practices.* New York: Teachers College Press.

This piece of literature provides a broad overview of the sociopolitical perspective on human development. Preservice and inservice teachers should understand and have specific knowledge about the sociopolitical perspective on human development. This perspective challenges Eurocentric/Western assumptions about development that historically has excluded minority cultural development.

MULTICULTURAL COMMUNICATION IN THE CLASSROOM

Adler, S. (1993). *Multicultural communication skills in the classroom.* Boston, MA: Allyn & Bacon.

Homel, P., Palij, M., & Aaronson, D. (eds.). (1987). *Childhood bilingualism: Aspects of linguistic, cognitive, and social development.* Hillsdale, NJ: Lawrence Erlbaum.

Magill, F. N. (ed.). (1992). *Masterpieces of African American literature.* New York: HarperCollins.

Ramirez, G., & Ramirez, J. L. (1994). *Multiethnic children's literature.* Albany, NY: Delmar Publishers.

Reyner, J. (ed.). (1992). *Teaching American Indian students.* Norman: University of Oklahoma Press.

Understanding the bilingual area of Hispanic Americans is complex because of the varieties of English and Spanish spoken by Hispanic Americans in the United States. An edited publication that synthesizes research studies of bilingual education and second language acquisition includes Homel, Palij, and Aaronson (1987). Information regarding Native American and low-incidence minority languages can be found in Reyner's (1992) *Teaching American Indian Students.* Courses in African American or multicultural literature taught through the English departments in colleges and universities would be helpful in building ethnic and minority perspectives for preservice teachers. If these courses are not available, Magill's (1992) *Masterpieces of African American Literature* and Ramirez and Ramirez's (1994) *Multicultural Children's Literature* provide valuable teaching resources (Smith, 1998).

CHAPTER 8

ASSESSMENT AND EVALUATION

*Students' test scores can mean the difference between a
remedial label and the gifted track—or between entry into a
selective college and a lifetime at McDonald's.*

—*The Education Trust*, Thinking K–16:
Good Teaching Matters *(1998)*

URBAN PERSPECTIVES

Elisabeth Snider
Urban High School Educator

The art of teaching occurs when teachers are able to help the students learn through the application of effective assessment strategies. Assessments take the form of everything from oral questions to probing to a final exam or to a six-week project.

"Life in the urban high school offers deeply rewarding experiences for classroom teachers," explains Elisabeth Snider. "What's amazing is the profound influence teachers have on awakening the limitless potentials of our students. With the right conditions and with vital support, teachers can make great strides in closing the achievement gap that currently exists between minority and White students. To maintain forward momentum of students' academic progress, teachers assess their students continually, and often individually, to make sure learning continues and builds."

Snider has spent the last fourteen years of her career at one urban high school that has met with significant changes throughout her tenure. "Staff turnover has been high over the years. Maintaining year-to-year consistency in curriculum and discipline decisions can be indeed challenging when new faculty, staff, and administrators come and go." Despite personnel changes, Snider contends that the maintenance of collaborative support systems among teachers is vital to the caring and understanding network that enriches and strengthens professionals in the urban school setting. She credits the establishment of the Critical Friends Group at her school for having developed strong collegiality and trust among the faculty participants.

Effective assessment requires that teachers hold students to high academic standards, according to Snider. She encourages conscientious, academic momentum in classes. "Although respectful and caring of the students," she continues, "the best urban teachers are firm and consistent with their expectations of students." She strongly advises that urban teachers: know well and gain confidence in their subjects taught; vary instructional delivery, while keeping the pace moving; reflect on anecdotal notations made of daily lesson and student activities in journals; model proper behavior and socially responsible language; diffuse tensions with humor, and forgive student mishaps or misspeaks without holding a grudge; establish private and compassionate connections with students that appreciate their varied, unique qualities; set academic and behavior expectations high; and establish varieties of assessments that best measure students' achievements. "*Rigor without rescue* is not good teaching," she cautions. "Assessment is a process that involves observing and valuing demonstrations of students' achievements, not just an act of determining grades for students. The art of teaching occurs when teachers are able to help the students learn through the application of effective assessment strategies. Assessments take the form of everything from oral questions to probing to a final exam or to a six-week project. Part of a teacher's planning process must entail how to scaffold and build on what students know, so that those students are able to reach higher levels of achievement."

Snider is as strong on students respecting and supporting each other as she is on the importance of teacher collaboration "Creating a community of learners in the classroom is an extension of the community of learners established between and among teaching colleagues. The intraschool community effectively supports teachers as learners, as well as its student learners."

THE TOOLS AND PROCESSES OF ASSESSMENT

An assessment used in the education of students is a test, or a planned procedure, that involves methods or tasks and is used to guide decisions about student learning, curriculum, and instruction (Moore, 2003). Assessments are both tools—providing the means to determine whether or not students are meeting learning objectives—and processes, the means to evaluate the quality of students' work as well as the success of the teachers' instructional practices. As testing tools, assessments collect data used to measure specific or general knowledge, behavior, performance, or attitude. They provide a reading or snapshot of learning outcomes. As processes, they play a vital role to improve student learning when teachers assess how successful students are learning and, based upon their analysis and judgment, elect to change instruction or revisit an idea, or change teaching pace, and so forth. Thus, rather than the typical last event of a lesson or unit of study that ends a specific topic or instruction, such as a grade or score, assessments serve as active teaching tools. They continuously collect and gauge each student's academic needs and set the pace for continued classroom instruction (Freiberg & Driscoll, 1996; Taylor & Nolen, 2005; Wiggins & McTighe, 1998).

Assessing what students know and do not know is an ongoing, day-to-day, and lesson-to-lesson process that takes students along instructional paths to their learning goals.

Regrettably, as early as second or third grade, students who are Black, Hispanic, or Native American begin patterns of low assessment that follow them through to the end of their education experience (The College Board, 2005). The nation's public education system is poised and determined to help students and schools elevate learning gains and, especially, close the achievement gap that exists between White and students of color.

McMillan (2000) emphasizes that effective teaching is "characterized by assessments that motivate and engage students in ways that are consistent with [educators'] philosophies of teaching and learning, and with theories of development, learning, and motivation" (p. 12). Using assessments as tools that generate significant academic data serves teachers and their students in an ongoing process to gather and analyze evidence indicating what students can and cannot do (Forte & Schurr, 2002).

Assessments are such an important part of teaching. As their ultimate purpose is to measure learning, they are also used as tools to *improve* teaching, curriculum, and conditions for student learning. To promote learning, for example, teachers use assessments to prompt students' thinking, or for review prior to beginning a lesson. Students might offer lists of information they know and identify about a particular topic of study. This strategy offers an understanding of how well-acquainted, knowledgable, and/or interested a student is in the newly introduced concept or field of study. It can shed light on what students do *not* know or on what topic they share confusion or erroneous perceptions. Further, offering vital feedback from assessments (for example, grades, stickers, positive or constructive comments) informs students about their learning, their understandings, and their accomplishments. This type of feedback is necessary for student learning and serves to motivate them to continue their academic successes, as well (Freiberg & Driscoll, 1996).

Assessments collect evidence that students are understanding the knowledge presented to them. To achieve this collection of evidence, effective teachers access a continuum of assessment methods that typically:

1. begins with informally checking students' understanding, using in class oral questions, observations, and informal dialogues;
2. includes administering quizzes and tests that are content-focused to assess facts, concepts, and discrete skills learned by the students;
3. includes academic prompts, or open-ended questions or problems, requiring students to think critically and prepare responses, products, or performances that demonstrate such; and
4. incorporates authentic performance tasks and projects, actual or simulated, that range in length from short- to long-term, and are multistaged, to mirror or replicate real issues or problems. (Wiggins & McTighe, 1998)

Overall, assessments need to cull and build upon the strengths that diverse learners transmit to the learning situation. The measures ultimately determine whether students have demonstrated gains in understanding useful information (Kulieke et al., 1990). Teachers use this information to plan the content and pace of their classroom instruction.

Results from frequent assessments offer valuable information on which effective teachers base their instruction (what they teach) and instructional deliveries (ways to teach it). This strategy can prevent students from falling behind, and from remaining behind grade-level achievement standards. Instruction that targets the strengthening of specific students' learning weaknesses leads to preventing academic failure later, and facilitates improvements in their overall achievement (WETA, 2004).

ADDING VALUE TO MEASUREMENT: EVALUATION

McMillan (2000) defines evaluation as "deciding the merit and worth of the data as applied to a specific use or context" (p. 12). Classroom teachers, as astute evaluators of student data, should gain whatever skills and knowledge possible to accurately and systematically analyze evidence of student performance, and make appropriate value judgments that correctly interpret what the results mean.

Evaluation entails the teacher making decisions about student learning. From observing or reviewing data from a student's academic performance (determined by an assessment), for example, teachers make judgments about the extent of the student's knowledge, behavior, performance, or the student's attitude, and thereby formulate an evaluation (Freiberg & Driscoll, 1996).

Evaluations are best accomplished through authentic and performance tasks that demonstrate how well students perform the skills teachers hope they acquire from classroom instruction. They provide evidence that students achieve understanding of the knowledge presented to them. They address what and how teachers assess the valued learning. Therefore, establishing evaluative criteria and performance standards at the outset of instruction keeps the teacher on track in content presented to, and participated in by, the students. Evaluative criteria presented to students prior to the teacher's instruction makes it clear what performance is expected of them, acceptable quality of performance, and what performance is considered "excellent" (Wiggins & McTighe, 1998).

In general, the teacher's knowledge and practice of sound assessment and evaluation principles and ideas benefit the students by offering enhanced learning opportunities. Additionally, teachers are benefitted as they create numerous avenues to refine instructional effectiveness (McMillan, 2000). As teachers continue to respect, plan for, and accommodate diverse student learning styles, attitudes, interests, and talents, and honor student efforts at all segments of the grading spectrum, the assessment process serves as the key vehicle that drives educational achievement forward (Forte & Schurr, 2002). The terms *test* and *assessment* are used interchangeably throughout this chapter to represent the documented measurements of students' academic progress.

HISTORY OF ASSESSMENT

Early Beginnings of Testing

Assessment, or testing, has been a part of the educational landscape for many years. As early as the second century B.C., tests were administered to measure an individual's abilities and skills to make judgments about his or her future behaviors. Earliest use of formal testing in schools dates back to the seventeenth century, having taken the form of written exams offered in Catholic universities in Western Europe. The emphasis on the use of tests as a major curriculum component in U.S. education was perceived negatively in nineteenth-century classrooms due to their use in schools to hold back or fail students. Teachers thought that if students proved not to be learning, it was the students' fault. The Progressive education movement of the 1930s and 1940s gave rise to educators attempting to ease student anxieties about testing and make school environments more amenable for all learners. Unfortunate consequences from this era included the practice of promoting students from one grade level to the next, regardless of

their test performances, notoriously known as "social promotion." Schools were discouraged from holding back students (retention), for fear of harming students' well-being and social adjustment. Thus, tests continued their use; however, as a complete turnaround from nineteenth-century practices, students were *not* held accountable for their performance in school (Ravitch, 2002; Schreyer Institute, 2004).

Standardized Tests/Assessments Emerge

From its documented beginnings in 1926, the standardized college admissions test, known as the Scholastic Aptitude Test (SAT), met with strong public enthusiasm, as it was immediately embraced as a national measure for school accountability. For the purposes of selecting the most promising high school students, SAT scores were found a better predictor of college potential than using high school grades (Hunter & Barbee, 2003; Johnson & Johnson, 2002). Commercially developed and distributed, normative-referenced (norm-referenced) testing programs—which used the achievement performance scores of one set of student test takers as a frame of reference for evaluating the performance of other like-individual student test takers, soared in popularity during the ensuing 1950s and 1960s. These programs of achievement tests, focusing on knowledge and skills learned in school, carry scientific credibility and tradition welcomed by the public in a competitive nation and world (Johnson & Johnson, 2002).

It was during the decades to follow that statewide testing became the norm, or standard and accepted means, by which achievement test scores were reported, analyzed, and interpreted. In the mid-1960s, scrutiny of these data brought dramatic changes to U.S. public education, as the focus turned to school accountability. Of particular impact during this era was a report titled "Equality of Education Opportunities" (Coleman 1990). Coleman examined national student achievement test scores (education outcomes), and compared the data against measurements of the distribution of resources and opportunities (input) among students of different races and ethnic heritage. As presented in historical context in Chapter 1, Coleman's study, based upon differing school populations and his reported findings, alerted the nation to profound discrepancies between input and education outcomes deserving immediate and critical attention and change. Since that time, the U.S. judges student test scores as indicators of student and school academic performance, as well as indicators of adequate educational preparation of tomorrow's leaders (Ravitch, 2002).

From the late-1960s emerged a congressionally mandated, national assessment gathering, analyzing, and disclosure institute, the National Assessment of Educational Progress (NAEP). The best source of long-term academic trends available from the federal government since the early 1970s, the NAEP scores and comparisons from state and national data, provide information about the educational achievement of U.S. students of different grade levels, ages, gender, racial and ethnic cultures, socioeconomic status, and so on. The score analyses are used publicly and politically to showcase and compare students' achievement standing to that of other students' progress among states or nations. In many cases, school systems use the data to urge schools and their faculties to increase productivity, and to encourage individual student and overall class score improvements in schools. Most revealing from NAEP data is its clear revelations verifying the large achievement gaps shown to persist between minority students and White students, beginning from the early years of their education until they complete their education (The College Board, 1999; Gredler, 1999; Stiggins, 2002). (NAEP graphs of fourth- and eighth-grade progress in reading and math illustrate achievement gap discrepancies per race/ethnic subgroups and can be observed at the end of this chapter.)

Public Support for Schools Based on Test Scores

There is significant public call for student and school performance comparisons. Because federal, state, and local government dollars support public education for all students, tax-paying citizens in the United States scrutinize comparisons of quality among schools and school systems based upon their respective reported assessment scores. A recent nationwide poll of public attitude toward education revealed that, compared to 80 percent in 1978 who viewed educational opportunities as the same for White students and minority students, today's public more passionately realizes great differences among the students' educational opportunities. There is greater public support for efforts to close the existent and profound achievement gap that demonstrates significant discrepancies in student subgroup test scores. Interestingly, they view it as the schools' responsibility to close the gap (Phi Delta Kappa International, 2004).

Further, in a 2003 "Voter Survey," the *Chattanooga Times–Free Press* in Chattanooga, Tennessee, asked the question:

> Do you support or oppose measuring of schools based on student *test scores, attendance,* and *graduation rates* as requirements for federal education program funding?
> Support: 58%
> Oppose: 29%
> Undecided: 13%
> (Chattanooga Times–Free Press, December 18, 2003)

Thus, reported student standardized test scores affect the degree of parental and public confidence in public education, and pique public concerns about funding schools.

Urban teachers, as well as teachers among other types of school settings, should continually search for and learn scientifically proven, creative, and engaging preparation methods that enable students to achieve the best success possible on standardized tests. In addition, professional development, teacher observations, university course offerings, and topic-specific seminars, workshops, and conferences, provide opportunities to learn the latest new and proven-successful techniques, methods, and knowledge of best instruction practices for urban classrooms (Gilman & Gilman, 2003). These opportunities are further explored in Chapter 10, "Opportunities for the Future."

The accumulated data from students' standardized test scores serve as a vital feature of one of the most costly, and arguably the most robust, of all academic expectations-based federal initiatives, the Elementary and Secondary Education Act of 2001, known as No Child Left Behind legislation (reviewed at greater length in this chapter). Policymakers at both federal and state levels seek, per analysis of student achievement test score performance, accountability of students, teachers, schools, and school districts.

RATIONALES FOR ASSESSMENT

Medical Assessments as Educational Assessments

Gandal and McGiffert (2003) draw upon the like-comparisons between medical tests and educational assessments and their importance, affirming that well-designed tests are an essential part of education, just as medical checks are an essential part of an individual's health. As medical tests diagnose and measure patients' conditions based upon optimum health standards (for example, cholesterol and blood count readings), so should educational assessments measure students' academic performances based upon optimum achievement standards. As medical tests determine relevant information regarding the patients' health status, so should educational assessments report the status of how well students meet state-established, grade-level standards. They assert that, similar to the usefulness of information gathered and the prescriptive needs fulfilled from individuals' regular medical checkups, "useful education assessments provide timely, specific, meaningful results that educators can use to target instruction [as prescriptions] to students' needs (Gandal & McGiffert, 2003). Targeted instruction can be determined by examining results of students' achievement tests, as well as daily results of teacher-generated (nonstandardized) assessments.

Year-end standardized assessments, as well as teacher-made classroom assessments, maintain a vital place in instructional planning and for devising strategies and activities that best assist students in meeting their respective academic progress goals (Guskey, 2003). The following sections discuss guiding positive student performance on standardized achievement tests, which are typically commercially prepared for nationwide use, and providing scores that reflect student levels of performance related to others of the same age or grade levels (Johnson & Johnson, 2002).

The Big Games as Educational Assessments

Papalewis and Fortune (2002) compare ongoing assessments—those which teachers initiate and record results—to ongoing athletic practices that occur prior to the "big game": students' performance on year-end standardized tests. In preparation for the game, coaches evaluate the players' day-to-day performances to know what players need to learn and practice what skill or exercise for best gametime performance. Just as coaches acknowledge preparation of their players to do their best, teachers evaluate and prepare their students for assessments that measure gained concepts deemed necessary for students to know and practice in life. Effective teachers among all school settings must help to prepare their students for "game day," be it the year-end standardized achievement test that demonstrates their learned skills and concept advances, or a launch into life that demonstrates their application of classroom-learned skills and knowledge of real-world events. Success—or winning—in the classroom is achieved when teachers continually assess what their students know compared to what set standards imply they should demonstrate that they know, and help them achieve school-based goals as an ongoing process that continues from year to year and grade to grade.

Purposes for and Benefits of Assessment

Effective educators regularly and continuously assess and evaluate student progress through fair and ethical practices. They are determined to keep abreast of each student's learning momentum and proven knowledge gains. The

National Association for the Education of Young Children (2004) encourages that educators who test students to determine their individual and class "strengths, progress, and needs," incorporate assessment strategies and methods that connect to specific, beneficial purposes, including:

1. making sound decisions about teaching and learning;
2. identifying significant concerns that may require focused intervention for individual children; and
3. helping programs improve their educational and developmental interventions.

Further, among their concerns for administering classroom assessments are that educators demonstrate developmental appropriateness (for example, selecting test formats that students can be truly capable of completing), as well as cultural and linguistic responsiveness (for example, assuring that students understand what is expected of them and what they are to accomplish to meet those expectations).

The following are indicators that serve to gauge sound assessment practice in all school programs, as cited by the National Association for the Education of Young Children (NAEYC).

NAEYC ASSESSMENT INDICATORS OF EFFECTIVENESS

- *Ethical principles guide assessment practices.* Ethical principles underlie all assessment practices. Young children are not denied opportunities or services, and decisions are not made about children on the basis of a single assessment.

- *Assessment instruments are used for their intended purposes.* Assessments are used in ways consistent with the purposes for which they were designed. If the assessments will be used for additional purposes, they are validated for those purposes.

- *Assessments are appropriate for ages and other characteristics of children being assessed.* Assessments are designed for and validated for use with children whose ages, cultures, home languages, socioeconomic status, abilities and disabilities, and other characteristics are similar to those of the children with whom the assessments will be used.

- *Assessment instruments are in compliance with professional criteria for quality.* Assessments are valid and reliable. Accepted professional standards of quality are the basis for selection, use, and interpretation of assessment instruments, including screening tools. The NAEYC supports and adheres to the measurement standards set forth in 1999 by the American Educational Research Association, the American Psychological Association, and the National Center for Measurement in Education. When individual norm-referenced tests are used, they meet these guidelines.

■ *What is assessed is developmentally and educationally significant.* The objects of assessment include a comprehensive, developmentally, and educationally important set of goals, rather than a narrow set of skills. Assessments are aligned with early learning standards, with program goals, and with specific emphases in the curriculum.

■ *Assessment evidence is used to understand and improve learning.* Assessments lead to improved knowledge about children. This knowledge is translated into improved curriculum implementation and teaching practices. Assessment helps early childhood professionals understand the learning of a specific child or group of children; enhance overall knowledge of child development; improve educational programs for young children while supporting continuity across grades and settings; and access resources and supports for children with specific needs.

■ *Assessment evidence is gathered from realistic settings and situations that reflect children's actual performance.* To influence teaching strategies or to identify children in need of further evaluation, the evidence used to assess young children's characteristics and progress is derived from real-world classroom or family contexts that are consistent with children's culture, language, and experiences.

■ *Assessments use multiple sources of evidence gathered over time.* The assessment system emphasizes repeated, systematic observation, documentation, and other forms of criterion- or performance-oriented assessment using broad, varied, and complementary methods with accommodations for children with disabilities.

■ *Screening is always linked to follow-up.* When a screening or other assessment identifies concerns, appropriate follow-up, referral, or other intervention is used. Diagnosis or labeling is never the result of a brief screening or one-time assessment.

■ *Use of individually administered, norm-referenced tests is limited.* The use of formal standardized testing and norm-referenced assessments of young children is limited to situations in which such measures are appropriate and potentially beneficial, such as identifying potential disabilities.

■ *Staff and families are knowledgeable about assessment.* Staff are given resources that support their knowledge and skills about early childhood assessment and their ability to assess children in culturally and linguistically appropriate ways. Preservice and inservice training builds teachers' and administrators' "assessment literacy," creating a community that sees assessment as a tool to improve outcomes for children. Families are part of this community, with regular communication, partnership, and involvement. (Reprinted with permission of the National Association for the Education of Young Children, 2004.)

Purposes for and Benefits of Evaluation

Grading students on a fair basis requires implementing clear goals and objectives, collecting reliable and valid evidence of student achievement, and designing ways to summarize the information that appropriately and fairly reports student progress (Taylor & Nolen, 2005). In tandem with federal guidelines mandating school systems to administer and report their students' yearly achievement test scores, the NAEYC also encourages that schools initiate regular evaluations of its students' progress in their school's program of study.

Below are indicators that serve to gauge sound evaluation practice in all school programs, as cited by the NAEYC.

NAEYC EVALUATION INDICATORS OF EFFECTIVENESS

- *Evaluation is used for continuous improvement.* The NAEYC recommends that programs undertake regular evaluation, including self-evaluation, to document the extent to which they are achieving desired results, with the goal of engaging in continuous improvement. Evaluations focus on processes and implementation as well as outcomes. Over time, evidence is gathered that program evaluations do influence specific improvements.

- *Multiple sources of data are available.* An effective evaluation system should include multiple measures, including program data, child demographic data, information about staff qualifications, administrative practices, classroom quality assessments, implementation data, and other information that provides a context for interpreting the results of child assessments.

- *Sampling is used when assessing individual children as part of large-scale program evaluation.* When individually administered, norm-referenced tests of children's progress are used as part of program evaluation and accountability. Matrix sampling is used (that is, administered only to a systematic sample of children) so as to diminish the burden of testing on children and to reduce the likelihood that data will be inappropriately used to make judgments about individual children.

- *Safeguards are in place if standardized tests are used as part of evaluations.* When individually administered, norm-referenced tests are used as part of program evaluation, they must be developmentally and culturally appropriate for the particular children in the program and conducted in the language with which children are most comfortable. There must be other accommodations as appropriate and valid in terms of the curriculum, and technically sound (including reliability and validity). Quality checks on data are conducted regularly, and the system includes multiple data sources collected over time.

- *Children's gains over time are emphasized.* When child assessments are used as part of program evaluation, the primary focus is on children's gains or progress as documented in observations, samples of classroom work, and other assessments over the duration of the program. The focus is not just on children's scores upon exit from the program. (Reprinted with permission of the National Association for the Education of Young Children, 2004.)

Urban schools are under great pressure to assure that all students reach established learning objectives. Teachers in those settings must now pay greater attention to test data than ever before. In using the data, they are continuously called on to prescribe instruction for their students. As is true in the medical field, the prescriptions must be based on analysis of data presented. Using test data to determine instructional strategies for students is expected and prudent.

ASSESSMENT DESIGN

Designing Culturally Sensitive Tests That Discourage Bias

Effective teachers, in general, demonstrate fairness in the assessments they design and in the assessment procedures they implement. They seek knowledge of how much students have learned, and wish to do so without trickery or surprise motive. When teachers design assessments or review those that are commercially made for use in their classrooms, they must be sensitive to infused bias. Bias occurs "when some factor, such as race, native language, prior experience, gender, or disability" impacts a student (of a culture or experiential base) group's performance scores differently from those of another (of a culture or experiential base) group's scores. The resulting scores are found to be influenced by the inclusion of foreign or irrelevant (to certain groups of students) criteria (Airasian, 2001).

On detecting and eliminating test bias, Taylor and Nolen (2005) conclude:

> Factors that affect scores other than the conceptual understandings and skills intended to be assessed constitute test bias. This occurs in assessment design when individuals of particular groups have an unfair advantage or unfair disadvantage on (test) items. When bias is determined, the instrument must be revised or items eliminated to make the assessment fair and a true measurement of student knowledge gains.

Effective, culturally sensitive urban teachers are careful to design measurements with test items that harbor no offensive references to irrelevant ethnic and socioeconomic backgrounds or to subgroups of student populations. They do not include anything that may perpetuate ethnic and gender stereotypes. For example, pictures used in assessments should characterize minority as well as majority races. Females should be represented as leaders and professionals, just as males are typically featured in those roles (Nitko, 2004). Tests that exhibit cultural bias are likely to offend or unfairly penalize people of certain ethnic backgrounds, gender, or socioeconomic status to the point that the test administered to such individuals has less predictive and construct validity. For example, students of cultures for whom English is their second language typically perform worse on standard American written tests than do their native-English-speaking peers (McDevitt & Ormrod, 2002).

Particularly true in urban schools, the ethnic and cultural heritage may differ between student and teacher. These cultural differences are reason to caution urban educators *not* to assess student learning and progress based on nonverbal student actions, for example. Students of some cultures are discouraged from drawing attention to themselves in groups, or displaying their expertise, and may be hesitant to volunteer verbal responses in class discussions. Or, students of certain cultural backgrounds may have learned that making eye contact with an adult is a sign of disrespect. Thus, such students may appear uninterested, unmoved, or even defiant. Effective urban educators take into consideration these types of cultural mores, and are careful *not to infer* from these types of student behaviors students' gained, or lack of, knowledge (Stiggins, 2005).

Assessments that include information irrelevant to the decisions for which the assessments are designed to help make are deemed invalid. Teachers should be careful to select and use testing procedures that do not offer unfair advantages to students of particular cultures, diverse native languages, certain genders, or with disabilities (Airasian, 2001).

An assessment that is fair and unbiased reflects strong test validity. Teachers experience the best success in assessing students when they:

- know what constructs to assess, the corresponding best format, and specific questions to ask;
- realize that any one assessment contains only a limited representation of learning targets;
- can identify the misuses of assessment and how to deal with them; and
- develop test accommodations that require their design of different methods of assessment for nontraditional, diverse students. (Nitko, 2004)

Further, good classroom assessments allow teachers to evaluate the diverse richness of their students' thought processes and opinions. It is beneficial for urban teachers to check their students' interpretations of assessment directions and required tasks to assure that all is understood before they proceed to respond to and complete test items. Important to the test's validity is the students' correct interpretation of their directions for accurate responding. Valid assessment results offer a clear understanding of the grade-level standard capabilities of each student (Nitko, 2004).

Backward Drafting: The End Determines the Means

Wiggins and McTighe (1998) encourage teachers to design, plan, and execute their assessments backward—that is, know the end results that demonstrate the learning that has taken place, and teach students the knowledge that moves them to the desired learning results. To do this, teachers must first identify what information/skills that students are to know and understand. Next, they determine what specific evidence will demonstrate results that prove students understand the identified information/skills. Finally, knowing what the results should be and how they will exhibit, educators plan their instructional activities that will achieve those student results. (Several excellent instructional delivery methods used to achieve desired student results are offered in Chapter 4, "The Urban Teacher.")

Four central criteria that lead to best test construction practices are:

1. Assessments should be designed *prior* to lessons. The assessment provides teachers their focus on instructional targets that guide what they teach.
2. Student assessment activities and/or projects include evidence of students' understandings of targeted, grade-level standards.
3. With these standards in mind, teachers design and orchestrate their teaching methods and the resource materials they use in their lessons.
4. The textbook may be only one of many supports to the standards-based curriculum and instruction. Rather than textbook use as the primary information focus, other valuable resources support the standards, such as Internet websites and other electronic media, guest speakers, field experiences, and so on (Wiggins & McTighe, 1998).

VARIETIES OF CLASSROOM ASSESSMENTS

Historically, teachers have practiced a wide variety of assessment techniques and formats, as they have used primarily self-constructed tests that assess student mastery or achievement (McMillan, 2002). Forte and Schurr (2002) offer a comprehensive listing of teacher-monitored classroom assessments that are vital to helping students learn.

teacher observations, recorded/documented

student journal entries

peer observations

performance tasks

products or projects

peer assessments

student or teacher interviews

role-playing vignettes

case study discussions or solution proposals

anecdotal records of student achievement or behavior progress

student self-assessments or reflective/evaluative comments

small or large group projects

formal tasks or authentic products

written or oral tests

written or oral quizzes

open-ended or guided responses

demonstrations or exhibits

visual designs

portfolios

interactive lectures or discussions

class or panel discussions or participation

lesson momentum, in general (the faster the students catch on to the information and prove they know it, the faster the pace of the teacher's introducing similar and/or new knowledge)

individual student responses

students' participation in class discussions

physical or facial messages and cues (Forte and Schurr, 2002; Izumi, 2002)

These ongoing classroom assessments fully engage the instructional process and are vital for helping educators plan and execute teaching strategies that help students learn (Guskey, 2003).

There are a multitude of techniques and issues educators consider when designing and implementing assessments. Effective classroom teachers use several assessment approaches, including those previously listed, that influence what students learn as well as the degree to which students meaningfully engage in the learning process. Because of their powerful effects on student motivation and learning, urban teachers would be wise to select from and offer varieties of assessments that include:

1. authentic or performance assessments that further student reflection, critical thinking, and problem solving, and offer feedback to students, along with opportunities for them to revise and improve;

2. portfolio assessments that engage students' intrapersonal (own) thoughts, as well as interpersonal (shared) thoughts, intelligences that include their exhibit of verbal, logical, visual, and naturalist intelligences, and that dynamically demonstrate signs of progress in examples of their work submitted;

3. student self-assessments that tend to increase the students' commitment to and sense of ownership in the testing procedures, criteria, and rubrics that students assist in designing, the quality of the scoring criteria and rubrics that students assist in designing, and their positive attitudes toward assessment; and

4. other varied assessments that confirm students' diverse intelligences, academic strengths, and specific learning styles. (Doherty, 2004; Forte & Schurr, 2002; Johnson & Johnson, 2002; McMillan, 2000; Nitko, 2004)

Creating Higher-Order Test Questions

To gain the best and most comprehensive and telling results, teachers who are effective in designing their assessments will incorporate in their tests higher-order questions and problems that measure students' decision making and problem solving capabilities. Higher-order inquiry not only engages students to create viable resolutions to challenging situations, and to interpret, analyze, and manipulate knowledge gained, but also it prods them to question ideas and propose investigations to solutions that will likely generate greater interest in learning (Izumi, 2002).

"Thinking Skills," reported by North Central Regional Educational Laboratory (NCREL) (2000), include higher-order thinking skills that:

- size-up and define problems that do not come neatly packaged;
- help identify facts or formulas necessary for solving problems;
- assist students in knowing where and how to investigate for more information;
- encourage brainstorming for possible ideas and ways to proceed further;

- require complex analyses, planning, management, and monitoring; and
- implement judgment in situations that are not clear-cut, yes-or-no varieties and exist beyond the typical routine to deal with unanticipated results.

FREQUENT ASSESSMENTS AS DIAGNOSTIC TOOLS

Classroom tests serve as effective diagnostic tools. Frequent and daily testing of student knowledge offers the means whereby teachers can identify current student skill strengths and skill weaknesses. Frequent assessment is encouraged in most school systems today. For the urban classroom, it is of utmost importance to monitor the learning taking place in order to maintain levels of instruction that neither create boredom with redundancy and/or slow pace, nor overly challenge students to the point of obvious frustration (Izumi, 2002).

This fluid and critical information provided by continuous assessment is vital to the teachers' providing the best classroom instruction. Continuous assessment helps teachers focus on students' individual skills development, thereby allowing teachers to tailor curricular goals to be compatible with the individual learning styles and needs of their students. These and similar types of indicators identify and discern for the teacher those in need of additional explanation or additional practice of the taught concept, those who are ready to learn the next set of concepts, and those who will benefit from further and enriched activities that enhance the knowledge gained.

Educators can monitor their own teaching strengths and weaknesses by means of their own frequently administered assessments. Those results enable them to reflect and improve instructional planning, be it changes needed to better the modes (visual, auditory, tactile) of content deliveries, to offer newly designed (shortened, lengthened, more or less stimulating) lesson presentations (Izumi, 2002).

Not only does frequent testing monitor student progress, but it detects *early* any academic weaknesses before becoming severe problems that might impede a student's ability to learn or block a student's academic progress to more advanced skills and complex problem solving. In this way, teachers implement assessments as useful tools that improve the quality of instruction. Through frequent analysis and gauging of skill level attainment provided by means of ongoing assessments, instruction works in tandem with assessment to move students forward in the curriculum. Frequent and regular assessment, therefore, better assures that students are dynamically challenged and progress to more challenging topics, information, concepts, and skills (Izumi, 2002).

Ongoing assessment and evaluation is vital to the success of urban teaching practices. In low-performing schools that deal with equity issues daily, effective teachers each day infuse classroom-based assessments and provide their students immediate feedback. Using a disciplined assessment approach, practiced throughout each day to identify students who have or who have not grasped certain concepts, offers valuable knowledge to teachers, students, and families. Changes in individual or group instruction may be indicated from the assessment results, as well as the encouragement for at-home practice and skill reinforcement. It is vitally important for this population of learners to maintain well-paced, instructional momentum (Beckum, 2004).

ENGAGING STUDENTS IN THE ASSESSMENT PROCESS

As an alternative to traditional test and records procedures dominated by teacher efforts, Stiggins (2002) suggests three tools that engage learners in the process of their own assessment:

1. *Student-involved classroom assessment.* Open the assessment process to include students as partners; under the teacher's guidance, allow students to assist in defining the criteria by which their assessment is judged. This builds trust between students and their teacher.

2. *Student-involved record keeping.* Through self-assessments, students monitor their own improvements in performance. Using portfolios, for example, students accumulate physical evidence (assessments) of their accomplishments, and record self-reflections about the improvements they demonstrate. This watch of their growth adds greatly to their self-confidence in their capabilities and potential.

3. *Student-involved communication.* Allow students to share information with others about their own academic successes. For example, student-led parent conferences shifts to students an internal sense of responsibility for the accomplishments, as well as a pride that fuels higher learning motivation levels.

For teachers to develop a student-centered approach to assessing what students are learning, Parkay and Stanford (2004) recommend guiding principles that lead to positive and constructive assessment environments, blending the following factors:

- clear and appropriate achievement targets (objectives, goals)
- effective communication about achievement
- high-quality assessment
- students as the key users and beneficiaries of assessment results

Student-involved approaches allow students to feel control over their own academic destiny. Assessment ideas and strategies are critical to students' success in school. When implemented, they may prevent students from giving up on themselves and/or their teachers. They may reenergize students on the verge of quitting school (Stiggins, 2002).

Factors Affecting Student Performance on Assessments

Effective educators are mindful that most students benefit by receiving assistance on test-taking strategies. Knowledge and implementation of the following factors, offered by Oosterhof (2001) and Nitko (2004), may greatly enhance students' self-efficacy, self-confidence, and comfort levels, and may likely and ultimately result in positive student test performance results.

1. *Familiarity with the testing medium.* Typically, tests administered to students are of the pencil-and-paper variety; however, there is current popularity for those that are computer-administered. Whatever type of test is used, students should be comfortable with the response format. If separate answer sheets accompany the test booklet, training and practice in their use is strongly advised. Studies have demonstrated that students tend to score higher when they are able to record their answers or responses directly onto the test itself.

2. *Timing.* Teachers should be sensitive to *when* the test is administered (time of day or day of the week), and under what conditions (timed or untimed). Teachers know what optimum test administration times and days are best for student concentration and quality performance.

3. *Test preparation.* First, teachers should familiarize students with the type of test items they will be answering. Then, it is best for students to get oriented to test-taking strategies (see "Getting Students Test-wise" in the following section). Test performance is impaired if students are sleepy, hungry, or have overeaten. The same effect will occur through over-stimulation by ingesting foods or beverages high in sugar or caffeine.

Discuss with students the content areas that will be covered on the test. Address point values that emphasize the importance of test responses, such as objective items versus essay items. Review with students the scoring criteria for the test. The students should understand the significance or relevance of their test scores, and how they affect their individual academic standings (Nitko, 2004; Oosterhof, 2001).

Getting Students Test-Wise

Nitko (2004) and Oosterhof (2001) offer test-wiseness principles that identify students' use of specific strategies to enable them to correctly identify and select the most correct responses to test items. The student examinees use characteristics of the test, or the test-taking situation, to perform their best and achieve their best scores. Test-wise strategies are those that relate to time usage, error avoidance, guessing, deductive reasoning, intent consideration, and cue usage.

Time Usage Strategy.   The student works rapidly with consideration to accuracy, paces progress throughout the test, marks omitted responses for revisit and further consideration, and uses remaining time to review and reconsider given responses. She should answer the highest-point questions and easiest test items first, and respond to the more time-consuming items last.

Error Avoidance Strategy. The student carefully considers the directions and instructions, pays prudent attention to what each test item requests, asks for clarification, if necessary, and checks all final answers and responses.

Guessing. If the test counts right answers only, students are recommended to guess; if eliminating options provides a sound way to determine a correct response, then the student is encouraged to narrow options and then guess; and, in the classroom assessments, students should never leave a question or test item unanswered.

Deductive Reasoning. Students should eliminate incorrect options and those that seem much like the incorrect options; and they should scrutinize other test items in search of related content that would help identify other correct responses.

Intent Consideration. Students should note, where possible, the test designer's emphases on certain concepts and ideas; they should read carefully the questions with careful consideration of specific details; and, as possible, they should respond as the test designer seems most likely to guide them toward a particular response.

Cue Usage. The test designer may have embedded consistent idiosyncrasies in test items that may hint to particular, desired responses, such as options that are

- lengthier than most;
- very qualified or very generalized;
- more false than true (statements);
- suspect in their positioning among options (e.g., middle placement among options);
- familiar expressions;
- grammatically at odds with the question item; and
- inclusive of relevant details and/or ideas that fit the item to the correct option selection.

Finally, research suggests that it does benefit students to change answers upon further reflection. However, lower-scoring students, or those who typically score poorly on assessments, tend to benefit less when changing answers than do higher-scoring students or those who typically score well on assessments (Nitko, 2004).

Follow-up Corrective Instruction and Enrichment Activities

Classroom assessments ideally inform teachers of who is ready to advance forward to learning more complex concepts, and who will need further presentation and practice of certain ideas that were taught. Re-presenting learning in unique ways, but not necessarily reteaching, and with enthusiasm that fully engages the students, provides corrective instruction to students in need that forms the solid foundation from which additional concepts are added and built. Corrective instruction seeks to remedy skill deficits or concept misunderstandings. Effective teachers continue to learn and introduce teaching strategies that accommodate students' individual learning styles. It is important to consider that no two students learn at the same speed, or learn best using the same prominent sensory modality, such as hearing, visualizing, and touching. To meet learning styles of those students who learn quickly, grasp concepts with full comprehension rapidly, and thirst for greater knowledge, for example, corrective instruction involves the creation and offering to these students needed enrichment activities. Both corrective instruction and enrichment activities are best facilitated during classtime and offered by the classroom teacher. As students become acclimated to the corrective instruction process, and realize its benefits to learning and their academic achievements, such activities can reposition from the classroom-based delivery to independent, tutorial, or homework assignments (Guskey, 2003).

ASSESSMENT MOTIVATION

Some students study hard, learn much, and subsequently test well. Other students, such as those lacking preschool knowledge or lacking any of the prerequisites to follow-up knowledge, become chronic failures and lose confidence. Educators must strive to assist their students to remain confident learners from the start and to initiate feelings of confidence among those as needed.

Motivating students using effective classroom assessment strategies as an ongoing process dramatically promotes their learning. As teachers continue to use *multiple* sources of student feedback that illustrate learning taking place in the classroom, the most meaningful and telling assessment information is that which is accumulated by teachers on a daily basis. As discussed, frequent assessments enable teachers to make immediate changes that help students achieve desired outcomes. As students successes build, their motivation for learning develops and expands (Forte & Schurr, 2002).

Further, in a safe, nonthreatening, classroom assessment climate, students feel less embarrassment and less discomfort when they happen to fail, especially when attempting to master new material or information. The effective teacher allows for failure at the start, and expects important improvement and success as continued learning resumes (Forte & Schurr, 2002; Stiggins, 2002).

Adopting Sound Testing Practices

For decades, noted scholar, physician, and clinical professor of student learning strategies, Dr. Mel Levine, has performed and written about cutting-edge, educational research in areas of the much-misunderstood needs of students who face learning challenges. Regarding assessments, Levine (2003) cautions teachers not to design those that exclusively ask for memorized facts or "straight regurgitation of skills and knowledge." Schools are to avoid testing practices that are prone to "inflict needless damage and unfair humiliation" on their students. The ideas cited below represent Levine's advice for administering assessments that do no harm:

1. *For those who do not test well, don't write them off as unsuccessful.* When students botch a test, attempt to determine why, and work toward correcting the deficit(s). Tests are not an end in themselves, but serve as a *call to action*.

2. *Vary assessments, because not all students demonstrate their strengths in the same manner.*[1] Allow a measurement of their own choosing, such as portfolios, theme papers, oral presentations, projects, or product development.

3. *Using assessment data, "leave no child behind."* Test scores should not be the sole justification for retaining a student, and research findings report that the practice of student retention proves ineffective.

4. *For proper student development, reduce undue focus on individual students' test scores.* Adult careers involve demonstrating capabilities that no test appropriately or accurately measures. Place emphasis on nurturing students' healthy thought processes and decision-making skills.

5. *Avoid teaching to the test.* With the pressure on teachers and school systems to push students to their greatest show of scores on standardized achievement tests, classrooms throughout the nation likely rehearse and trial-test students, presenting prestandardized test administration preparations. When teachers adopt a curricula designed to teach to the test, rather that test what is taught, their students perform less well than they would otherwise. (Levine, 2003)

As students understand that their minds work like muscles, strengthening and expanding with use, they gain confidence in their abilities and efforts in the test-taking arena. Skills of self-efficacy and developing positive mind-sets assist students in gaining better study habits, grades, and test scores. For example, studies of students taking difficult tests prove their significant gains in year-end grade point averages due to lessened anxiety, a can-do attitude, and exposure to role models who have triumphed over similar academic struggles (Aronson, 2004). Effective urban teachers serve as powerful influences to instill testing

---

[1]Compared with White students, African American eighth graders are nearly four times less likely to be assessed using hands-on activities per grading period (The Education Trust, 2001).

strategies and winning attitudes that make significant differences in their students' classroom performance results.

Incorporating Technology with Assessments

In years dating back to the 1983 *A Nation at Risk* report (see Chapter 1), schools and school systems have sought to reform and introduce curricula with assessment that supports the educational needs of children. To best assure that students achieved meant that schools measured each student's academic gains. The need to measure students' abilities that connect what they learn in school to real-world applications is found in technology: computer hardware and software, Internet websites, and other electronic resources. Technological applications have been proven to deepen students' understanding of what they learn per grade-level academic standards, for example, and to link that knowledge to relevant life events. Moore (2003) identifies evidence to support that technological applications, while engaging students in reality-type tasks among collaborative learning opportunities, can effectively support high-order, complex thinking skills: "technology has provided us with the tools to link academic standards with higher-order thinking skills that are necessary in properly assessing the competency of the learner."

Tests, such as the Measures of Academic Progress (MAP), are electronically administered and scored achievement tests that measure individual students' academic growth. The test administrator links to an Internet host that downloads student data from previous tests, and provides individualized student achievement testing. Each test automatically adapts the level of difficulty to each student, once she has completed the first set of test items. Computerized tests can include the features and benefits that traditional assessments offer, along with additional benefits, such as:

- appropriately challenge 97 percent to 99 percent of students, including those with special needs;
- measure individual student achievement;
- provide data ready for comparisons and analysis across learning areas and variables;
- more closely engage educators and other stakeholders in the learning process. (Woodfield, 2003)

McMillan (2000) suggests that as teachers have increased opportunities for using computer-based methods, including computer-adapted and online testing, item banks, electronic grading, Internet resources, and state-of-the-art reporting of test results, they become more proficient in technology.

It is an unfortunate fact that, as Barton (2003) reports, "in schools with a higher percentage of minority students, there is a low percentage of students who have computers available in the classroom than in schools with a smaller percentage of minorities: 77 percent compared with 84 percent." Across the nation, however, technology in the classroom is making gains. Market Data Retrieval's report "Technology in Education 2001" found that computer access to students is improving (Moore, 2003).

STANDARDIZED ACHIEVEMENT TESTS

In today's U.S. society, all students are expected to meet high academic standards. They are to become competent readers, writers, and mathematical problem solvers. Sound instructional practices, guided not only by daily classroom assessments but also by students' annual standardized assessment data, are positively sustained when students continue to be motivated (Stiggins, 2002). Assessments, offered annually at a time nearing the completion of the official school year, yield results that are reported publicly by schools and stand as record of the school systems' levels of academic success. The scores are typically interpreted by the public to reflect the quality of a school, its teachers, and overall educational program. Although determined as an academic snapshot of a school's academic performance, the scores are not, however, the ultimate measurement of the students' educational attainments, nor the definitive evaluation of a school's progress (Hunter & Barbee, 2003).

Assessments and the Achievement Gap

To judge students' educational advances and benefits from year to year, schools closely examine results of classroom achievement test scores. Nationally collected, and when compared, graphed standardized achievement test scores demonstrate the current achievement gap. The gap represents disturbing and unacceptable score disparities between minority (African American and Hispanic) and nonminority (White) students. Over an approximate twenty-year span of time, from the mid-1970s through to the mid-1990s, the National Assessment of Educational Progress (NAEP), as discussed earlier in this chapter, reported score increases in standardized test scores of African American 17-year-olds that exceeded gains made by White students of the same age (Hunter & Barbee, 2003). Since 1988, however, the achievement gap between the groups of students has widened, showing declines in minority students' scores in both reading and math. Over time, gains in minority students' test scores have proven relatively small and inconsistent (Doherty, 2004; Irvine, 1999). For many urban-educated, typically minority students, standardized testing offers no opportunity to showcase their strengths (Levine, 2003). Progress in closing the achievement gap between White and students of color appears to have now stalled. Proposed reasons for standardized test score differences that create or contribute to the achievement gap include racial, environmental, economic, and institutional differences that diminish minority students' abilities to perform at the same rate as White students (Hunter & Barbee, 2003).

Popham (2004b) advises anyone who works to reduce achievement gaps to become *assessment literate*—to be knowledgeable of the fundamentals of educational testing, including spotting the strengths and weaknesses of achievement tests. Secondly, they should scrutinize testing documents to ensure that tests

- measure only "a modest number of curricular aims of extraordinary significance," so that teachers may best focus on a reasonable number of curricular targets;
- describe curricular goals in ways that enable teachers to best design meaningful instruction; and
- provide score reports that identify for teachers which aspects of their instruction prove effective versus not effective.

Studying achievement test content helps teachers provide the instructional support necessary to enable students to gain the knowledge needed to fairly meet high expectations and accountable goals. In other words, when teachers understand what students are expected to know from their instruction, and aim instruction directly at the curricular goals—rather than at particular test items—they have the ability immediately at the start of the semester to facilitate classroom lessons that offer the best instructional impact (Popham, 2004a).

Advantages of Standardized Tests

Standardized tests do have their place in assessing student achievement. As noted by Johnson and Johnson (2002), there are several advantages that make these tests most worthy of local, regional, and national attention and use. First, they are easily administered; and, in doing so only once a year, they distract minimally from teachers' day-to-day instruction and classroom routines. They give teachers a fairly concise reading of students' academic strengths and weaknesses to identify and direct further instruction. All examinees of particular ages or grade levels answer the same questions, and are evaluated according to like-criteria. As permanent records of academic behavior, test scores allow for easy comparisons between and among other students and schools, locally, regionally, nationally, and globally. Finally, not only are standardized tests respected for their scientific credibility, but they prove strong predictors of how students fare in their continued academic pursuits such as success in college coursework (Johnson & Johnson, 2002; McMillan, 2000).

Disadvantages of Standardized Tests

Johnson and Johnson (2002) caution educators regarding the disadvantages of standardized test usage. First, as tests tend to measure principally factual information recall and some verbal skills (for example, recognition vocabulary), they lack measuring depth of comprehension or integration of conceptual knowledge. They cannot assess students' capabilities of processing or expressing information or their correct implementation of sequential steps. The tests are of little help in the ongoing diagnosis of students' specific academic strengths and weaknesses that determine remediation or special assistance, because they are offered only once a year, and the test items are *not aligned directly* to specific topics and concepts that teachers cover in their daily, weekly, and monthly instruction. Further, standardized tests cannot assess goals that involve higher-level outcomes, so they are not helpful in assessing what students have learned *specifically* as a result of knowledge gained from certain courses. The tests most typically emphasize basic skills, omitting the higher-order reasoning skills that teachers strive for students to learn and practice. Finally, although standardized tests are sound predictors of students' abilities to continue as learners in school settings, they fall short of predicting students' career choices (Johnson & Johnson, 2002).

An unfortunate liability of the current focus on standards-based teaching and achievement testing is the perception that schools may become "test-preparation academies" that discount or set as low-priority the noncore subjects of art, history, and music. However, although not emphasized in standardized achievement tests, these subjects remain vitally necessary in offering students a well-rounded, diversified curriculum in education (Gilman & Gilman, 2003).

Standardized tests are usually based on a traditional one-test-fits-all design that excludes regional uniqueness and variations outside the average range of stu-

dents. They do not always match well each state's regional or local academic requirements or curriculum preferences. True student assessment involves a succession of measurements occurring week to week, throughout the school year, that demonstrate students' knowledge and comprehensions through various methods. Standardized test scores should *never* be used as *the sole basis* for defining students' academic potential or for making important decisions about them, their teachers, or their schools (Charp, 2003; Hunter & Barbee, 2003; McMillan, 2000).

CLASSROOM ASSESSMENTS: NONSTANDARDIZED OR NORMED

As presented previously, standardized tests offer final school year composite scores for individual students and classes, and those scores are published and presented as normed and ranked for comparison-analysis and reporting. The teacher's use of classroom assessment results is fundamental to the instructional process, central to helping students learn, and motivating to those whose scores identify their grasp of the subject matter or concepts (Guskey, 2003).

The best gauge of learning and the motivation of learners and its impact upon day-to-day instruction is acquired by educators through daily classroom assessments. Developed and used by the teachers themselves, they gather reliable information about student learning daily, weekly, and monthly, using the information to benefit instruction for students individually or together as a class. If flaws or irregularities develop in the continuity or consistency of this achievement reporting system, student end-of-year achievement test scores are negatively impacted (Stiggins, 2002). Classroom assessments and grading are essential ingredients of effective, overall instruction (McMillan, 2000).

Teacher-made, -created, or -designed class assessments are best suited to guide improvements in student learning. Conceived not as one-time or do-or-die isolated assessments, these tools provide continuous readings of students' gains and relate directly to grade-level standards and to the teacher's specific instructional goals. Validity is typically sound, in that the tests cover what the teacher has addressed in her presented unit of study (Guskey, 2003).

Paul and Elder (1999) offer valuable, constructive suggestions that help guide teachers in their design of classroom assessments. They advise following guidelines that compel teachers to reflect upon the purposes and desires for outcomes of their designed assessments. Simply put, teachers need to predetermine:

- *what* should be assessed, and *why?*;
- probing and evaluative questions that *reflect understanding* of the concepts;
- the *specific information* that accurately determines that students know and understand concepts;
- reasonable and practical *application of criteria or standards*;
- *judgments* to be rendered that relate to expectations fulfilled (or not) by student responses;
- *implications* that will follow judgments; and
- *reality checking* for coherency, logic, realism, and practical nature.

Advantages and Disadvantages of Teacher-Made Classroom Assessments

Researchers who accumulate and report pedagogical strategies related to varieties of assessments report the strengths and limitations of teacher-made, objective tests. Advantages of their design and administration include:

- broad sampling of knowledge;
- ability to assess quickly and efficiently;
- ease of scoring and analysis; and
- prevention of bias in scoring.

Limitations that plague the use of these types of tests include:

- requiring great amounts of time to construct;
- highly subjective choice of test items;
- difficulty in designing unambiguous test items;
- reliance upon recall of facts and information;

- established, specific, correct (no variance or creativity of) responses; and
- penalty on poor readers.

Effective teachers develop their classroom assessments to meet state grade-level standards, which become the major part of their academic curriculum. They then provide instructional material that directly relates to their curriculum and to the state's curriculum based on those established standards (Charp, 2003). They provide their students continuous and timely feedback, which also enables teachers to evaluate student progress, reflect upon the effectiveness of their instructional practices, and make sound adjustments and judgments that enrich their teaching for best learning results to occur (Forte & Schurr, 2002).

With regard to ongoing assessments, such as the use of portfolios and projects, Wenglinsky (2002) urges supplementing them with forms of traditional testing, such as formative written tests, to assess student progress. In order for students to perform well on standardized tests, for example, teachers should devise their classroom, self-designed tests to focus on higher-order thinking skills, as opposed to an emphasis on students' recalling isolated facts or specific pieces of information (Wenglinsky, 2002). Accordingly, to further prepare students for the look and feel of their annual achievement test, teachers should infuse among their assessment strategies the use of selected-response items, such as multiple-choice and matching, and some practice taking objective tests (McMillan, 2000).

To help students gain confidence in their assessment performances, Stiggins (2002) suggest that teachers begin the school year with assessments designed that allow all students in the class opportunities to achieve academic success. He touts that even the smallest or most obscure successes initiate self-confidence in students, and encourage their continued academic efforts. As more and more successes are realized, students' academic self-concepts take on positive changes. With experienced academic success follows self-confidence, which is followed by motivation that leads to continued learning.

Students who experience academic success on classroom assessments are willing to trust that devoting their energies and efforts pays off, and they learn, as a result. If academic successes for some students are *not* forthcoming, teachers are encouraged to assist those effected by analyzing their needs and assisting them with new and different, more effective strategies for learning. Classroom teachers' use of moment by moment, continuous assessment, places their noble efforts at the crossroads that connect classroom assessment and the schools' effectiveness (Stiggins, 2002).

High-Quality Classroom Assessment

Successful urban teachers are often those competent in their classroom assessment practices. As an ongoing, continuous process, documenting and recording various types of student assessment performances offer a comprehensive and reliable profile of student achievement. Well-designed tests and records reflect student academic growth that correlates well with standards-based, classroom instruction. Lack of high-quality, classroom assessment, however, diminishes instruction efficiency, student achievement, and the schools' overall effectiveness. Schools or courses that work to enhance teachers' learning to design quality classroom assessments result in demonstrable student gains. For example, optimum student test performance results occur when students are actively involved in the assessment process itself, they assess their accomplishments with a clear picture of the goals they attempt to gain, and they receive from teachers ongoing and essential feedback (Stiggins, 2002).

For designing instruction that, based upon assessments, helps teachers gauge what and how skills and concepts are best introduced and taught, teachers should know and understand what academic standards and targets their students are challenged to achieve. They should keep appraised of their progress related to their students' achieving the grade-level standards. Students need to understand the importance of learning, as well as the relevant applications of gained knowledge. Notwithstanding, it is important that they realize the importance of the achievement test as an overall snapshot of their school year of learning (Stiggins, 2002).

Urban teachers, more than their suburban counterparts, must understand the many nuances of assessment. Understanding the strengths and weaknesses of various assessment methods is an important understanding for teachers as they are expected to use assessment data to develop instrumental strategies.

EVALUATING AND USING DATA FROM STANDARDIZED ACHIEVEMENT TESTS

For the most part, data accumulated from tests are used to improve teaching and academic performance of students. Through their availability to and use by educators, schoolwide student test data, grade-level student test data, or individual student test data is significantly important for purposes of curriculum and instructional planning. For example, comparing achievement test scores related to specific skills attainment from year to year will demonstrate the academic strengths and weaknesses of groups of students—as well as those of individual students—useful and helpful to schools for purposes of grade-level skills analysis and planning for instruction of all related disciplines (Izumi, 2002).

In an elementary school in California, for example, standardized test data was used to group students in one of four instructional-level categories:

- intensive (students needing much assistance in a content area);
- strategic (students performing just below grade-level proficiency standards);

- benchmark (students demonstrating adequate proficiency on grade level); or
- challenge (students demonstrating high scores and need for content enrichment). (Izumi, 2002)

This example of categorizing is just one of many ways to determine instructional focus per each student's needs, based on standardized test measurement data. Accordingly, *challenge* students would be considered advanced per their demonstrated achievement data, and thus would be challenged with enrichment activities of greater complexity or depth of subjects studied. *Benchmark* students suggest by their test scores that they are absorbing grade-level standards as anticipated. Those students who fall in the *strategic* category may be marked as those who are quite capable and need extra attention and skill reinforcement to remain at grade-level knowledge stratum. Students in the *intensive* category would likely benefit from skill enhancement and practice activities, as well as varieties of instruction options and opportunities.

Teaching to the Test versus Testing What I Teach

With school systems feeling the pressures of accountability—for all their students to demonstrate achievement that meets minimum percentages of improvement for the year—teachers may regard their daily instruction as derived from a curriculum that is based upon teaching to the test. The belief of teaching to the test meets with mixed controversy and serves to disadvantage the practice of standardized achievement testing (Moore, 2003). Teaching to the test entails adhering to a practice of incessant drilling of skills, and emphasizing shortcuts to learning isolated facts and information that is likely featured on the year-end achievement test. Research confirms that teaching to the test is an ineffective instructional delivery plan and makes for a poor curriculum design. Data confirm that educators who emphasize the set grade-level standards in their daily instruction, and assist their students in improving content mastery, demonstrate better student performance on standardized achievement tests than do those who incorporate the skill-and-drill methods—or teaching to the test. We do not condone teaching to the test strategies as the basis for teachers making instructional or curriculum decisions. Rather, teachers should test what they teach, which entails focusing on achieving curricular goals using their teacher-made, subject-based product, process, or observational assessments that directly measure how well their students are learning (The Education Trust, 2003; Guskey, 2003).

Using Assessments to Improve Instruction and Student Learning

Students need to experience *success* in initial teacher-designed assessments. This serves to help students realize the positive rewards of their hard work and efforts, especially those who are prone to academic struggles. The successes help instill in students feelings of deep trust in their teachers (Guskey, 2003; Irvine, 1999).

Effective urban teachers are sensitive to their students' apprehensions over their respective test performances. They can seek to lower student test anxiety and improve course/test/grade results by using not only important test-wiseness training, discussed previously in this chapter, but also by the following strategies.

- Realize that at-risk students exhibit higher levels of test anxiety than typical achievers.
- Attempt to convince students that the assessment is *not* overwhelmingly difficult.
- Offer posttest, item-by-item feedback.
- Arrange test items from easiest to most difficult.
- Test students more often so they sense the assessments as routine.
- Lessen auditory and visual distractions.
- Instruct students to concentrate attention more on *assessment tasks* and less on distractions from the tasks, rather than reassure them with responses of "don't worry" or "you'll be fine." (Nitko, 2004)

Classroom assessments serve as meaningful sources of information, representing concepts and skills emphasized in classroom instruction that are aligned with grade-level standards and objectives. Individualized feedback from assessment results gives students an idea of what skills they've mastered and those that need additional understanding and practice. These assessments identify for teachers what was learned well from their instruction, and what concepts or skills need additional attention, so that students gain better understandings or grasps of concepts or skills.

Assessments are useful as a guide for teachers' daily classroom instructional activities. They inform teachers when to move on to the next level of information, when they need to ask students more questions, when to enhance discussions with further examples, and what responses to student questions best help their comprehension (McMillan, 2000). Further, as teachers take the time to study the results of each assessment, noting items students get right versus those missed, it becomes apparent how to proceed with instruction for each student and for the class as a whole (Guskey, 2003). Teachers need to utilize assessments as a source of confidence (Stiggins, 2002). Further, instruction-based assessments with consequences, such as grades attached, arguably serve as catalysts that change behavior (Bernauer & Cress, 1997).

When evaluating classroom assessments, each test item deserves attentive teacher scrutiny. For example, if several students miss a particular test item, the way the question or answer selections are worded may be the culprit. Each test item addresses the knowledge, understanding, or skill that it declares to measure (validity). Rather than for teachers to be discouraged if students as a whole perform poorly or do not meet their expectations on a particular test, they must keep in mind that the assessment demonstrates what the students are able to accomplish. Despite the most dynamic lesson plan and instructional delivery, if assessments prove that instruction needs to be tweaked or changed to move students forward in their learning, teachers should refocus their institutional strategies to accommodate the learning shortcomings. Tests administered immediately following a lesson will offer the teacher valuable evidence of student learning and the teacher's instructional effectiveness (Guskey, 2003).

CURRENT ASSESSMENT ISSUES: *NO CHILD LEFT BEHIND*

The reauthorization of the Elementary and Secondary Education Act (ESEA) of 2001, known as the No Child Left Behind (NCLB) legislation, adds significant accountability provisions to which school systems must adhere (for additional information on NCLB, see Chapter 1). Each state is required to establish clear timelines for improving student achievement, and to demonstrate the closing of achievement gaps between low-income and minority students and their peers. In "ESEA: Myths Versus Realities," the Education Trust (2003) clarified, in brief, the following NCLB assessment stipulations for each of the fifty states.

1. *Standards and assessments.* States are required to designate grade-level standards, develop assessments, and identify schools that need to demonstrate improvement in their students' annual achievement test scores.

2. *Test administration.* Beginning in school year 2005–2006, all grades 3 through 8, and in grades 10 through 12, are required to administer and report scores from its students' annual standardized achievement testing results.

3. *Data collection.* States are required to collect and report data on student achievement as groups of students' scores that fit into eight categories[2] of learners, or *disaggregated data.*

4. *Accountability.* States are responsible for students to meet the state-set standards for proficient yearly achievement within twelve years. Disaggregated data must demonstrate each year that all student groups are making adequate yearly progress. (The Education Trust, 2003)

Types of Standards according to No Child Left Behind (NCLB)

To assist educators in determining instruction based upon what their students need to know, educators look to so-called standards developed by state and local education agencies. Academic content standards, according to NCLB legislation, are required to be *challenging* and to identify the knowledge, concepts, and skills in subject areas that students are required to learn at each grade level. *Challenging* refers to content that is deemed worthwhile and aspiring to high-levels of

---

[2]Student score data is reported by states that school systems determine fit among the student categories: African American, Asian American, Hispanic or Latino, Native American, White, limited English proficiency, low-income, and special education (The Education Trust, 2003).

student performance and accuracy, as set by the "academic performance standards." These performance standards, explained in greater length later in this chapter (see "Current Issues of Assessment"), refer to the desired levels of proficiency, or competence, related to the content standards that students must master. Again, the NCLB legislation stipulates that state-determined, academic performance standards must be challenging, and hold students to high levels of achievement. States assess, through analyzing students' performances on end-of-year standardized achievement tests that are aligned with their established grade-level content standards, whether or not schools have met their thresholds of adequate yearly progress (AYP). Schools must meet these thresholds to remain in good standing with federal government education goals (Popham, 2005).

Under the provisions of the NCLB legislation, standardized achievement assessment reports ensure that all students' academic strengths and weaknesses are identified, recognized, and scrutinized by the students and their parents and teachers. The annual reporting of these scores serves to inform school administrators and school system leaders, as well as state departments of education, as to whether each school has successfully met its responsibility to assist its students in meeting the designated grade level standards. Where schools report higher than expected student scores that demonstrate lack of adequate grade-level progress, the ESEA provides funding to assist schools and their students in realizing their identified achievement goals (Charp, 2003; The Education Trust, 2003). As emphasized earlier, standardized test scores should not, however, be the sole determining factor in making academic or placement decisions regarding students, teachers, and schools. Where curriculum is concerned, teachers should adjust their instruction to that which is designed to align with state-enacted, grade-level academic standards. Based on these standards, the test scores serve as one central, independent, and reliable source of scientific evidence that supports effective teaching and holds schools accountable (Charp, 2003).

Popham (2004b) acknowledges that what gains most public attention of NCLB is the "annual assessment sweepstakes": the reports comparing student performance on standardized achievement tests. Student subgroup scores should make statistical gains in their adequate yearly progress (AYP) quotient. Determined by reports of their accumulated student achievement test scores, schools are identified as having exceeded, met, or failed their respective AYP target scores.

Categories of Achievement

For reporting score purposes defined in NCLB, the National Assessment Governing Board (NAGB) presents achievement level results that fit among three ranges:

- basic;
- proficient; or
- advanced. (National Center for Educational Statistics, 2004)

ACHIEVEMENT-LEVEL POLICY DEFINITIONS

Basic   *Basic denotes partial mastery* of prerequisite knowledge and skills that are fundamental for proficient work at each grade.

Proficient   *Proficient represents solid academic performance* for each grade assessed. Students reaching this level have demonstrated competency over challenging subject matter, including subject-matter knowledge, application of such knowledge to real-world situations, and analytical skills appropriate to the subject matter.

Advanced   *Advanced represents superior performance.*

An example of national test score reporting is offered by the National Center for Educational Statistics, 2004. Figures 8.1 and 8.2 illustrate a brief history of student racial and ethnic subgroups according to standardized achievement test performances in reading, grades 4 and 8, and in mathematics, grades 4 and 8.

The mathematics graphs of fourth and eighth graders in subgroups (Figure 8.1) illustrate that in both fourth and eighth grade, percentages of White students, Black students, and Hispanic students at or above "basic" and "proficient" achievement levels were *higher* in 2003 than in previous years of assessment data. Thus, the subgroups demonstrate gradual improvements in mathematics over the past years. Students of Black, Hispanic, and American Indian/Alaskan Native heritages need intense assistance to raise their test performance scores nearer to those scores of students of White, Asian and Pacific Islander heritage.

The reading graphs of fourth and eighth graders in subgroups (Figure 8.2) illustrate that improvements were *not as evident* as in the mathematics data graph. In grade four, since 2002, no significant changes were detected in percentages of students at or above "basic" and "proficient" achievement levels. Percentages of White, Black, and Asian Pacific Island students testing at or above "proficient" were higher in 2002 than in 1998. Percentages of White and Black students at or above "basic" were higher in 2003 than in 1992. No significant changes were detected in the percentages of Hispanic students at or above "basic" or "proficient" in 2003, when compared to either 1998 or 2002. These graphs dramatically demonstrate the need for greatly improved reading skills among students of Black, Hispanic, and American Indian/Alaskan Native heritages. Disturbing is that test scores of American Indian/Alaskan Native students have steadily declined since the year 2000.

The graphs also illustrate that at eighth grade, the percentages of Black and Hispanic students at or above "basic" were higher in 2003 than in previous years of assessment data exhibited. Percentages of American Indian/Alaskan Native students at or above "basic" declined from 2002 to 2003, and no significant changes were detected in the percentages of American Indian/Alaskan Native students at "proficient" achievement levels. These graphs dramatically demonstrate the need for greatly improved reading skills among students of Black, Hispanic, and American Indian/Alaskan Native heritages.

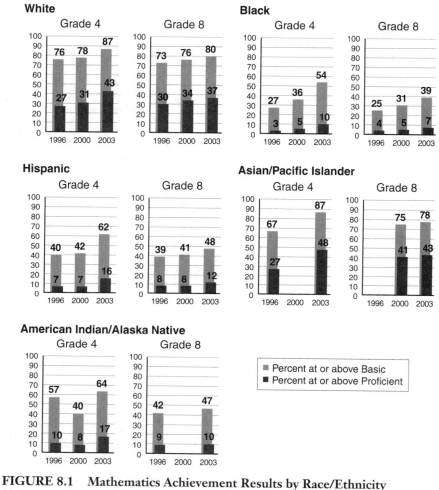

FIGURE 8.1   Mathematics Achievement Results by Race/Ethnicity (Accommodations Permitted)

Source: U.S. Dept. of Education, National Center for Education Statistics (NCES), Nation's Report Card, 2003.

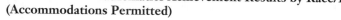

At the time during which this book goes to print, President Bush has expressed the desire for additional testing of reading and mathematics each year in grades 9 through 11. He has proposed creating programs to help struggling middle and high school readers, backing those initiatives with a $200 million fund. And to reward teachers who effectively influence closing the achievement gaps through his accountability resourcefulness, President Bush has proposed a $500 million "Teacher Incentive Fund" authorized for states and their school districts to distribute (Robelon & Davis, 2004).

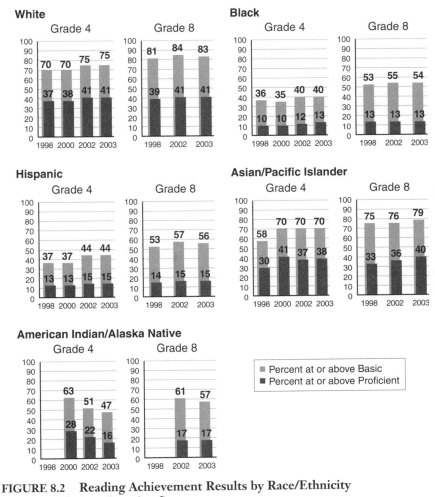

FIGURE 8.2   Reading Achievement Results by Race/Ethnicity (Accommodations Permitted)

Source: U.S. Dept. of Education, National Center for Education Statistics (NCES), Nation's Report Card, 2003.

Good Start, Grow Smart and Head Start Initiatives

While NCLB targets children at the elementary and secondary school levels, the Bush administration (2004–2008) initiated a Good Start, Grow Smart program that focuses upon the prereadiness academic skills of the youngest members of our national population. The program proposes to assess skill levels of Head Start students, provide additional training for Head Start teachers, develop state-defined "quality criteria" on which to base early childhood education programs, and support public awareness campaigns to promote effective strategies that best prepare preschoolers' readiness for school (Vandivere, Pitzer, Halle, & Hair, 2004).

Federal, state, and local education proponents have determined that academic standards must be high and apply to all students. These standards should be aligned with good quality assessments. Failure to properly teach the challenged learner is unacceptable. And every child is deserving of a challenging curriculum (The Education Trust, 2001).

SUMMARY

Assessments and evaluations have evolved with changing impact on learners and their schools over many centuries. When carefully planned for optimum effectiveness, both are valid, reliable, and very useful indicators of student learning progress. The design of assessments deserves prudent scrutiny, be they assessments commercially made or teacher constructed, to assure no cultural bias, sound guidance in curriculum and lesson planning, appropriate applicability to the age and readiness of the test takers, higher-order test items, that they do no harm, and they foster associations with advanced technology. Differences in the types of tests lead to varieties of uses and extrapolations of their results. Finally, No Child Left Behind legislation has made profound changes in the relevance of student achievement test scores to support schools and providing funding to help schools meet academic goals. All public schools are held accountable to advance all students to expected and projected academic gains. Administratively and legislatively, there will inevitably be opportunities for measures that enhance, improve, and strengthen NCLB in ways that retain its spirit, offer greater credibility of its goals, and provide necessary funding to get the job done.

Most minority children attend urban area schools. Thus, the implications for accountability to assure that all students learn at high levels fall to a great extent upon urban teachers. It is in the classroom that challenges will be greatest. Both standardized and teacher-designed assessments take on greater importance than ever before. Teachers cannot simply note test results. It is important that they use the results to drive effective, general instructional decisions and individual student decisions. Utilizing test information wisely is a powerful, potent tool in helping students to meet academic goals.

CHAPTER QUESTIONS

1. How do assessments differ from evaluations?

2. In what ways are standardized achievement tests like
    medical assessments?
    the "big game?"

3. From the earliest of documented tests, what improvements have they encountered that make them so useful to educators today?

4. Why are the following NAEYC stipulations important to
   assessment?
   evaluation?

5. Offer three solutions that will reduce or eliminate test bias.

6. Justify with three reasons the importance of students learning strategies that help them become test-wise?

7. What are the advantages and disadvantages of
   standardized achievement tests?
   teacher-made classroom assessments?

8. What is the difference between educators testing what they teach and teaching to the test?

9. Has the No Child Left Behind legislation helped or hindered current assessment practice in schools? Explain your response.

SUGGESTED WEBSITES

American Association of School Administrators
www.aasa.org/issues_and_insights/assessment/

Can Performance-Based Assessments Improve Urban Schooling?
www.ericdigests.org/pre-9218/urban.htm

Funderstanding: Classroom Assessment Techniques
www.funderstanding.com/classroom_assessment.cfm

Good Start, Grow Smart
www.whitehouse.gov/infocus/earlychildhood/toc.html

IOX Assessment Associates
www.ioxassessment.com/

Less Tests, More Redress: Improving Minority and Low Income Students' Educational Access in the Post-Brown Era: Educational Access and Academic Achievement in Public Schools
www.urbanedjournal.org/articles/article0015.html

National Assessment of Educational Progress: The Nation's Report Card
www.nces.ed.gov/nationsreportcard/

National Center for Education Statistics
www.nces.ed.gov/nationsreportcard/reading/results2003/raceethnicity.asp

Performance Assessment.org
www.performanceassessment.org/

Practical Assessment, Research and Evaluation
PAREonline.net

Urban Academy
www.urbanacademy.org/learn/urbanstand.html

U.S. Department of Labor Bureau of Labor Statistics
www.bls.gov/data/home.htm

U.S. Office of Elementary and Secondary Education (OESE) Website
www.ed.gov/about/offices/list/oese/index.html?src=mr

REFERENCES

Airasian, P. W. (2001). *Classroom assessment, concepts and applications* (4th ed.). New York: McGraw-Hill.

Aronson, J. (2004). The threat of stereotype. *Educational Leadership, 62*(3), 14–19.

Barton, P. E. (2003) Parsing the achievement gap: Baselines for tracking progress. *Policy Information Center, Educational Testing Services,* 1–36.

Beckum, L. C. (2004). WestEd: Center for Educational Equity. Available: www.WestEd.org/cs/we/view/pg/17.

Bernauer, J. A., & Cress, K. (1997). How school communities can help redefine accountability assessment. *Phi Delta Kappan, 79*(1), 71–75.

Charp, S. (2003). Editorial: Assessment and accountability. *T.H.E. Journal, 30*(6), 8.

Coleman, J. S. (1990). *Equality and achievement in education.* Boulden, CO: Westview Press.

The College Board. (2005). Researching the educational benefits of diversity. Research Report N. 2005-4. Available: www.collegeboard/research/pdf.

Doherty, K. M. (2004). Assessment. *Education Week on the Web.* Available: www.Edweek.com.

The Education Trust. (1998). *Thinking K–16: Good Teaching Matters, 3*(2). Washington, DC: The Education Trust, Inc.

The Education Trust. (2003). *ESEA: Myth versus realities: Answers to common questions about the new No Child Left Behind act.* Washington, DC: The Education Trust, Inc.

Forte, I., & Schurr, S. (2002). *The definitive middle school guide* (rev. ed.). Nashville, TN: Incentive Publications.

Freiberg, H. J., & Driscoll, A. (1996). *Universal teaching strategies* (2nd ed.). Boston: Allyn & Bacon.

Gandal, M., & McGiffert, L. (2003). The power of testing. *Educational Leadership, 60*(5), 22–25.

Gilman, D. A., & Gilman, R. A. (2003). Overcoming the side effects of standards-based teaching. *Principal, 83*(November/December), 44–48.

Gredler, M. E. (1999). *Classroom assessment and learning.* Reading, MA: Addison Wesley Longman.

Guskey, T. R. (2003). How classroom assessments improve learning. *Educational Leadership, 60*(5), 6–11.

Hunter, R. C., & Barbee, R. (2003). The achievement gap: Issues of competition, class, and race. *Education and Urban Policy, 35*(2), 151–160.

Irvine, J. J. (1999). The education of children whose nightmares come both day and night. *Journal of Negro Education, 68*(3), 6–12.

Izumi, L. T. (2002). *They have overcome: High-poverty, high-performing schools in California.* ERIC ED No. 469 963.

Johnson, D. W., & Johnson, R. T. (2002). *Meaningful assessment, a manageable and cooperative process.* Boston: Allyn & Bacon.

Kopetz, P. B. (2003). Understanding the at-risk student: Vital teacher knowledge for success-ful classroom management and instruction. In D. W. Rea & R. Stallworth-Clark (eds.), *Fostering our youth's well-being: Healing the social disease of violence.* New York: McGraw-Hill.

Kulieke, M., Bakker, J., Collins, C., Fennimore, T., Fine, C., Herman, J., Jones, B. F., Raack, L., & Tinzmann, M. B. (1990). Why should assessment be based on a vision of learning? *North Central Regional Educational Laboratory,* 1–12.

Levine, M. (2003). Celebrating diverse minds. *Educational Leadership, 61*(2), 12–18.

McDevitt, T. M., & Ormrod, J. E. (2002). *Child development and education.* Upper Saddle River, NJ: Pearson.

McMillan, J. H. (2000). Fundamental assessment principles for teachers and school adminis-trators. *Practical Assessment, Research and Evaluation, 7*(8).

McMillan, J. H., & Lawson, S. R. (2001). Secondary science teachers. *Classroom Assessment and Grading Practices.* ERIC ED No. 450 158.

Moore, W. (2003). Facts and assumptions of assessment: Technology, the missing link. *T.H.E. Journal, 30*(6), 20–26.

National Association for the Education of Young Children. (2004). Organization Guidelines.

National Center for Education Statistics. (2004). *NAEP 2004 mathematic and reading achieve-ment levels.* Washington, DC: U.S. Department of Education.

North Central Regional Educational Laboratory. (2000). Thinking Skills. Available: www.ncrel.org/sdrs/areas/issues/students/atrisk/at6/k.htm.

Nitko, A. J. (2004). *Educational assessment of students* (4th ed.). Upper Saddle River, NJ: Pearson.

Oosterhof, A. (2001). *Classroom applications of educational measurement* (3rd ed.). Upper Saddle River, NJ: Prentice-Hall.

Papalewis, R., & Fortune, R. (2002). *Leadership on purpose: Promising practices for African-American and Hispanic students.* Thousand Oaks, CA: Corwin Press.

Parkay, F. W., & Stanford, B. H. (2004). *Becoming a teacher* (6th ed.). Boston: Allyn & Bacon.

Paul, R., & Elder, L. (1999). The miniature guide to critical thinking concepts and tools. *The Foundation for Critical Thinking, 17.*

Phi Delta Kappa International. (2004). The 36th annual Phi Delta Kappa/Gallup poll of the public's attitudes toward the public schools. Available: www.pdkintl.org/kappan/0409pol.htm.

Popham, W. J. (2004a). A game without winners: Striving to reduce the achievement gap with-out reforming testing is an impossible dream, *Educational Leadership, 62*(3), 46–50.

Popham, W. J. (2004b). Tawdry tests and AYP. *Educational Leadership, 62*(2), 85–86.

Popham, W. J. (2005). *Classroom assessment: What teachers need to know* (4th ed.). Boston: Pearson.

Ravitch, D. (2002). A brief history of testing and accountability. *Hoover Digest, 4.* Available: www.hooverdigest.org.

Robelon, E. W., & Davis, M. R. (2004). Bush's school agenda will get a 2nd term. *Education Week, 24*(11), 1, 26–27.

Schreyer Institute for Teaching Excellence. (2004). Test administration. *Pennsylvania State University.* Available: www.uts.psu.edu/Test_Adminstration.

Stiggins, R. J. (2002). Assessment, student confidence, and school success. *Phi Delta Kappan.* Available: www.pdkintl.org/kappan/k9911sti.htm.

Stiggins, R. J. (2005). *Student-involved assessment for learning* (4th ed.). Upper Saddle River, NJ: Pearson.

Taylor, C. S., & Nolen, S. B. (2005). *Classroom assessment: Supporting teaching and learning in real classrooms.* Upper Saddle River, NJ: Pearson.

Vandivere, S., Pitzer, L., Halle, T. G., & Hair, E. C. (2004). Cross currents. *Child Trends, 3,* Publication 2004-24. Available: www.childtrendsdatabank.org/pdf/ecls-k.pdf.

Weinberger, E., & McCombs, B. L. (2001). *The impact of learner-centered practices on the aca-demic and non-academic outcomes of upper elementary and middle school students.* ERIC ED No. 458 276.

Wenglinsky, H. (2002). How schools matter: The link between teacher classroom practices and student academic performance. *Education Policy Analysis Archives, 10*(12). Available: http://epaa.asu.edu/epaa/v10n12/ (2004, March 10).

WETA. (2004). *Reading rockets: Components of effective, research-supported reading instruction.* Available: www.readingrockets.org/article.php?ID=47.

Wiggins, G. P., & McTighe, J. (1998). *Understanding by design.* Alexandria, VA: Association for Supervision and Curriculum Development.

Woodfield, K. (2003). Getting on board with online testing. *T.H.E. Journal, 30*(6), 32, 34–37.

CHAPTER 9

PARTNERSHIPS THAT WORK IN URBAN SETTINGS

The responsibility for promoting and establishing a positive perception of school is the combined responsibility of parents, teachers, counselors, administrators, and the support staff.
—Denyce S. Ford, Howard University professor, 1986

URBAN PERSPECTIVES

Zary Colón, High School Educator
Native of Columbia and Venezuelan Citizen

Hispanic families are typically hard-working individuals who have sacrificed much to settle and work in the U.S. They desire to be contributing, partnering citizens in their new country, to pursue the best education for their children.

Moving to the United States in 1995 was a lonely experience for Zary Colón. She discovered the English language challenging to learn and speak, especially while, at the same time, assimilating the extraordinarily different and fast-paced surroundings of her new country. The fear of practicing her recently-acquired English language skills with Americans intimidated her, and discouraged her eagerness to collaborate with schools or in her new community, in general—a response that isolated her otherwise natural, vivacious qualities.

Colón is much aware of the daily influx of Spanish-speaking neighbors settling into urban and suburban pockets throughout the U.S. She shares deep concern for the perplexing experiences that these Hispanic immigrants will undoubtedly encounter, likening them to her own bumpy ride. Her work at local schools allows her to witness the interactions (or lack thereof) of new students and their parents as they become involved in their new country's educational system. For these "new" families, she is motivated to reach out to advise and assist them of otherwise unknown, U.S. education–based facts and information that she has come to learn on her own.

"I encourage parents of school children to learn and speak English as soon as possible. They must take advantage of ESL (English as a second language) or ESOL (English speakers of other languages) classes offered at local community centers or sponsored by churches."

She advises teachers of these children that "they need to know that the Spanish-speaking community is here to stay. Educators must keep an open mind about helping them adjust, and offer them a respectful welcome for the students that they are."

Further, she cautions teachers about making wrong assumptions. "The Spanish-speaking students and parents may continue to struggle with the English pronunciations and meanings of words and phrases, but that *in no way* suggests that they are less intelligent beings. Spanish-speaking families are typically hard-working individuals who have sacrificed much to settle and work in the U.S. They desire to be contributing, partnering citizens in their new country to pursue the best education for their children."

Colón convinces her Spanish-speaking friends to share their culture in the schools, and encourages teachers to receive this teaching in their classrooms. "Those of my heritage can bring to American classrooms a cultural richness that students and their teachers would otherwise be unaware, or only read about in books or on websites."

Finally, it is her fervent desire that teachers not only reach forward to connect with newly-arrived immigrants, but to certainly expect and maintain high standards of achievement for the foreign-born English as a second language (ESL) students. "Teachers must keep them involved and challenged in the schoolwork, and keep them enthused, so that they are making gains that please the teachers, school, and parents. With this kind of momentum, Spanish-speaking students will work diligently to meet and exceed all set expectations."

ESTABLISHING COOPERATIVE VENTURES

This chapter presents a variety of models for developing and maintaining partnerships between schools and communities in urban settings. The challenges and solutions in forming and working with partnerships are discussed and guidelines are established for building and maintaining effective partnerships from which urban preservice and beginning teachers can learn. Educators recognize today, more than ever before, that if urban children are to succeed in school, collaboration with the home is critical. Parents must be persuaded to become partners in their children's learning. (See previous chapters for strategies that can achieve effective collaboration.)

In addition, teachers are in a key position to form small partnerships with groups of parents and/or community leaders with the aim of providing support for their school or individual classroom. Chapter 5 encouraged urban teachers to assume a greater role in educational leadership; effectiveness in that role requires teachers to work in forming partnerships with parents, churches, community agencies, and businesses.

The notion that teachers can educate children in isolation is no longer a reality. Teachers are responsible for building partnerships with the individual parents of the children in their classrooms. Teachers as leaders need to look beyond individual collaborative efforts toward forming larger and more inclusive partnerships. Urban communities are filled with valuable and often willing resources. Teachers must be astute in finding these resources and leading efforts to engage a wide variety of partners in the educational enterprise. There are a number of different models, each unique and yet having certain commonalities. Chief among the challenges and work in partnerships is that of developing trusting relationships. Initially, prejudice often exists among potential partners. Preservice and inservice teachers need to understand and become proficient in the skills needed to develop trust within urban communities. Working partnerships are a key element in bringing about change in the urban environment, and there is research evidence that community involvement positively impacts student achievement.

Powerful collaborations among various community partners, such as business, universities, service learning, and school-linked service programs, if properly implemented, can "enhance students' achievement and well-being, build stronger schools, assist families, and revitalize communities" (Sanders, 2003, p. 173). An example of one such partnership is the Urban Community–School Collaboration (Underwood & Frye, 1995), one of which is in Oakland, California. This collaboration began in July, 1990 using key representatives from the University of California campuses and local school districts and community organizations to create working models for long-term collaborations. Each of these entities collaborated toward solutions to the issues defined appropriate to the specific locality's problems regarding social, health, and educational issues.

The school, university, and community recognized the unique strengths that each one brought to solve these problems. However, as they came together to discuss and find common ground to achieve their goals, they found themselves struggling with their own biases and perspectives. Conflicts emerged over the divergent interests of each group. Each group had its own language, vocabulary, and culture to address the needs and solutions for the academic achievement of urban youth; and, therefore, little common ground was found to the problems and solutions of urban education.

> In the case of Oakland, for instance, the university people perceived the problem as a general failure in the areas of curriculum development, teacher professional development, parental involvement, as well as the impoverishment of a large proportion of the student population served. The school people saw it as a function of budgetary constraints, curriculum issues, and a general lack of external support for education. The community people, on the other hand, generally saw the problem as the pervasive neglect and abandonment of their children's physical, spiritual, cognitive, and cultural needs by the mainstream institutions of the larger society. In brief, each saw the problem as one in which they themselves had been consistently engaged, without the informed support of the others. In fact, each saw the other constituencies as almost perversely disinterested and unhelpful in addressing what they saw as the "real" problem.

Yet as they worked to resolve these conflicts, they discovered a new social process that assisted in breaking down the distrust when all three of the parties were present that was *not* present when just two parties were present. Over a period of time, each distinctive partner began to see common interests and expectations and where they could begin to work together toward common goals, using common language.

Out of this successful trust-building process, a desire was created to implement similar processes with school, community, and university partnerships within the surrounding area. The Oakland Urban School Field Station pilot study was developed from this work with a vision to create other sites in the district built on this model. The building of trust among the collaborative partners continued to be a slow and difficult process. Once built, however, strong interests and goals kept the partnerships working together to change the urban profile. Community, university, and school members continued to work together to come to a common agenda regarding social, health, and educational problems facing the school and community. Together they have worked toward solutions to the problems the school and community face. Each has contributed to the common vision based on each others' unique strengths. Ultimately, this collaborative model is used to bring change to urban schools and the communities surrounding the schools and across the United States, and remains in effect today. (Additional website information concerning beginning and sustaining efforts of this kind can be found at the end of this chapter entitled Oakland Urban School Field Project.)

PARTNERSHIP TYPES AND MODELS THAT BENEFIT SCHOOLS AND STUDENTS

The following examples of partnerships and collaborations include many different types and models in their implementations. The Comer School Development Model, as well as four other effective university partnership examples, share insights into the challenges of forming effective partnerships and guidelines to meet those challenges more effectively. Each are organized differently and involve university partnerships with surrounding school districts, businesses, grants, and community foundations. Three examples focus mainly on the need for the recruitment and effective preparation of qualified teachers for urban schools. The last example shows the results of a community-wide effort toward the revitalization of a downtown urban area. All show the positive gains made in communities that take partnerships among various groups seriously. Without the partnerships of all those entities involved in urban communities, changes in schools and achievement for urban students cannot be accomplished.

Family, School, and Community Involvement

Students are influenced by three spheres: school, family and community. When these three spheres interact and collaborate effectively, then students' academic and social well-being are enhanced (Epstein, 1987, 1995, 2001). Epstein lists six types of family, school and community involvement (Epstein, 1995):

> Type 1: parenting or helping all families establish home environments to support children as students;
>
> Type 2: communicating or designing effective forms of school–home and home–school communication;
>
> Type 3: volunteering or recruiting and organizing families to help the school and support students;
>
> Type 4: learning at home or providing families with information and ideas to help students with homework;
>
> Type 5: decision making or including parents in school decisions and developing parent leaders; and
>
> Type 6: collaborating with the community or identifying and integrating resources and services from the community to strengthen schools, students, and families. (p. 705)

Schools with comprehensive programs of school–family–community partnerships address all six types of involvement through activities directed toward specific goals and student outcomes (Epstein, 1995, 2001).

An example that includes all six types is the Comer School Development model. In "Mobilizing the Village to Educate the Child," Maholmes (1995) discusses the Comer School Development begun in 1968 toward the end of the Civil Rights movement, as another example of a collaborative model that works to bring about higher achievement in urban schools. This model, based on the African proverb "It takes a whole village to educate the child," formed a collaboration among the school, community, and parents. The model contains three organizational tools that allow this plan to be successful:

1. *Three Mechanisms*: The School Planning and Management Team, the Mental Health Team, and the Parents' Program
2. *Three Guiding Principles*: Consensus Decision-Making, Collaboration, and No-Fault Problem-Solving
3. *Three Operations*: The Comprehensive School Plan, Staff Development, and Assessment and Modification

Using these three tools, low-performing schools in the New Haven, Connecticut, district have since become among the highest achieving schools.

A new endeavor to implement this Comer model began in 1992 with an innovative school located in a northeast urban center. The Nouveau School is a unique collaboration of a charitable foundation, a public community school district, and a private nonprofit organization. The collaborative group had a vision of the school as a hub for community activities, health resources, and educational high standards. Therefore, the school along with its partners created four resources that implemented this vision: a Health Center providing health and wellness services to children and families; the Family Center, a multiservice resource center that creates linkages between the home, community, and school; the Extended Day Program that extends the academic instruction; and the Residential Campus that provides year-round learning experiences for students and families.

Key to the success of any urban renewal process is the ownership of the parents in the vision for educational change. In promoting home and school partnerships through comprehensive, long-lasting programs that involve parents with the educational development of their children (Comer, 1980; Epstein & Dauber, 1991), urban students begin to achieve academically in the school setting. Comer (1980) realized the importance of engaging the parents of low-income and diverse populations in this vision. If the parents of these students were not included and considered a valued partner in this process, then it would not be successful. The strategies of the Nouveau School to involve parents included three levels: gaining general participation, joining the parent organization, and becoming a representative on the school planning and management team.

At the first level, parents are encouraged to attend activities at the school involving their children. Included in this first level is the effort on the part of school personnel to give more positive than negative feedback to the parents about their children, thus building a more trusting relationship with the parents. As part of building relationships, the school received funding to develop a family center to provide a broad array of activities to support the needs of the families in the community. At the second level, the parents are encouraged to participate in classroom and school activities and to join the parent association at the school. A strategy called *class parent representatives* (Comer, 1980, p. 18) was developed in order to improve communication between classroom and home. The representatives are assigned to a classroom and assist in sharing information about school programs and activities with the other parents and act as a liaison to ensure parent feedback in the planning and management of the school. A needs assessment was developed and conducted in the community to determine the type of programs that would best benefit them. Some of the programs that were implemented based on this assessment included a teenage support program, holistic health and stress management, African studies, parents' club, single parent support group, GED classes, and Saturday basketball. At the third level, the parents became representatives on the school planning and management team and thus join with others in making decisions about the school's management and direction.

Three major categories of issues that needed to be addressed were relationship/trust issues with parents, educators' attitudes and beliefs about high-level student success, and the political and organizational structure of the school. Because these three areas of concern were appropriately identified and addressed, success for all students became evident throughout the school. (For current information concerning the Comer Schools, refer to their website at the end of this chapter.)

University Partnerships

University of Wisconsin–Milwaukee.   Howey (2000) speaks to the issue of powerful partnerships in bringing about change in urban communities in *A Review of Challenges and Innovations in the Preparation of Teachers for Urban Contexts.* The report draws on work accomplished by nine urban partnerships among schools and colleges of education that are part of the Urban Network to Improve Teacher Education (UNITE).

The main goal of the partnerships in UNITE is to strengthen the recruitment, preparation, and retention of teachers in urban contexts. A major assumption for bringing about reform efforts in urban environments is that major improvements in teacher preparation will not occur unless major changes are made in instruction and curriculum at the university level. These changes also need to be aligned with the first years of teaching. In order to achieve these changes, Howey emphasizes the importance of bold partnerships that are interinstitutional in nature and that integrate key chairpersons in both the educational arena as well as the business, political, community, and religious arenas.

One example is the partnership of the Milwaukee Academy (Howey, 2000). The members of this academy include the superintendent of the Milwaukee Pubic Schools (MPS), the chief executive officer of the teachers' union, the president of the school board, the president of the Greater Milwaukee Chamber of Commerce, the chief executive officer of the Private Industry Council, the president of the Milwaukee Area Technical College, the chancellor of the University of Wisconsin–Milwaukee (UWM), the deans of the School of Education and Arts and Science at UWM, and parents from the community. They meet on a regular basis and share the leadership among the chancellor of the university, the superintendent of schools, and the executive director of the teachers' union.

One of their major goals is to place more teachers of color into the public classrooms. Eighty-two percent of the students are students of color, yet only 29 percent are teachers of color. One strategy for accomplishing this is to develop a career lattice for the aides and paraprofessionals who assist licensed teachers. Because a large percentage are African Americans, the aim is to assist them in preparing for a teaching career. This challenge includes coordinating a reasonable curriculum between the area technical college and the University of Wisconsin–Milwaukee as well as negotiations between the school board and the teachers' union to provide for their continued education. Both the Chamber of Commerce and the Private Industry Council work together to bring about scholarships and fellowships for paraprofessionals. As the curriculum designed for these nontraditional students involves extensive changes, both deans of education and liberal studies are involved in making decisions in this process. Once these students have completed their licensure requirements, they will need a position in the district and support for their first years of teaching, which requires collaborating with the board of education and the teachers' union to accomplish these tasks (Howey, 2000).

This type of effective collaboration requires a strong commitment on the part of the key administrators involved in each area of the partnership. Deans at the university and CEOs of the various organizations and associations must all be willing to make this initiative a priority in their schedules. However, when leaders in the community have a common vision and are willing to work together toward the accomplishment of that vision, then these goals can be achieved.

Boston Teacher Residency Program. The Boston Teacher Residency (BTR) is an alternative certification program collaborating with the Boston Public Schools, the Boston Plan for Excellence, and the Strategic Grant Partners, which is funding the program for the first two years. The goal of this program is to create qualified teachers of classrooms where every child can succeed. It is a twelve-month program designed to recruit, prepare, and certify highly-qualified candidates who already have their four-year degree and want to make a difference in the lives of urban children. The program is based on the medical residency model. After a month of initial coursework and training, teacher residents spend a school year working with a master teacher in their classroom. Residents are able to observe and learn from an experienced teacher as he manages the classroom, conducts lessons, and assesses students. The master teachers are able to give guidance, advice, and training to the resident as they begin teaching in the classroom. Every Friday, residents attend seminars led by both professors and practitioners. This model of working side-by-side with a mentor teacher for a full school year, being able to observe that teacher, as well as receive feedback from that teacher on lessons presented in the classroom and behavior management, is an innovative method being implemented by various states across the country to meet the demands for highly qualified teachers. The traditional route is for student teachers to have part of a semester in a classroom with an experienced teacher, usually not a complete year. With this method, resident teachers are supported and guided in good classroom practices by an experienced teacher while receiving coursework on classroom theory and management practices. Theory and practice come together to create a more effective and experienced beginning teacher. Teacher residents earn a Massachusetts Initial Teacher License, dual certification in special education, and a master's degree in education. (For more information about this program visit the website provided at the end of the chapter.)

Project Site Support.   A third partnership, called Project Site Support (PSS), involves Johns Hopkins University, Morgan State University, the University of Maryland–Baltimore County, the Baltimore City Public School System, and other Maryland school districts. The program is an innovative teacher-training and development program designed to recruit, prepare, support, and retain new teachers to meet the diverse needs of urban K–12 students in the Baltimore city area. This alternative licensure program is designed for career changers and recent college graduates who have not yet earned teaching certification. PSS provides three pathways to a teaching career at the elementary or secondary level: a master's level school immersion internship, a master's level two-year resident teacher program, and the undergraduate internship. Tuition grants and stipends are provided through a grant from the U.S. Department of Education and support from the Baltimore City Public School System. Students throughout their time in the program receive mentoring from experienced teachers and content-area experts. They will also participate in an electronic learning community that links students to fellow teachers and leading educators across all participating schools and universities. This nontraditional method of training highly qualified teachers is meeting the needs of school districts that are losing many teachers to retirement as well as to a high turnover rate in the urban districts. (For more information regarding Project Site Support, see their website at the end of the chapter.)

University of Tennessee–Chattanooga.   Another example of what partnerships can accomplish is the Chattanooga partnership for the revitalization of its downtown area, involving local charitable foundations, the University of Tennessee at Chattanooga (UTC), local businesses, community and business leaders, local neighborhood associations, and the local Hamilton County school district. Beginning with the vision for building the aquarium in downtown Chattanooga, other foundations have contributed and invited growth in the downtown area. Old downtown buildings that were once deserted are now being revitalized as apartments and businesses. UTC is considered a vital part of Chattanooga's vision for economic growth in that robust education is necessary to produce the healthiest economy.

UTC's College of Health, Education, and Professional Studies has been aggressive in partnering with the Hamilton County Department of Education (HCDE) to promote teacher quality and enhance classroom learning. Since its beginning, the partnership has expanded to include seven other key partners who are stakeholders in pre-K–16 education: the Office of the Mayor, the City of Chattanooga, the Hamilton County Commission, the Lyndhurst Foundation, the Public Education Foundation, the Osborne Foundation, and the Benwood Foundation.

Working together, this diverse partnership has produced new initiatives—such as Each One Reach One, which recruits and prepares African American men to serve as elementary school teachers—and the Urban IMPACT grant, which is a project funded by the U.S. Department of Education's Teacher Quality Enhancement Program. The Urban IMPACT program has a regional emphasis, serving urban schools and educators in Chattanooga and Knoxville. This initiative helped create a more stable urban educator workforce in the urban schools by developing a mentor training program that trains experienced teachers in urban schools as mentors for new teachers to the urban environment. Also through the grant, the Urban Specialist Certificate Program was developed and implemented to enhance the knowledge and skills of those teachers already working in urban schools.

The UTC–HCDE partnership together engaged numerous partners to fund and construct two new downtown community elementary magnet schools: H. H. Battle Academy of Teaching and Learning and Tommie F. Brown Academy of Classical Studies. Students who live in the urban core communities can choose either school; the remaining slots are made available to families who work downtown through a lottery system. These schools are an example of the integration of inner-city and downtown workers' children and high-poverty and middle class students learning together.

In 2001, nine underperforming urban elementary schools were placed on notice by the state. A local philanthropy, the Benwood Foundation of Chattanooga, pledged to improve conditions in these nine schools ("the Benwood schools"). The Benwood Foundation awarded a $5 million grant to the Public Education Foundation (PEF) to facilitate the grant with PEF adding $2.5 million in matching funds over a five-year period. The funds were used to improve literacy and attract high-quality teachers to these schools. By the year 2003, significant gains had begun to be made, with 35.9 percent of the students at or above grade level in reading. In comparison, in 2001 only 22.6 percent of the third-grade students read at or above grade level. As a result of this work, urban student achievement has increased and urban teacher retention has declined (PEF, 2004).

In 2003 and in connection with the Benwood Foundation's initiative, another Chattanooga foundation, the Weldon F. Osborne Foundation, has given $1.5 million to support the teachers in the Benwood schools in achieving their master's degree over a five-year period, with PEF adding another $500,000. UTC was chosen to deliver the Osborne Fellows Urban Masters Program through a rigorous and competitive proposal process including numerous universities. The initiative was recently extended to five urban feeder middle schools.

In conclusion, the UTC–HCDE partnership is developing an integrated learning environment of pre-12 students, preservice and inservice teachers, and UTC College of Education and Arts and Sciences faculty. Together with other stakeholders in the Chattanooga community, the partnership is working toward

a shared vision of what Hamilton County's urban schools will become and a shared plan for how to achieve that vision. (For further information concerning the Benwood schools, the Osborne Fellows Urban Masters Program, and the Brown and Battle academies, see the websites at the end of the chapter.)

CHALLENGES TO EDUCATIONAL PARTNERSHIPS

Urban parents and urban communities present challenges to the educational environment that need to be addressed and overcome if urban students are to be successful in the school environment and in the world at large. Urban parents are like their suburban counterparts in that they too have strong desires for their children to succeed in life. They understand that an education will help their children succeed, but they often do not know how to go about encouraging and positioning their children for success in school. Quite often, urban parents themselves have had difficulties and negative experiences with school (Hale, 1986). In many urban schools, distrust exists both within the teachers and administrators at the schools and within the parents and communities that connect with the schools. "School personnel assume that parents will be apathetic, adversarial, or challenging to deal with. . . . The assumption is that school personnel, especially those in urban areas, possess all the wisdom about teaching and learning" (Hulsebosch & Logan, 1999, p. 34). While urban teachers are frustrated with lack of family involvement in school academics, urban parents are skeptical about the schools' attitudes toward African American and Hispanic children. They sometimes consciously decide not to become involved in the schools' activities and participate only with the teachers whom they feel respect and value their children (McDermott & Rothenberg, 2000).

In order to address the challenges that urban schools and communities face, two choices are available. One approach emphasizes the students', parents', and community's needs, deficiencies and problems while the other discovers the urban families' and community's capacities and assets. The assets of a community include individuals, associations, businesses, and institutions. Instead of looking at the negatives, it focuses on the positives that the communities bring to the table (Kretzmann & McKnight, 1993). All too often the abilities, experiences, strengths, and culture that urban students, their families, and their communities bring with them to schools are often ignored. However, when parents and communities are seen to be equal contributors to the education process, then a strong foundation of mutual trust and acceptance is laid and can begin to be built upon. Chang (1993) writes,

> The difficulty involved in creating an effective collaborative process should not, however, be underestimated. The success of a collaborative is often determined by the ability of the individuals involved to respect each other as equals, establish trust, and work constructively together. But group dynamics can be shaped by historical power relationships that are neither respectful nor equal. . . . building trust . . . is perhaps the biggest challenge to developing effective collaborations. (pp. 220–221)

Teachers and administrators in urban schools need to implement effective strategies to build relationships with urban parents and urban communities. Business, religious, and social leaders in the urban community can serve as liaisons with the schools and assist in building the capacity of parents to network and become advocates on school issues. Parents and teachers working together on an equal footing can provide positive changes to bring about the success of students in urban schools. We cannot underestimate the importance of training preservice education students and new teachers how to develop strong, trusting relationships with urban families and communities.

ORIENTATION AND TRAINING FOR TEACHERS AND PRESERVICE TEACHERS

Promoting Positive Home–School Relationships

Comer (1987) suggests that preservice education training should include theoretical and applied courses in child development and behavior early in their coursework. Gaining this knowledge and the application of it in early field experiences better prepares students for creating an equitable social classroom environment in which students are able to imitate, identify, and internalize the attitudes and values of the staff. He also suggests that future teachers should be taught the reasons for distrust between the home and school and given skills to create a power-sharing organizational structure in their classrooms. Within their educational training, preservice students should learn how to promote positive home–school relationships in order to minimize the intimidation that many urban parents feel when they enter the school environment. Current Comer websites that detail high-performing Comer schools and provide further important information about the development, implementation, partnerships, contacts, and funding for these schools can be found at the end of this chapter.

In *A Framework for Understanding Poverty*, Payne (2003) addresses the importance of creating trusting relationships. She draws from the work of Covey (1989) that regards an emotional bank account where one makes emotional deposits and withdrawals. Deposits are the positive speech and actions that build trust in a relationship, and the withdrawals are the negative speech and actions that break apart a relationship. If teachers understand deposits that are valued by students from poverty, they can then create a strong bond with their students. Some of the deposits to an individual in poverty are appreciation for humor and entertainment provided by the individual, acceptance of what the individual cannot say about a person or situation, respect for the demands and priorities of relationships, using the adult voice, and assisting with goal setting. Likewise, some of the withdrawals made from individuals in poverty are put-downs about the humor or the individual, insistence and demands for full explanation about a person or situation, insistence on the middle-class view of relationships, using the parent voice, and telling the individual his goals. For students and adults in poverty, the main reason that they will succeed, do well in school, and go on to finish high school or college will be because of the relationships that they have built with teachers and other role models that support and encourage them to go on and become all that they can be.

Examples of trusting relationships that lead to changes in the lives of urban students are those of youth organizations that are often part of the urban community (Heath & McLaughlin, 1993). Preservice and inservice teachers can learn from and use these organizations as a model for building relationships and establishing trust with youth in urban areas. If teachers in urban schools can act as mentors to urban students, then the students will have assistance and support in leading different lives with meaningful goals. These organizations such as the YMCA and Boys' and Girls' Clubs provide a stable caring environment for inner-city youth looking for a safe haven from the chaos that often surrounds their everyday lives. Through the relationships formed with those who run these organizations, youth are able to gain another perspective on life. They form mentoring relationships with mature, caring adults who can influence and guide them to a productive life. Forming trusting relationships with those involved in these local organizations provides a way out of a life filled with hopelessness and despair. (For further reading and information concerning the work done by Heath and McLaughlin, see the websites listed at the end of the chapter.)

Additional Collaborative Solutions to Urban Problems

The Massachusetts Avenue Project (Welborn, 1995), located in Buffalo, New York's west side, is a project in a neighborhood-based organization that grew out of a block club organized in 1990. The block club had two main purposes: (1) to bring property owners and tenants together for increased security, and (2) to pressure absentee landlords to maintain their property better and take responsi-

bility for their tenants. The Massachusetts Project brought people together from local businesses, union, police departments, academic and human service organizations, and churches, as well as the local city and county representatives. An eleven-block area was targeted for long-term and comprehensive change. Two areas of focus were vital to success: empowering residents in the neighborhood by involving them in the process and involvement from all racial, ethnic, and class lines in the community.

Several serious issues regarding the neighborhood needed to be addressed. More homes needed to be occupied by the owners, thus giving more ownership within the community. Low poverty, single-parent households were in need of family support services, and jobs were scarce due to declining steel manufacturing in the area. Training and education were needed to prepare members of this community for work. These issues began to be addressed, but the central issue of creating a secure and healthy environment for the children of the community remained the focus of beginning efforts. In 1993, the community began to organize five hundred volunteers for the Playground Project. Assistance and funding came from a nearby company, a West Side Neighborhood Housing grant, and city bond funds.

The committee decided on a process to involve the community by working with area schools to set up a Design Day. Architects talked to the students in their classrooms about designs for the playground, asking for their ideas and drawings. The project created a sense of community as members from all race, ethnic, and socioeconomic status came together to build something good for the children. Through the children at the Boys' and Girls' Club, the committee was able to reach out into the community to let residents know about the project and invite them to participate. Because the children, parents, and members of the community were of all races and socioeconomic groups, the playground became a multicultural space where neighborhood relationships continue to grow. The momentum that began with building the playground continued to be sustained through addressing other areas of concern in the neighborhood, including needed services such as reproductive services, health services, an immunization program, family planning services, and parenting education. Models of economic revitalization continue to be investigated. (Current information concerning the Massachusetts Avenue Project can be found on the websites listed at the end of the chapter.)

Another model derives from "The Role of the Black Church in Changing Times: Empowering the Community for Survival" Moore (1995). Africans who were brought to this country under the system of slavery carried with them rich spiritual and religious traditions. Initially, the Black church served as a means of support and survival, and during the Civil War was used as a network for slaves seeking freedom through the Underground Railroad. After emancipation and based on this rich heritage, African American churches became symbols of freedom from White rules and influence. By 1906 there were approximately 36,477 Black churches and today they claim more than nineteen million members.

Multiple challenges face African Americans growing up in the United States today, such as the percent of female head of households, school dropout rates among adolescents, unemployment, drug use, AIDS, and incarceration. The Black church is in a position to be a leading force in empowering the Black community if the church leaders see the role of the church as assisting in social activism. Black church leaders and their members can come together to set a national agenda to address the problems, develop strategies for meeting the agenda, and pool its resources for this purpose.

Related to what the Black churches can do, *Restoring At-Risk Communities: Doing It Together and Doing It Right*, Perkins (1995) establishes ways in which the Christian community can come together to affirm the dignity of people, motivate them, and help them take responsibility for their own lives. Perkins challenges Christians in communities with their churches to relocate and live among the poor, to reconcile people to God and to each other, and to redistribute skills and resources to ameliorate the problems of the urban community. He believes that the people of God together can overcome the problems of the urban communities. He began his work in Mendenhall, Mississippi in 1960 where he returned after many years to help rebuild his rural home community. He has developed principles and guidelines that led to economic development and job opportunities for many in Mendenhall. Hundreds of Christian communities across the United States and in cities around the world are using these defining principles of Christian community development and finding them effective agents for spiritual transformation and socioeconomic development for the poor.

Full-Time Family Partnership Specialist

The model used with the Family Partnership Specialist is based on the research by Epstein, the director of the National Network of Partnership Schools at Johns Hopkins University. If school districts or state entities are interested in developing strong school, family, and community partnerships for student success, they are invited to join the National Network of Partnership Schools (Sheldon & Epstein, 2002). The model depicts how schools can engage families in educational activities that specifically highlight increasing student achievement. It represents a framework that allows for differentiating the activities to the needs of various schools. (Information about this partnership can be found in the website listed at the end of this chapter.)

Under this model, the position of the Family Partnership Specialist is expected to engage families and the community in the education process of their children and to support the school in accomplishing the following goals:

- 100 percent of third graders reading at or above grade level;
- students participating in the after-school program will move from the bottom quartile to the proficient or above proficient level as measured by TCAP/CRT subtests in reading, language, and math;
- Tennessee Value Added Assessment System (TVAAS) will measure more than 100 percent gain in all five subject areas as measured by this test;
- survey data will show 90 percent parent and teacher satisfaction; and
- student attendance will be above or at least at 95 percent.

Family Partnership Specialists are an integral part of the school's leadership team by engaging families and communities in meaningful ways that improve student performance and help them understand the school's expectations and goals. The qualifications for this position include the following:

1. a bachelor's degree with a minimum of two years experience working in public education;
2. strong oral and written communication skills;
3. work well with others and outstanding organizational skills;
4. competencies in Microsoft Word, Excel, Outlook, and PowerPoint;
5. the ability to work with factual data elements to direct the program's initiative, including but not limited to locating, disaggregating, assessing, and communicating data with families and school staff; and
6. action-oriented, high energy, able to multitask, and the ability to work flexible hours.

Some of the responsibilities related to this position involve:

1. facilitating the development and implementation of a school–family–community partnership plan that is directly connected and completely interwoven with the school improvement plan;
2. identifying and organizing a representative mix of community members and school staff to generate an action team that will develop and carry out the school–family–community partnership plan that engages families to achieve the school improvement goals;
3. coordinating an after-school literacy tutorial utilizing community-based organizations, consulting teachers, and other community resources that yields measurable academic improvement;

4. planning and/or conducting workshops and trainings for parents and teachers to increase their capacity to work together on student achievement and school improvement goals; and

5. using students and school data to communicate to families how their children and school are performing.

(Further information concerning the Family Partnership Specialist position can be found at the website located at the end of this chapter.)

SUMMARY

To conclude, numerous guidelines can be developed and utilized by preservice and inservice teachers from these various models that have been presented in this chapter. Regarding university partnerships, Howey (2000) found that a strong commitment and common vision on the part of chief administrators in various city and county organizations allowed the building of a network to address the need for people of color to be trained as certified teachers for the Milwaukee public schools where 82 percent of the students were students of color. In both the alternative certificate programs in Boston and Baltimore that were described, innovative teacher training methods were implemented in order to gain highly qualified teachers committed to teaching in diverse urban settings. One of the main features of these programs was that of the master/mentor teacher who guided and supported the learning of the teacher-in-training within the practical setting of the classroom. These teacher training programs utilized the intersection of theory and practice to create effective beginning teachers trained in urban settings.

In Chattanooga, Tennessee, the common vision for the revitalization of the downtown area by local businesses and philanthropists was the catalyst for many changes in the urban community. One such change was the collaborative project of building two new downtown elementary magnet schools where low and middle socioeconomic and Black and White students learn together. In addition, two local foundations partnered with nine low-performing elementary schools to fund instructional changes in these schools. One of the foundations has funded an urban master's degree for the teachers in these nine schools in partnership with the University of Tennessee in Chattanooga. Having a common vision and community, university, and city leaders committed to that vision has yielded positive results in places like Milwaukee and Chattanooga. These types of partnerships can prove successful in any urban area.

Another partnership that was discussed found that when three partners came together it was more effective in breaking down the distrust than when only two of the partners worked together. Although building trust takes time, this model is being used in other areas around the nation. The Comer School Development program is another effective model that was developed in 1968 and is still used today. The components of the model that have proven successful are three organizational tools that involve decision-making and problem-solving skills, parental involvement, and a comprehensive school plan. As part of their vision, the school and its partners created four resources to implement this vision: a health center, the family center, the extended day program, and the residential campus. These centers fulfill the vision that the school be a center for community activities, health resources, and educationally high standards. Another important feature of this model is the engagement of parents of low-income and minority populations as valued members of this initiative. As urban parents are included as a vital part of the decision-making, planning, and implementation of these various centers, they are causing this vision to succeed.

Another successful project that grew out of a block club became the Massachusetts Avenue Project. This project was successful because they empowered residents by involving them in the process, and they sought involvement from all racial, ethnic, and class lines in the community. Since the main focus of the block club was to create a secure and healthy environment for the children of the community, the community organized five hundred volunteers for the Playground Project. The project created a sense of community as all the various members of the community were included in designing and implementing this playground. Through the sense of community that was built with the Playground Project, other concerns of the neighborhood began to be addressed.

Throughout the partnership models, issues related to the building of trusting relationships among diverse groups surfaced many times. It is vital to remember that trust is a foundational issue that must be resolved before any meaningful partnership work can be accomplished. Urban school teachers and administrators must examine their attitudes toward their students and their parents. Parents do not want to work with school staff who do not understand and respect them or their children. Educators need to see the urban students, parents, and community as having assets that they bring to the learning environment. Creating a power-sharing organizational structure in the classrooms, along with parents and teachers working together on an equal footing, can be a powerful force to bring about trusting relationships that in turn bring about the success of students in urban schools. Teachers and administrators can look at the models that the YMCA and Girls' and Boys' Club have developed as they work with youth in inner-city neighborhood areas. These organizations have developed trusting relationships with youth that have led to significant positive changes in the lives of these young people. Working partnerships are the key to bringing about change in the urban environment that allows for student achievement and thus student success in the world at large and in their lives.

CHAPTER QUESTIONS

1. Your school is asked to form a partnership with the nearby university, several local businesses, parents from your school, and community leaders. You have been asked to organize this partnership. The purpose of this partnership is to

increase the student achievement at your school. Using some of the models in this chapter, what guidelines would you use to create an effective partnership?

2. You are a business leader in your urban city. You are concerned about the low achievement levels of the students in the area schools. What are some strategies you might use to connect with the local schools and help them gain in their student achievement scores?

3. You are a teacher at an urban school and you have many students whose parents you have not yet met. They do not come to any of the parent conferences, parent teacher organizational meetings or special student events. What are some strategies that you might use to build relationships with these parents?

4. You are a leader of a youth organization in the inner city. Your organization provides tutoring to students who attend the local school. How might you connect with the school in a way that your organization would be more effective with their tutoring program?

5. You are a teacher in an urban school. Think about your relationships with parents and members of the urban community. What biases and perspectives do you have that might hinder a trusting relationship with them? What might help you overcome those?

6. You are an urban parent and you are concerned that your child is not being held to high expectations and thus is not doing the quality work of which you know he is capable. You did not finish high school and you want your child to have the skills to finish high school and perhaps even go on to college. You feel that the teacher of your child does not think he is capable of doing high-level work. What would you do to change the perception of the teacher about your child?

SUGGESTED WEBSITES

THE ACHIEVER: "Education News Parents Can Use"
www.ed.gov/news/av/video/edtv

Advocates for Children and Youth
www.acy.org/relatedlinks.shtml

Boston Teacher Residency Program
www.bpe.org/btr

Cities Alliance
http://www.citiesalliance.org/citiesalliancehomepage.nsf

College of Education Outreach Programs
http://edtechoutreach.umd.edu/Outreach/urban.html

Comer Collaboration Projects
www.emich.edu/coe/collab_ed/comer.html
www.emich.edu/public/collab_ed/comer.html
www.ncrel.org/sdrs/areas/issues/educatrs/leadrshp/le2con8.htm

Epstein—family–school connections
www.csos.jhu.edu/p2000/new_research.htm

Family Partnership Specialist
www.pefchattanooga.org/www/docs/7.340/community_engagement_home.html
www.albany.edu/aire/urban/anderson-butcher.html
www.stanford.edu/dept/news/pr/95/950502Arc5247.html

Heath and McLaughlin: inner city youth
www.uic.edu/depts/soci/yrp/comp/pages/resob.html

Kretzmann and McKnight: building communities from the inside out
www.northwestern.edu/ipr/publications/community/buildingblurb.html

Massachusetts Avenue Project
www.volunteersolutions.org/uwbec/org/3361863.html

National Center for Urban Partnerships
www.thenationalcenter.org/

National Network of Partnership Schools
www.partnershipschools.org

New Schools, Better Neighborhoods
www.nsbn.org/about/

Oakland Urban School Field Project
www.ucop.edu/urbancoll/urbcollpg2.html

Project SITE SUPPORT
www.SITESUPPORT.org

Public Education Foundation of Chattanooga
www.pefchattanooga.org

SUNY–Oswego's Project SMART
www.oswego.edu/prosmart/

University of Kentucky Center for Poverty Research
www.ukcpr.org/RelatedLinks.html

REFERENCES

Chang, H. (1993). Serving ethnically diverse communities. *Education and Urban Society, 25,* 212–221.

Comer, J. P. (1987). New Haven's school–community collaboration. *Educational Leadership, 44,* 13–16.

Comer, J. P. (1980). *School power: Implications of an intervention project.* New York: The Free Press.

Covey, S. R. (1989). *The seven habits of highly effective people: Powerful lessons in personal change.* New York: Simon & Schuster.

Epstein, J. L. (1987). Toward a theory of family-school connections: Teacher practices and parent involvement. In K. Hurrelman, F. Kaufmann, & F. Losel (eds.), *Social intervention: Potential and constraints* (pp. 121–136). New York: Aldine.

Epstein, J. L. (1995). School/family/community partnerships: Caring for the children we share. *Phi Delta Kappan, 76*, 701–712.

Epstein, J. L. (2001). *School, family, and community partnerships: Preparing educators and improving schools.* Boulder, CO: Westview.

Epstein, J. L., & Dauber, S. L. (1991). School programs and teacher practices of parent involvement in inner-city elementary and middle schools. *The Elementary School Journal, 91*, 289–305.

Hale, J. E. (1986). *Black children: Their roots, culture and learning styles* (rev. ed.). Baltimore: Johns Hopkins University Press.

Heath, S. B., & McLaughlin, M. W. (1993). *Identity and inner-city youth: Beyond ethnicity and gender.* New York: Teachers College Press.

Howey, K. (2000). *A review of the challenges and innovations in the preparation of teachers for urban contexts: Implications for state policy.* Milwaukee: University of Wisconsin–Milwaukee.

Hulsebosch, P., & Logan, L. (1999). Inner-city parents co-construct better schooling. *The Education Digest,* (January), 33–39.

Kretzmann, J. P., & McKnight, J. L. (1993). *Building communities from the inside out: A path toward finding and mobilizing a community's assets.* Chicago: ACTA Publications.

Maholmes, V. (1995). Mobilizing the village to educate the child. In D. Koritz, P. R. Mattai, S. Phelps, K. Railey, & J. Riley-Hunt (eds.), *Crossing boundaries: Collaborative solutions to urban problems* (pp. 15–26). Selected proceedings of the First National Conference on Urban Issues, November, 1994 Report No. UD-031-354. Buffalo: State University of New York, Buffalo. ERIC ED No. 403 333.

McDermott, P., & Rothenberg, J. (2000). Why urban parents resist involvement in their children's elementary education. *The Qualitative Report, 5* (3, & 4). Available: www.nova .edu/ssss/QR/QR5-3/mcdermott.html (2004, March 3).

Moore, S. E. (1995). The role of the Black church in changing times: Empowering the community for survival. (1995). In D. Koritz, P. R. Mattai, S. Phelps, K. Railey, & J. Riley-Hunt (eds.), *Crossing boundaries: Collaborative solutions to urban problems* (pp. 162–176). Selected proceedings of the First National Conference on Urban Issues, November, 1994 Report No. UD-031-354. Buffalo: State University of New York, Buffalo. ERIC ED No. 403 333.

Payne, R. K. (2003). *A framework for understanding poverty* (3rd ed.). Highlands, TX: aha! Process.

Perkins, J. M. (ed.). (1995). *Restoring at-risk communities: Doing it together and doing it right.* Grand Rapids, MI: Baker Books.

Public Education Foundation. (2004). *Many strategies, one goal.* Chattanooga, TN: Public Education Foundation.

Sanders, M. G. (2003). Community involvement in schools: From concept to practice. *Education and Urban Society, 35*, 161–180.

Sheldon, S. B., & Epstein, J. L. (2002). Improving student behavior and school discipline with family and community involvement. *Education and Urban Society, 35*, 4–26.

Underwood, D. F., & Frye, H. T. (1995). Collaboration as a social process: Inter-institutional cooperation and educational change. In D. Koritz, P. R. Mattai, S. Phelps, K. Railey, & J. Riley-Hunt (eds.), *Crossing boundaries: Collaborative solutions to urban problems* (pp. 1–14). Selected proceedings of the First National Conference on Urban Issues, November, 1994 Report No. UD-031-354. Buffalo: State University of New York, Buffalo. ERIC ED No. 403 333.

Welborn, G. S. (1995). The Massachusetts Avenue project: Community revitalization on Buffalo's west side. In D. Koritz, P. R. Mattai, S. Phelps, K. Railey, & J. Riley-Hunt (eds.), *Crossing boundaries: Collaborative solutions to urban problems* (pp. 117–139). Selected proceedings of the First National Conference on Urban Issues, November, 1994, Report No. UD-031-354. Buffalo: State University of New York–Buffalo. ERIC ED No. 403 333.

CHAPTER 10

OPPORTUNITIES FOR THE FUTURE

The proof is growing that all teachers—regardless of race, ethnicity, or gender—who care about, mentor, and guide their students, can have a dramatic impact on their students' futures, even when the students face tremendous barriers related to poverty, racism, and other social ills.

—Profoundly Multicultural Questions, *Best of 2002–2003 Educational Leadership*

URBAN PERSPECTIVES

Amanda McKinney
Elementary School Teacher

I express to my students that they can *be successful, and I spend my energies emphasizing to them that there is so much more to life than what they currently know and experience.*

Amanda McKinney enjoys teaching third-grade students in her urban elementary school placement. "From my seven years of teaching in urban schools, I have learned to understand and appreciate the attitudes, values, and desires of this population of learners," she smiled. "I am able to reach them, and take them to academic levels where they need to be. It's so important that we, as teachers, keep academic expectations high."

For her students' futures, she emphatically maintains high optimism. "I express to my students that they *can* be successful, and I spend my energies emphasizing to them that there is so much more to life than what they currently know and experience. As they grow and enjoy their academic successes, I expect that they will indeed 'educate their way' out of poverty and/or their often-unstable home and community environments."

McKinney does not allow her students to be excused from nonperforming in class or on assignments due to their disadvantages or depressed living conditions. "We cannot blame parents for the environment they provide their children. My students live as they live, and we must accept that; but I so want them to realize that much, much more awaits them! I can lead them there."

Her years of service to urban students have been met with numerous challenges, she laments. "It's often shocking to hear my students describing to me their personal experiences of abuse, police activity, or violence that occur in their homes and community. Although most live with some sort of parental figure, like a single mom, an aunt, or a grandparent, I see these children, for the most part, as raising themselves. So I do all I can to *enable* these 'little adults,' offering them not only the academic skills they need to know, but also introducing to them tools and strategies that build their life skills."

She radiates optimism and the promise of unforeseen opportunities available for students in her classroom. "We talk about their graduating from high school and heading for college, similar to my former and current experiences and expectations," McKinney continued. "I explain my personal goals and responsibilities, and values and morals, in hopes of positively influencing the students' attitudes and how they internalize this world they live in."

To teachers new to the urban school environment, McKinney offered critical counsel: "Collaborate with your professional peers for advice and guidance, that's a must," she recommended. "With your students, be honest, and firm and consistent in your classroom management—although expect that there will be times when rules won't apply to some situations. Design your classroom as a safe and welcoming climate for students. Make your academic environment a place where students will want to be"—as hers proves to be.

CHANGES FOR BETTER EDUCATIONAL OPPORTUNITIES

From Past to Present

The early years of education in the United States, recorded from its pre-Colonial era through its Industrial era, reflects nearly three centuries of change in schools. Originally religious-based, schools offered to only the elite, and principally White males, the right to learn with supervised instructors or teachers. White females were homebound, learning skills as housewives and mothers. Formal education bypassed both males and females of color, who were instead trained and expected to perform duties of manual labor and chores that were typically gender-specific. For example, males would tend to horses and house repairs, and females would assist in raising children. Discrimination of equal rights was commonplace in our nation's youthful years.

Following the Civil War, schools slowly began opening their doors of educational opportunities to females, as well as to all students of color. They would join White males to receive the benefits of structured lessons and supervised learning. Schools at the time were racially segregated, legally separate but equal, until the 1950s, which marked the beginning of reforms to integrate schools. It was a simple idea that was to become unnecessarily complex in its implementation, and met with outrage by the concerned majority of White citizenry and politicians.

Since President Lyndon B. Johnson's administration, and through to the latest administration of President George W. Bush, billions upon billions of federal dollars have poured into federal education programs to react to and right the gross racial inequities inherent in most all of America's school systems, creating bureaucracies that attempted to make the necessary adjustments to state education and local school systems. Federal aid for nationwide education initiatives has grown dramatically since the beginnings of the Bush administration in 2000. Congress has provided more than the president has requested, totaling nearly $60 billion in discretionary spending for 2005 (Robelon & Davis, 2004).

The two most challenging trends that affect education in our nation today—a growing school population of students of color and the aging of the current population at-large—place a heavy financial burden on the U.S. economy. Education funding is and will continue to be tight. There is and will continue to be stiff competition for resources needed to meet needs of America's youth, as well as its aging population (Webb, Metha, & Jordan, 2003).

For a country that prides itself in educating the masses, early disappointments in implementing equal educational opportunities for all mirror the current predicament of significant achievement gaps that exist between low-income students of color and higher-income White students. Educational evaluations, analyses, studies, and reports have indicated that while educating children in kindergarten through grade 12, the majority (White, nonpoor learners) on the whole has performed adequately or excelled at each grade level. Meanwhile, minority children of color and low-socioeconomic status on the whole have struggled to maintain stability or consistency in exhibiting adequate academic performance. The unfair struggle waged to gain for persons of color equal rights to educational opportunities and fair treatment in public schools is a shameful embarrassment at best to the U.S. government's past political leaders who have

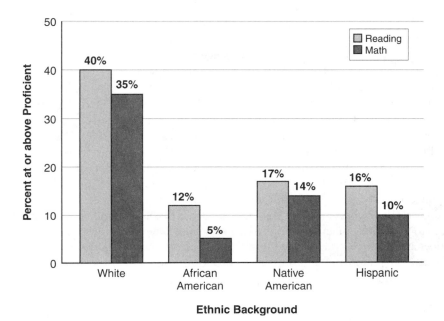

FIGURE 10.1   Fourth-Grade Student Achievement Gaps: National Assessment of Educational Progress, 2000

Source: U.S. Department of Education *No Child Left Behind Report*, 2004.

governed and claimed to have fought for the public good of our nation for more than two centuries. Against such discrimination and bigotry were our country's forefathers who worked diligently to establish such protections of equal justice for all American citizens, despite race, religion, or gender. Granted, they could not have foreseen nor accurately anticipated the decades of legal battles, political angst, and firm unwillingness of our nation's public to change and embrace contemporary efforts offering guarantees of greater equality of social justice and educational opportunity in schools. Nevertheless, history represents the past. It cannot be changed, but can be instructive for the future.

The nation's urban schools today face an emergency assistance stage. After years of falling or flat profiles of student test scores, states now bear responsibility to demonstrate action that leads to educational improvements, as illustrated in annual student test score reports. Figure 10.1 illustrates comparisons of reading and mathematics achievements among fourth-grade students in the year 2000. The differences between White students and students of color (African American, Native American, and Hispanic) are dramatic. With extraordinarily low scores when compared to those of White children, it is easily observed from this illustration that America's schools must firm up their expectations of and employ much more efficient instructional strategies for reaching and teaching students of minority populations. The responsibility falls squarely upon the shoulders of American teachers.

The pressure is undeniably on urban teachers to improve student performance and address standards-based assessment accountability issues. In many school systems, such demands likely discourage creative and novel instructional ideas, as those will take a backseat to strict content standards and preparation for mandated student assessment programs. Amidst such a backdrop, and given what teachers must teach and students must know, the urban school environment is charged to remain flexible, embrace change, and figure out methods by which to adapt and cope with current education demands. For example, if or when municipal officials exert power and influence to guide urban school systems in ways that suit their own established priorities or agendas, urban teachers and teacher leaders must strive to collaborate with and educate those political officials who very much need better, more accurate, and more positive guidance concerning how children learn best (Webb, Metha, & Jordan, 2003). Skill and compromise are key to promoting such meaningful relationships that enable best pedagogical practices and positive student-benefit initiatives. Trusting partnerships, explained in Chapter 9, created among politicians, educational personnel, and community leaders, in general, is essential to improving the urban academic landscape for currently enrolled and future urban students.

This book offers descriptions for the contemporary states of need in urban school settings so that readers have much better understandings of the primary concerns plaguing today's urban education system. There is importance for those who teach or plan to teach in urban schools to understand how those concerns evolved, and what schools—through critical analysis, evaluation, discretion, and direction of knowledgeable and capable educators, staff, parents, and community leaders—need to do to fix the problems.

Chapter 2 provided an in-depth review of urban school and neighborhood demographics. Reading about the effects of poverty on children is certain to generate anger in the hearts and minds of readers pursuing strategies to help these affected students enjoy an education that will benefit them in all realms of life, not to mention an education that is their ticket out of regrettable living conditions and arrangements.

Low-income urban communities strive to survive. Schools are challenged to make learning interesting and enjoyable, and comfortable and safe. The objective is to allow urban students, no matter what they experience, to leave any troubled homelife experience(s) at the classroom door in exchange for fresh and invigorating classroom activity. Despite overcrowded living conditions, in which urban students experience deficiencies in health, nutrition, clothing, shelter, supervision, and stability, urban teachers can champion marvelous opportunities to make substantial differences in the lives and futures of their economically disadvantaged students.

Chief Goal: Meeting High Expectations

Chapter 3 emphasized several academic and behavioral goals that effective urban educators prove fortifies their professional philosophy to leave no child behind to failure in meeting his or her learning potential. Urban educators must continue to assist their students to meet and/or exceed grade-level or individualized education program objectives and goals, and push them academically. They must prepare for and assist in delivering to students challenging curricula. Where urban students host diverse populations of students that represent a multitude of languages, cultures, and values, the teachers must sharpen their skills to manage the potential for unexpected inconsistencies or inevitable student conflicts.

Overall, according to former U.S. Secretary of Education Rod Paige, students in urban schools learn significant character values from urban teachers who demonstrate moral leadership; who endeavor to reduce achievement disparities, or gaps, between and among disaggregated groupings of students; and who build the bright, proud, considerate, and responsible citizens of tomorrow. With these goals in mind, Urban (2004) assures readers that educators in the urban schools will strive to accomplish what they can, given the resources available, combined with the will of the students—yet cautioning that "Most urban teachers and administrators are well-intentioned mortals—not heroic figures" (Urban, 2004, p. 2).

These effective "well-intentioned mortals" of urban schools recognize and acknowledge that poverty conditions yield barriers to affected students' learning. Students' only way out, their ticket to dreams, or literally their only hope is the place that proves consistent warmth, comfort, attention, love, and encouragement from adults—their school. Knowing this, teachers cannot conduct instruction in class with a business-as-usual mind-set. There is too much at stake. With the right teachers, the school improves, moves forward, and remediation and discipline concerns subside markedly.

Regard for the Intrinsic Worth of All Students

The current focus on positive educational outcomes of today's student achievements sets the stage for more long-needed, fair, and mindful considerations, particularly in urban school settings. Shields (2004) offers education professionals sound advice as they seek to deliver academic excellence and social justice to all their populations of learners. Teachers should:

- ground themselves in "bedrock moral principles of social justice and academic excellence" for all students;
- observe closely and attend to relationships, understandings, and dialogue;
- ensure that all students, despite diversities—including levels of ability, ethnic backgrounds, sexual orientation, religion, or socioeconomic status—feel accepted as participants in the school;
- respect and value each and every student;
- use listening skills, and be there for students, to create the sense of belonging that so many children seek to find;
- seize opportunities to establish relationships with and among individuals who are stakeholders in educational efforts, which includes students, teachers,

school personnel, parents, administrators, board members, legislators and community leaders;

- develop a just and caring environment for students by providing a full range of programs and activities that address various student needs, interests, abilities, and endeavors;
- extend opportunities for success to all students, thereby creating a learning community that is based upon academic excellence and is sensitive to issues of social justice. (Shields, 2004)

A civil atmosphere in urban schools breeds learning. Such aura is seen, heard, and felt by all who approach or enter school buildings or classrooms when students and school personnel demonstrate and treat each other with due dignity and respect. Teachers greet students by their names and chat with and among them in demonstrations of trust and caring. When school participants feel safe, honored, and cared about, the natural progression results in students who stop misbehaving and teachers who focus more on teaching (McCloud, 2005).

SUCCESS IN SCHOOL

The Educational Victory Achieved

John Stuart Mill once said, "The pupil who is never required to do what he cannot do will never do what he can do."

We must continue to build in schools today a community of learners, with the understanding that as students achieve they develop stronger self-esteem. Urban schools that endeavor to engage all varieties of students in assortments of programs, where student successes abound, help develop in their learners a can-do attitude that is reflected even in annual standardized achievement test scores. In order to instill this mind-set among all who work or are served in the school, teacher teams or administrators are challenged to monitor its students' participation in the activities it offers its student populations. For example, incentives, from small to significant, are established to appropriately reward and recognize student achievements in activities; likewise, they may hold meetings to discuss problems that impede the inclusive nature of the school's participation and success initiatives. Meadowland Elementary, in Sterling, Virginia, for example, established successful school activities, such as Poetry Masters and Running with Math, programs that the school identified resulted in their students' advanced academic achievement results and high scores earned on statewide assessments (Young, 2004).

Chapter 3 charged urban schools to operate as no less than the most effective schools. Urban schools must demonstrate strong administrative leadership, with principals who have clear and desired visions for their schools, along with a commitment to improve instruction, participate in decision making, and buffer and support faculty devoted to leave no child behind in achievements. Urban schools must offer safe and orderly environments, with working conditions that support teachers amidst an atmosphere conducive to both best teaching and learning. High performance standards should be expected of all students, with sensitivity to students' culture and individual differences. Students should be appropriately rewarded for their school accomplishments and systematically assessed to keep them in step with grade-level goals. Urban schools should supply sufficient resources (for example, personnel, materials, professional developmental opportunities, planning time for collaboration) that enable teachers to motivate students to meet their school-based objectives. And, all-important, the schools' own culture must reflect the positive human interactions between and among students, faculty, staff, parents, and community, along with those that encourage innovative practices and strategies to best promote teaching and learning (Webb, Metha, & Jordan, 2003).

CONSIDERATIONS FOR EDUCATIONAL PROGRESS

Recommendations for Teaching in the Multicultural Environment

Among the urban population of learners, effective educators are sensitive to how students from diverse cultural backgrounds interact and think differently from one another. Understood is that, ultimately, students of all shapes, sizes, colors, and backgrounds will be working with and among each other for most of their lives. Ormrod (2003) offers practical suggestions helpful to urban teachers in their mission to accommodate student diversity.

Urban teachers provide multicultural education in their curriculum when they:

- infuse in their teaching curriculum various types of cultural values, beliefs, and traditions (special events and/or holidays and awareness of the "greats" of many backgrounds and heritages);
- discourage ethnic stereotypes (the tagging of cultural features, such as sombreros or headscarves or chopsticks);
- encourage positive interactions among different ethnic groups;
- build upon and infuse diverse background experiences within the curriculum;
- emphasize significant accomplishments of individuals from various cultures;
- use local community leaders to represent role models and have them speak to the class;
- assist students to become better acquainted with each other, using teams to achieve goals;
- learn about and better understand each student's diverse culture and ethnicities; make home visits;
- design instruction that meets unique needs and characters of each learner, free of bias or favoritism. (Ormrod, 2003)

In addition, Dore (2004) suggests the following strategies and activities that serve to bring awareness of diversity issues from the media and local community to the classroom.

1. Use local newspapers to find stereotypes in writings or in advertising.
2. Encourage students, via assignments, to scrutinize and report on television programs that feature individuals in stereotypical roles.
3. Ask a colleague to observe classroom operations and instruction for sexual or racial bias.
4. Translate newsletters into other languages for parents who do not speak English.
5. Make sure that working groups involve all students.
6. Integrate curriculum that features historical perspectives (whence occurrences originate).
7. Encourage formulations of diversity clubs or organizations.
8. Incorporate service opportunities and learning programs that promote outreach to the local community and its citizenry.

Taming Tendencies or Factors Leading to Teacher Burnout

Earlier chapters mentioned teacher burnout as a hazard, yet an avoidable one, to once-enthused professionals in this line of work. What leads to burnout, or teacher disparagement that builds to the point of quitting the career and/or moving on to a different professional job path? Teaching in urban settings, although significantly emotionally rewarding, can be greatly challenging for several reasons, such as impoverished student situations, poor school–family communication, and lack of support from students' homes. College and university programs—designed to prepare our saints and warriors for the profession—are keen on following state and national criteria that stipulate a plethora of varied methods, strategies, and experiences, necessary to attain to become certified or licensed to teach young people. Entering the field of teaching, and happily remaining in the career, deserves adherence to well-thought guidelines. For example, problematic situations that teachers at all schools endure are typically multiplied or intensified in the urban schools, due to factors that place many urban school children at risk of failure. Urban teachers who may sense overwhelming stress, anxiety, and feelings of isolation are bound to identify with the burnout experience when faced with the following, or combinations of the following, negative situations in their classrooms:

- disruptive student behavior
- teacher-perceived, low self-efficacy (in classroom management)
- teachers' feelings of alienation. (Brouwers & Tomic, 2000; Kopetz, 2003)

Preventing burnout requires that teachers be wise to self-monitoring their feelings to identify the early warning signs of physical, mental, or behavioral stress that often lead to burnout. Alert to the signs of job stress that lead to burnout, teachers are encouraged to manage the negative symptoms using techniques like:

- backing off and focusing on taking slow, deep breaths;
- relaxing muscles with tension-and-relax exercises;
- taking a five-second calming pause prior to reacting to irritating situations;
- visualizing peaceful scenes; taking time out for a minivacation;
- don't sweat the small stuff;
- using that sense of humor;
- asking assertively for what is needed;
- refusing stressful requests of your time and energies. (Bradshaw, 1991)

These techniques offer sound survival advice, along with noting additional lifestyle changes that help relieve stress, such as adopting a proper diet and exercise plan, as well as engaging in sports activities, hobbies, friendships, television programs, movies, and similar diversionary activities. It is all a matter of caring for oneself, contemplating one's life goals, and anticipating and accommodating necessary changes.

Finally, curbing future problems or frustrations leads to emotions far better spent. The greatest frustrations experienced by new teachers that easily lead to burnout are problems they face with classroom management, time management, lesson planning, and student behavior issues. Recommended to counteract teacher frustration or burnout are experiences offered to and encouraged for all teachers:

- professional development (see page 334);
- mentor opportunities;
- meetings with school system administrators;
- providing adequate classroom supplies;
- programs that monitor and support new teachers; and
- adequate preservice preparation. (Bolich, 2001; Tapper, 1995)

Traditional approaches to discipline *do not work*. For example, typically reacting to misbehaviors by assigning punishments that exclude students from their peers (for example, detention, suspension, or expulsion) is indeed reactive, punitive, and exclusionary. By contrast, in Chapter 6, we urge urban teachers to adopt classroom management approaches that are proactive and positive, making the most of those teachable moments to demonstrate, explain, and counsel youth to assume better self-control and more appropriate behavior choices (McCloud, 2005).

Mentoring Programs Are a Must

School systems should provide quality mentoring and induction programs as remedies. The main focus of the mentoring program is to support new teachers in the classroom so that they will be retained in urban settings. The team is trained in an initial two-day session with a follow-up day several months later to provide additional assistance and support after the mentoring program has been initiated in the school. The mentors are paid a stipend at the end of each school year.

Mentors can be chosen to fill this role in two ways. The first way is for the principal to select teachers who have the following characteristics: good interpersonal, relational, and communication skills, listening and people skills, collaborative skills, effective instructional leadership skills, excellent pedagogical and content matter skills, excellent classroom management skills, and reflective skills. A mentor should be willing to be a role model for others and willing to learn from others and be a lifelong learner. The second method of filling this role is having teachers apply for the position. It then becomes a selective process with a team in place that reviews the applications, holds interviews and makes a selection based on the process.

Continuing Need for Professional (Staff) Development

Professional (staff) development is the organized set of ongoing learning opportunities available to teachers and other education personnel through their schools and districts. With the onset of continued, challenging situations in schools, from diverse populations of learners to meeting new and fastidious state academic standards, this type of teacher education is requested and valued more than ever before (Rebora, 2004). "The importance of good teaching is better understood *now* than ever before," announced by the Education Trust (The Education Trust, 2003c).

Implementing ideals and standards stipulated in the No Child Left Behind legistation, every school and school system is accountable to academic performance standards that pertain to all students. By raising academic expectations for especially the previously underserved, low-income, and minority students, commonly taught in urban school settings, expectations of teachers are also raised. Many education professionals express that they are not adequately prepared to meet the new challenges expected of them. Professional development that offers teachers the latest scientifically-proven instructional strategies, particularly in academic areas such as literacy and mathematics improves the quality of teaching that can assist all students to meet state standards (The Education Trust, 2003b).

The strong correlation between teachers' knowledge and skills and students' academic achievement leads educators, and others interested in education, to construe the importance of quality teaching (McCarthy & Frederick, 2000). Investing in improved teacher quality through professional development strongly and positively impacts teachers' classroom practices (Wenglinsky, 2002).

Professional staff development can introduce and maintain the classroom teachers' repertoire of contemporary and proven instructional skills. For urban teachers to learn about and engage in best practices that meet the needs of the at-risk student population, and to assist all students to meet or exceed state and national academic standards, professional development initiatives such as the Accelerated Schools Project (ASP) provide seminars designed by the teachers themselves. For ASP seminars, the teachers formulate goals that meet their own instructional goals, as well as the needs of the school in general. In doing so, members of the community, including administrators, school personnel, teachers, parents, and students, participate in activities aimed at contributing to the success of the school. "Rather than being the targets of change," claim Mc-Carthy and Frederick (2000), "school communities became the initiators of change."

Professional staff development will vary in intensity and delivery of information, depending upon budgets and program goals. Sometimes, staff development is an orientation of learning goals and objectives, an overview of the curriculum or fundamental academic requirements that teachers will impart during the school year. More creative and beneficial staff development exercises occur when topics are shared that relate to proven instructional strategies: ideas that fully engage students in their participation in learning activities; methods that enhance understanding and valuable instruction to students with special needs; student assessment and its benefits to the continual progress of student achievement; and immediate and practical advisement in matters that relate to better communication skills, interpersonal skills, and cultural awareness. Planned activities that serve as follow-up to professional development seminars provide continuity that can assess, for example, how newly-learned techniques are (or are not) best utilized, or whether the seminar information helped improve classroom management or individual students' self-control issues (U.S. Department of Education, 2000).

As a learning experience, easily facilitated as a professional development activity, Matsumoto-Grah (2004) suggests distributing to educators checklists that assess their individual efforts to scrutinize curricular materials, their instructional strategies, their values, their interactions with students, and general self- and professional considerations, topics that influence teachers' sensitivity to teaching fairly to a diverse population of learners. The following is a list of suggested ideas that professional development participants find useful as criteria for assessing their urban classroom materials.

- Integrate women and different cultures in curriculum materials.
- Minorities (e.g., race, religion, and for gender) are represented in the community *and* displayed in nonstereotypic fashion.
- Offer accurate and appropriate information regarding religious beliefs.
- Exhibit accomplishments of not only famous individuals, but also those of lesser means who work hard and responsibly to meet goals.
- Exhibit ideas that offer encouragement and opportunities for all students to participate and gain success. (Matsumoto-Grah, 2004)

Related to self-analysis and profession considerations, Matsumoto-Grah finds it an important and practical professional development activity to query teachers' feelings that assess their own

- knowledge about students' backgrounds and their communities;
- demonstration of respect for individuals of diverse origins, beliefs, and status;
- perceptions of demonstrating sincerity and respect for others of all types of demographics;
- ability to locate resources that teach about diversity and multiculturalism;
- treatment of all students; and
- handling of student *value conflicts* based on diverse backgrounds and beliefs. (Matsumoto-Grah, 2004)

Another professional development plan involves improving schools by changing teaching and learning through a restructuring initiative called Comprehensive Schoolwide Reform (CSR). Successful CSR models implemented in school systems nationwide support necessary professional development activities and support planning time for their teachers as well. CSR requires time to effectively orient teachers to proven methodology and entails curricular development, preparations, planning, and collaboration opportunities for faculty to exchange ideas and strategies. The type, level, and quality of professional development strongly determines the CSR model's successful implementation. CSR teams provide orientation and training in areas of instructional design and delivery; effective strategies for collaboration to promote cooperation and understanding between and among parents, teachers, and students; and collaborative opportunities for teachers to share and brainstorm types of instructional ideas. Desimore (2000) contends that "Professional development tailored to (the teachers') specific needs is the most helpful, as are models that provide substantial information about implementation." Teachers implement best the CSR model when the design teams offer nearby assistance, a clear vision of the plan and direction of changes made, and planning for organizational change (Desimore, 2000).

Finally, ideas incorporated into professional development programs that bring cultural awareness, concerns, and celebrations to the forefront of importance in today's urban schools include suggestions such as:

- the understanding and valuing of cultural differences;
- contributions made by different cultural groups;
- language and literacy development in culturally diverse groups;
- culturally appropriate referral and assessment methods and procedures;
- enhancing students' self-concept among those of diverse cultures;
- culturally responsive education and instruction;
- learning and behavior styles based upon cultural influences;
- behavior management and culturally diverse students; and
- relating multicultural content (e.g., art, music, tales) to general education curriculum. (Obiakor, Utley, Smith, & Harris-Obiakor, 2002)

Staff development can create an ongoing learning curve for urban teachers of all ages and years of experience. As new strategies, ideas, and procedures are introduced, implemented, evaluated, and analyzed, doors to change open, teacher community builds, and instructional expertise spreads. Based on data-driven school improvement plans, necessary and contemporary, best practices are introduced to the faculty by way of professional development or teacher inservice workshops that offer valued opportunities that promote teachers' personal reflections, self-improvement opportunities, "critical friends" advice, and the designing of trial-and-error, relevant instructional strategies (Berry, Johnson, & Montgomery, 2005).

FUTURE CONSIDERATIONS

Facts and Ideas and Advice

The success of our nation, and of humankind in general, is based upon "mutual respect and appreciation of others"; Dore (2004) alerts readers to consider the following facts:

- Minorities in the United States are expected to become the majority.
- Diverse student backgrounds will become the norm throughout United States school systems.
- To reach success among students of diverse races and ethnicities, teachers are challenged to examine and resolve their own biases and prejudices of their expectations of their students.
- In designing their policies and standards, organizations must plan with respect to diversity.

- Students' uniquenesses and diverse backgrounds are to be considered every day in working with them.
- Schools model communities based upon justice and the celebration of its members similarities and differences (Dore, 2004).

If implemented with conscientious direction, improvements to current educational programs in urban schools promise to offer children more positive prospects and outlooks in life. Considering that present-day kindergarteners may have bleak educational futures (see Figure 10.2) there is no time like the present to shape up and infuse powerful, tested-proven strategies into traditional teaching practices that provide these children greater hopes for their futures.

Urban teachers need continued awareness of the struggles faced by all their students, with the goal in mind to narrow the achievement gap and provide valuable educational/instructional challenges that urge students to meet established, high expectations. As a teacher's learning never stops, the following list provides constructive advice.

Of Every 100 African American Kindergartners:

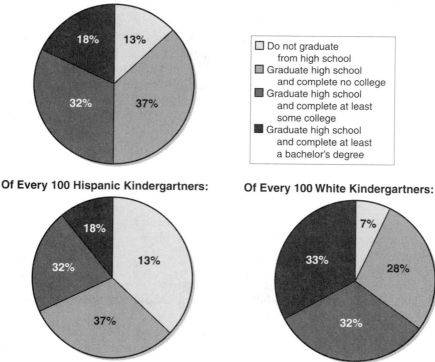

☐ Do not graduate
   from high school
☐ Graduate high school
   and complete no college
■ Graduate high school
   and complete at least
   some college
■ Graduate high school
   and complete at least
   a bachelor's degree

Of Every 100 Hispanic Kindergartners:

Of Every 100 White Kindergartners:

FIGURE 10.2   Present-Day Statistics for Kindergartners

Source: The Education Trust, Inc., 2004: *Achievement in America, 2003.*

■ Know the pipeline—learn about the numbers of education graduates who elect to teach, remain teaching, or leave the field altogether. Take measures that help to better the odds for teachers, especially those with excellent promise, to continue their efforts in urban classrooms.

■ Gain knowledge in the content areas to be taught, and in classroom management techniques. Independently seek out the most current information and strategies in periodicals that include those categorized as info-journals, as well as those that are peer-reviewed or juried to reflect sound credibility and integrity. Enroll in further academic study, and/or learn from continuing education or distance learning offerings.

■ Learn from observations of teacher practice in the classroom, and from feedback offered. Ask to visit the classrooms of more seasoned teachers who have reputations for demonstrating effective classroom achievements and practices.

■ Collect information on effective approaches and continue to learn what works. Take note of educational programs, videos, televised specials, or local seminars that provide contemporary initiatives found to benefit our nation's learners. Share your relevant, learned information among teaching colleagues, and/or use the ideas to generate interest for action and inservice teaching presentations or activities. (Bolich, 2001)

Understandings to Live By

In the following, Clark (2004) sums up what all teachers can do to "bring education to life," and in "lighting a fire in the hearts and minds of their students," with suggestions to make a significant impact on the lives of students in the classroom.

■ "Don't underestimate the power of your words." Exhibit care to inform students of their qualities in positive ways. Focus, too, on their talents and abilities.

■ "Teach to reach all students." All individuals learn in unique ways; no two learn alike. For all students to achieve success in school, instruction should incorporate as many of the students' senses as possible: vision, hearing, smelling, touching, and tasting.

■ "Nurture the relationship between teacher and students." Firm and consistent rules of behavior, consideration, and discipline, mixed with enjoyment in the learning atmosphere, and a likeable teacher, complete the ticket for accomplishing successful student achievement and satisfaction in the classroom (Clark, 2004).

   Despite rocky encumbrances to traditional methods of instruction, the responsibility of our current society, of which teachers are primarily accountable, is to endeavor to close the achievement gap between racial minorities and racial majorities. Schools cannot be expected to achieve this goal on their own. Educators have a direct connection and influence for motivating students to perform their best on standardized achievement tests. Yet, closing the achievement gap is a far more complex issue than inspiring students to demonstrate best efforts on assessments. According to Hunter and Barbee (2003), there are three compelling reasons for seeking to eliminate the achievement gap:

1. The achievement of significantly higher minority education levels is *essential to long-term productivity and competitiveness of the U.S. economy.*
2. If minorities are to enjoy the full benefits of their recently won civil rights, they need formal-education-dependent knowledge and skills much closer in quantity and quality to those held by Whites.
3. The maintenance of a humane and harmonious society depends to a considerable degree on minorities' reaching educational parity with Whites.

Today's urban teachers are pioneers in their own right, as demonstrated by star schools, districts, states, and teachers. America's future holds captive to their spirit and ingenuity to break from the old ways of teaching in favor of instruction that actively engages learners. Beginning the schoolyear anew, and knowledgeable of their subject content and their students needs, teachers confront daily challenges in urban schools everywhere. They do so armed with aggressive plans to motivate their children to achieve high academic expectations. Today's teachers have tremendous opportunities to defer to exercise contemporary and proven effective practices of instruction, assessment, and classroom management—strategies that literally change the game rules of traditional education. They hold the tools to repair the disconnects that still continue to exist in urban schools.

America has been a land of tremendous achievements and a beacon of democracy for the entire world. Our success stands as testimony to the foresight of the great men who put forth our constitution more than two hundred years ago. They foresaw the many advantages of an American society that allowed all citizens equal opportunity. The cornerstone of equal opportunity lies within our educational system.

We have learned, much to our shame, that equality of educational opportunity has not existed during any period in our history. In spite of that, we have managed to achieve greatness. Many Americans today perceive our success as waning. They are concerned about the future and whether we can continue to be the great nation of opportunity.

There is universal agreement that our educational system is the engine that powers our future. Thus, it is easy to believe that we are a nation at risk when we learn almost daily of the failures of our schools. Our nation has changed greatly and is today home to a wide diversity of cultures. That diversity is centered heavily in our urban areas, which have become major clusters of poverty. Demographers tell us that the minority population in American is growing more rapidly

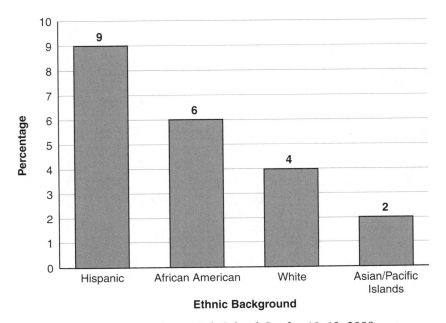

FIGURE 10.3   Dropouts from High School Grades 10–12, 2000

Source: Higher Hispanic Dropout Persists, by V. Honawar, 2004, *Education Week Online, 24*(12), 6.

than the majority. It is likely that our urban areas will represent America's last stand. If schools fail here, will today's children be prepared to take on the reins of leadership to keep American strong?

The answer to that question depends not upon the education system at large, but upon every individual teacher and the skill and commitment they bring to their classrooms every day. If our schools are to produce students who are literate and academically advanced, they will do so in each individual classroom. The burden then falls upon our teachers.

As illustrated in Figure 10.3, a demonstrated challenge in closing the achievement gap, particularly in urban schools, is that of assisting students of color, Hispanic students in particular, to remain in school and graduate from high school. Honawar (2004) identified from year 2000 data that nearly 9 percent of Hispanic students, 6 percent of African American students, 4 percent of White students, and 2 percent of Asian/Pacific Island students entered high school but exited during grades 10 through 12, failing to achieve coursework necessary to graduate. This unfortunate rate of student high school noncompleters has changed very little over the past three decades, despite the importance American society places on achieving a high school education for entry into the labor market or to higher education opportunities (Honawar, 2004).

There is much talk today about the lack of skill and commitment on the part of our teachers. We are not prepared to abandon our teachers at the very time that they hold the future of our great nation in their hands. We believe there is a new future ahead. For the first time in our history, our schools are fully integrated, and we now have laws that insist that children learn at high levels, and hold teachers and administrators accountable for student academic performance. The pressure is admittedly stressful, but it is long overdue.

Dr. Martin Luther King, Jr. believed in a dream that all children would be free to reach their maximum potential. We share that dream, and believe that we shall see it become an American reality. Our confidence is buoyed when we witness the quality of students in our teacher preparation institutions. They are better prepared to meet the challenge, their skills are sharpened, and their levels of commitment are rock solid.

We believe in our hearts that they will lift our classrooms from the shackles of failure, and build American citizens who will continue our proud traditions and shine our light brightly for the rest of the world to follow. They can feel America's breath at their backs, and it propels them forward.

This new generation of teachers is a federation of skilled, caring individuals, prepared to take whatever risks necessary to motivate children to succeed in school, as well as in life. Schools have waged war on mediocrity, and the country cannot afford to lose its battles. As we pass this awesome responsibility of better preparing our urban population of learners on to the current teaching force, we do so with our utmost support and our deepest prayers.

We, as a nation, cannot afford to allow our children to fail in schools. As educators, it is our moral obligation to this chosen profession to exercise social justice and uphold each and every student's right to a fair and equitable education. So endorsed by President George W. Bush, "For this great land called America, no child will be left behind."

CHAPTER QUESTIONS

1. What federal legislation led to current laws that protect children from discriminatory educational practices?

2. Regarding fourth-grade math and reading scores, why is there such concern among the public citizenry that current education is not working well enough?

3. Why is "meeting high expectations" our chief goal in preparing today's students for the future?

4. Identify examples that illustrate how educators respect their learners' intrinsic worth?

5. What are at least four methods teachers can employ to demonstrate their interest in, respect for, and accommodation of student diversity?

6. Offer three recommendations that teachers should consider to offset burnout in their education careers.

7. How do mentorships help new teachers?

8. For at least what three reasons is it helpful to teachers to engage in professional (staff) development seminars?

9. Given the advice, facts, and reflections offered in this chapter, what can schools do to move forward in closing the achievement gap that exists today?

SUGGESTED WEBSITES

Advocates for Children and Youth
www.acy.org/relatedlinks.shtml

American Institutes for Research
www.aasa.org/reform/

Internet System for Education and Employment Knowledge (ISEEK)
www.iseek.org/

Midcontinent Research for Education and Learning (MCREL)
www.mcrel.org/products/csrd-eval.asp

National Center for Education Statistics (NCES)
www.nces.ed.gov/nationsreportcard/reading/results2003/raceethnicity.asp

New American Schools Driven by Results
www.naschools.org

WestEd, Excellence in Research, Development, and Service
www.Wested.org/

REFERENCES

Berry, B., Johnson, D., & Montgomery, D. (2005). The power of teacher leadership. *Educational Leadership, 62*(5), 56–59.

Bolich, A. M. (2001). *Reduce your losses: Help new teachers become veteran teachers*. Atlanta, GA: Southern Regional Education Board. Available: www.sreb.org/main/HigherEd/Teacher.

Bradshaw, R. (1991). Stress management for teachers: A practical approach. *The Clearing House, 65*(September/October), 43–47.

Brouwers, A., & Tomic, W. (2000). *Disruptive student behaviors, perceived self-efficacy, and teacher burnout*. Paper presented at the 108th Annual Meeting of the American Psychological Association. ERIC ED No. 450 120.

Clark, R. (2004). The power of the positive: Four rules for success. *Middle Ground, 7*(4), 12–15.

Desimore, L. (2000). The role of teachers in urban school reform. ERIC ED No. 442 912.

Dore, E. (2004). *Classroom Connections*. Columbus, OH: National Middle School Association.

The Education Trust. (2003a). *ESEA.* Washington, DC: The Education Trust.

The Education Trust. (2003b). *In need of improvement: Ten ways the U.S. Department of Education has failed to live up to its teacher quality commitments.* Washington, DC: The Education Trust.

The Education Trust. (2003c). *Telling the whole truth (or not) about highly qualified teachers.* Washington, DC: The Education Trust.

The Education Trust. (2004). *Achievement in America, 2003.* Washington, DC: The Education Trust. Available: www.edtrust.org.

Haberman, M. (1995). *Star teachers of children in poverty.* Indianapolis, IN: Kappa Delta Pi.

Hendrie, C. (2004). In U.S. schools, race still counts. *Education Week.* Available: www.edweek.org/ew/ew_printstory.cfm?slug=19Brown.h23.

Honawar, V. (2004). Higher Hispanic dropout persists. *Education Week Online, 24*(12), 6.

Hunter, R. C., & Barbee, R. (2003). The achievement gap: Issues of competition, class, and race. *Education and Urban Society, 35*(2), 151–160.

Jerald, C. (2003). Beyond the rock and the hard place. *Educational Leadership, 61*(3), 12–16.

Kopetz, P. B. (2003). Understanding the at-risk student: Vital teacher knowledge for successful classroom management and instruction. In D. W. Rea & R. Stallworth-Clark (eds.), *Fostering our youth's well-being, healing the social disease of violence.* New York: McGraw-Hill.

Matsumoto-Grah, K. (2004) Diversity in the classroom: A checklist. *Eisenhower National Clearinghouse.* Available: www.enc.org/professional/learn/equity/selfassessment/document.shtm?input=ACQ-111594-1594_001.htm.

McCarthy, J., & Frederick, B. (2000). *Eisenhower National Clearinghouse, 9*(4), 43–45.

McCloud, S. (2005). From chaos to consistency. *Educational Leadership, 62*(3), 46–49.

Obiakor, F. E., Utley, C. A., Smith, R., and Harris-Obiakor, P. (2002). The comprehensive support model for culturally diverse exceptional learners: Intervention in an age of change. *Intervention, 38*(1), 21.

Ormrod, J. (2003). *Educational psychology, developing learners* (4th ed.). Upper Saddle River, NJ: Pearson.

Rebora, A. (2004). Professional development. *Education on the Web, Hot Topics,* 1–6. Editorial Projects in Education. Available: www.edweb.com.

Robelon, E. W., & Davis, M. R. (2004). Bush's school agenda will get a 2nd term. *Education Week, 24*(11), 1, 26–27.

Shields, C. M. (2004). Creating a community of difference. *Educational Leadership, 61*(7), 38–41.

Tapper, D. (1995) Swimming upstream: The first-year experience of teachers working in New York City public schools. *Educational Practices Panel,* 1–55. ERIC ED No. 460 085.

U.S. Department of Education. (2000). *Summary: Extending learning time for disadvantaged students.* Washington, DC: Planning and Education Service, U.S. Department of Education.

U.S. Department of Education. (2004). Education Department announces launch of CETAC online. *The Achiever.* Available: www.cetac.org/pageTemplate.cfm?centerTemplate=News%20Events/newsDetailBox (2004, February 17).

Urban, L. (2004). Meeting challenges in urban schools. *Educational Leadership, 61*(7), 64–69.

Webb, L. D., Metha, A., & Jordan, K. F. (2003). Foundations of American Education, (4th ed.) Upper Saddle River, NJ: Merrill Prentice-Hall.

Wenglinsky, H. (2002). How schools matter: The link between teacher classroom practices and student academic performance. *Education Policy Analysis Archives, 10*(12).

Young, D. (2004). Seeing behind the averages. *The Achiever.* Available: www.ed.gov/news/newsletters/achiever/2004/020104.html (2004, February 1).

INDEX

PHOTO CREDITS